MYSTERIES
of the
BRIDECHAMBER

MYSTERIES
of the
BRIDECHAMBER

THE INITIATION OF JESUS
AND THE TEMPLE OF SOLOMON

VICTORIA LEPAGE

Inner Traditions
Rochester, Vermont

Inner Traditions
One Park Street
Rochester, Vermont 05767
www.InnerTraditions.com

Excerpts from *The Zelator* by David Ovason, published by Arrow Books, are
reprinted by permission of The Random House Group Ltd.
Excerpts from *Jung and the Lost Gospels* by Stephan A. Hoeller, published by Quest
Books, are reprinted by permission of the Theosophical Publishing House.

Library of Congress Cataloging-in-Publication Data
LePage, Victoria.
  Mysteries of the bridechamber : the initiation of Jesus and the temple of Solomon /
Victoria LePage.
    p. cm.
  Includes bibliographical references and index.
  ISBN-13: 978-1-59477-193-4 (pbk.)
  ISBN-10: 1-59477-193-6 (pbk.)
  1. Jesus Christ—New Age movement interpretations. I. Title. II. Title: Mysteries
of the bridechamber.
  BT304.93.L47 2007
  299'.93—dc22

                                                                    2007028362

Printed and bound in the United States by Lake Book Manufacturing

10 9 8 7 6 5 4 3 2 1

Text design by Jon Desautels and layout by Priscilla Baker
This book was typeset in Garamond, with Copperplate used as a display typeface

To send correspondence to the author of this book, mail a first-class letter to the
author c/o Inner Traditions • Bear & Company, One Park Street, Rochester, VT
05767, and we will forward the communication.

CONTENTS

LIST OF ILLUSTRATIONS

ACKNOWLEDGMENTS

U ltimately, much of the inspiration for this book springs from my childhood memories of endless dinner table discussions, sometimes acrimonious, always intense, by my French-Jewish-Australian forebears on the subject of Religion—religion as occulted by the wondrous rising star of science. And eventually Theosophy added its voice to the Great Debate. My thought world has therefore been greatly influenced by the spirit of ardent inquiry that emanated from that displaced and somewhat rootless generation, and I owe it many thanks.

Nearer to hand, I owe a deep debt of gratitude to my late husband, Rayner, and to my son, Lamaan, for their unstinting support and encouragement in researching and writing this book; to Peter Martyn, without whose secretarial and computer wizardry the work might well have never found its way into print; to Tracy Cooper of Maverick Designs for her beautiful graphics; to the editorial staff of Inner Traditions/Bear & Co. for its guidance and expertise; and last but by no means least, to all my friends in the Southern Highlands for their enlightened contributions.

I would like to thank Quest Books, the imprint of the Theosophical Publishing House, for permission to reprint quotes from *Jung and the Lost Gospels* by Stephan A. Hoeller, who holds the rights to the work. I would also like to thank Arrow Books, an imprint of Random House, for permission to reprint excerpts from *The Zelator* by David Ovason. Indeed, my thanks are due to all those rich and diverse literary sources whose recent rediscoveries have opened up the ancient Wisdom of the Heart that brought Christianity into being, and in doing so have made this book possible.

SOLOMON'S TEMPLE REVISITED

Most Jews remain to this day ignorant of their esoteric heritage, regarding it as a strange pursuit of the exceedingly Orthodox . . . Yet it cannot be denied that the Kabbalistic schools are the sole representatives of the Mystery religions that have continued uninterruptedly from the day of their foundation until the present.

JOSCELYN GODWIN

In 70 CE Jerusalem fell to the Roman army, and the second Jerusalem temple, prime monument to a Yahwist version of monotheism, was burned down as King Solomon's had been in 586 BCE. Of that first temple no archaeological trace remains. The search for it takes us back to a time before the Hebrew Bible was written and before rabbis wove the myths of Hebrew history, back into the deep past of the Hebrew people when historical fact and fantasy merge in the mists of yesteryear. Not until the fourth century BCE and the Jews' return from their Babylonian exile are we on sure historical ground. Around that time a second temple was built in Jerusalem, and it was on its modest foundations that the Idumean Arab-Jew King Herod (d. 4 BCE) raised his stupendous edifice. His was believed to be the largest temple then known in the Roman world, certainly one of the most magnificent, and its fall was great.

For forty years or more the city had been in turmoil, seething with rumors. The Jewish scholar and author the late Dr. Hugh Schonfield sketches several illuminating studies of that climactic period in Palestine that saw the birth of Christianity. In *The Pentecost Revolution* he describes how two reforming preachers had come to Jerusalem with their separate bands of followers, prophesying that the temple was soon to be destroyed and its blood sacrifices made obsolete. A Day of Judgment was imminent that would usher in a new messianic age.[1] The two teachers were foreigners, Hebrews from the outlandish northern provinces, where the Torah was tainted by old forbidden teachings. It was even whispered that the two might be prophets, though the prophetic orders were now outlawed and had long been exiled far to the north among the heathen.

Certainly the two foreigners were no rabble-rousers but men known to be of high repute, healers and miracle workers who brought in their wake supernatural signs such as had never before been seen. It was also said that they might be baptizing magi from the Delta city of Alexandria in Egypt, where—so rumor had it in informed circles—the old Mystery teachings of Solomon were being revived in collaboration with Greek and Egyptian philosophers. Thought to be cousins, initiates of the Nazarean line, the two men were preaching not behind closed doors but directly to the people, on riverbanks and hillsides and in the synagogues, their tongues golden with a kind of heterodox wisdom that had not been heard openly in Judaea for as long as people could remember. The doctrines they voiced had long been outlawed by the Jerusalem authorities, creating in the populace a ferment of speculation and controversy.

It was incumbent on Jews of the day to attend the temple in the holy months, there to buy what livestock they could afford, a pigeon, a lamb, or a goat, and take it to a priest as a sin offering to be ritually slaughtered. Besides paying the temple tax, that was the sole extent of the religious obligations required by the temple. The practice of blood sacrifice for the atonement of sins was widely detested. The British historian A. N. Wilson tells us that the renowned first-century Greek magus Apollonius of Tyana, although a seasoned traveler, refused to visit Judaea because of his abhorrence for the animistic Yahwist cult of animal sacrifice. He considered it polluted the country and the people.[2] Many Jews agreed with him—especially the liberalized, well-educated, and cosmopolitan Jews of the diaspora, those settled in great Hellenized cities like Alexandria.

The two northern teachers came to Judaea on the cusp of one of the greatest periods of religious reformation in Jewish history, bringing with them, among other things, an alternative to animal sacrifice. Instead, John the Baptizer, a famous spiritual leader, practiced free baptism in the Jordan River for the remission of sins; and during their separate missions both men brought conversions, exorcism of spirits, and initiation into forbidden esoteric teachings. It was said that the second preacher, Yeshua ben Joseph, even spoke cryptically "for those with ears to hear" about the Mystery teachings of the bridechamber, a topic long banned by the temple though still familiar to the populace. For contrary to modern assumptions, remnants of the pagan Mystery religions like the cult of Tammuz, with its *hieros gamos* or sacred marriage rites, still survived in Jerusalem in the first century, although long driven underground. Officially, the Great Goddess had been banished, as had her secretive royal rites, but among the people there still lingered memories of the pageantry and celebrations of the ancient Mystery cycle that had lain at the heart of temple worship.

Popular unrest increased when the execution of these holy men, one by beheading and one by crucifixion, was followed at a Pentecostal assembly by a wave of euphoric mass conversions to their cause. Thousands from every walk of life embraced the new revelation they had brought, including many of the younger priests of the temple who were dissatisfied with the venality and abuse of power that they witnessed there, and others from the sects of the Pharisees and the Essenes. Dangerous and incendiary rumors swept anew through the city, fueled by those who had undergone the Pentecostal spiritual transformation: the Messiah had come, or his reign was imminent; the laws of caste defilement were to be repealed, the sacrificial system made obsolete, the temple theocracy abolished, a new egalitarian dispensation begun, and the temple itself destroyed.

The second temple, magnificent though it was, had never won the same reverence from the Jews as had King Solomon's legendary first temple. The present one, built at vast cost and dedicated to a Yahwist cult cast in a legal-ritualistic mold, had never been able to replace the earlier one in the Jewish heart and imagination. Like King Herod himself, the high priests and the senior clergy were despised as corrupt and autocratic quislings of the Roman power; and the temple, for all its grandeur, shared something of the spiritual impoverishment and general decadence that had befallen Judaism since the ascension to power of the Hasmonean priest-kings nearly two centuries before. As A. N. Wilson comments, "[T]he temple, for all its marble and gold, was really a magnificently constructed abattoir designed to ease and ritualize relations between humanity and the Unseen."[3] It could not compete with the aura of sanctity that surrounded the legend of the first temple, which had been destroyed, so it was said, by the Babylonian king Nebuchadnezzar in the sixth century BCE.

The rich mythology surrounding Solomon, the Hebrew Sun King, is regarded by archaeologists as one of the West's strangest legacies from the remote past. For although modern researchers can find no trace of the first temple, nor of the king who built it, nor of his united monarchy,[4] according to scripture Solomon was the great Sun King who brought untold wealth, power, and prestige to his united kingdom of Israel and Judah, establishing an empire in the tenth century BCE that stretched from the Euphrates to the borders of Egypt (1 Kings 4:21). A figure of folk fable, the philosopher king of Ecclesiastes "was the wisest man who ever lived, master of magic and the secret arts, whom even the demons must obey."[5]

The mystical lore of Solomon and the temple he built for Yahweh has reached as far as Afghanistan and India; and yet, recent investigative research into the Palestine of the tenth century BCE has cast doubt on the historicity of King Solomon, his temple, and his united monarchy.[6] A certain miasma of folk legend attaches to this great and wise king, veiling him in deepest mystery. Why is he so important to the Western esoteric tradition, indeed to the esoteric traditions of all three religions of Semitic origin? And why have his great knowledge and powers fascinated in turn the Essenes, the Therapeutae, the Qabalists, the Shi'ite Sufis, the Knights Templar, Freemasons, Rosicrucians, and other Jewish, Christian, and Islamic fraternities for the past two thousand years, seeming to lie in some mysterious way at the very root of the whole Western religious tradition? Can it be that the genesis of these esoteric movements is in some way linked to the Hebrew Old Religion, the forgotten Mystery tradition that King Solomon represents?

The fall of Jerusalem and of the entire state of Israel, and the rise thereafter of a distinctive rabbinic Judaism, has become an important watershed in religious history. Until recently the books of the Hebrew scriptures, edited in the main by early Talmudic rabbis, were the only source of information scholars possessed about the world of the ancient Israelites before they were carried off in the thousands to Babylon. The picture painted was of a people uniquely embracing monotheism and so establishing a sublime faith threatened by crude fertility practices borrowed from the Canaanites, by tribal fetishes and royal apostasy, and marked by the struggles of the prophets of Yahweh to carve a true Hebrew religion out of the surrounding pagan plasma. But this picture was effectively challenged when the Hungarian anthropologist and biblical authority Raphael Patai, himself Jewish, published his groundbreaking work *The Hebrew Goddess* in 1976.

Patai argued that the kings of Judah's monarchic period officially worshipped not only Yahweh but also the Sun god El, his son Baal, and other Canaanite gods. As well, they worshipped the goddess Asherah, whom they called the "Mother of the Gods" and "Queen of Heaven," the titles of the Egyptian goddess Isis and the later Christian Virgin Mary. Asherah, the mighty Near Eastern goddess of shamanistic skills, she who had been El's wife since Neolithic times, became in turn Yahweh's consort and was inseparable from him in Israel's devotions.[7]

"Solomon," says Patai, "built many sanctuaries for Asherah in the 'high places' of the countryside, planted her sacred tree, the terebinth, beside each one, and possibly placed her image in the temple on Mt. Zion; and the kings of Israel after him, and the court, the priests, and all the people worshipped her." The reverence for this ubiquitous Canaanite deity, Patai asserted, is undeniable, "an integral element of religious life in ancient Israel prior to the reforms introduced by King Josiah in 621 BCE."[8] He notes that the Zohar, or Splendor, the most influential medieval Qabalistic work, gives great reverence to the Divine Couple and calls the Supreme Mother the Companion of God because his love never departs from her.

> The Father and the Mother, since they are found in union all the time and are never hidden or separated from each other, are called "companions" . . . And they find satisfaction in permanent union. (Zohar III 4a)

The medieval Qabalists, whom Patai closely studied, believed that the key to this theme of divine conjugal love running through Jewish history lay in the fact that Solomon's temple had been built, not for the worship of Yahweh alone, but as a bridechamber for the Divine Couple. There the most ancient Mysteries were conducted by the reigning king and high priestess according to the rites of the hieros gamos, which celebrated the heavenly union of Yahweh and his wife Asherah. And there also, in somber ceremony, the ritual killing of the king and the reinstatement of the new god-king were carried out.[9] Other modern scholars besides Patai agree with the Qabalists. One recent authority has written, "It is generally (although not universally) agreed that a ritual involving a dying god, a divine marriage, and a ceremonial procession, was found in Israel."[10] According to Geo Widengren, distinguished Professor of Religious History at Uppsala University,

> we are thus able to assert that there was just such a ritual mourning in Israel as there was in Mesopotamia after the death of Tammuz, and that this lamentation festival was celebrated in connection with the Feast of Booths, *after the jubilation ceremonies of the sacred marriage.*[11]

According to the Zohar, the marriage of the supernal King and Queen (God and his consort) "could not be celebrated until Solomon had built the temple at Jerusalem, which was to serve as their wedding chamber, and thereafter their bedroom."[12] The Queen, surrounded by her handmaidens, repaired each midnight to the couch set up in the temple, and there the King, come down from his heavenly abode accompanied by songs of praise, embraced and kissed her in sexual union. So it would seem that the first Hebrew temple was regarded by medieval Qabalists as quite literally an earthly bridal chamber sacred to the Divine Couple. Although Patai himself refrains from drawing such a conclusion, it is obvious that the fifteenth-century Zoharic text in which this description occurs is describing the classic Mystery rituals enacted by the high priestess and the reigning monarch or prince of an ancient Hebrew royal court.

The Hebrew scriptures also say that King Solomon placed the Ark in the temple Holy of Holies as a sacred receptacle of two stone slabs inscribed with the Ten Commandments that Moses received from God on Mount Sinai. But Patai is of the opinion that in the beginning there must have been two images in the Ark, those of the Divine Couple, and that these "two images, or slabs of stone . . . represented Yahweh and his consort." Patai further notes that in Solomon's time the holy receptacle was said to be guarded by two golden cherubim carved in the likeness of the traditional winged Egyptian cherubim, angelic beings who guarded the Egyptian Mysteries, but he notes that in the second temple a strange change had occurred: one cherub was male and the other female, and they were to be found twined together in the Holy of Holies in matrimonial embrace, even though such images were officially forbidden. The historian writes,

As late as the third and fourth centuries, the memory of the original function and the significance of the Cherubim in the Sanctuary survived among the Babylonian Talmudic masters. According to a certain Rabh Qetina, "When Israel used to make the pilgrimage, they [the priests] would roll up for them the *Parokhet* [the Veil separating the Holy from the Holy of Holies], and show them the Cherubim which were intertwined with one another, and say to them: 'Behold! Your love before God is like the love of male and female.'" Rashi, the eleventh-century commentator, explains the passage: "The Cherubim were joined together, and were clinging to, and embracing each other like a male who embraces the female."[13]

This practice had the effect of throwing the populace gathered in the temple forecourt into a festive sexual orgy, a practice forcibly curbed by the priests only a short time before Jerusalem's fall. It becomes apparent therefore that in the first century the Jewish people were by no means dead to memories of their more colorful past. Restricted as they were to the dry legalities and cultic proscriptions taught in the synagogues by the scribes and Pharisees, many of them would no doubt have joyfully greeted the healers from the north. For these were preachers whose words, however strange and inscrutable at times, evoked memories of the Old Religion and the sacred union of the Divine Couple.

SACRED MARRIAGE, SACRED DEATH

Patai's work has begun a revolution in our picture of early Judaism that still continues, throwing into confusion the traditional approaches to Israel's past. Perhaps we can no longer take at face value the story of King Solomon—that great philosopher king and national hero of unimaginable wealth and wisdom who married a pharaoh's daughter—but that is not to say that the post-Exilic authors did not draw on old oral traditions for their own purposes. However, these purposes, Dr. Thomas Thompson suggests, were didactic rather than historical, concerned with creating a vehicle for spiritual instruction rather than with historical narrative.[14] Thompson, who is the Professor of Old Testament Studies at the University of Copenhagen, claims that, like the Qur'an, the Bible is a magnificent theological, philosophical, and mystical teaching vehicle; but it is not history.

The burden of Thompson's thesis is that in the Hebrew Bible's books of Kings and Chronicles we have not history but a Solomonic romance not unlike the Western Arthurian romances, an allegory that conceals the teachings of a monumental Mystery cycle once practiced in Israel and in all the surrounding nations of the period. Such occult teaching vehicles are found in the Sumerian epic of King Gilgamesh's search for wisdom and immortality, in medieval Europe's tradition of the alchemical marriage, and in the great chivalric saga of King Arthur and the Grail Quest—all variations on the same immemorial theme of the sacred marriage that runs through the biblical Song of Songs imputed to Solomon. In such a view the Sun King, his brilliant reign and achievements, and his messianic personality are fables. As in the sagas of the ancient god-kings, it tells us in epic style about the search for wisdom, the adventures, and the temptations of a Hebrew royal initiate and outlines the universal nature of his Mystery background. This interpretation of the Solomonic legend as mythic has indeed always existed in certain esoteric circles, for whatever he may or may not have been in historical reality, in occult symbolism King Solomon, like the Egyptian pharaohs, has always epitomized the Son of the Sun, the supreme adept, the initiate of the Solar Mysteries illumined by the Sun's divine power of Life and Knowledge combined.

Ongoing research in the Holy Land is revealing the full extent of Israel's participation in the Solar Mystery religions of the ancient East. As far back as the middle of the third millennium BCE, when the pyramid complex at Giza was in the process of being built, the Semites of Palestine were carrying on a thriving trade with Egypt and thereby absorbing all the cultural elements of its high civilization, including its religious traditions.[15] From the fifteenth century BCE until the end of the Bronze Age the Levant was virtually a province of Egypt, the northern hegemonies of Phoenicia and Syria, in particular, faithfully reflecting all aspects of the superior Egyptian culture: its Solar cult, its immense temple learning, and its fertility rites. Israel was surrounded by such Mystery religions and borrowed elements from all of them in the creation of its own cultic mysteries.

These formed a two-tiered or double-phased sacred cycle, one that was to remain at the root of all subsequent religious institutions—the foundation, however deeply hidden, of all exoteric religions up to the present day. The first phase was matriarchal, tantric, and fertility-centered; the second patriarchal, messianic, and wisdom-centered. The first celebrated the earthly sexual joys of the god-king, the second his immolation as the heavenly redeemer of his people. The scriptures are full of cryptic allusions to this foundational cycle, a cosmic drama in which the whole of humanity is involved. Thus in the biblical myth of the Garden of Eden, we find that both the Tree of Life and the Tree of Knowledge are central to the development of the human story, but one Tree is permitted to Adam and Eve, the other is not. And so too in the history of religion a public celebratory light shone only on the first phase of the Mystery cycle, while the second, the ritual sacrifice of the god-king, was shrouded in mystery and denial. Until the rise of Christianity, the great fertility rites of the hieros gamos dominated the popular religious scene, while the sacrificial messianic rites were unknown to the people and hidden in deepest shadow. Indeed, even today Judaism officially denies the presence of ritual regicide and human sacrifice in general in the annals of Jewish history.

Nevertheless, the myths that once dramatized on earth the divine coupling in heaven, from the crude theater of the village medicine huts to the ritualized pomp of the great hieratic courts, were everywhere in principle the same, in Palestine as elsewhere. Immeasurably old, they held universal sway in royal courts in Hebrew, Sumerian, Phoenician, Ethiopian, Indian, and Babylonian hieratic city-states, and in those of northern Europe, Shang China, and the rest of the Far East as well. Even in the New World there is evidence of the same Solar mythology. And wherever they ruled, the high priestess and the king were the earthly representatives of the Divine Couple—the High Goddess, Giver of life, and the High God, Lord of death and rebirth—acting out their celestial marriage in similar forms of pageantry and ritual.[16]

Of the two-thousand-year-old Eleusinian Mysteries and their rites of the *pastos,* or bridal chamber, the Egyptologist Jane Harrison notes that "the rite of the Sacred Marriage and the Birth of the Holy Child

. . . were, *I* believe, *the* central mystery."[17] Robert Turcan, Professor of Roman History at the Sorbonne, similarly suggests that the rites of the pastos celebrated in the ancient cult of the Goddess Cybele and her castrated priests conveyed the centrality of the hieros gamos, as did those of other Syrian Mother cults of the time.[18] And in an Indus Valley seal of about 2300 BCE that records the sacred copulation of a priestess and a king, the female tantric rite is accompanied by a priest who stands nearby swinging a censor "to purify the god and the goddess before their connubium . . ."[19]

Closer to home, we find prime evidence of the hieros gamos in the Song of Songs, that most richly lyrical and erotic of love poems, which was written down in about 100 BCE and included in the Hebrew scriptures. Once regarded as a celebration of God's love for his chosen bride Israel, and still later as a hymn celebrating Christ's love for his Church, it is now more generally agreed to be part of an ancient liturgy that accompanied the Hebrew king's participation as bridegroom in the temple rites of the sacred marriage, probably at his coronation.[20] The delight in the sensuous beauty of nature and the innocent ecstasy of love flows like nectar in the Hebrew poetry as the high priestess invites the king into her sexual garden: "milk and honey, apples and pomegranates were all the fruits of her garden, images of her fertility and the fertility of the land generated by the rite of the sacred marriage."[21] The genre goes back to the oral traditions of the second and third millennia BCE, to the exquisite love songs of the Sumerian goddess Inanna. In just such rhapsodic phrases did Inanna praise her gardener lover and bridegroom Dumuzi, and so too did the Babylonian goddess Astarte sing the praises of her doomed young husband Tammuz.

In this archaic coronation rite a king received the wisdom and divine authority of his office only through sexual intercourse with the high priestess of the temple, which represented and indeed embodied the spiritual power of the Great Goddess herself. In point of fact, the queen herself was often the high priestess; but such a transmission was possible only where the hierophant was a true spiritual adept, trained to control the transformation of sexual energies involved and through them to bestow mystical enlightenment. This was certainly the case in archaic Egypt, where the same nuptials were once celebrated between high priestess and pharaoh in the temples of Isis and Osiris: he was her consort and lover; she his initiatrix, his spiritual mentor, his guide.[22]

It is significant that Solomon is proverbial for his prodigious knowledge, for the hidden name of the Goddess Asherah was Wisdom, later to be known as Sophia in the Jewish Wisdom writings and still later as the Shekinah of Judaic lore. Asherah would have had her priestesses and her secret schools of female wisdom, and we can confidently assume that, following the Egyptian model, female sacerdotal orders played no small part in the cultural life of ancient Israel. This is an assumption strengthened by the findings of archaeology and biblical research. Carol Myer, an American archaeologist and Professor of Religion at Duke University, notes that Israelite life in the early monarchic and pre-monarchic period was relatively free of gender bias and that an unusually large number of prominent and powerful women prophets were to be found in it. Moses' sister Miriam is cited as an influential prophet in the book of Exodus, and in the book of Judges the prophetess Deborah is also a judge, an office that carried with it the highest intertribal authority.[23] Early Talmudic rabbis have written the women's orders out of the Hebrew scriptures, but in 2 Kings 22:3–11, Huldah the prophetess has escaped the scribal editing of a later age. We learn that she lived in the Jerusalem college around the time of the prophet Samuel, a woman evidently of great spiritual prestige who offered oracular information and counseling to the temple officials. Female priestcraft can therefore be assumed to have been well established in ancient Israel at that time.

Some scholars who base their views on Bible study dispute this, claiming that in the words of Roland de Vaux, an archaeologist and Catholic priest, "no women ever held a place among the Israelite clergy [in the Jerusalem temple]."[24] But such statements cannot be taken seriously, since no original Hebrew texts have ever been found to show that the Deuteronomic laws pertaining to the status of Hebrew women go back so far. On the contrary, everything we are now learning about the Solar symbology and its relation to Moon symbology in ancient Hebrew religion, particularly as it emerges in the classic story of King Solomon, demands the contrapuntal participation of both male and female priesthoods.

> The language of symbolism is universal, and the sun, whether it be feminine as in the Germanic tradition, or masculine as in the Hindu and Greek traditions, always has a spiritual or celestial significance in relation to the moon, which . . . stands for earthly or human perfection.[25]

Therefore, if Solomon is to be given the accolade of Sun King, we can only suppose that massive editing has been at work in the Hebrew Bible to excise the figure of the high priestess, his Moon counterpart. No doubt in the major Levantine towns of that period temples and shrines had their presiding priestesses, and the ruling chieftain or princeling would have played out the traditional role of Sun to the high priestess's Lunar role, uniting with her in the temple in the coronation rites of the bridechamber. Under such circumstances, the practice was a folk fertility rite at one level and at another a holy sacrament, a king-making initiation of great power that could generate the wisdom and inner powers needed for the king to govern his land.

But this beautiful sun-filled idyll is incomplete: the Bible tells us only half the tale. Cast into deepest obscurity and relegated to the forgotten margins of history is its somber coda. Ritual regicide was once the second and final stage of the Mystery cycle. In secrecy, in silence and mourning, the ancient custom was played out whereby the king was sacrificed a fixed number of years after his coronation. Performed by priests, the symbolic rites of scourging and humiliation ended with his immolation—or that of his substitute, generally his own son or daughter or a noble captive of war.[26] This was the other face of the bridechamber, dark, solemn, yet most hallowed. Although there is no record of human sacrifice in Egypt such as was entailed in the death of the god-king in other cultures, the mythologist Joseph Campbell suggests the sacrifice of the Apis bull replaced that of the pharaoh. The first kings of Egypt were from Ethiopia, where ritual regicide certainly was practiced, and the Isis and Osiris mysteries clearly reflect vestiges of the Bronze Age custom, which must have been modified at an early stage of Egyptian history.

Regarding it as the skeleton in Judaism's cupboard, the Hebrew Bible has concealed beneath euphemisms and silence the fact that the kings of Israel and Judah, or rather their substitutes, were subject to the same age-old practice of human sacrifice as all the pagan god-kings of deep antiquity. Yet the Bible has not been able entirely to obliterate from view the killing field that once lay just outside the walls of Jerusalem. There, in the Valley of Ben-Hinnom, the burning, smoking pit known as the Tophet—the "Place of Fire"—was located, which the prophet Jeremiah called "the Valley of Slaughter" (Jeremiah 19:6). This ominous place, lit at night by the glow from its fires, became Gehenna, the Hebrew word for "hell," where, as the British investigator Patrick Tierney says, "sinners suffered the eternal torment of fire."[27] The immolation in the Tophet of sacrificial victims, at night and to the accompaniment of wild music, seems to have continued until the sixth century BCE, when the Babylonian exile brought the practice forcibly to an end. Jeremiah says: "They have built a shrine of Topheth in the Valley of Ben-Hinnom, at which to burn their sons and daughters" (Jeremiah 7:31). We know, for example, that King Ahaz of Judah worshipped at this Tophet, substituting his sons for himself.

> He also burnt sacrifices in the Valley of Ben-Hinnom; he even burnt
> his sons in the fire according to the abominable practice of the nations.
> He slaughtered and burnt sacrifices at the hill shrines and on the hill-
> tops and under every spreading tree. (2 Chronicles 28:3–4)

It has always been thought that the practice was dedicated to the heathen god Moloch; but archaeological research has uncovered evidence that the Hebrew word *mlk,* which can mean victim, has probably been mistranslated as Moloch, and that there never was a god of that name: the victims of the Tophet were dedicated to Yahweh.[28] And this is what the prophet

Isaiah declaims in his ecstatic war song of victory and sacrifice:

> With the downsweep of His arm and the crash of His voice, with His staff Yahweh will beat the victim, with hot wrath and flame of consuming fire He will make him cower.
>
> Every passage of the rod of His punishment which Yahweh will lay upon him will be to the sound of timbrels and lyres . . . For his Tophet has long been prepared . . . Yahweh has made its firepit deep and wide, with fire and wood in abundance. The breath of Yahweh, like a torrent of sulphur, sets it ablaze! (Isaiah 30:29–33)

Does this throw light on the cryptic story of Abraham and his beloved and only son Isaac? Did God really save the Hebrew patriarch and clan prince from sacrificing his son on Mount Moriah, or did the consecration go ahead? Esoteric tradition interprets Genesis 14:18 as a passage in which Abraham is initiated into the fertility rites of a Jebusite Mystery religion dedicated to El Elyon, the High God of Canaan.[29] "The whole episode," says Guénon, "enacts a true 'investiture,' almost in the feudal sense of the word," but with the difference that it is a spiritual investiture. On Mount Moriah Abram meets Melchizedek, King of Righteousness, the Jebusite priest-king who proffers him the timeless symbols of initiation. "Melchizedek king of Salem brought out bread and wine; he was priest of El Elyon, God Most High. And he blessed him . . . and Abram gave him a tenth of everything." After this tithing, Abram receives the new spiritual name of Abraham, in accordance with the age-old usages of initiation. So would not Abraham's new religious allegiance demand a living sacrifice—in other words, his own son?

And what of King David, of whom it was said in Psalm 110:4, "the Lord has said and will not change his mind, 'thou art a priest forever after the order of Melchizedek'"? Does this not mean that David also was initiated into the Order of Melchizedek, as his ancestor Abraham had been? And would he not thus be made subject to the somber ordinances of El Elyon's Mystery cult, and be obliged, like Abraham, to offer a human sacrifice? Here we cannot help noting that the Bible text also gives considerable space to the stories of David's two overly ambitious sons, Absalom and Adonijah (2 Samuel 1:5; 1 Kings 1:5), who are ostensibly killed in battle for their sins. But were they actually given to the Tophet in punishment for trying to seize the throne? Were they in this way given the opportunity, as it was believed, of earning their soul's redemption?

For inhuman cruelty was not in essence the original sense of such immolations. On the contrary, ritual regicide was altruistic at its source; it was a celebration of the noblest ideal known to humanity, the impulse to self-sacrifice for the good of others. The archaic god-kings of the Neolithic age, so Joseph Campbell tells us, went to their deaths voluntarily, for this reason assured of the full forgiveness of their sins and an instantaneous translation to the divine realm. They acquiesced in their sacrifice to the extent that as late as the sixteenth century a god-king of Malabar, in southern India, was observed to sacrifice himself, cutting off parts of himself with sharp knives until he nearly fainted from loss of blood, whereupon he slit his own throat.[30] Says Campbell,

> These [sacrifices] are not gifts, bribes, or dues rendered to God, but fresh enactments, here and now, of the god's own sacrifice in the beginning, through which God became incarnate in the world process. All the ritual acts around which the village community is organized, and through which its identity is maintained, are functions and partial revelations of this immortal sacrifice.[31]

Accordingly, the rites of regicide were given the highest honor; they were a second and higher initiation in the bridechamber that prepared the king, through intensive spiritual instruction, for his messianic role in the afterlife. Resurrected to the astral world, he would intercede for his people as their heavenly benefactor and judge, rain blessings on their crops, and succor them in times of need. And so, prepared by initiation into the highest wisdom of his race, in death he was divinized, honored, and worshipped as a risen god, the supreme example of the spiritual adept.

Campbell points out that among the Indus Valley seals of about

2300 BCE are depictions of the goddess Kali's consort as the Lord of Yoga. He who would be immolated like countless others of Kali's victims in the sacrificial rites is portrayed as a yogi, a prototype of the god Shiva, seated cross-legged in meditation upon his throne and surrounded by adoring beasts.[32] The king became divine precisely by his attainment of the enlightenment associated with sacrificial death.

The ancient Egyptians also believed that the tragic regicidal office was synonymous with the downpouring of divine Light and divine Power, the bestowal of Life and Knowledge. According to the *Egyptian Book of the Dead,* written in the second millennium BCE, there were priestly rites designed to bring about the inner transformation of the dying pharaoh that would make him "one with the light."[33] Highly mystical and esoteric *Pyramid Texts* and *Coffin Texts,* which have been preserved for a thousand years in the Osirian temple at Abydos, bear the title "Transfiguration Texts: texts to bring the dead to the divine light."[34] Behind these hieroglyphic records we glimpse the darker presence of the rites of human sacrifice that were once conducted in the Sun-temples along the Nile, in which the sacrificial victim was first given spiritual instruction for his soul journey to the stars.[35] There in an astral heaven he would thenceforth live on as the celestial redeemer of his people, continuing to intercede for them and bless the life of earth. In Israel he became Isaiah's Suffering Servant and the early prototype of the Messiah.

In the royal funeral rites, initiation was conducted under the auspices of a male priesthood especially charged with exoteric knowledge, with an understanding of the secret laws of nature, of the human body, and of the greater universe—in other words, all the spiritual and secular knowledge on which civilization depended—so complementing the tantric knowledge of the female orders. Both initiations were celebrated in the bridechamber, but the first was carnal, the second spiritual, or "unsullied." For the masses, deprived of initiation, the sacred cycle was mythic, celebrating the rising and dying fertility of the spring and autumn festivals, but in sacerdotal circles it was a hidden teaching based on a science of Light, a twin-pillared theosophy of supremely mystical significance.

This was Israel's Old Religion that flourished in the legendary days of its kings. No archaic culture known to us failed to enact this Mystery cycle regularly in one form or another, for there was a universal belief that the divine creative fission that engendered the universe—the Many out of the One—must be continually repaired by human love and sacrifice so that the Many might return to the One. The goal was cosmic union, nothing less than the union of the cosmic polarities, the healing of the cosmic rupture in the sanctity of the bridechamber. Only then would humanity be blessed and civilization prosper.

It was against such a background that the two prophets from the north entered Judaea with their revolutionary teachings on the ancient theme of the bridechamber. They came to revive the Old Religion, but in a new form. They sought to establish what had never before been known: a messianic age and a new type of Mystery religion—the sacrificial Christ Mystery.

CHRISTIANITY:
THE GREAT DIVORCE

*Where the Greeks were all verve and inquiry, poetry and
caprice, high nobility and spirited debasement, the Romans
homogenized the uneven scene with a genius for system.
The Roman talent was for empire and law—sword and
conscripted pen. With these they fashioned Europe's future.
Both the patrons of the Middle Ages—the Holy Roman
Empire and the Papacy—drew for much of their structure
and motivation on the bequest of old Rome.*

BRENDAN LEHANE

*The esoteric is the heart of human civilization. And should
the outward forms of a human civilization become totally
unable to contain and adapt the energies of great spiritual
teachings, then that civilization has ceased to serve its function
in the universe.*

JACOB NEEDLEMAN

For more than a hundred years, esotericists have been predicting the
moral and spiritual collapse of Western civilization. Long before
the turn of the twentieth century, the German philosopher Friedrich
Nietzsche foresaw the coming of an age of greater materialism and
voiced his pessimism regarding the future of European civilization. So

also did Édouard Schuré, the controversial French esotericist. "Today neither the Church, imprisoned in its dogma, nor science, locked up inside matter, any longer knows how to make men whole,"[1] he warned, prophesying a grim reckoning to come. Another celebrated French Qabalist and Sufi writer, René Guénon, in *The Crisis in the Modern World* spoke of the history of Western civilization from the Middle Ages to the present day as an accelerating downward spiral, and regarded its inexorable cataclysmic outcome as linked to the loss of a true religious tradition.

Decades later the ill omens evident in the arts, sciences, and politics of society were becoming equally apparent to Western historians. "We have to accept the fact," said William Irwin Thompson in the 1970s, "that we now live in a time when the esoteric traditions of Christianity are dead, and the esoteric traditions of Western science are fast dying, so that the whole light of civilization that came out of Christian Europe is flickering toward a new age of darkness."[2] Not much later this presentiment was being shared in scientific circles as well, as the catastrophic ecological and sociological effects of postindustrial technology were felt.

In a sense, these omens of catastrophe seem no longer valid. New spiritual currents are bathing the West: the wind of a changing zeitgeist blows through the world of the third millennium, promising a renewal of the spirit. And yet the widespread resurgence of interest in soul care, in the occult, and in a spectrum of meditational and yogic practices from the East—in a word, the reawakening of a sense of the transcendent—is highlighting as never before the depth of the cultural/social crisis that besets us. Is it, some ask, the beginning of a spiritual renaissance or the last efflorescence of a dying organism? As the Eastern giant stirs, the rising sun at its shoulder, it is surely time to consider the situation: for the West, time is short.

After all the prophecies warning that Western civilization is dying, the imminence of the fact raises some interesting questions. Why has it been so violent, so rapacious, so loveless a reign? Why has it been so brief at its apogee, contrasting with the Egyptian civilization, which lasted for nearly three thousand years? Above all, to what extent has Mother Church been at the root of our malaise, fostering a materialistic power lust that has now spread to every corner of the earth? While perfecting society's most advanced means of physical comfort and communication, and the most advanced machinery for the destruction of enemies that the world has ever seen, has the West the Christian religion to thank for its otherwise poor performance?

The Canadian author John Ralston Saul believes we belong to an unconscious civilization, meaning one that lacks self-knowledge.[3] Seduced by its new marketplace mythology, it lacks awareness of the underlying societal realities inherited from the past and therefore of its true condition. Quoting Cicero, Saul says: "He who does not know history is destined to remain a child."[4] But if he is right, it would be fair to say that the unconscious condition of Western civilization stems from the fact that it has been built on the foundations of an unconscious religion. Christianity too may be said to lack self-knowledge, to lack an effective grasp of its warlike history, its divisive philosophy, and its negative options for a peaceful future. Even more cogent is its lack of awareness of the antiquity and worldwide spread of its roots, or of its debt to pagan religious traditions that were old when the pyramids were built.

For nearly two thousand years the whole thrust of Christian doctrine has centered on one very powerful emotive belief: the salvific efficacy of Jesus' death on the cross and his resurrection—a cosmic event that vicariously atoned for the sins of the world. But for many in the West, that belief has now lost its force and its meaning. What drives the spiritual search today is of a more pragmatic nature: the need for a holistic philosophy that transcends racial and ideological differences, a moral and social vision capable of unifying rather than dividing peoples, a teaching that synthesizes the individual's highest evolutionary aspirations.

This longing for unification—of the soul, of nations, of ideas—although frequently inarticulate, evokes the mood of the earliest phase of Christianity. The apocryphal gospels found at Nag Hammadi speak repeatedly of a bridechamber rite that offers the possibility of rebirth into the unitive consciousness of Christ, a rite of self-transformation in which the primal opposites find their resolution, conflict between the soul's polarities is transcended, sorrow ceases with the coming of peace, and the soul at last "enters into her rest," a phrase that occurs frequently in the Gospel of Philip. This bridechamber sacrament, unknown to us today, was once the pivot on which the whole Judaeo-Christian movement turned, yet many centuries have passed since the mainstream Church celebrated it or aspired to its ideal of holy love.

Instead, competitive and adversarial attitudes have developed in the Church that divide rather than unite. Beneath all the pious declarations of accord there is a sense of extreme discord: ruptured relations between science and religion, between faith and knowledge, between individual and society, between the sexes, between humanity and Nature, and a barrier of fundamentalist intolerance between Christianity and the rest of the world religions—a far cry indeed from the Sermon on the Mount. This confrontational style is a massive obstacle to the spirit of inclusiveness and synthesis that sped the infant religion on its way, and must bear much of the responsibility for the carnage that is now rapidly consuming our entire world.

The fact that a yoga of love is the engine that once secretly drove the very heart of Christianity is only one of the corrections that need to be made to our innumerable misconceptions of what makes up a genuine religion. Dr. David Tacey, the author of *The Spirituality Revolution,* suggests that for the younger generation especially, less piety and more informed knowledge of religious history would be welcomed.[5] Tacey, the Associate Professor of Religious Studies at La Trobe University, in Melbourne, believes that even though the sacred motifs of the religion are now losing their potency in their traditional form, their symbolism—their essence, or universal spiritual meaning—must be understood if they are to be reborn in a form more effective for the times. Yet for such a task, the Christian establishment seems ill equipped.

Our present institution reflects almost nothing of the rapture of spiritual creativity that poured forth from the core of the new Jesus movement during the first and second centuries. In those days its agenda was nothing less than to shift the locus of control, both emotional and intellectual, from the externalized government of the gods and goddesses of pagan antiquity to *the inner governing center of every human being*. This elevation of the Self over the authority of the Community was so radical a change in spiritual direction that it could scarcely be conceptualized, but remained a powerful underlying motive force in the new religion that overcame all before it. The pagan world, although uncomprehending, found it irresistible. It is impossible now for Christians to recapitulate that early spiritual magic, for the shift from outer to inner authority and power is no longer possible in its original form. The sacramental mechanism by which it was effected—that is to say, the bridechamber rite within a system of graded initiation—was excised from the religion within three centuries of its birth. That sacrilege is now returning to haunt us.

Today Christianity is the only world religion in existence that has no sanctioned esoteric tradition, no body of transcendental science at its core that can be accessed by an institutionalized system of individual initiation. Every other world religion has incorporated into its overall belief system an inner yoga or wisdom tradition to which the believer seeking greater understanding of his faith can turn. Through initiation he can enter a more advanced path that will take him to higher levels of enlightenment and spiritual fulfillment, one that will offer a more informed overview of the doctrines he lives by and the universe he inhabits. But despite the existence of monastic orders supposed to fill this need, such a course is no longer available to Christians, and has not been for many hundreds of years.

"Only in the western Christian movement," says the American theologian and writer Elaine Pagels, "do we see a suppression of this kind of mystical tradition [evident in other religions]." As more and more critics are insisting, the inadequacy of the Christian tradition reveals what the Renaissance magi knew, that almost from the beginning there has been a mutilation of the original revelation, and indeed a major extirpation of the very heart of the faith. The discovery of the

Nag Hammadi codices has merely reinforced the conviction, long held in esoteric circles, that what began as a gnostic Mystery religion has become little more than a ritualized tribal mythology.

These long-forgotten Gnostic scriptures recovered from the sands of Egypt suggest that if the roots of Christianity are to be rediscovered, we should be approaching Jesus' teachings as we would the "whispered teachings" of the Upanishads, as belonging in the tradition of the great yogic schools of India, whose "twilight" wisdom was transmitted only through initiation. This is what Jesus himself recommends in the Nag Hammadi texts. In the elliptical language of paradox and dissent, time and again he reverts to the inner mystery of the Kingdom of God, dropping hints that he is transmitting in secret "what no eye has seen and what no ear has heard and what no hand has touched and what has never occurred to the human mind"[6] (Thomas 17).

Indeed, the idea that from the beginning Christianity may have contained a Mystery doctrine with Gnostic overtones secretly transmitted to the few has received confirmation in the famous document that Dr. Morton Smith, the late Professor of Ancient History at Columbia University, found in 1958 in the library of the Greek Orthodox Mar Saba monastery in Palestine.[7] It was an eighteenth-century copy of a fragment of a letter, subsequently authenticated by numerous experts, that had been written by Clement of Alexandria (ca. 150–240), one of the earliest, most erudite, and most gnostic of the church fathers, to one Theodore, evidently a trusted friend.

The letter indicates that a hitherto unknown gospel, written by Mark in Alexandria around 90 CE, had been based on an earlier Aramaic gospel and translated into Greek. Smith quotes Clement as saying that after Mark wrote his canonical gospel in Rome soon after 70 CE, he had written an account of the Lord's deeds in this secret gospel, about "whatever makes for progress towards knowledge *(gnosis)*." Clement continues:

Thus he [Mark] composed a more spiritual gospel for the use of those who were being initiated . . . When he died, he left his composition to the church in Alexandria, where it is even yet most carefully guarded, being read only to those *who are being initiated into the great Mysteries*.[8] (author's italics)

Another instance of the Mystery grades in Christianity appears in the work of a Gnostic named Theodotus, who wrote in Egypt during the 160s: Clement of Alexandria quoted from him a report that Jesus taught his disciples

at first by examples and by stories with hidden meanings, then by parables and enigmas, but in the third stage, clearly and nakedly, in private.[9]

Morton Smith cites many other instances, including ones in the Christians scriptures that suggest the existence in the primitive Church of a hidden tradition that had been taught by Jesus to those considered worthy of his mysteries, which for a time was transmitted in an initiatory structure of progressive grades. These could be accessed by every member of the Church who was prepared to undergo the necessary purification, study, and acts of penance. The professor refers especially to Paul's letters: Rom. 5:3 ff, 1 Cor. 12:12 f, Gal. 3:26 ff, 2 Col. 9:3–4, which connect baptism with a visionary ascent of consciousness into the heavens. "Why else did so very many gnostic sects," Smith asks, "spring up so early in so many parts of the Christian church?"

It seems likely that the primitive secret tradition of Christianity will prove the most important single factor in solving one of the major problems of the history of Gnosticism. Groups that seem gnostic occasionally appear in paganism or Judaism, but nowhere else is there anything like the quantity and vigor of the Christian development. This has to be explained, and the explanation must be something in Christianity. What else but the secret tradition?[10]

What we find in primitive Christianity is that beginners faith built largely on external factors were distinguish those who had acquired knowledge of inner realities: in other words, an outer circle of neophytes was distinguished from an inner circle of initiates in the classical manner of the temples. Early Christian communities were thus organized into three ranks, whose members were known as *hylics, psychics,* and *pneumatics,* respectively.[11] The lowest spiritual initiation was for catechumens or hylics, for whom the ordinary baptismal rite was appropriate. The second initiation, that for psychics, took place at the Paschal Vigil, which was an all-night baptismal service preceding Easter Day, in which certain elements of Mark's secret tradition were transmitted by insertion into the liturgy. But the third initiation, for pneumatics, the true Gnostics, involved an unwritten tradition that Mark never openly divulged and which was transmitted in more private circumstances.[12]

The first rank was likely to be composed of poorly educated and at best semiliterate men and women, who made up a large part of Near Eastern society in the first century. As Origen, the great Christian theologian, born in Egypt in 185 BCE, admitted, that was because in the world he inhabited "the illiterate necessarily outnumber the educated."[13] Above the hylics were men and women of a considerably more literate quality. The highest group was of a generally superior intelligence, education, and thirst for spiritual understanding. It alone would become cognizant of the secret tradition. As pneumatics, its members were free to enter small initiatory study groups, closed to the two lower grades, in which an advanced Christology was taught. They were likely to become as familiar with Platonic and Neopythagorean philosophies, with Qabalah,* even perhaps with the metaphysical doctrines of the gymnosophists of India, as any other of the intellectual sophisticates of great cities of learning like Edessa, Antioch, and Alexandria. Such Christian initiatory schools were frequently held in private homes and could be

---

*The usage and spelling of *Qabalah, Kabbalah,* and *Cabala* are critical in understanding cultural and historical differences. *Kabbalah* or *Cabala* is the Judaic system of esoteric knowledge. *Qabalah* is the Greek spelling, which is employed by Christians and others. *Qabalah* is a much broader system of knowledge that includes Christianity, Gnosticism, Sufism, and current interdisciplinary scholarship. Both forms are used in this book; however, I have kept *Kabbalah* in italics as it is used by scholars referring to the Judaic body of knowledge.

entered only by invitation. For two to three hundred years this triune initiatory structure prevailed in Gnostic circles, until it was denounced as heresy and eradicated. As long as it survived there is evidence that the Church possessed a high wisdom tradition no less rarefied than that of any Roman Mithraic cell or the Egyptian Serapion.

Even before the discovery of the lost Gnostic scriptures and Mark's secret gospel, there were courageous thinkers like Walter Bauer who attacked the Roman Church for its obsession with heresy. Bauer believed Christianity had begun as a Gnostic religion in which a whole spectrum of attitudes and beliefs, both gnostic and conservative, were at first able to coexist peaceably, without accusations of heresy on either side.[14] This is only what we would expect of an institution in which ascending grades of instruction and practice culminated in visionary experiences of the Christ Spirit incommunicable to those below: and not only visionary experiences, but also theosophical and cosmological insights of an esoteric nature that utterly transformed the worshipper's worldview.

Indeed, it is highly probable that originally the four canonical gospels were chosen from among many others for inclusion in the Christian scriptures because of their suitability for the lowest, most numerous and most exoteric of the three initiatory grades. More esoteric texts, such as the Gospel of Thomas, the book of Clement, and the Gospels of Barnabas, Peter, Mary, and Philip, which we now refer to as apocryphal, may well have been regarded as suitable only for the higher grades and reserved for private readings.

"The imposition of a standard 'orthodox' belief came only later," says another commentator, with the concentration of authority in the hands of the Roman Church successfully replacing the older apostolic tradition.[15] Despite such revelations, the official and still largely unopposed view of the modern Church establishment is that the Gnostic vision had no part in Jesus' message, but was a later development. Thus Bentley Layton, possibly the foremost authority on the Gnostic texts found at Nag Hammadi, denies the possibility of a gnosticism older than the first or second century CE, asserting that none of the gnostic myths "can be earlier than the first serious efforts of Christian theologians to come to grips with Platonic philosophical myth . . ."[16] It was an opinion shared by his second-century heresy-hunting predecessors. They too regarded Gnosticism as foreign to Christianity, a relatively late pagan infiltration of the true Christian faith.

But Morton Smith was one authority who disagreed. He contended that Jesus himself was Gnostic in outlook, and that he taught a new kind of Mystery tradition to his inner circle of disciples in conjunction with a secret nocturnal baptism that freed them from Judaism's purity laws. This "pneumatic" baptism some see as having been more particularly the gateway to the bridechamber and its gift of spiritual illumination. Smith believed the practice was regarded in orthodox circles as heretical and was the reason for the bitter opposition to Jesus maintained by the Pharisees and the Levitical authorities in Jerusalem.[17] However, the new Judaeo-Christian sect would probably not have survived, he argues, had not Jesus' brother James taken over its leadership in Jerusalem after a period of extreme persecution in which thousands of converts, including Peter and others of the apostles, had fled the city. James, an orthodox Nazarite from birth, effected a shift in doctrinal direction toward a strict observance of Mosaic law, after which "relations with the Pharisees markedly improved and there developed a party of strong observants who stood even to the right of James."[18]

This doctrinal shift succeeded in returning the Judaeo-Christian community in Jerusalem to the exoteric stance from which it had originally distanced itself. Once again, the outer Law became more important than the inner voice of conscience, more important than individual moral authority. Dr. Smith contends that from then on until the Jewish Revolts in 70 and 135, the Jamesian Church of the Circumcision imposed its orthodoxy on the radical message brought by Jesus, thus altering the entire thrust of his breakaway movement. In Jerusalem, the esoteric Christian impulse was forced underground almost before it was born. Only in the Hebrew diaspora was the original apostolic faith, carried forth by Paul, the disciple from Tarsus, in southeastern Turkey, able to survive for several more centuries.

Walter Bauer and Morton Smith are by no means alone in suggesting that the Christian religion simply cannot be understood without reference to Gnosticism, nor the bridechamber sacrament without reference to the Gnostic initiates who disseminated it in obedience to their Master Jesus. Gnosticism was the term applied to a number of salvation sects that arose in the final centuries before the Common Era and which represented an amalgamation of Hebrew mysticism, Greek philosophy, and the Hermetic traditions of Egypt and the Near East. As one authority says,

> Although Gnosticism's origins and philosophy are essentially pre-Christian, it became linked with Christian ideas at an early stage and, because of Christianity's influence, is still identified as an "heretical" doctrine.[19]

Christianity was swept into existence on the crest of a Gnostic tide that had first seeped into the popular culture in the wake of Alexander the Great's conquests, and numerous scholars have insisted that it is only against this historical backdrop that the Christian religion reveals its intrinsic meaning.[20] What emerged under mysterious circumstances in a flood of mysticism of an entirely new kind became loosely known as Gnosticism, a coined term derived from Gnosis. The primordial Gnosis was a body of sacred knowledge, a wisdom repository believed to have been given to the human race from the earliest times. From the sixth century BCE, Greek and Phoenician traders and adventurers had carried home in a secularized form the sacred arts and sciences they discovered on their travels abroad, and it was thus that many of the secrets of the Bronze Age temples began to flow out to the masses.[21] By the third century BCE, the Hellenic enlightenment was spreading across the Mediterranean world and beyond, bringing in its wake a body of Gnostic speculation and temple practice that helped to offset the divisive influence of the new secular religions, such as Zoroastrianism, Confucianism, Reformed Judaism, and to a lesser extent Hinayana Buddhism.

These were populist religions that rejected the sacred sciences and secret magical rites of the temples, caring little for the Gnosis but a great deal for the victory of righteousness over evil. They represented an altogether new spirit of interreligious competition, diversity, and conflict; were loyal only to their own community; understood only their own doctrines; and were united only in their indifference to higher learning. Had it not been for the leaking of the Gnosis from the temples into the public arena, and especially into the Judaeo-Christian movement, our priceless wisdom heritage might have been lost forever. In any event, the Gnostic influx helped to democratize the ancient closed caste system and revolutionized the nature of civilization as it had previously been understood.

Gnostic ideas infused all the new mystery cults, of Mithras, Serapis, Isis, Cybele, and others that were emerging in the Hellenic period, but in Jesus' Judaic movement the Gnosis found its most favorable environment and crystallized at once into a popularly realized form opposed to Reformed Judaism. Christian Gnosticism was a mystical path, a psychological tool, and a complex cosmology in one. Transmitting a knowledge potentially available to all, such as we find in the esoteric paths of Vedanta, Qabalah, and Hermetic and Sufi alchemy, Gnosticism was deeply concerned with the individual self and referred to immediate inner experience, to direct awareness of sacred things through self-knowledge, and to insights intuitively apprehended from within rather than from objective reasoning. Among the Christian pneumatics, it promoted psychospiritual methods that went beyond vocal prayer and ritual and included hitherto secret temple techniques: meditative disciplines and techniques of trance, the application of a science of subtle spinal energies, and the harnessing of symbological systems whereby what was known by such means could be practically controlled and utilized in the service of the spirit. This was a revolutionary innovation in first-century agricultural Palestine, a profound awakening of the mind nurtured by men and women for whom Jesus was the great Master who had said, "I am the intellectual spirit, filled with radiant light."[22]

Many of Jesus' most famous sayings are gnostic. The first Christian communities established in Mesopotamia and Egypt were gnostic. They were led by gnostic luminaries and professed beliefs that were gnostic, numinous, and concerned with a Christology that incorporated the Qabalistic Tree of Life icon. Although such beliefs were more prevalent at the higher stages of initiation, they influenced the whole. Gnostic Christians welcomed women disciples and slaves and gave them administrative and prophetic roles; they spoke of the Mother-Father God; and they gave every Christian member the opportunity, through ascending grades of tuition, to rise in wisdom from a simple mythological basis to a state of true enlightenment.

These "children of the bridechamber" also believed that love and wisdom spring from the same root, that the two are interdependent. The first Christians therefore sought nothing less than personal union with the Divine through means that led into intellectual as well as devotional paths of self-transformation. To further their quest, many of them read widely and thronged the various religious academies of Alexandria, Rome, Ephesus, and Antioch. The result was startling. A new courage to think for oneself, to value independence of thought, led before long to expressions of individual opinion on even the most sacred subjects, in a show of intellectual independence and creativity that would amaze and mystify modern Christian congregations. From both pagan and Christian sources we learn of the contentious arguments that raged among Christians on such topics as the Resurrection, prophecy, the role of women in the new sect, whether to obey episcopal authority, the value of martyrdom, the meaning of the Crucifixion, and countless other things that would presently become too sacred to question. For a time, this intellectual vigor was the hallmark of the religion and, despite opposition, a prime reason for its success.

How had it been achieved? What was the secret dynamic at the heart of the new Jesus movement that so rapidly distinguished it from the many mystical cults that were emerging at that time and rendered it a very different religion from the one we know today?

SPIRITUAL KINGSHIP
AND THE ROYAL CULT

The myth that ignorance is of little moment in matters of religion, that it is no barrier to holiness and may even be conducive to it, is an invention that has plagued Christianity since the fourth century, when the Gnostics were finally outlawed and their initiatory schools closed down. Since then the notion among theologians that the early faith was an intellectually unsophisticated movement built solely on prayer and unlettered enthusiasm has survived to the present day with the tenacity of a cult belief and is undoubtedly connected to Jesus' supposed low social status. A well-known writer has recently enlarged, for example, on the fact that in Alexandria, Christians competing with their well-educated peers "had to become more sophisticated, transcending the simplistic message preached by Paul to his largely untutored flock."[23] The same source quotes the British scholar E. R. Dodds: "If Christianity was to be more than a religion for the uneducated it must come to terms with Greek philosophy and Greek science."[24] Such views reflect the prevailing patronizing assumption, almost universally held today, that Jesus was an uneducated, untrained, and unsophisticated tradesman: virtually an illiterate peon who founded a religion that appealed only to the most ignorant level of the population.

But great world religions are not built on "simplistic messages." In the past all the visionaries or *avatars* who have founded world religions—the Vedic sages, Moses, Zoroaster, the Buddha, Mani, Muhammad—have emerged from their respective spiritual traditions as initiates adequately equipped with the most advanced spiritual learning of their day. Nor do we find their first converts to be ignorant peasants but rather men and women similarly trained in a religious setting, though perhaps earning their living by humble means—as did Paul, a sailmaker educated to a high standard in the rigorous law schools of the Pharisees. The most recent research into the beginnings of Christianity suggests that Jesus and his followers did not depart appreciably from this universal norm. Indeed, by claiming to be a scion of the line of King David, the Jesus of the gospels seems to be stressing this very point.

Throughout the canon there are numerous instances in which Jesus presents himself to the populace in the archetypal image of the King: sometimes as the ancient god-king of the Mysteries, at other times as a descendant of King David, or, again, as the one whom the prophet Isaiah immortalized as the Suffering Servant of Israel. This royal scapegoat (or his animal surrogate) was either sent out into the desert to die or burned alive in the Tophet, so atoning for the sins of the community. Indeed it was in the latter sense that the charge must be read that was written so derisively above Jesus' head on the cross: "The King of the Jews."

But all these cult heroes of the past, though monarchs, were considerably more than monarchs, more than key figures in the stately ritual and pageantry of court obsequies: they were also vessels of the most sacred knowledge of their race. Whether represented as mighty rulers like Solomon or as sacrificial victims of the Tophet, they were learned men initiated by their priests into the highest Mystery wisdom of their day. Similarly, in all the early scriptures available to us, Jesus too proclaimed by his followers a Jewish king, exhibits all the trained knowledge and skills of a royal initiate.

The spiritual brotherhoods that formed small communities in the wilderness areas of Syro-Palestine, especially in the Transjordan and along the banks of the river Jordan, were all schools of arcane learning; and it was in these areas that we know Jesus roamed with his followers, teaching and healing. It was a world of scriptural and occult scholarship, of prestige and social status, a closed system whose initiates possessed the secret of powers and sciences inconceivable to the common man. There can be no doubt that Jesus possessed, and would have passed on to his closest disciples, this higher knowledge withheld from "those outside" (that is, the uninitiated), as was customary among the hermetically sealed spiritual brotherhoods of his day.

> Jesus said . . . "To you has been given the secret of the kingdom of God, but for those outside everything is in parables; so that they may indeed see but not perceive, and may indeed hear but not understand; lest they should turn again, and be forgiven." (Mark 4:11)

Matthew too relates that Jesus spoke in parables to "those outside," saying to his disciples: "To you it has been given to know the secrets [literally, "mysteries"] of the kingdom of heaven, but to them it has not been given" (Matthew 13:11).

In the royal cult it was to the king that the priests transmitted their entire body of knowledge, and the king at his death would bear it with him to the stars, where he would become a god and would dispense judgment and salvation to his people on earth. There were many layers of symbolic meaning in Jesus' monarchic ascriptions and self-identifications: they were a certification of scholarship as well as supreme authority. Far from being the faith cult it later became, primitive Christianity embodied an ancient Hebrew tradition that mirrored that of Egypt and India, one that associated royalty with privileged sacred knowledge. Thus Jesus' claim to kingship gave his movement an intellectual underpinning of incomparable strength and richness of texture, and it emphasized at an even deeper and more hidden level the core of the royal cult, its very raison d'être: the sacred marriage rite. Secretly celebrated though it was, the bridechamber sacrament was the real key to Christianity's success.

The canonical gospels make one or two guarded references to "the children of the bridechamber" and to Christ as bridegroom (Matthew 9:15); but it was the Gnostics who fully developed the theme of the sacred marriage, according it a pivotal importance in their apocryphal gospels. Bishop Irenaeus, of Lyons in Gaul (ca. 130/40–200), was the first to record for posterity the existence of this sacrament in the course of his diatribe *Against Heresies*. Some Gnostics, he said (probably meaning the Valentinians),

> prepare a "bridal chamber" and perform a mystic rite with certain invocations, for those who are being consecrated (perfected), and they claim that what they are effecting is a "spiritual marriage."[25]

The fact that Irenaeus needed to explain the bridechamber sacrament makes it evident that it was already moving onto the heretical margins of Christianity even by the late second century and was little known among mainstream Christians. It was not until 1946, when the Gospel of Philip, thought to have been written in the late second or early third century, was rediscovered among the Nag Hammadi documents, that scholars began to puzzle over the hitherto unknown bridechamber sacrament. After nineteen centuries of suppression, the Gnostic Gospel of Philip disclosed it as the culmination of five ascending degrees of Christian initiation, claiming, "The Lord has done everything in a Mystery, a baptism, and an anointing [a chrism], and a Eucharist and a redemption and a marriage-chamber."[26]

What, wondered biblical historians, was this Gnostic marriage chamber that had been described by Irenaeus—and to which, according to the Gospel of Philip, Jesus himself had subscribed? The other sacraments were derived obviously enough from their Judaic parent: purification by ablutions in water, a scaling ceremony by anointing with oil, a sacred meal, and what was probably an act of penance—all these were simply variations on standard Judaic practices. But from whence came the spiritual marriage chamber? The modern German scholar Dr. Kurt Rudolph, one of the first to research Gnosticism in depth, concludes that the ceremony was evidently a kind of sacrament for the dying, accompanied by unction and recitations, and was intended to be a reunification of the soul in the afterlife with Christ Jesus as bridegroom.

> The bridal chamber is the "Holy of Holies" and ranks above the other sacraments. The object in view was evidently to anticipate the final union with the Pleroma (represented as a bridal chamber) at the end of time and realizing it in the sacrament; though not by a sexual act or a kissing ceremony, as was frequently assumed . . . There is an explicit contrast between the earthly and celestial marriage: the latter is the "unsullied marriage."[27]

Was this marriage chamber related to the one that, according to Jewish Qabalists, took pride of place in Solomon's temple? Was it connected to the union of the Divine Couple? Or could it be associated even more pertinently with the statues of the two embracing cherubim, one male and the other female, that made of the Holy of Holies in King Herod's second temple a similarly erotic bridechamber? True, two illustrious visitors to the Jerusalem temple seem to deny this possibility: both Philo Judaeus and Josephus strove to give the impression that the Holy of Holies was empty. But Raphael Patai notes that they did so with such self-conscious and self-contradictory circumlocutions that the opposite impression is conveyed.[28] He concludes that, despite official claims to the contrary, there is sufficient historical evidence to accept as fact the presence of the embracing cherubim within the innermost Jewish sanctuary.

That an implicit relationship—and clear differences—existed between the Jewish bridechamber and the Christian sacrament Dr. Rudolph makes apparent when he emphasizes that the latter is not a sexual act or "kissing ceremony"—not, in short, like that imputed to the Hebrew cherubim. Although the Levitical priests assured visiting pilgrims that the cherubims' embrace in the Holy of Holies was purely symbolic of God's love for Israel, Patai points to a historical event that renders undeniable the mythological connection of the statuary to the ancient hieros gamos of the Mysteries.

Patai's researches into Talmudic sources reveal a historical incident in which Gentiles broke into the inner sanctuary of the temple—a dark chamber officially declared empty and devoid of images—and there discovered the hidden erotica. Since Judaism was famous for being an aniconic religion devoted to the worship of the invisible God, the invaders (according to rabbinic records) carried the two cherubim entwined in conjugal embrace out into the streets of the city, parading them to the accompaniment of much ridicule. "You used to say this nation was not serving idols. Now you see what we found and what they were worshipping!" they jeered.[29]

Patai believes this incident, so embarrassing for the Jewish priests, may be dated to 170 BCE, when Antiochus Epiphanes, the Seleucid king of Syria (175–164 BCE), took Jerusalem and looted the second temple, bearing away all its treasures, no doubt including the cherubim statuary. The treasures were eventually restored, and the historian suggests that the embracing cherubim too were restored to their traditional position in the Holy of Holies, probably remaining there until the

destruction of Jerusalem.[30] If he is right, the inner sanctuary, all official dogma to the contrary and however symbolically intended, indeed
served as a mystical bridechamber and a secret memorial to the forbidden Judaic Mysteries.

We find the same Mystery tradition being continued in the Jesus
movement—yet apparently with a profound difference. While the
bridechamber in the Jewish sanctuary clearly refers to the first tantric
phase of the Mysteries and the ancient fertility rites of the king and his
high priestess, the Christian bridechamber is not admitted to have any
such overt meaning. Its "unsullied" celestial marriage celebrates rather
the second phase of the Mystery cycle, the last rites of the dying god-
king. As we have seen, his tryst in the bridechamber is spiritual rather
than carnal. He is done with the passions of the flesh and his end is a
lonely one. Taken from the court and from the side of his queen, he is
sequestered in a solitary place and initiated into all the sacred practices
and knowledge of his race before being delivered to his death. Thus
on a higher initiatory arc than at his coronation, the god-king's soul
ascends to union with the Divine Light.

The Christian belief in a spiritual marriage seems to have been based
on a variation of this same primal theme. It rested on the idea that when
the soul descends to earth only a part of the individual incarnates. The
lower self lives its life on earth, as though spellbound, estranged from
the angelic higher Self, which remains in the worlds of spirit. The goal
of the spiritualization process therefore is a resurrection of the lower
unit and a reunification of the sundered elements. "The pneumatics or
gnostics," states Rudolph, "are understood as brides of the angels, and
their entrance into the world beyond as a wedding feast."[31]

The Mysteries of ancient Egypt enshrined the same ideas. A rare
mural in an Egyptian temple at Abu Simbel portrays the resurrection
ceremony following the death of Osiris, at which Isis and her son Horus
are officiating with initiatory tools. Horus holds to the back of Osiris's
head a long rod with a tuning fork at its end, called the rod of resurrection, which Horus situates at the seventh chakra in the king's spinal
system.[32] Other tools are shown in the mural that further facilitate the

king's spiritual metamorphosis and ascension to the Light. Love is the dominant theme throughout the Egyptian Mystery cycle, but the love the dying Osiris now embodies is not eros but agape. Delivered from passion and ignorance, his is a marriage on high, a union in a celestial analog of the earthly bridal chamber, culminating in rebirth.

This ancient Egyptian theme was recapitulated in the Christ Mystery. Gnostic gospels state repeatedly that the progression of the Christian sacraments was toward an ultimate union with Christ in a ritual marriage chamber, offering the possibility of regeneration to every participating soul. Taking place in a sacred inner space, an inner citadel, it clothed the soul in the garments of life and light and crowned it with glory. Andrew Welburn, a well-known author and Fellow of New College in Oxford, agrees with Morton Smith that there is much evidence in the gospels that Jesus conducted a secret nocturnal baptism that initiated his inner circle of disciples into a heightened state of consciousness known enigmatically as the Kingdom of God or the Kingdom of Heaven; and Welburn identifies this ritual activity with the bridechamber sacrament.

"The evidence of a baptismal Mystery," he asserts, "sheds a direct light on some of the most perplexing passages of Jesus' teaching."[33] He refers to the story about Nicodemus, the influential Pharisee who at night sought rebirth from Jesus, and to the parable about the king who invited guests to a great wedding feast but found among all those assembled in the marriage chamber one who was not wearing a wedding garment. "This," says Welburn, "surely suggests that the garment in question was the white baptismal robe worn by all Christians, without which the bridechamber initiation was invalid." He stresses too the prevalence of light symbolism in the Gospel of Philip, which the author continually couples with references to the marriage chamber. The candidate comes in the night to be initiated into the "light of a higher consciousness that will dawn in him,"[34] and thus

> [e]very person who [enters] the bedroom will kindle the light and it will be manifest to him or her alone hidden not in darkness and the night, but hidden in a perfect day and holy light. (Philip 107:14–16)

The Mystery cycle of antiquity represented a unified field whose function it was to be a kind of mystical transmitting station that continuously radiated the energy of love and wisdom from the temples out to the common people. The Christian bridechamber rite accomplished a similar result. It wove into this living energy field a new law of social compassion and transformed the archaic goddess of fertility into Sophia, the goddess of wisdom, of spiritual knowledge. Love and wisdom thus transformed the initiates of the Christian bridechamber into accomplished servants of Christ.

Although they were few in number compared to the rest of their community, the initiates of the bridechamber became community leaders, healers, and prophets, and acquired extrasensory gifts such as telepathy and clairvoyance as well as the noble character traits required to use those gifts wisely. It was in the bridechamber, in short, that the leaders of Christian congregations were incubated as warriors of the spirit and architects of a new and more enlightened society, for love was conceived of as being far more than the magnetic emotional bond between humans. It was the creative energy that also organized the raw material of ideas into meaningful conceptual patterns. Love was the basis of a winged intellect, the very mother of wisdom.

Why, then, did such a metaphysically vibrant and enquiring Christian climate, so different from the Church today, so soon die out? Resentment at what was seen as elitism was not the only factor in the reaction against the Gnostic model. Christianity also had its rivals in the pagan world, which tested to the utmost its new creed of communal love, as the tidal wave of change that had swept Gnostic thought from the temples out into the greater world had led to the emergence of a whole crop of new mystical cults that all too strongly resembled the Judaeo-Christian movement. Competitive pagan schools like those of Serapis of Egypt and Mithras of Rome, which beckoned a new well-educated middle class and could be entered by the requisite financial outlay, were increasingly viewed by the more conservative Christians with suspicion and antipathy. At least two of them, the Mithraists and the Mandaeans, also practiced the bridechamber rite. By the third century, the mysticism professed by

these rivals was being seen as the work of Satan, or at best as a blasphemous imitation of Christ's revelation to man, alienating many Christians
from the Gnosis.

Yet in his writings, René Guénon repeatedly questions the traditional Christian attitude to other faiths, emphasizing the heterodox
nature of Christian origins.[35] He believed that all the great religions
of antiquity were rooted in one common Wisdom tradition, the sole
primordial Gnosis for this planet, and that therefore their differences,
over which so many tears have been shed, wars fought, and civilizations
destroyed, were fundamentally illusory. Indeed, scholars have long
noted that a strong family likeness is apparent in Christianity and the
other Mystery cults of Jesus' time. Their similarities include personal
salvation, redemption through repentance, and, in the case of the Osirian religion, circumcision, confession, baptism, and a cult of the Holy
Family.[36] As well, the virgin birth of Isis's second son, Aion, was celebrated on the sixth of January, the date of the Epiphany of Christ.[37]
Mithraism, too, although it had become a closed military sect, included
a *nymphus,* a sacred bridal ceremony in an initiation chamber.

The rite featured baptism and water and light symbolism, and like
Christianity was the apex of a series of initiations corresponding to the
planetary system.[38] The initiates, or *mystai,* of several such cults were
said to be "born again" and all ritually celebrated their union with the
Divine by participating in a sacramental meal akin to the Christian
Eucharist.[39] These likenesses seem to be not so much borrowings from
each other as clear evidence of family kinship, and indicate that the
other cults and Christianity were born of a common parental stock.

Both systems, the early Christian and the Mithraic, saw the spiritual journey of the soul in terms of esoteric astrology—that is, as the
mounting of the initiated soul through the "stargates" of the planetary
spheres that surround the earth—although the goal of both was to rise
beyond the zodiac to the divine, eternal, and unchanging Absolute that
reigned above it. Central to the Mithraic mythology was the sacrificial
ordeal in which Mithras seized the primal bull by its horns and, hoist-
ing it onto his shoulders, dragged it to his cave, where he plunged a knife

into its spinal cord, thereby releasing a cornucopia of wheat and wine . . . "whence the bread and wine of the sacramental meal."[40] The painful transitus of both hero and bull corresponded with the Via Crucis of the Christian path and was intended to symbolize the trials and sufferings of the initiate, who must sacrifice the energies of his animal soul on the way to illumination so that the spiritual soul might be born.[41]

Even by the second century, many Christian leaders were moving away from the idea of initiation into the Gnosis and what they saw as an unwelcome threat to their own power base; and the mysterious bridechamber rite was especially suspect. Faith, they believed, was more important than knowledge: St. Paul was said to have declared that spiritual knowledge encouraged hubris—was vanity and from the devil. Some leaders, like Bishop Irenaeus, began to assert that the only priests suitable to be accepted by the laity were those who repudiated secret teachings and initiation into gnosis, and who refused to take part in private meetings that had not been authorized by the bishop. He added, pointedly,

> It is also necessary to hold in suspicion other [priests] who depart from the primitive succession, and who assemble themselves in any place whatsoever, regarding these as heretics, or schismatics, or hypocrites . . . who cleave asunder and divide the unity of the church.[42]

Very soon all references to Christ Jesus as an adept with occult powers were suppressed. Secret knowledge was discouraged and its transmission by separate initiatory conclaves within the Church regarded with hostility. Although for some centuries the tradition of Jesus as a great magus learned in all the spiritual arts continued to circulate among the common people, as recent researches testify,[43] within the official Church structure his image became strangely polarized. Paradoxically, the founder of the religion became on the one hand the divine and only Son of God but on the other was demoted to the illiterate peasantry and excluded from all the benefits and freedoms of education and the privileges of ecclesiastical training. He was known as a *naggar,* a term that means either a carpenter or a scholar, a man of learning, but the second meaning was ignored and eventually lost. So too his claim to be the true king of Israel was abandoned as the religion spread into foreign lands.

Consequently, the resuscitation of the Hebrew Mystery tradition was to have a brief life. Bishop Irenaeus, the first to formulate the orthodox response to Gnosticism, wrote the massive, five-volume *Refutation and Overthrow of Falsely So-called Gnosis* filled with ill-informed invective in which he confessed himself horrified at what he saw as "enormous fictions . . . absurd and inconsistent inventions without authority . . . an abyss of madness and blasphemy against Christ."[44] Henceforth, all ecclesiastical polemics against Gnosticism were to indulge in a similar kind of dogmatism.

Within a mere three centuries, Gnostic Christianity had disappeared. With it, the closely related concepts of Jesus as Messiah and Bridegroom, the New Covenant, the Angel of Wisdom, the cult of agape, and the bridechamber tradition had disappeared as well. The latter, the source of what may justifiably be called a true Christian yoga, became merely the bland rite of holy matrimony. None of these transcendental ideas had ever been properly understood or appreciated by the majority of Christians; nevertherless, their departure tore out the heart of the religion, and century by century has increasingly bled it of sacral meaning. The very pillars that had once sustained the faith had been brought down, and the circuit connecting them to the Mystery field of love and wisdom was irrevocably broken. Thereafter, the Church was forced to take an entirely new direction in its search for institutional power.

A WITHERING WIND

The degeneration of the Christian impulse began from the time the Church made its formal alliance with the Roman state. That was when Christian worship moved decisively from a basis of inner personal experience to one of theological dogmas learned by rote from others. At the root of the breakdown was the intrusion of Gnostic ideas into an unready society, introducing esoteric sciences of a psychospiritual nature that were not understood. The whole suprasensible assemblage was increasingly seen as anarchic and blasphemous, a pagan element that had no part in the purity of Jesus' original transmission. But there was also a political dimension to the rejection of Gnostic Christianity. We can date the decline from the holding of the Council of Nicaea in 325, which was attended by all the bishops and presided over by the emperor Constantine.

This was the historical watershed in Christianity's devolution and destroyed far more than its innately mystical character and its tolerance for universal discourse. It was then, and at the Council of Constantinople in 360 under the patronage of Constantius II, and again in 381 at the Second Ecumenical Council in Constantinople, attended by Theodosius the Great, that Christianity took the fateful step that wed it to the Roman state and to partnership in a repressive Caesero-papist system that stripped it of its original gnostic character.

The papist system was in fact born only at that juncture, in the fourth century. The doctrine of apostolic succession had first been made known in about 180 CE, when a document known as *Proof of the Apostolic Preaching* was written. In it, without any evidence, the apostle Peter was declared to have become the first bishop of Rome. A list of twelve more bishops succeeding Peter was then promulgated as proof of the system, although as only one of these bishops can be traced in the history of the Church, many believe the list is a fabrication.[45] But it was not until the fourth century, after the Second Ecumenical Council, that Damasus, then the bishop of Rome, used the above work to bolster his assertion that he alone spoke with the infallible authority of Christ. Much to the anger of the Byzantine emperor and other bishops, Damasus took to referring to them not as "brother" but as "son," and demanded to be called "Father." Before that, Eusebius, bishop of Caesarea in Palestine, and Athanasius, bishop of Alexandria in Egypt, had been the leaders of the Church.[46] Thus arose the ascendancy of the Roman see in the West and the consequent secession in high dudgeon of the Byzantine Empire from Roman Christendom.

Constantine had inherited a tottering empire debilitated and divided by civil wars. By the fourth century, the old Republican religious traditions were almost dead, and a spiritually empty emperor cult had bred a dangerous skepticism and a mood of insurrection throughout the imperium. Constantine realized, more clearly than any other Roman emperor, that only a strong state religion could contribute the bonding power now needed to hold together the aging empire. His aim was to create a single state religion and to draw from it sanction and support for imperial authority. For the purpose he chose Christianity, although the Sol Invictus or Mithraic cult seems to have been a close or even an equal contender for the honor. Wielding the powerful weapons of military threats on the one hand and bribery through munificent gifts and privileges on the other, he ceased all persecution of the Christian communities carried on by previous emperors, put himself at the head of the Church, and proceeded to mold the Christian faith to his own political ends. It was a tragic end to the Christian socioreligious revolution and to any further development of a true Christian gnosis.

The Church has consistently pointed to the Gnostic movement as constituted of the poorly educated, lower class, and more credulous Christians who were easily led into heresies by clever magicians and mountebanks posing as men of God; but the boot was rather on the other foot. Gnosticism was the metropolitan product of a small, well-educated, highly intellectual elite[47] and appealed to those of a reflective disposition. Kurt Rudolph has pointed out that research shows Gnostic leaders to have been of high creative intelligence, members of the more thoughtful upper class in whatever society they inhabited, and the first to frame a Christian theological philosophy, after which orthodox writings were forced to develop purely as a refutational response.[48] Rudolph cites A. Von Harnak in his *History of Dogma,* in which he says that the first authoritative ecclesiastical system, that of Bishop Irenaeus of Lyons, arose directly out of his opposition to the Gnostics. Once the work of these gifted and illuminated men was suppressed, the Church became an easy prey to less favorable influences.

In order to project a strong and unified religious image modeled on that of the Roman state itself, one that would appeal to the people and particularly to the huge, highly influential army, the emperor closed down internal debate in the Church. Dissent was outlawed, gnostic spirituality discriminated against, the creed standardized, the laity disempowered, and the bishops elevated to a hierarchical and authoritarian autocracy. The Gnostic sects in particular were suppressed by two edicts, of 326 and 333, that prohibited their meetings and ordered all gnostic literature to be burned. Thus the bishops were empowered by the highest state authority to brand Christian Gnostics as heretics and eliminate all trace of their activity in the Church.

On the exoteric path that the Christian religion thereafter chose to take, its cousinly relationships to other Greco-Roman cults were vehemently denied, but exist they did, and, despite the Church's growing antagonism to its gnostic heritage, they survived until the fourth century. At that point, the Roman emperor Constantine had appeared on the scene and destroyed any tolerance that may have lingered in the Church for a rapprochement with other belief systems. Thus the heterodoxy that lay at the heart of Christianity was effectively suppressed for good in 386 CE, when Priscillian, the bishop of Avila, in Spain, was executed for teaching gnostic, hermetic, and Qabalistic doctrines from Egypt as authentic ingredients of the Christian faith.[49] The event was to be the last dying recognition that the intellectual illumination fostered by the bridechamber tradition was a legitimate part of mainstream Christianity. The tradition would reappear only in the Manichaean religion, the Celtic church, the medieval Grail legends, the Renaissance schools of Europe, and other such mystical deviations from orthodoxy.

After the fourth century, the Roman state decreed that among Christians, well-funded social service was preferable to the pursuit of spiritual knowledge, and in place of the latter, the adoption of popular pagan ideas was encouraged. As a consequence, both intellectual and moral standards declined and corrupt church politics were condoned; bishoprics were bought and sold regardless of good character or spiritual qualifications;[50] bishops became merchant bankers, real estate speculators, and governors of provinces, as well as church administrators and distributors of alms. Exoteric rituals and mythological dogmas replaced the inwardness of the living faith, and the image of Christ on the Cross began its long degeneration into fetish.

The corruption of the Church hierarchy was augmented by a further evil. Constantine suppressed all competing religions and cults by state law, leaving orthodox Christianity the lone unchallenged victor, supreme in a subservient universe. And Constantine's sons, Constans and Constantius II, proceeded even more rigorously against the pagan cults. Decrees had already been passed—closing temples and punishing magical practices and soothsaying. In 391–392, all sacrifices were outlawed, the cult shrines and temples closed, and divinization by inspecting the entrails of animals punished as high treason. In 393, for the same religio-political motives, the Olympic games were discontinued and soon after the Eleusinian Mysteries were abolished. The mere possession of gnostic writings, once as respectable an element of Christian literature as the recently canonized texts, was now a criminal offense under state law, punishable by excommunication and, in certain cases, such as that of Bishop Priscillian, death. The result was catastrophic.

Those Christians who fell foul of the new orthodoxy because of their esoteric beliefs and practices were excommunicated or fled by the thousands to the Syrian and Egyptian deserts. There they formed a radical opposition in the shape of the first hermitages and monastic foundations, where the outlawed Mystery teachings could find refuge. But the Church never ceased to pursue and exterminate or to regularize by subtle controls. Distance from civilization was no guarantee of safety. So it came about that in 367, more than a dozen apocryphal codices, incorporating fifty-two separate Gnostic works, were destined for burning, according to the written instructions sent by Bishop Athanasius to the head of a Coptic monastery five hundred miles down the Nile.

Soon after this letter was received at the monastery, the offending leather-bound books of gnostic persuasion were secretly buried in a sealed earthenware jar in the desert sands close to the monastery and near the town of Nag Hammadi. Discovered in 1945 and eagerly scrutinized by antiquarian scholars, their existence under such circumstances tells a sad tale of mounting bigotry in the Church and truth suborned to political ends. Were it not for the fortuitous discovery of these texts, we would know almost nothing of the great heterodox currents of thought that launched nascent Christianity on the world. Of the fifty-two Gnostic texts published in 1977 in the Nag Hammadi Library, forty-one had previously been unknown, their very existence unsuspected. Over the intervening centuries, virtually all traces of this seminal form of Christianity had been destroyed.

Wellburn points to yet a further perspective on the rapid decline of Christianity, indeed its total spiritual volte-face in the first few centuries of the Common Era. This was when the barbarian tribes of Goths, Vandals, and Visigoths were sweeping over the civilized world in waves that were "something between an invasion and a gold rush,"[51] motivated by little more than a hungry grab at the centers of power. In 410, Rome fell to the Goths and so did Christianity. The masses of barbarian immigrants who thereafter accepted the Christian faith changed it drastically, for they had never belonged to the highly socialized Mediterranean civilizations[52] but subscribed instead to more archaic culture patterns.

> They came straight out of prehistory, in the strict sense that they came from oral cultures based on tribal divisions . . . They interpreted the gospels accordingly. Lucifer became a bad feudal baron who had not obeyed his overlord, and was punished according to their laws. Christ became a good feudalist who taught obedience, loyalty, and contentment with one's lot . . . These tribal inheritors of the Roman world grew up into a distinctive culture.[53]

Under new Roman-Goth management, the universal Church reflected the imperialist hubris of Rome and adopted a rationalistic and legalistic style modeled on Roman rhetoric, and in general Romanized its theology, its ecclesiastical structure, its worldview, its social ethos, its canons of literary self-expression, its evaluation of its own purpose in the world, and indeed every possible aspect of its spiritual destiny to a degree not always adequately recognized today. By the time the Roman Empire in the West had crumbled, the Church was already well trained and sumptuously equipped to take over the reins of imperial power in Byzantium.

But high intelligence found no place in Byzantine society either, writes the historian Cyril Mango, Professor of Byzantine and Modern Greek Language and Literature at Oxford University and an acknowledged authority on the Byzantine period, which ended only in the twelfth century.[54] The fate of Byzantium, we should note, holds a lesson for the modern world with its rising tide of religious fundamentalism. In the Byzantine Empire in the East, the intellectual elites were persecuted as they had been in the West; popular thought rose no higher than theater and horse racing; religious philosophy and theological speculation disappeared underground and were replaced by doctrinal fundamentalism. Urban violence became endemic.[55] As the Dark Ages approached, bands of fanatical Christian activists reminiscent of today's terrorists destroyed the campuses of the empire, burning books, denouncing teachers suspected of pagan sympathies, beating up opponents. "Elites" were suppressed, and higher learning abandoned; plagues appeared, the cities died, universities disappeared along with lawyers and professors; and primary education, purely for boys, consisted of learning the Psalter.[56]

For hundreds of years thereafter, Christian Europe was marginalized, cut off from the thriving Chinese and Islamic civilizations and rendered poor, culturally backward, and spiritually isolated, partly as a result of the loss of its Eastern trade routes, but primarily from contempt for what it saw as dangerous intellectual elitism. Having suppressed its enlightened Celtic branch as well as the surviving centers of Greek learning, Christianity lost the art of civilized converse with its peers and stagnated as a religious tradition at the unacceptably archaic, ill-informed, and provincial level that customarily accompanies intolerance, without being aware of having done so. By the tenth century, a condition approaching spiritual rigor mortis had set in, the very antithesis of the verve and creativity that flows from metropolitan learning at its best.

Christianity's loss of its esoteric dimension has been one of tragic cultural consequence that is still casting its long shadow over the Western world. We are really only just emerging from a protracted dark age. This has meant the loss of those luminous mythic images that lead into the heart of philosophy and the arts, the loss of the very archetypes wherein are found the higher energies that give life, intellectual power, and healing to a civilization. It has reduced the teachings of the Christian founder to a banal social ethos of increasing irrelevance and has denied generations of Christians the opportunity for a more intelligent understanding of their faith. If the loss is not redressed, it seems likely that Christianity will not be able to regenerate and will be replaced.

Again and again the West has been aware of this danger and has striven to meet it. In the medieval Grail romances and their chivalric songs and poetry, the bridechamber tradition managed to survive by an underground route; and again it surfaced during the Italian Renaissance, when the liberating ideas of Sufi and Qabalistic scholars, defying ecclesiastical suppression, swept through Christendom. As a result, electrifying Hermetic-Qabalistic and alchemical texts were being translated, printed, and studied for the first time in Europe and hope grew that the true mystical Church of Christ could be revived.

It was argued by the *cognoscenti*—men of the adventurous fifteenth century like Marsilio Ficino, Pico della Mirandola, and Francesco Giorgi—that the Roman church was the repository of sacred knowledge it no longer knew it possessed. Moses and Solomon, they said, had been Hermetic adepts and magicians as well as mystics. Moses had received not only the Law on Mount Sinai but also its esoteric interpretation, which was passed down secretly and orally in the Judaic Mysteries. This transmission was the Qabalah, the true heritage of Christianity. A new universal religion was envisaged by these Renaissance illuminati based on Christian Qabalah, a synthesis of Greek and Egyptian gnostic thought, and the mystical learning of Hebrew Hermeticism.[57]

A hundred years later, a rising Rosicrucian brotherhood was to reawaken the spirit of the original New Covenant, a contract with God that was independent of ecclesiastical power structures. The new impulse gave radical force to the idea of human dignity, the idea of "the dignity of Man as Magus . . . having within him the divine creative power, and the magical power of marrying earth and heaven . . ."[58] The rebirth of this kind of unitive mysticism was closely bound up with the resurgence in Spain of a Jewish culture in which mystical literature, philosophy, grammar, and biblical exegesis flourished alongside Hebrew poetry, song, and hymn. The unquenchable Jewish spirit, demonstrating an intellect undimmed by the most violent forces of oppression, was the catalyst for a new European vision of humankind as free and self-responsible, even as had been envisaged by the early Christians.

Even the nascent Protestant movement was infected by this glorious vision of human freedom, perfectibility, and spiritual power. Briefly it became a family of love, and Calvinist Prague became the center of radical Hermetic-Qabalistic and alchemical ideals in Europe. But in the sixteenth century, the Roman church set up, or rather refined, its already existent infamous Inquisition to deal with such heresies. The Thirty Years War followed in 1620, devastating Europe and crushing the incipient Enlightenment. Once again the bridechamber was desecrated. Dame Frances A. Yates, the British doyenne of Renaissance literature, called this disastrous event "the failed Renaissance, or premature Enlightenment, or misunderstood Rosicrucian Dawn."[59] It meant in any case the death of the religious hopes of the European Renaissance.

The consequence of that historic failure is that Christianity is now being accused of lack of substance, of offering nothing to our postindustrial culture except an outdated mythology without meaningful roots—its history problematic, its founder a shadowy figure whose violent death provides his only claim to renown. This harsh judgment has led millions to turn to Eastern systems for spiritual meaning, believing that Christianity has become little more than a tribal cult dedicated to socialized ritual and taboo. It has had, and still has, enormous cohesive advantages in society and the family because of its festive rhythms and codified mores, which provide the continuity, stability, and regularity that are indispensable to tribal well-being; but virtually nothing is left of the underlying sacred science.

The Roman mind-set hidden parasitically within Mother Church, now disguised in a more up-to-date garment, still dominates the West's secular and rationalistic culture, operating just below the surface to vitiate the resurgence of any effective spiritual tradition. The exoteric Roman outlook, the Roman penchant for logic and system, the Roman intellectual aridity and contempt for feminine sensitivities still dominate the Church. As Brendan Lehane, a chronicler of Celtic Christianity, says,

> The lasting quality that Rome added [to Christianity] is best described as an intellectual discipline, a system of logic, a kind of mental code of laws—arbitrary perhaps to unattached philosophers, but of a superb and enduring practical value.[60]

Practical it may be, but a withering wind to the creative spirit. There is a widespread perception that the Western bloc we still call Christendom needs to rediscover a more meaningful language of the numinous and the sacred lest it go the way of Byzantium. Yet most modern minds, Lehane asserts, are "still willy-nilly in the confines of Roman discipline."[61] Its legacy has helped to preserve the modern Christian faith as an anachronism, its conservative and unreflective attitudes appropriate to an insular, politically dominant, militaristic society like that of ancient Rome, but not to the global democracies of modern times. Many of the dogmas Christianity has espoused, as well as the theological scholarship brought to bear on them, are tenable only in an isolated culture in which the checks and balances of religious cross-reference are impossible, or have been made impossible by state law, as happened in Rome, and where the elegant universal intuitions of the Gnosis have been cut off at the root.

> Since the seventeenth century, science has been contending with philosophy, with organized religion, and with the arts for dominion over Western civilization and society ... In the years following 1945, Western culture embarked on a new age of scientific rationalism and

scepticism. Anything pertaining to the "irrational," anything sugges-
tive of "magic" or "superstition," was not just ignored, but regarded
with active mistrust, alarm, and hostility.[62]

This aberrant development has led to a growing realization that the
Roman rhetorician, the modern physicist, and the deconstruction-
ist theologian are closer bedfellows than one might suspect. All are
destructive of the living symbology that sustains religions. Until the
last few decades, "Roman discipline," hand in hand with the physical
sciences, rational, skeptical, literal, aggressively exoteric, and, above all,
disdainful of "unseen powers" and "unseen realms," has been the ghost
that stalks the Western banquet, its reminder of mortality, its nem-
esis. Perhaps it is only now, with the dead hand of the past at last being
lifted, that the West can begin to understand the true import of its
Christian heritage.

2

FORBIDDEN PATHS

*Beneath the surface of Judaism there has always been a strong
Mystery content. Philo forbade his people to take part in pagan
initiations, suggesting that there were Mysteries in their own
faith to which they might aspire.*

JOSCELYN GODWIN

In *The Birth of Christ* Dr. Percy Seymour notes that on September 15,
7 BCE, a triple conjunction of Jupiter and Saturn in the constellation
of Pisces heralded in astrological terms the birth of a king and a great
leader. Dr. Seymour equates this extremely rare stellar event—one that
had never before taken place in recorded history—with the birth of Jesus,
who came as an embodiment of the Christ Spirit on earth, an avatar who
would usher in the new Piscean age and the new world order to come.[1]
However, no one knows for absolutely certain when Jesus was born. For
political reasons, Pope Liberius declared the event to be on December
25 only in the fourth century, arbitrarily commemorating it on the same
day as the birth of the god Mithras in order to bring Christianity into
line with the popular Roman Mithraic cult. Until then, Christians had
not regarded Jesus' date of birth as important: the chief Christian winter
festival had been the Epiphany, on the sixth of January, which celebrates
his baptism by John in the Jordan River.[2] But whatever his astrological
date of birth, Jesus was born into a world undergoing the turmoil of a
great evolutionary transition. His birthplace, Palestine, was in many ways
a reflection in miniature of this enormous cultural upheaval.

The naive assumption entertained by biblical scholars that in the first century CE Palestine was culturally asleep and that Jesus spent his life there in a kind of bucolic cultural vacuum suffered a major setback in the nineteenth century, when part of the apocalyptic Book of Enoch was translated into English, first in 1821 and again, more completely, in 1893. Enoch revealed that, contrary to current belief, at Jesus' birth Palestine was imbued with the new Hellenic arts and philosophies pouring into it from both East and West, fermenting in the process deep ideological divisions and intractable enmities among its various religious communities. Due to subversive literature like that of the Enochic texts, the land seethed with new currents of creative and innovative thought, much of it at odds with the Mosaic tradition.

As a consequence it was a fractured world, outwardly submissive to the monotheistic orthodoxy established in Jerusalem but secretly riven by dissent. The northern provinces had only recently been annexed by force to Jerusalem, and on that account alone, political tension was high; but as well, a network of sects arose that were opposed to the fundamentalist style of Reformed Judaism, all of them forced into postures of extreme secrecy. Many of the sectarian texts written at that time and uncovered among the Dead Sea Scrolls acquaint us for the first time with hymns of numinous and revelatory beauty, rhapsodic passages that speak of visions of God, even union with God, of cosmic flights of consciousness, meetings with angelic agencies, and many other mystical topics derivative of the new Alexandrian Egypto-Judaic school. Therefore, the notion that persists to the present day that somehow Jesus alone, of all the spiritual teachers of his day, remained immune to this great cultural efflorescence says little for the Church's commitment to historical fidelity.

Under the influence of Hellenism and a prosperous lifestyle, literacy was burgeoning in the Jewish expatriate community in Alexandria. There the new occult philosophies sponsored by Hellenism had already gained a firm foothold in educated Jewish circles. But in Judaea, religious and nationalist conservatism backed by military power forbade all such innovations and ignored the people's simmering discontent. As a consequence, a vast literature was produced by Egyptian Jewry aimed at a covert undermining of the second-temple hierarchy in Jerusalem. The controversial literature opened up a political rift between Alexandria and Jerusalem that was never to be healed. Probably the most popular of all this new-age literature was the pseudepigraphic Book of Enoch, which first began circulating throughout the Jewish diaspora around the third century BCE.

The five Sections of the Book of Enoch were written anonymously in Aramaic or Greek, probably from a far older oral tradition, and the later Sections by Jewish expatriate scholars such as the Essenes. The Dead Sea Scrolls have revealed the ongoing Mystery orientation of the Essenes, particularly as demonstrated by The Thanksgiving Psalms, which express so clearly the sufferings and crises of initiation. These psalms, thought to have been composed by the Essenes' leader, the Teacher of Righteousness, many years before Jesus' birth, are very relevant to the Enoch literature and reveal

> a Mystery flourishing in the heartland of Judaea, a *gnosis* with its own rites of initiation, a sacramental meal, and an esoteric understanding of the Jewish scriptures; [bestowing] an experience of "illumination" and vision of the eternal, [teaching] a doctrine of cosmic spirits of Light and Darkness, and such esoteric topics as astrology and physiognomy. Any remnants of the notion that Palestine in the time of Jesus or immediately before was out of the sphere of influence of the Mysteries had to be abandoned.[3]

Enoch was an intrinsic element of that Mystery stream. It has frequently been said that a great deal could be learned not only about first-century Palestine, but also about Jesus' intellectual milieu and general religious background by studying the apocalyptic Enochan texts, and yet they remain to this day almost unknown outside specialist circles.

The adventures of this ancient prophet, who was famously taken up into the heavens in a type of winged chariot or spaceship, began to appear as an oral tradition at much the same time as a Reformed Judaism based on Zoroastrian principles was being imposed on Judaea by its Persian overlords. For another five hundred years Enoch continued to enchant the many Jews disaffected by the new temple regime.[4] The last three pre-Christian centuries, those that saw Enoch's growing popularity, were rich in cultural development for Judaism and covered the period in which the Hebrew biblical texts were being collected and written down, many for the first time. The Book of Enoch was still in great demand in Jesus' lifetime and was enormously popular among his followers for at least another two to three centuries. Why, then, has a literature so relevant to Christian origins been almost ostentatiously neglected?

Although books and visions in his name were once widely known and very influential, in the early Christian centuries Enoch became unpopular with both Talmudic rabbis and Christian bishops. There is no Book of Enoch in the Hebrew Bible and the prophet is mentioned only once, in Genesis 5:18–24, as being in the seventh generation from Adam and the father of Methuselah: a wise man who "walked with God and he was not, for the angels took him." For fifteen centuries, Enoch likewise vanished from the ken of Christendom, yet he was once of global importance, a universal figure of legend whose story crossed all racial boundaries. He was identified with the seventh and wisest king in Sumer's antediluvian king list, and in Egyptian mythology with Thoth, the ibis-headed god of the Egyptian wise arts, and also with Hermes, the Greek god of wisdom; while to the Arabs he was Idries, equated with their prophet hero Elijah.[5] In some scriptures he is regarded as the archangel Michael. Raised aloft and translated in heaven into Metatron, the Angel of Judgment, Enoch has been given a close association with the equally legendary figure of Melchizedek and may well have emerged from the same literary tradition.[6]

The work bearing Enoch's name is in the same ascension genre as a number of other pseudepigraphic biblical books ostensibly written by famous prophets who, like Enoch, were taken up to the heavens in a type of winged chariot-throne (a *merkavah*). As he ascends into the heavens in his chariot-like craft and looks down on the wrinkled seas and mountains receding below him, Enoch seems to us to resemble a modern astronaut; and yet his ascent is also a psychological one, an ascent of consciousness and a spiritual journey to cosmic realms full of supernatural features. He ascends through the four worlds and sees a crystal wall surrounded by fire, a palace whose ceiling is stars and lightning, and within it another palace of fire. Within the latter are cherubim and a chariot throne with shining wheels, and on it the Great Glory sits, the Lord of Spirits in radiant white robes.

Thus, without having gone through the metamorphosis of death, Enoch becomes an exalted being of angelic stature and in the course of his celestial journeying a man of encyclopedic knowledge—knowledge that is based on experience at once natural, psychic, and spiritual. Among the stars he learns the laws of the cosmos, of medicine, dreams, astronomy, angelology, and magic, and undergoes instruction by the angel Uriel that renders him a high adept, an equal to the archangels and a prototypical Messiah.[7]

In the same vein, the prophet Elijah in 2 Kings 2:11–12 ascends to God in a quasi-physical type of space vehicle without undergoing death. His disciple Elisha watches his ascent as Elijah is taken up into the heavens, never to die, in a chariot of fire drawn by fiery horses. "My father, my father! The chariot of fire!" cries Elisha, and sees Elijah no more. And so too does the prophet Ezekiel witness the descending and reascending of a shining, thunderous vehicle throne that features rimmed and spoked wheels whirling on their axles, a fiery engine, and bronze body, all controlled by four great winged cherubim who move through space as one as the Spirit wills, almost like the figureheads of an aerial ship (Ezekiel 10:9–17). And the book of Isaiah, especially the judgment passage of Isaiah 1:1–17, has a marked though different kind of affinity with that of Enoch.

These prophets form a homogenous group and are associated with an extremely ancient mystical science called the Chariot tradition, or merkavah mysticism. Their books are believed to have been written by Jewish sectaries at much the same time as that of Enoch, with the same religio-political protest in mind. All are touched by something very mysterious to the modern mind: a unified, weblike view of the universe and human experience that is peculiarly blended with the physical, psychic, and spiritual—an ideology in which the supernatural is woven seamlessly into the natural order. The prophetic genre into which the Book of Enoch falls exemplifies this unbounded perspective, the peculiar hallmark of the Hebrews' Old Religion.

Of all the Enochan books, the oldest Section, the Book of the Watchers, was the favorite reading matter of early Christians.[1] Enoch was their daily fare and could be read on three different levels, probably depending on the reader's grade of initiation. The Watchers recounts the mysterious legend in Genesis 6 concerning the Sons of God *(bene 'elohim)*, a band of evil angels who rebelled against the sovereignty of Almighty God and in their fall from heaven descended upon Mount Hermon in Syria, where they intermarried with humans. These Watchers, or Rephaim (related to the Hebrew verb *rapha,* to heal), fathered a mysterious race of demigods of ambiguous reputation called Nephilim. "The Nephilim were on the earth in those days, and also afterwards," recounts Genesis 6:4, "when the sons of God came in to the daughters of men, and they bore children to them. These were the mighty men that were of old, men of renown."

The rabbis described the Watchers' progeny as monstrous beings infamous for their cruelty; but many sectaries, including the Essenes and early Christians, regarded them as their spiritual forebears, "a race mighty in knowledge and magical skills,"[8] and the ancestors of their own healing and medicinal traditions. Stephan A. Hoeller, director of the Gnostic Society of Los Angeles, declares that "the Gnostics of Nag Hammadi . . . viewed themselves as spiritual kin of both the rebellious inhabitants of Sodom and Gomorrah and of the *Rephaim* as well."[9] Hoeller believes this declared kinship gives a clear indication of an alternative tradition devoted to secret knowledge and practices, one that was opposed to the established Judaic and Christian orthodoxies.

Enoch passes harsh judgment on the Sons of God and on their sexual practices, and because of their wickedness hurls them into the Dead Sea's boiling water of bitumen as an eternal punishment. In effect, he demotes the time-honored image of the Great Goddess as a sexual icon, she who for thousands of years had presided over the people's great fertility festivals. True, she has not disappeared altogether; she is active still in the Enochan texts as a wisdom figure, as the Tree of Life, "rooted in tree, vine, earth, and water as well as in the human creation of the city"; and as judge (Enoch 91:10) and savior (Enoch 92:1), "interceding to save her people as the goddess Ishtar had interceded to save humanity from the Flood."[10] But although lauded as a magisterial figure of wisdom and authority, in Enoch the Goddess has been denuded of her traditional procreative role: her sexual proclivities and her well-known sexual license are no longer acceptable; her temptation of the evil angels is tacitly condemned. This is probably the first historical sign of changing times in the Near East, auguring the great patriarchal shift that even then was developing under the influence first of the Persians and then of the Greeks.

In the legend of the Watchers, the Jerusalem priesthood saw nothing but a satanic influence at work in the environs of Mount Hermon. The Watchers' dark mythology, the clergy believed, had laid its curse on all the apostate sectaries of Syro-Palestine—a region that took in Samaria, the Galilee, Phoenicia, and the Upper Transjordanian and Damascene areas. The land of Damascus in particular, the territory that had once included Elijah's homeland of Gilead, was regarded in Jerusalem as the cradle of dark occult and magical lore centered on Lebanon's sacred mountain and its brood of evil angels. The mountain's malign influence, it was said, emanated from the region of Baalbek-Heliopolis in Lebanon, a stronghold of the hieros gamos and many of the Syrian Baals and Baalats such as Atargatis the Fish goddess and the Phrygian Mother-goddess Cybele,[11] all of them steeped in licentiousness.

And yet according to biblical scholars, Mount Hermon was also the site of Jesus' spiritual Transfiguration, which was attended by the prophets Elijah and Moses (the latter of whom has replaced Enoch by the hand of some pious scribe) (Mark 9:1–5).[12] For early Jewish Christians, therefore, Mount Hermon was sanctified, and Enoch's chronicles had all the weight of canonical scripture; they were essential reading. Up until the third century CE, the prophet was mentioned respectfully in the writings of most of the great Christian leaders, like Clement of Alexandria,

Origen, and Bishop Eusebius, and the Enochan books were known and used all over the Christian world. But in the fourth century, when Jesus was deemed to be divine and consubstantial with God, the Enoch literature was condemned by the bishops as heretical and suppressed so successfully that it became completely unknown to subsequent generations. It was rediscovered, at least in part, only two hundred years ago in Ethiopia and taken back to England for antiquarian study.[13]

When the Ethiopic texts, written in the Geez language, were eventually translated, scholars were stunned to discover that they anticipated not only the idiom, language, and vocabulary of the Christian scriptures, even to specific phrases and sentences, but also all the theological themes hitherto regarded as unique to the Christian religion: divine election, the Son of Man title, most of the Sermon on the Mount, doctrines of redemption, the harrowing of hell, resurrection and ascension, the Second Coming, and Judgment Day. These were all themes Christians believed had been brought to earth by Christ for the first time in the first century CE, yet they seemed to be familiar to the authors of the Enoch corpus at least three centuries before Jesus' birth. What could it mean?

The early Christians themselves, it seemed, had regarded Enoch as prefiguring the Christ as a heavenly judge of men and angels, and the Irish Canon R. H. Charles, the foremost authority on the contentious work, scandalized his peers by claiming in 1893 that Enoch was "the most important Jewish work written between 200 BC and AD 100."[14] Jesus and his New Testament biographers, Charles declared, quoted from the Book of Enoch; Paul took it with him wherever he went.[15] Despite fierce opposition, Charles continued to defend his view:

> [T]hese are the books that built the frame of reference and furnished the thought forms, idioms, vocabulary, doctrines, and ideas of Jesus and Paul and their contemporaries . . .[16]

The transcendental ideas developed in the Enoch books have only recently entered into public awareness and are a revelation to modern readers. They introduce a numinous and visionary world uncannily like that of early Gnostic Christianity but entirely at odds with either Orthodox Judaism or what we may call Augustinian Christianity. Indeed, the polemic of a first-century rabbinic commentary on Genesis (Genesis Rabbah 25:1) regards Enoch as a prophet foreign to the Jerusalem tradition, condemning him as wicked and hypocritical and insisting that he was taken up to heaven only to prevent his further wrongdoing on earth!

The Book of Enoch is the first intimation historians have been given that there may once have existed a Judaism quite different from today's rabbinic tradition, an esoteric version in opposition to Orthodox Judaism and with close affinities to the ancient Mysteries. "What type of Judaism was this," asks one commentator on the Enochan texts, "which had no real place for the [Mosaic] Law and none for the sacrificial cult?"[17]

Enoch furthermore introduces the suspicion that, like Judaism, Christianity may once have been *fundamentally different* from the religion we know today. The Book of Enoch provides us with the first hint that Jesus may have belonged not only to a quite different spiritual tradition from that of rabbinic Judaism, but also to one completely unknown to the Christian Church that developed a couple of centuries after his death.

We in the West tend to assume that the one and only legitimate form of Judaism must have been the one Jewry knows today, the official one presented by the Hebrew Bible and the later Mishnaic and Talmudic rabbinic writings, the one in fact from which we believe Christianity must have emerged. But with the discovery of the Qumran documents in general and the Enochan literature in particular, we find that a vastly different Judaism unfolds to our view.

We are reminded that, according to recent studies, in the period of Jerusalem's second temple there were numerous regional Judaisms of widely differing religious perspectives, all of which, however, have since been excised from Jewish history. Yahweh temples once existed at Elephantine and Hermopolis in Egypt, in Jerusalem, Arad, Araq-el-Amir,

Cyrenaica, and Beersheva in the Sinai,[18] and all were associated with esoteric sectarian activity similar to that of the Essenes. Samaria had its own temple on Mount Gerizim, with its own priesthood, scriptures, and liturgical tradition and its own Mysteries. Near Alexandria, home of the Essenes known as the Therapeutae, a Jewish temple built by the exiled high priest Zadok of Jerusalem stood in the city of Leontopolis, its influence just as powerful as that of Jerusalem. All these religious centers claimed equal degrees of cult legitimacy, and all offered differing religious perspectives. These versions, writes Professor Thompson,

> were the Judaism of Elephantine, as well as of the many variant historical forms of *benei Yisrael* Judaism that dotted the Palestinian landscape and the shores of the Mediterranean. They included the *shomronim* of Samaria, as well as the Samaritans and Jews of Alexandria.[19]

As a result, highly diverse and competing versions of Judaism were once to be found in Egypt, Ethiopia (where some say the Ark of the Covenant rests), Samaria, the Negev, Arabia, and the prophetic territory of Syria, and all had clandestine sectarian links with the Mysteries. Enoch had much in common with these centers.

In the Book of Enoch there is a great emphasis on astronomical knowledge, something foreign to Orthodox Judaism, and also a devotion to the first-temple Solar calendar rather than to the lunar one used in the second temple. There is no reliance on sacrificial rites or scriptural authority, no Mosaic teachings, no talk of Israel's sins, and no consignment of the dead to Sheol, the shadowy underworld concept that official Judaism shared with many other Mediterranean races. We read instead of a hierarchy of heavenly afterworlds, of angels and demons interacting with human beings, of a messianic Redeemer of human origin called the Son of Man, and of a High God worshipped as the Great Glory or Lord of Spirits. The principle of sacred kingship is upheld, the supremacy of the jealous God Yahweh rejected, and the priests of the second-temple theocracy in Jerusalem are regarded as the perpetrators of an evil regime.

Central to this alternative version of Judaism is the belief that the pursuit of a scientific knowledge of Nature properly belongs with the spiritual arts and sciences and with occult practices leading to enlightenment. Spiritual adepthood is synonymous with kingship, with the divine right to govern. The human soul, according to Enoch, came from the stars and when enlightened will return to them. Man is an angel being in training, his destiny deification. He exists before the Creation as the firstborn of the Godhead, and although he has now forgotten his godlike nature will one day inherit all knowledge, both natural and spiritual. He will know himself as a great stellar being of divine provenance who has fallen asleep in a world that is not his own.

According to this unfamiliar theology, humanity's problem is not its state of sin so much as its ignorance of reality, the solution to which is not primarily expiation for wrongdoing so much as the acquisition of greater spiritual and moral understanding. Nor is our fall into the realm of matter primarily our own fault, but rather the consequence of cosmic forces beyond our control, for which we need help from above.

Despite these revelations, little long-term interest was aroused in academia by the texts from Ethiopia until a further huge cache of Enochan fragments was discovered among the Dead Sea Scrolls in 1947 and again in Cave 4 in 1952, revealing how voluminous the literature must once have been. Fragments of copies of eleven different manuscripts were identified, written by different authors, attesting to Enoch's immense popularity in antiquity.[20] The recognition that the Books of Enoch must have been in full flood in the first century and must indeed have been familiar to Jesus and his disciples, and later to his New Testament biographers, created a fresh furor in scholastic circles. Dr. Norman Golb, of the Chicago University, reiterated Canon Charles's long disputed contention, declaring that the Books of Enoch have influenced the idiom of the Christian scriptures and the early literature of the church fathers more than any other writings of the Jewish Apocrypha and Pseudepigrapha.[21]

Margaret Barker, a British Anglican priest and a leading figure in Anglican theological circles, made an intensive study of Enochan material in *The Lost Prophet,* published in 1988. Her highly informative insights helped to fan a more widespread interest in this strange prophetic figure emerging so opportunely from the mists of time, for it was recognized by liberal researchers like herself that the Enoch chronicles were revolutionary, opening up new possibilities of enlightenment concerning the origins of Christianity, and that indeed they would enforce radical changes in the present Christian worldview and its theological premises.[22] (Unfortunately, Ms. Barker's confident expectations have not materialized as yet. Once the initial interest died down, twenty-first-century theologians have been as distrustful of Enoch as fourth-century theologians were, and the prophet seems to have been cold-shouldered back into oblivion.)

In her study, Barker observes that the pseudepigraphic group of prophets headed by Enoch harks back to the imagery, ethos, and general thought of an earlier period in Israel's history. She believes there are solid grounds for concluding that Enoch was the work of a party opposed to the religious innovations brought back from the Babylonian exile and instituted by the Persian official Ezra. Instead, the group was loyal to the royal cult and great ceremonials of the first temple of Solomon:

> What we have in Enoch is the writing of a very conservative group whose roots go right back to the time of the first temple, when there were still kings in Jerusalem. If this is correct, it is of very great importance for our understanding of Christianity, for the central theme of Christianity is that Jesus was the Messiah, the Anointed, the true king of Israel.[23]

Since, as Barker comments, "Ezra was associated with the Law; whereas the Enochan group kept the ancient Messianic ideal and had no place for Moses,"[24] Enoch was deeply subversive of post-Exilic Reformed Judaism. The aim of the Enochan group was to dethrone the Hasmonean dynasts in Jerusalem and bring back the Judaic Mysteries and the messianic role of the anointed kings of Israel. Jesus, Barker believes, inherited that agenda:

Enoch has no real place for the Moses and Exodus theology, but there is a great emphasis on . . . the world of the first temple, the world in which the Enochic writings claim to have their roots. Those who built the second temple, say the Enochic writings, were impure and apostate.[25]

Barker hypothesizes that Jesus and his new movement was not the cause of the longstanding schism in Judaism but rather its consequence. The Jewish archaeologist Gaalyah Cornfeld supports Barker's hypothesis. In his work *The Archaeology of the Bible: Book by Book,* this highly respected Jewish author recognizes an extreme polarization of Jewish society around questions of religion in the final pre-Christian centuries. It was a schismatic crisis that has not been admitted in Jewish historical records, but which had much to do with the eventual hiving off of the Jesus sect.

The Persian domination of Judaea's religious life meant that a strict Zoroastrian type of monotheism replaced the more tolerant Old Religion that prevailed in the first temple. Despite a great deal of covert resistance, after the return of the Jews from their Babylonian exile the Hebrew Goddess and all her tantric works were demonized. Her groves were cut down and her women's orders dissolved. Monotheism further purged the Jerusalem ideology of its customary hierarchy of divinities under the One God, banning its agricultural Ba'als and Ba'alats, its god-kings and soothsaying prophets, and its families of nature gods, devas, and angels, and wedded it instead to the idea of a single great God of Heaven: male, omnipotent, and implicitly superior to the deities of all other races. Reformed Judaism was thus born under the domination of a theocratic priesthood deeply resented by many Jews for casting off Israel's ancient and much beloved agricultural Mysteries.

In this thoroughgoing religious revolution, Persian-trained officials from Babylon like Nehemiah and Ezra the scribe, whom we meet in the Hebrew Bible, also enforced a new emphasis on the Mosaic purity laws as set out in the book of Deuteronomy. Gaalyah Cornfeld notes that as a result of these Zoroastrian reforms, the Hebrew population was increasingly split into two hostile camps long before Jesus was born. One camp accepted the legalistic principles of Reformed Judaism as taught in the synagogues, while the other, especially in the northern provinces where sectarianism flourished, clung to the more liberal Mysteries of antiquity and were more sympathetic to Hellenic philosophical principles:

> One [camp] hewed to orthodox ethnic and religious exclusivism; the other was more cosmopolitan in its social attitude and was led by the high priest, the Assembly and the upper class . . . Hostility and trouble followed. Mosaic law was enforced, but latent liberalism remained under the surface.[26]

The Book of Enoch, then, reflected the views of the second, rebellious group. The two camps were forced even farther apart by the conquest of the Levant by Alexander the Great and the rising dominance of Hellenic culture, centered on an amalgam of freethinking philosophies and ancient Mystery traditions. Scholars have noted that the Enoch texts become more militantly opposed to the second temple during the Hellenic period, and at last openly hostile. The Maccabees, a priestly family that had usurped the high-priestly office and eventually taken over the government of Israel, continued to enforce such fundamentalist reforms and such a rigid interpretation of Deuteronomic law as to render insurrection inevitable. The increasing clash with the Jerusalem priesthood led to the second of the Enochan Sections, The Similitudes, frequently, though perhaps erroneously, classed as a Christian work because of its adoption of tenets so widely at variance with those of Orthodox Judaism.

We hear a great deal about the bitter struggle of the Jewish populace against the Roman occupation but a great deal less about this internecine religious war. The unfamiliar picture of a Judaean society deeply divided along *theological* rather than nationalistic lines gives little traction to some of our pet theories about Jesus. He can hardly be seen as a pious Jew who founded a movement essentially conservative and rabbinic in tone—an interpretation especially favored by modern Jewish scholars—in the light of his sectarian connections and northern dismissiveness of Mosaic law. Nor is there any warrant for classing him an insurrectionist against the Romans, as is frequently attempted, when it was precisely sectaries of a mystical rather than a nationalistic bent such as the Essenes, Nazareans, and Ebionites, as well as young priests in revolt at the venalities of the temple clergy, who flocked to Jesus' spiritual call at Pentecost. Besides, Jesus is often referred to as a prophet, and Cornfeld insists it was the prophets who most strongly resisted the Levitical party's rise to power under the aegis of Reformed Judaism.[27] Undeniably, the picture of the Christian founder the Book of Enoch implicitly presents us with is that of a teacher of the Mysteries, a religious reformer, one aligned to spiritual principles foreign to the Jerusalem establishment.

Enoch is in fact a very strange document and provokes a great many questions that are, unfortunately, rarely addressed. Why was it sinful for angels and human beings to cohabit—if indeed it was genetically possible? Why, if the fallen angels were so evil, did so many Jewish sectaries revere them as their spiritual ancestors? And how could the Watchers, offspring of an evil union, be seen as a benign superrace that had left behind a legacy rich in supernatural knowledge? And why, if it was so congenial to early Christians, did the world of Enoch die out so completely from our Christian heritage, so much so that few now know it ever existed?

THE WATCHERS AND THE
ORIGIN OF THE BRIDECHAMBER

As has been said, a great deal of Hebrew lore came from the land of Egypt. Not surprisingly, therefore, we learn that the Watchers were also active in ancient Egypt, where they were worshipped as benign demigods. The Pyramid Texts found in the burial chamber of the pyramid of Unas, an Egyptian pharaoh who reigned from 2356 to 2323 BCE, reveal that the Egyptian Watchers were lesser divinities mediating between the elder gods and humanity, and are represented as an advanced race that brought the civilizing arts and sciences to an Egypt sunk in barbarism at the very beginning of its history.[28] Raphael Patai refers to them as the Heru Shemsu, the illustrious Companions or Initiates of Horus who ruled predynastic Egypt for thousands of years and were the originators of Jewish alchemy.[29] They were said to be exceptionally tall and high-skulled, and had come from the Karakorum settlements of central Asia, where they were known as the Sons of the Sun.[30] In Egypt, then, the race of Holy Watchers was an integral part of the great Osiris-and-Isis religious tradition and was worshipped as a source of blessing to the human race.

Like the Egyptians up to a point, Margaret Barker gives a positive spin to this mysterious race whom occult circles regard as advanced beings who came from the star Sirius. As a consequence of her Enochan studies, Barker concludes that the rebellious angels and their progeny were indeed a group of exalted human beings, spiritual adepts who played an important role in remote prehistory. Lest we question her identification of the Watchers as human beings like ourselves, she points to a remarkable code system used in the fourth Enochan Section called the Book of Dreams.[31] Herein, ordinary human beings such as you and I are classified under the heading of animals, while initiates and spiritually advanced persons in general are variously classified as "men in white," true humans, men of angelic stature, sometimes as kings or more simply angels or gods. "This code of 'animals' for human beings and 'men' for angels," says Barker, is important for understanding early Christian writings.

> The angel figures in [Enoch's] history are described as "men"or "men in white," and there are three notable people who are born as animals and yet become "men." Decoded, this means that Noah, Moses [i.e., Enoch], and Elijah began life as mortals and achieved the status of angels.[32]

Likewise, putting on white garments or being anointed with oil was a sign of angelic stature and linked angels to Israel's royal figures, to the Messiah, and to the Son of Man. 2 Enoch 22:8–10 describes how Enoch is anointed by the archangel Michael with sweet ointment and given a robe of glory, which "transforms him into an angel."[33] Many anomalous stories in the book of Genesis can now be explained. Why did Lot in Genesis 19:1–4 ply two angels visiting the city of Sodom with refreshments of bread, venison, and wine if not because they were actually human beings, high initiates rather than immaterial spiritual beings? By the same token, in Enoch's story the fallen angels led by Semihazah can be interpreted to mean a class of shaman masters who incarnated in the Levant and whose practices apparently became morally questionable. For them, therefore, mating with women was not genetically miraculous—indeed impossible, as it would be if they were truly angelic beings—but simply socially irregular and probably taboo for reasons of racial purity.

Leaving aside the interesting idea that our distant ancestors regarded human beings as potentially part of the angelic kingdom, we are left to deal with the concept of a group of two hundred or so highly developed human adepts disobeying a divine injunction and acting in an aberrant if not a sinful manner. In first-century Palestine the sectaries pondered these historical conundrums as they pored over the papyri smuggled in from Egypt, studying in their light the hidden Egyptian origins of Hebraic wisdom and prophecy. Until the fall of Jerusalem, this study of forbidden material, most of it originating from Alexandria and from the pen of Hellenized Jews living in that city, continued in sectarian enclaves all over Palestine, and even in Jerusalem itself. As Dr. Charles contended, such material would have been familiar to peripatetic spiritual teachers like Jesus and therefore to his followers as well, providing a rich source of philosophical enquiry.

Jerusalem had become by the first century a large and imposing Hellenized city. Thanks to the prodigious building projects of the Idumean tyrant king Herod, it was an important trading center, its population swollen by prosperity and by the pilgrims who converged on the temple every year, its culture opened up to the international advances of Greek learning and literacy. Roman civilization then was to a large extent Greek civilization; Greek was the lingua franca that united all Rome's subject people, the international language of good taste. In the Upper City, where the king and the high priest and other dignitaries lived, the avenues were paved with fine slabs of white stone and lined with opulent palaces and mansions built in the Grecian style with colonnades and porticoes and surrounded by beautiful gardens, trees, and fountains. Great colonnaded forums and porticoed markets were to be seen, along with a gymnasium, a theater and hippodrome, and athletic contests and games dedicated to Greek gods. Greek coins, architecture, and domestic customs were the norm, and the majority of urban well-to-do Jews now wore Greek dress and reclined on couches to dine.

In the Lower City, however, the crowded hovels of the poor were in dire contrast. Here Jewish customs and traditions were fiercely guarded, Hellenization resisted with peasant religious passion. As in the small towns and villages throughout the country, among the poor there was a burning hatred for the new heathen lifestyle of the rich. As a consequence, Jerusalem's affluence and superficial air of sophistication masked profound social and religious tensions. Outwardly, the Judaean people had never enjoyed so many multicultural advantages; but beneath the splendor lay dark and incendiary passions, not the least of which was a wasting hatred of foreigners and the alien ideas that foreigners brought with them. The climate of repression was stifling. Even the most violent antipathies had to be cloaked in piety, and were all the more deadly for it.

It was in this dangerous environment, under the very noses of their enemies, that the sectaries pursued their secret studies. Next to the Lower City, on the Ophel overlooking the ravine of the Kedron Valley and the Mount of Olives, the Essenes and the Nazareans had their separate, hermetically sealed quarters, the former accessed by a path that led out of the city by the Gate of the Essenes. Next to the Nazarean quarters, which lay on what had been Mount Zion and the site of the Jebusite fortress that became the City of David, was the quarters of the young priests of the temple.[34] Theirs was a group composed equally of poverty, rabid piety, and discontent with the corruption of the upper class of clergy. In these claustrophobically closed and dangerous condi-

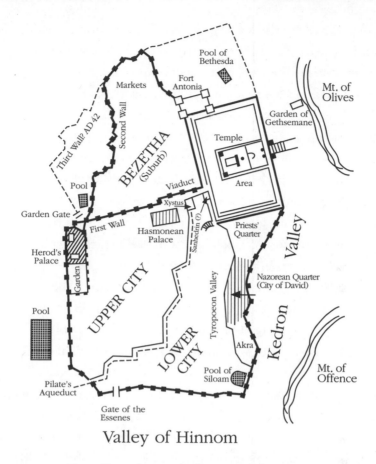

Fig. 1. Jerusalem in the first century CE

tions, rebels of all kinds continued to read the new Greek/Jewish literature infiltrating the city from Egypt: the newly developing Greek Qabalah, alchemy, works on esoteric astrology, and astronomy (a science for which expatriate Jews were famous), the new Wisdom literature pouring out of Alexandria, and especially the Books of Enoch.

Beneath the Enochan material the sectaries were able to decipher a second, encoded level of meaning pertaining to the bridechamber tradition. According to this secondary and more informed level, the myth of the evil angels had a genuine historical basis. In its older oral form, it was giving expression to the folk memory of a great crisis in the evolution of the race that occurred at the end of the last ice age. Greek lore as interpreted by the English esotericist and author John G. Bennett, who had close links with the Sufi master George Gurdjieff, suggests that this planetary crisis had a most positive significance for the evolution of human consciousness. Bennett believes that, because of critical changes in the earth's climate, it became the custom for prehistoric adepts, shamanic Sons and Daughters of God, to mate with members of backward communities in order to improve the genetic stock of the race and so increase its chances of survival.[35] Thus by means of the mighty Goddess's phallic rite of initiation, the hieros gamos, dynastic lines of god-kings were laid down of which we occasionally hear faint echoes in historical studies of Paleolithic and Neolithic societies, and even in some primitive societies at the present time.

The hieros gamos was once practiced all over the earth. It was a deeply secret rite and the bridal site was therefore kept hidden from the uninitiated. In the bridechamber, which was probably most often an isolated forest shrine of some kind far from the tribal compound, shamanic adepts practiced the sacred marriage that raised a chosen mortal from animal to angelic status—that is to say, to the "human" stature of an initiate. This elevated condition provided the basis for an improved royal stock. The Scandinavian scholar Jurgen Spanuth claims that the prehistoric bridechamber was established on moated islands to which the rest of the tribe was excluded, and there the Mysteries of later ages first evolved.[36] The transmission of higher energies by such a sexual method as the hieros gamos, undertaken by an adept, had the effective power of a genetic science and was capable of creating deep physiological and psychological changes in the royal line.

What is hinted at here, of course, is the science of spinal energy centers in which the later Solar temples excelled, and which involved the Gnosis of the heart practiced by Christians of a later age. The same science that Jesus introduced to his inner circle of disciples was the key to the forest rites that had long ago raised the consciousness—and indeed changed the DNA—of members of even the most primitive and undeveloped tribes. But how could an extraordinary genetic experiment like this have occurred as far back as Neolithic times? And how could it have succeeded so outstandingly that, as we are now realizing, humanity's evolutionary course was forever changed by it? Some researchers into this prehistoric mystery, Bennett among them, claim that in paleolithic times there were to all intents and purposes two human races, one far more advanced than the other. Due to their specialized spiritual practices, shamans had evolved more rapidly than the majority of the tribe, becoming biologically and genetically a superior subspecies that enjoyed godlike powers, which they were able to deploy without the slightest understanding or resistance from the overawed members of the tribe. They were, as Bennett puts it, the servants of the Demiurge. In time these Masters of Wisdom lived separately from the lower race, which was still hunting and food gathering, and lived according to higher standards of civilization and took on the mythic quality of heavenly beings, of angels or gods.[37] The rebellious angels of legend may then be recognized as a group of Neolithic master shamans who created the cult of the sacred bridechamber as a means of genetic racial control in a time of environmental crisis.

Historians from the Greek Diodorus (60–30 BCE) to Robert Heine-Geldern, a modern anthropologist, have commented on the ancient practice of the bridechamber, calling the hieros gamos "one of the sacred mysteries of the Megalithic Age."[38] It evolved into a highly institutionalized religion around the fourth millennium BCE, at the same time as ritual regicide arose, and depended on a practical knowledge of occult physiology, as already described. This knowledge led to trance techniques enabling consciousness to rise through sexual intercourse from the lower chthonic energy centers to higher ones, especially to the heart, thus generating new civilizing qualities in the tribal stock. But it was a method open to immense abuses of power.

Barker finds there are several versions of this story in the Enochan texts, and one version in the third Section, the Astronomy Book, suggests that the group of Watchers introduced a great deal of this advanced genetic knowledge into the human race at too early a stage, when human beings were not morally and intellectually mature enough to use the gift wisely. Another version tells how the Watchers had corrupted the creation by passing down the secrets of their immense knowledge of the natural order—such as medicine, metallurgy, mathematics and engineering, weapon-making, writing, and the magical arts—to a primitive race that abused that knowledge. As yet it lacked the moral maturity to cope with the high ethical demands of a complex social organization.

The Watchers are also accused of revealing too early the secrets of their astrological and healing arts. Mention is made in the Astronomy Book of a cosmic covenant that the superior race had broken. It had acted without divine authorization and had erred through pride. There was a strong difference of opinion as to the wisdom of its genetic program and the passing on of dangerous technological knowledge.[39]

> Enoch describes how Asael, a powerful angel who knew the secrets of the creation, came to earth and taught humankind some of those secrets. This heavenly knowledge gave men godlike powers, and thus they corrupted the earth.[40]

A belief reigns in esoteric circles that in the end a compensatory course of action had to be undertaken to neutralize the evil that had been unleashed on the earth, and this was achieved with the coming of the Christ Spirit. The Book of Enoch was a preparation for it by creating a new mythology centered on higher moral values. Certainly, in the Enochan literature, written under the patriarchal influence of Greece, a subtle but very fundamental change has occurred: Enoch is about morality, about judgment. It is not the hieros gamos or the Divine Couple or the surrogate king and high priestess who now take center stage; it is the figure of Enoch, the heavenly Judge. Earthly joys are subject to a heavenly tribunal. The sacred marriage is now aimed not at a mortal union but at a higher one involving the celestial order. Righteousness must prevail. The king must atone for sins committed in passion, be instructed in wisdom, and undergo purification, death, resurrection, and ascension to the highest heaven in the Pleroma. There he must become judge and jury of all that takes place on earth and in heaven, and be kept in that secret place until the time comes for his return to Earth as its Redeemer.[41]

Nevertheless, misconceived or not, the bridechamber tradition was originally motivated by a spirit of the highest altruism, and this was how sects like the Essenes and the Sethians responded to it. It had led to prehistoric initiates relaxing the taboo that had traditionally segregated adept communities from the ordinary tribes, involving them instead in the evolution of their younger brothers and sisters. By offering spiritual initiation through the hieros gamos to selected tribe members, they refined the quality of inferior races and secured dynastic succession in the royal houses thus founded. The mixed Neolithic communities led to the breaking down of old tribal patterns, to a class system, institutional religion, arts and sciences, trade, urbanization, and the modern world. Legends preserved in a great many races declare that miscegenation finally spelled the doom of the Neolithic god-race, but not before it had passed on its wealth of sacred knowledge to subsequent lines of kings and prophets. Both these institutions, the royal and the prophetic, were therefore feared for possessing the most powerful science known to humanity: the Chariot science of genetics, the science of evolutionary ascension.

Now, this was the third level of meaning lying hidden at the very heart of the Enochan texts. To the sectarian *illuminati,* the Chariot tradition was the key to the entire bridechamber mythology. Enoch's allegorical story of ascension to the stars was essentially a manual of instruction for initiates, preparing them for the physiological transformations and elevations of consciousness whereby they could gain access by stages to the spiritual world. Z'ev ben Shimon Halevi, a Western Qabalist, states that Enoch's secret initiatory lore with its recitations of ecstatic "heavenly ascents" and "heavenly journeyings" was known among the prophets and holy men of the Levant from the earliest days of Israel, and was then called the Work of the Chariot (Maasah Merkavah) or simply *merkavah* mysticism, the spiritual science of self-transformation.[42]

The chariot-throne, so central to Enoch's story, was a metaphor for the ethereal Light body believed by initiates to permeate and surround the physical human body as the vehicle of a spiritualized consciousness. By the first century, its secrets were at last entering the public domain, clandestinely, it is true, but nevertheless irrevocably. Gnostic Christians were enthralled with the Chariot tradition and worked with it for at least two centuries, and after it was prohibited by the church fathers, it was taken over by the Persian prophet Mani and enshrined in the Manichaean religion. The Hermetic and alchemical traditions knew of it. The Cathars of southern France continued it until the twelfth century. It was the great taproot that invisibly fed all the numerous mystical pathways and Mystery religions known to the West, all of them eventually outlawed, marginalized, or tacitly condemned as heretical by the church fathers.

This corpus of sacred knowledge enshrined in the Chariot tradition originally spread out from central Asia to form the basis of the Solar Mysteries of all peoples. In the Hebrew scriptures, several of the prophets are recorded as making heavenly flights in a type of fiery chariot; and of course Josephus, in his description of King Solomon as the golden charioteer driving a team of Sun horses, implicitly places him at the very head of the tradition. Ancient Egypt had long had its own Chariot mythology. In the Theban temples, a belief prevailed that four gods, identified with four stars of an Egyptian constellation called the Chariot of the Gods, were guardians of the initiatic lore connected with the dead, and this belief played a significant role in the Egyptians' mystical Light teachings.

> *The Chariot of the Gods* in Egyptian star lore is probably the square marked out by the stars (Dubhe, Merak, Phekda, and Megrez) of our Ursa Major. Certainly, by the end of the Egyptian civilization, the Chariot was referred to more specifically as the Car of Osiris, and sometimes depicted as a boat.[43]

Later the priests of the Heliopolis temple reformed the Theban system by identifying the divine Light with the Sun and raising Re, the Sun god, to a new eminence. Accordingly, in the Egyptian boat of the

Sun—the Car or Chariot of Osiris—souls at death were enabled to ascend to the upper worlds and to the Halls of Judgment, where they were weighed in the Scales of Justice. The Hebrew prophets drew on this Solar belief system, as did the authors of the Enochan literature.

However, many of the rabbis were hostile to all things Egyptian and held the Chariot tradition in as much distrust as they did the Books of Enoch, declaring that merkavah mysticism was a fraudulent and dangerous path. In texts like the Book of Edras, written at the end of the first century CE, rabbinic teachers claimed that visionary ascensions were impossible or, if not, too perilous to attempt. "I never went down into the deep or as yet into hell, neither did I ever ascend into heaven," says 2 Edras: 4–8. No one had gone up to heaven, insisted the rabbis, nor had the light of God ever descended to earth.[44] In any case, they added warningly, the saintly rabbi Akiba was the only holy man who hadn't come to grief through such escapades.

Were these protests simply a ruse to deflect attention from secret matters too dangerous for the masses? Modern research suggests that may have been the case. In his informative studies of early Christianity, the late Dr. Hugh Schonfield, a noted religious historian, has described the Pharisees as a sect of outwardly legalistic pedants, but in secret, savants who shared none of their great esoteric learning with the people they instructed in the synagogues. The Pharisees were as secretive as the Essenes, the Sethians, the Ophites, the Nazareans, and all the other beleaguered minorities, and were almost certainly studying the Book of Enoch even as they disowned it. Thus, it was clear that the Enochic message needed a far more open medium of dissemination than the Pharisaic schools could provide. That became the task of Christianity.

HERESY IN JERUSALEM

The Qabalah was another vehicle for the Work of the Chariot that was circulating in the Jerusalem underground in the first century, under the title of the *Bahir* or "Illumination," a work authored by R. Nehunia.[45] A theosophical system developed in Alexandria by Greek, Hebrew, and

Egyptian philosophers, the Qabalah employed the Tree of Life glyph to reveal the underlying structural principles of both man and the universe. It featured ten basic cosmic principles called sephiroth, the glyph enclosed at its center the Tiphareth principle, a symbol for the human heart. In many respects the Qabalistic Tree of Life was a moral tract, though a great deal more than that. It was also a cosmology, and at the same time a ground plan of the soul's way back to God, a method sometimes known as "going down in the Chariot." Indeed, the Qabalah and Enoch were the first public productions of their kind and shared much the same symbolism; one system explained the other.

In the *Bahir* we are familiarized with a Gnostic cosmology that

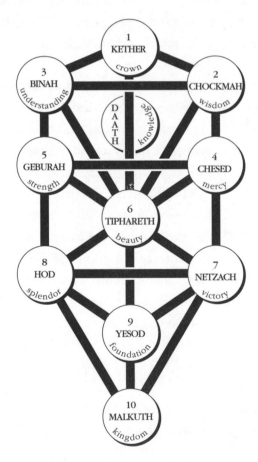

Fig. 2. The Tree of Life

took the form of an active mystical experience rather than a speculative system. It was a hymn to the divine processes of mercy and justice, grace and retribution, and it charted the passage of souls and star systems back to their Source. We learn how the Divine Light in the beginning of Creation fragmented into millions upon millions of divine sparks that fell to earth to illumine matter, and how the Divine Will has determined that all these lesser lights must find their way back to the One Light. The *Bahir* is, then, a manual of the Work of Creation and reveals the Way of the Great Return whereby all created things return to God.[46] The Hellenistic Jewish philosopher Philo Judaeus (ca. 30 BCE–45 CE), a leader of the large Alexandrian Jewish community, was one of the first to teach this theosophy.

Both the age and the provenance of the Qabalah are the subject of much fierce controversy. That it is not confined to the Jewish race is demonstrated by the fact that, according to the New Zealand scholar and author Kieren Barry, the Greeks were developing literal Qabalah into a viable system of alphabetic mysticism as far back as the seventh century BCE, when seafaring Greek adventurers discovered the Phoenician alphabet.[47] Known to specialize in divinatory and magical practices consisting of manipulation of the Greek alphabet and numbers as well as magical rites and spells, literal Qabalah was introduced into the ancient East in the fourth century BCE. It was at that point, says Barry, and no earlier, that Alexandrian Jews were able to adopt the Greek alphabetical and numerical system that then led to their scholars developing a Qabalistic gematria—that is to say, a method by which the Hebrew scriptures could be interpreted according to alphabetical number symbolism. It was Philo, according to Barry, "who first applied Neopythagorean traditions to Hebrew scriptures and so introduced the Greek idea of scriptural exegesis to the Jews."[48]

The root QBL originally meant to receive, reveal, or accept, but has come to mean "hidden tradition," one that illumines the yoga or mystical philosophy of the Western races. Although the Qabalah lies at the heart of the whole of the Western Mystery tradition, with the exception of an esoteric elite its existence was hardly acknowledged before the twentieth century, even by the majority of Jews. Less than a hundred years ago it was regarded by most people, Jewish as well as Christian, as simply Hebrew witchcraft. The late Gershom Scholem, a noted Israeli Qabalist, called it "a veil for forbidden heresies," and it is still rejected as such by Reform, Conservative, and non-Hasidic Orthodox Jews.[49]

Hebrew Qabalah began to emerge into the public domain only in the thirteenth century, when the *Sefer Hazohar,* or "Book of Splendor," which is the most influential work in all the esoteric literature of the Jews, appeared, the work of the Spanish Qabalist Moses de Leon. It was, however, by his own admission inherited from earlier Qabalistic texts written in the first century CE and known as *Maasah Merkavah,* literally the "Working of the Chariot."[50] R. Akiba and R. Simeon ben Yohai have also been named as second-century Qabalistic masters. Akiba was executed by the Romans for being involved in the Second Jewish Revolt in 132. It is said that Simeon ben Yohai and his blind son, who hid for twelve years in a cave as refugees from the roving Roman soldiery, traveled the roads of the diaspora giving out the great Qabalistic teachings in an oral form.

In effect, the Qabalah is a universal language whose vocabulary can be used to define the basic principles of the Gnosis in countless different spiritual contexts; and it is in that sense that its concepts thread their way through the Christian scriptures. Barry provides us with persuasive evidence that in the development of Christian Gnostic doctrine, the Qabalah played a prominent part:

> There is no doubt that the early Christians made extensive use of the Greek Qabalah in all its forms, and that they were in large part responsible for its refinement and development in the opening centuries of the Current Era. It is clear from the evidence that there was an inner Christian gnosis of Greek Qabalah and isopsephy, and that this was heavily indebted to the Gnostics.[51]

In *The Dead Sea Scrolls Uncovered,* Robert Eisenman and Michael Wise, both eminent scholars and translators in the field of Dead Sea

Scrolls research, allude to the clear evidence of an early Qabalism in the Qumran sectarian texts and also in the earliest known Christian writings. The authors point to the "sublime and incredible beauty" of many of the passages in the Qumran texts, and stress that

> texts of this kind border on what goes in Judaism under the name of *Kabbalah,* and indeed it is difficult to see how there cannot have been some very direct relationship albeit an underground one.[52]

This suggests that the Qabalah was circulating among the Palestinian sects well before the first century CE, and no doubt in Jerusalem's sectarian quarters as well as at the Qumran settlement on the shores of the Dead Sea. Morever, Eisenman and Wise have discovered in the fragments of documents from the Qumran caves significant parallels between the Christian scriptures and the Judaic Chariot tradition.[53] There are, the authors say, unmistakable traces of Qabalistic terminology and patterns of mystical Qabalistic thought that recur throughout the Christian scriptures; and the two scholars stress, for example, the ecstatic Qabalistic tone of certain of the apostle Paul's letters, written only a decade after the Crucifixion. In these Paul speaks of "hidden mysteries" and "secret wisdom" (1 Corinthians 12:2–4). Some of the Qumran texts are hymns and psalms overflowing with similar ecstatic imagery of great beauty. They refer to "chariots of glory" and allude to a document called the "Mystery of Existence," and also to "mystical ascents" and "mysteries of the highest angels," terms that are prominent in the Qabalah. Positing a virtual identity of the Scroll terminology with that of both Jewish Qabalah and Christian scripture, Eisenman and Wise note that the Qabalistic "perfection" imagery in particular evokes the language of the Christian scriptures. Perfection imagery, the authors point out,

> fairly abounds in the literature at Qumran, often in connection with another important notation in early Christianity, "the Way" terminology. For Acts, "the Way" is an alternative name for Christianity in its formative period in Palestine from the 40s to the 60s AD . . .[54]

The Way as a synonym for the initiatory path is employed in most religious cultures, from the ancient Egyptian to modern Sufism, and is found in rhapsodic form in the Hebrew Bible in the book of Isaiah (40:3). Long before the Bible was written, the Greek god Hermes called the path of initiation the Straight Way or the Ancient Road.[55] We also find John the Baptist coming forth from the Wilderness paraphrasing Isaiah's words and calling for a new, more righteous Way: "Prepare ye the Way of the Lord, make His paths straight" (Matthew 3:3, Mark 1:3, Luke 3:4, and John 1:23). And even before that, the Essenes' mysterious Teacher of Righteousness, the leader of the pre-Christian Community of the New Covenant, was similarly calling for reformation: "In the wilderness clear the path of [Yahweh]; make level in the desert a highway for our God." Thus the demands of the Hebrew prophets for a new Path or Straight Way for the worship of God that echoed and reechoed down the post-Exilic centuries had a hidden significance that may be lost to modern readers. It would seem that Christianity was a crystallization of the call for reform that had been long reverberating through Palestinian lands.

By the beginning of the Common Era, Palestine was entering its terminal phase of religious dysfunction. Particularly at the lower end of the social spectrum, where the basic insularity of the peasantry was augmented by illiteracy and extreme poverty, the fundamentalism of the Levites found fertile ground. The Hebrew race, a mixture of Indo-European and Hamitic blood, had matured at the crossroads of the major trading routes of the ancient world, a tiny pastoral enclave encircled by powerful empires and molded by centuries of invasions, counterinvasions, deportations, and unceasing colonization. As a consequence, Hebrew psychology was a volatile mix in which high ideologies and peasant xenophobia continually jostled, while centuries of repression by a series of conquerors—Egyptians, Assyrians, Babylonians, Persians, Greeks, and finally Romans—had made it proud, insular, and intransigent in its loyalties, especially in the matters of religion.

By the time of Jesus' birth, the conservative Mosaic cult was in implacable opposition not only to the Roman army garrisoned at its very door, but also to the Greek spirit spreading its doctrinal heresies into a host of new Jewish sects. Nevertheless, a further element in the general climate of ill will must be laid at the door of the sectarian mind-set itself, which was harsh, xenophobic, and fanatical. Translations of the Qumran Scrolls have illuminated with increasing clarity the unforgiving values and ethos of the sectarian world in the years leading up to the birth of the Christian movement, despite the mystical beauty of many of the passages contained in its texts.[56] Nor were the sects even of one mind; they disputed bitterly among themselves.

It is evident that at least one of them, namely the Zealots, were pro-establishment and brutally militaristic and nationalistic, while the antiestablishment Essenes, who called themselves the Sons of Zadok, had no patience with the conservative Ebionites. These latter sectaries, although professing peace-loving principles, were so unbending in their allegiance to the minutiae of the Law as to seem a tolerant sect only in name. Again, we know from the Christian scriptures that the Nazareans were extremely hostile toward the Pharisees, a sect that had become so influential in the synagogues or schools of Mosaic law and so identified with the temple establishment that its sectarian status is generally overlooked. All these factors must have contributed greatly to the ominous darkening of Judaea's social climate as the first century got under way; but it was the purity laws codified in the synagogues that were mainly responsible for the exaggerated xenophobia that afflicted the last days of Jerusalem.

We hear little about pre-Fall Jerusalem as a web of secretive enclaves plotting against each other and against the temple authorities in the best oriental manner; but research is gradually unveiling the reality behind the imposing facade. The Pharisees, one of the three dominant Judaic sects of the time, wielded considerable influence as teachers of Mosaic law, but not enough influence to be able to ameliorate the general obsession with the purity laws. Ritual purity was originally enjoined only on priests to ensure the effective outcome of their ceremonies, a means of lending wing to the liturgies and supplications they directed to heaven; but under the Maccabees, the purity laws became a closely structured religious way of life for the ordinary Jew as well, in lieu of higher spiritual knowledge. So stringent had the cult of ritual purity become in the synagogues that the Talmud, the later body of rabbinic commentary on Jewish law written between the third and fifth centuries CE, says of the first century that "the impurity of a knife was more important to Israel than murder."[57]

Ritual purity, it should be noted, is strictly speaking neither physical nor moral cleanliness, but is rather associated with the inner body or etheric life body that forms the direct causal background to the physical body. Ritual impurity is a material condition contracted by a kind of osmosis set in motion by touching any impure thing and can be cured by material means. Such a form of impurity can be contracted by touching a dead body, by the impure secretions of the opposite sex, and from a low-caste person or a foreigner. The impurity of objects can be associated with human manipulation, such as fired clay as opposed to "natural" clay (for which reason stone utensils for eating and cooking were favored in first-century Israel rather than pottery). Ritual impurity is regarded as contagious and is cleansed by bathing in consecrated baths or *miqva'ot,* as the skin or surface of the physical body is generally the mediating agent of the impurities; whereas according to Judaic law, nothing can atone for the deeper state of moral *sinfulness* except sacrifices and repentance. Hershel Shanks, an authority on the Dead Sea scriptures, notes that

> the concern for ritual purity was at its height in the first century . . . There is considerable archaeological evidence of the extent to which purity requirements were adhered to by the Jewish populace in general. Ritual baths are found by the dozen, especially in the Jerusalem area, during the period almost precisely contemporaneous with the scrolls—250 BCE to 70 CE—but not nearly so many before or after.[58]

The period mentioned by Dr. Shanks coincides with the rise to power of the Levitical priesthood, presided over by the priestly family of Maccabees, and coincides too with the suppression of the prophetic orders and the rising of Pharisaic influence. During the Maccabean era, ritual purity became incumbent on all Jews, effectively cutting them off from their neighbors. If strictly interpreted, these laws forbade Jews to enter a Gentile's house or receive a Gentile into their own houses, much less eat with one. "To touch a Gentile, or his clothing, or any object he had sat or lain on, made one impure."[59] In areas populated by Samaritans and Idumeans, archaeology has found very few miqva'ot, and therefore these folk, although otherwise observants of Judaic law, were regarded by Jews as unclean foreigners and shunned. Samaritans in particular were targeted for this kind of racial discrimination.

It is worth noting, however, that there was yet a further reason for the xenophobia, and it was political. The critical times were the culmination of centuries of chronic political instability in Palestine and by successive conquests from outside, beginning with the Egyptian armies and then by the Assyrians. The following Persian conquest with its enforcement of foreign Zoroastrian ideas on the Palestinian provinces was seen by many Jews as a threat to their new sense of national identity;[60] and their mood of resentment intensified when Alexander the Great, on conquering Palestine in the fourth century BCE, unified the region as a single Greek province and made its capital Samaria rather than Jerusalem.

At that time, Samaria was by far the most cultured, prosperous, and liberal center in Palestine, and Hellenization gave it an even greater cultural eminence. The Greeks introduced sophisticated secular ideas, customs, and values to the region, which served, however, to increase the competitive climate between the two states, Samaria and Judaea. Samaria's elevation to the capital of Palestine was a move that Jerusalem must have bitterly resented, for before long the Hasmonean ruler of Jerusalem mounted a series of military attacks on the northern state that utterly decimated and ruined it. With this signal conquest in the middle of the second century BCE, Jerusalem became for the first time in Palestinian history politically and religiously dominant over Samaria, for so long the leading partner in the Judaea–Israel axis. The southern state now exercised its powers ruthlessly, aiming to permanently destroy Samaritan ascendancy in Palestine. Samaritans, it was said in the synagogues, were of all peoples especially impure—in fact, they were not Jews at all but rather were following a false form of Judaism.

Although Dr. Thompson's demographic researches into the genetic mix in ancient Judaea have uncovered no evidence that it was any more genetically pure than its neighbors, Samaritans were singled out as foreign, heathen, and un-Jewish. And the earlier Mystery form of Judaism retained by Samaria was one Jerusalem branded a Godless non-religion—a fiction that gave license to a great deal of religious and racial intolerance. Divorce was enforced on any Jew marrying a foreigner, particularly a Samaritan, and the children of such polluted alliances had to be disowned. Yahweh was proclaimed the God of the Jews alone, and fundamentalist assassins lurked among the Jerusalem crowds like vengeful vigilantes, ready at an unwary word against the Jewish God to kill the apostate, the blasphemer, or the defiling foreigner. Hugh Schonfield, himself Jewish, comments:

> Some now said that all the earth beyond the holy land of Israel was impure and that the people of God could not suffer contact with such ritual impurity. Others declared that all Gentiles and all their works, even their crops and animals, were equally impure. Arguments raged over the minutest details. Was bread lawful when baked in an oven inadvertently heated with wood cut by a Gentile? Did a weaver's shuttle cut from foreign wood make lawful cloth?[61]

We are speaking here of an indoctrination so profound that in Reformed and Orthodox Israeli circles it has scarcely been overcome to the present day. Morton Smith points out that the strictest observants—those belonging to Judaic sects besides the Pharisees, such as the Sadducees and Essenes—thought even ordinary Jews unclean, and hence closed their meals, houses, and schools to them and lived in rigidly segregated communities.[62] Although the higher echelons of these sects were themselves in possession of the riches of merkavah mysticism and secretly studied Enoch and the Qabalah, it was against their laws to share these arcane teachings either with their own lower initiatory grades or with the masses, whether Jewish or Gentile. So the hermetically sealed boundaries that separated Jew from Gentile also separated the small, enclosed coteries of Jewish initiates one from another and from the mass of ordinary Jewish noninitiates. The latter, however often they washed in the miqva'ot, offered sacrifices, and studied the Torah in the synagogues, remained in the eyes of the Elect an unwashed peasantry.

Noninitiates lived as people beyond the pale. They knew nothing whatever about the secret doctrines that illuminated the religious life of their superiors, such as the names of God, the Work of the Chariot, the fourfold structure of Creation, the immortality of the soul, reincarnation, resurrection, magical formulae, the worlds of divine angelic beings, the astrological meaning of the End Times, and many other Qabalistic matters studied in the sectarian schools; nor could they expect an afterlife in the Kingdom of Light. These same impermeable barriers divided sect from sect, adding to the general climate of discord, divisiveness, and insularity.

In effect, a spiritual caste system operated in ancient Judaea that set sect against sect, initiate against noninitiate, and Jew against unbeliever, creating a xenophobic climate of suspicion and ill will on every side. At the same time, no love was lost by the general populace on the aristocratic priesthood, that huge body of officials who, swollen with power, ran the temple and watched coldly for heresies. History has glossed over the full malignancy of which this body was capable, but the sectarian writings found among the caves at Qumran, and believed by most scholars to be those of the Essenes, tell their own story of terror and persecution. They are clearly those of an endangered underground movement enduring a repressive regime.

The Essenes, like the Nazareans and other such sects, were influenced by Philo's development of a number symbolism, or gematria, from the Greek Qabalah that could provide an allegorical (rather than a literal) interpretation of the Hebrew scriptures,[63] and had adopted many Neo-Pythagorean beliefs about the soul, the afterlife, reincarnation, heaven, and hell, a general resurrection, and a Messianic kingdom to come, all concepts circulating in the diaspora but vigorously rejected by the official temple cult in Jerusalem. Furthermore, the social manifesto of the sectaries, the New Covenant, was nonethnic, being based on a revolutionary principle of racial tolerance, and therefore a direct flouting of the temple's ethnocentric policy. The Essenes also proclaimed their opposition to slavery, unequal wealth, militancy, and animal sacrifice, and claimed that membership in their sect was based on love of all humanity and "not as a matter of race."[64] In other words, although presenting themselves as strictly observant Jews, secretly they had heterodox and multiracial leanings that were very much in defiance of official Judaic policy.

The Qumran writings tell us as much. They are secretive, encoded; they name no names, they offer no incriminating details in their account of the sect's history under hostile authorities: first, the Maccabean/Hasmonean high priests and then the Herodian. Deeply guarded in tone, the sectarian scrolls that reveal the esoteric interests of the writers were hidden among copies of the more orthodox scriptures in desert caves outside Jerusalem and were clearly not intended for general perusal. But no city could survive for long in such a schizoid state. It would probably be wrong to impute to either the Roman occupation or the Judaeo-Christian ferment, or indeed any one single factor, the primary reason for the fall of Jerusalem and the breakup of the Jewish state. Rather, the extremely polarized social and cult conditions in the Holy City had made it eminently ripe for destruction. Even before the first century, it had become evident that reform was urgently needed, but that the birth of a new ethos was going to be accompanied by much blood and sorrow.

3

JESUS, UNIVERSAL MAN

*Without initiation or mystical intuition a philosopher is
restricted to the narrow field of rational speculation in which
he can only pace to and fro like a caged lion, ignorant of what
true freedom can be.*

JOSCELYN GODWIN

Commenting on the reactionary religious climate in Judaea in the
first century, Thomas Thompson writes that more than one book
of biblical scholarship

> has explored the possibilities of radical political parties forming
> around a Taliban-like fundamentalist core of religious bigots . . .
> Slogan-like references to "Yahweh Alone!" as a rallying cry for such
> groups echo through many of our texts, and might well reflect such
> socially destructive movements.[1]

By the first century, religious bigotry combined with a secrecy amounting to paranoia ensured that the majority of Judaean Jews were psychologically incapable of adjusting to the harsh constraints of foreign
conquest or the impact of Hellenism on their religion. Under a profane and alien pressure, Jerusalem could no longer bend; it could only
implode.

Into this inflammatory scene came the Nazarean initiate Jesus ben Joseph with his band of disciples, a prophet whose brief but incandescent career ignited forces that would help to set the city ablaze and reduce Judaea to ruins. He was almost certainly not working alone: revolutionary reforming forces originating in the diaspora were gathering in northern Palestine of which Jesus was only a part—but a pivotal part. One of the most mysterious figures in history, he flashed across its skies like a meteor, blazing with the pressure of a task that had all too little time for its accomplishment.

From the beginning of his ministry, Jesus was a wanted man, burdened by a mission anathema to the Jewish Levitical priesthood and haunted by the prospect of the same fate that had overtaken the Baptist. John had recently been beheaded by Herod Antipas, the ethnarch of the provinces of Galilee and Peraea and a friend of Jerusalem's priestly establishment. Jesus' movements about Palestine can be traced in the gospels to show how the enmity of the Herodean ruler (and behind him the temple hierarchy) pursued him from place to place, forcing his escape from Galilee into the relative safety of the Syrian wilderness, down into Peraea, then back into Galilee and danger, and finally southward to Jerusalem, where the greatest concentration of his enemies awaited him. A relative stranger to Judaea, Jesus was speaking literally as well as metaphorically when he said, "The foxes have their holes and the birds have their nests, but the Son of Man has no place to lay his head and rest" (Thomas 86).

According to the records, Jesus survived for three years at most, after which he was arrested, tried, and crucified. In that time he laid the foundations of a new Mystery religion destined to spread into every quarter of the globe, yet many modern scholars still cast doubt on his spiritual agenda. They persist in identifying his cause rather with the politically motivated insurrectionists and freedom fighters from Galilee such as Judas of Galilee and other Zealots described by Dr. Schonfield in *The Pentecost Revolution*. These rebels, Schonfield says, were nationalistic "Zealots for the Torah; they were anti-Gentile because of the contamination of heathenism; and they were opposed to Caesar or any foreigner as their ruler."[2] But these were the sentiments of the Maccabean/Levitical party, policies that were strongly contested by more-liberal elements in Jewish society and not in any sense descriptive of Jesus himself. To the contrary, several early authorities inimical to the Christians, including the Talmudic rabbis writing in the third century CE, have stated that Jesus was executed not for political reasons at all, nor for inciting the populace to insurrection, but for Egyptian magical practices—for being an occultist from Egypt and a teacher of alien doctrines.[3] This was undoubtedly at least in part the cause of the alarm in high places that led to Jesus' arrest: he was a carrier of the radically new ideas of the Egyptian diaspora that were fermenting so much hostility and political anxiety in Jerusalem. Even worse, he was preaching them openly to the masses.

Historians tell us that the overt basis for Jesus' arrest and summary crucifixion on the eve of the Passover Festival was a civil one; he created a disturbance among the people. The disturbance is generally agreed to be threefold: first, he claimed to be the legitimate king of Israel, which would have been a charge taken with the utmost seriousness by the Romans, since the terrorist and Zealot Judas of Gamala had made a like claim not long before, disrupting the peace with years of incessant guerrilla warfare.[4] Second, Jesus predicted the destruction of the temple; and third, he created a furor in the temple, at that time crowded with pilgrims, by overturning the tables of the moneychangers. Caiaphas the high priest brought the charge, seemingly backed by the ruling legislative body of the Sanhedrin; the Roman governor Pontius Pilate delivered the death sentence. Any one of these crimes might have been grounds for the execution of a troublemaker according to the rough-and-ready methods of crowd control under Roman colonial law, and the three felonies may in truth have been all that had concerned the Roman governor. But there are cogent reasons for imputing to Caiaphas a darker agenda.

There is an early tradition that John the Baptist also was associated with Egypt, the land whose reputation for harboring the most occult, pagan, and forbidden elements in the Jewish religion was so resented by the authorities in Judaea. It would seem, therefore, that the stream on which Jesus and John were swept into Palestinian affairs came from a quite different direction from that of the Galilean political rebels, though no doubt adding surge and momentum to their militant program, and that the mission of the two prophets was obstructed by the temple authorities for reasons other than civil security. Both were carriers of a religious message that the temple authorities—that is, the highly conservative Levitical party, which included the aristocratic sect of Sadducees—believed could destroy them.

Some scholars, reluctant to admit that the Levites connived at Jesus' death, point out that the council of the Sanhedrin was legally entitled to have him stoned to death if he were found guilty of a religious crime rather than the civil one with which he was actually charged and delivered over to the Romans. But a telling counterargument to this view is that it would have been unwise in the extreme for the temple clergy to be seen by the populace to be executing such an important and charismatic figure: better if it were done by stealth.

For Jesus was no ordinary troublemaker from the rank-and-file, no "peasant nobody" or "Mediterranean peasant," as the Catholic priest and author John Dominic Crossan has dubbed him, but a major force to be reckoned with. This eminent Jesuit author has clearly not studied the abysmally wretched and underprivileged conditions of the peasantry in the Mediterranean world of late antiquity, nor, most pertinently, the class strictures that made life at that time a prison for the illiterate agricultural serf, tenant farmer, builder, or laborer. Such a man lived barely above the starvation line and was not free to leave his place of work without permission. Still less could he gain access to the closed spiritual schools, all of which required social status, literacy, and financial means as basic requirements of their members. The historian and foremost authority on the Byzantine culture, Cyril Mango, says that in the first century the Mediterranean peasant was little better than a slave, "one of degraded and anomalous status,"[5] and that the artisan and trader class suffered only a slightly better fate.

Consequently, the idea that in the caste-dominated world of Jesus' era a peasant outcaste, untrained, uneducated, and socially disdained, would be allowed to teach in the temple or could succeed in filling the teaching office of the prestigious synagogues—preaching and reading the Sabbath lection, as Jesus is reported in the gospels to have done— flies in the face of the social realities of his day. No one who has studied the dynamics of social caste in traditional societies, both in the past and equally today in such countries as India, Tibet, and Indonesia, could easily accept such a notion. Even at the present time, in Indonesia, the servant class and the peasantry are not permitted into the esoteric schools that flourish there; these are reserved for the educated and affluent urban class alone. The unspoken embargo can become quite explicit should a member of the lower classes forget his place in society and attempt such a thing.

Whatever Jesus was or was not, the stereotype of the illiterate serf as applied to him is wildly inappropriate. His freedom of movement, geographically wide-ranging activities, and forays into the scholarly synagogues and homes of wealthy and privileged citizens underscore the impression he gives of high-caste stature. The culture of privilege is distinctive; Jesus' simplest utterances betray the cultivated mind and, more, the highly individuated consciousness not of a serf but of a spiritual master reared and trained in a privileged social milieu.

For most modern Jewish scholars Jesus was, by virtue of being a Jew, a strict adherent of Mosaic law, a rabbi. "This is only what we should expect," writes Schonfield. "It is no longer tenable that Christianity at its inception . . . was distinct from contemporary attitudes within Judaism."[6] But this of course begs the question, Which Judaism? In what section of the diaspora? Geza Vermes, like Schonfield, has written extensively about Jesus as a simple and observing Jewish *nabi* of his time, a holy man of impeccable orthodoxy.[7] His portrait of the Christian founder as a charismatic Galilean healer and exorcist, a Hasid in the mold of countless other such Jewish holy men of the northern provinces, is currently perhaps the most popular of all Jesus' possible personas. But behind the picture of the saintly provincial faith healer there still lurks the old stereotype, the stigma of the unlettered village shaman that has attached to Jesus for so long. Indeed, Morton Smith saw him as so similar to countless other rural wonder workers of the time that he regarded Jesus' impact on religious history as a mere fluke.[8] Others have stressed the rustic simplicity and humanity of Jesus' character, which is indeed undeniable:

> [Jesus is] forgiving and imaginative, tolerant, generous . . . strikingly compassionate . . . and associated in life with acts of gentleness, with flowers, birds, animals, and of course children.[9]

A. N. Wilson reinforces this portrait of a simple rustic healer by stressing that Jesus lacked a wide education; he was a peasant visionary who worked, presumably alone, solely in the rural areas among the common people, avoiding the sophisticated Galilean cities and the intellectual cosmopolitans who inhabited them. With the Greek-educated cognoscenti of the cities, Wilson implies, Jesus had little in common.[10] This again is a stereotype that has had its day. Margaret Barker stresses the fact that the figure of Jesus familiar to us from the Christian scriptures, "a simple teacher surrounded by ordinary and largely unlettered folk who withstood the sophisticated religious leaders of their time," simply cannot be a true one in the light of his Enochan background.

> The points at which Enoch illuminates the New Testament show that ours is far from being an accurate picture. 1 Enoch is not a popular work, not the simple religion of Galilean peasants and fishermen. It represents an enormous body of learning, sophisticated in its own way—ancient, intricate, and highly developed. If teachings such as these were known to the New Testament writers, then the New Testament itself may be no more than the tip of an iceberg.[11]

A much deeper picture of Jesus as the agent of a worldwide religio-social reformation emerges from the three arguably earliest (and therefore most reliable) written Christian sources, produced perhaps only a decade or two after his death: Paul's letters, the Fourth Gospel by John, and the Gospel of Thomas. It has long been known that Paul's letters, written from ca. 40 to 60 CE, are the earliest known record of his Master's work on earth. The Fourth Gospel and that of Thomas, the latter of which comprises 114 sayings of "the living Jesus," were once thought to be late productions, but some scholars now doubt that presumption and date both to a period likely to be contemporaneous with Paul's communications or very little later.[12]

In other words, the Gospels of John and Thomas could conceivably be apostolic, or at least the work of someone drawing on firsthand testimony to Jesus' life and teachings, and therefore of inestimable value as source material. All three documents are distinctly mystical and gnostic in tone and are the ones that most decisively transpose the figure of Jesus from a homely folk level to the intellectual elevation enjoyed by other great illuminati of history. Contemporary studies of the Dead Sea Scrolls also remind us that today a radically new picture of Jesus is emerging.

> The New Jesus [is not] the uneducated faith-healer and miracle-monger of Galilee alleged . . . to have spoken only colloquial Aramaic (the first Yiddish), to have written only on the ground with his finger, and to have been quite ignorant of the wonderful Greek paideia and Roman civilization of his time. Careful study of the Essene scrolls . . . confirmed by the Egyptian Gnostic codices from Nag Hammadi, reveals him to have been not only well-versed in the knowledge and culture of Rome, Persia, Athens, and Alexandria, a wide traveler, and a great teacher, but also an original independent thinker and a dedicated existential empiricist . . .[13]

In this new picture the father of Christianity comes across as an ecstatic in the mold of the sixth-century-BCE Taoist Lao-tzu of China or of the nineteenth-century Hindu saint Ramakrishna, or again of Guru Padma Sambhava, the learned Indian mystic who took Buddhism to Tibet in the seventh century. But Jesus is even more closely akin to the Persian prince Mani (200–275), the brilliant mystic, magician, sage, artist, and healer who founded the religion of Manichaeism, which rivaled

Christianity for so long.[14] All these men were spiritual luminaries of genius. Like them, Jesus too was evidently a man of unusually diverse spiritual talents that ranged from highly developed shamanistic powers to an eloquent grasp of the learning of his day, a healer and exorcist whose magisterial authority of bearing and magnetic personality reminded his hearers of the prophet Elijah. His powers of oratory evidently swayed thousands, and he was also a miracle worker and magus who knew the secret of controlling others—who could say "follow me" and be instantly obeyed. This is most certainly the portrait not of a "peasant nobody" or an illiterate village shaman, but of an initiate trained in one of the great inner brotherhoods.

Jesus' high mission in history was centered on religious reform. He aimed to liberate Israel from the straitjacket of collective law, from a theology that had become shackling to the spirit, even though knowing that by doing so he was offending a deeply entrenched power system. Geza Vermes has repudiated this commonly expressed assessment of first-century Jewry as being obsessed by the Law, and claims that it springs from the misleading polemics of Christian opponents of Judaism.[15] But as we have seen, the many modern *Jewish* studies of Palestinian society at the time of the writing of the Dead Sea Scrolls leave an overriding impression of just such a legalistic malaise in Judaea, amounting to almost a national psychosis. Arguments for and against this conclusion can of course be summoned, as Vermes brilliantly attests, but the real point at issue is not the strength of "the yoke of the Law," but whether there is or is not a higher moral imperative that overrides it—that is, whether there is not an evolutionary need to develop an *inner locus of control* that wrests moral power from external forces and authorities and vests it in the individual soul. Christianity testifies that this higher imperative, which had always operated in the lives of initiates, was indeed at the center of all Jesus' teachings.

What Israel needed more than political freedom, from either the Romans or the upstart Herodian house, was spiritual freedom. The idea, generally imputed to St. Paul, that Christ's mission was aimed at transcending the strictures of Jewish Mosaic law, is not a popular one today, yet it cannot be discarded lightly. Paul expressed a belief, shared by many Judaeo-Christians from the very beginning of the movement, that beyond a certain level of evolution the life of the soul cannot with impunity be subjected to legislation; thereafter, the inner being needs freedom for growth. Jesus found a nation already schooled for hundreds of years in priestly and scribal law and expert in keeping the purity regulations and sacrificial rites of the temple, but one that, except for a very small elite, was unfree and excluded from spiritual enlightenment.

Despite opposition in high places, in the short time at his disposal Jesus opened up a gate to greater self-awareness, to an autonomy that went far beyond tribal law. Zoroastrianism had split the world into two, claiming that it was ruled by the Good God Ahura Mazda and his eternal opponent, the evil Ahriman, the Great Lie. Jesus' teachings sought to transcend that duality. As a revival of the Gnosis taught in the temples, the Christian path provided a stairway by which the soul could ascend by ordered stages of initiation from this world of duality to the unitary consciousness of the Kingdom of Heaven, which is above good and evil. By means of the bridechamber rite, Jesus laid the foundations of such an initiatory path, providing practices that all could follow according to their level of need, strength, and understanding. The Gospel of Philip in particular reveals a baptismal Mystery "involving death-rebirth, illumination, enthronement, and mystic marriage"[16] as practiced by Jesus himself. This revolutionary reform that may have already been begun by John the Baptist in his baptismal ceremonies in the Jordan—a liberation of the masses who were normally excluded from contact with the Gnosis—broke major taboos, sexual, social, and religious, and was a scandal to the temple clergy.

Christianity evolved from the beginning as a religion of the individual, concerned with selfhood and the unique needs of each human soul rather than with formal collective structures. The trend toward a greater concern for the individual ego was already under way throughout the ancient East, but the Jesus movement brought it to its fullest flowering. Unlike either Judaism or Islam, Christianity was not founded as a sociopolitical system based on scriptural authority; it was not a "religion of the Book," although it has been turned into one, but was originally a mystical path leading beyond the fixed boundaries of cultic and societal institutions. This is both Christianity's strength and its weakness, as the checkered history of Christianized Europe attests.

Even today, when so much of the original intention has been lost, the dynamism of the Christian impulse shines through. Its concern for personal conscience and the rights and values of the individual suffuses its teachings with a spiritual luster that its excesses cannot entirely dim. This concern for the individual—every individual, including women, slaves, children, criminals, and outcastes—combining with our Greek heritage, has created an egalitarian mind-set unique to Western culture. Clement of Alexandria (ca. 150–214) declared that since Christ's coming "divinity now pervades all humankind equally . . . deifying humanity, the slave equally with the master."[17] In principle, this is still true. Christianity's innermost "seed truth" declares to the present day that each human being is a child of the Divine, each individual, however lowly in social status, is a singularity, a unique center of decision gifted with the divine privilege of freedom of conscience and choice.

This concept of inner liberty flowed from the dynamics of the bridechamber rite, which involved a water baptism and a sealing with oil. Since oil burned when ignited, it was equated with the element of fire, symbolizing pure mentation, while water symbolized the emotions. As we have seen in the previous chapter, in the bridechamber these two elements, mind and emotion, hostile to each other and traditionally regarded as forming the primary polarity, were united. Spirit united with soul.

> Soul and the spirit are constitiuted of water and fire; a child of the bride-chamber is constituted of water, fire and light. Fire is chrism; light is fire—I do not mean worldly fire, which has no form, but another kind of fire whose appearance is white—which is beautifully luminous, and which bestows beauty. (Philip 58)

Although the bridechamber experience remains something of a mystery, its pivotal place in early Christianity is becoming more and more

evident as the unitary principle underpinning it emerges. "The reconciliation of the opposites," Stephan A. Hoeller reminds us, "is the key
that unlocks the storehouse of limitless psychic energy"[18]—an energy
which in turn augments a hundredfold the awareness of selfhood and
its potential for autonomous functioning. Thus Dr. Seymour states that
with the coming of Christ, the seeds were sown for a radical shift in
human thinking which had begun with the Greeks, who believed that
at least in principle it lay within each person's own power to think and
judge for himself.

> This was new . . . Christ may well be said to have spearheaded a new
> direction in religion . . . The last two thousand years have therefore
> been a history of Christianity's struggle to come to terms with the
> notion of individual and personal authority . . .[19]

This elevation of individual rights and individual liberty of conscience to the status of a religious principle is precisely why tradition
has always assigned to Jesus a unique eminence and an altogether more
esoteric function in religious history than that of either Moses or
Muhammad.[20] But because his mission has too often been skewed to
the orthodox Mosaic viewpoint, its profoundly psychological, individualistic, and gnostic orientation, a startling innovation in his day, has
been completely obscured. Its debt to the bridechamber rite has indeed
never been acknowledged.

Writing before the final forced expulsion of Christians from the
synagogues, the narrators of the canonical gospels, particularly the three
Synoptics, were eager to put Jesus in a favorable light with their fellow
orthodox Jews and to convince them that he never deviated from total
loyalty to the Torah: the Lord's teachings, they insisted, were strictly in
conformity with "the law and the prophets." But the apocryphal gospels
contradict this view. They present a picture of Jesus that is infused with
Alexandrian nonconformist ideas, reminding us that in Egypt, Philo
was at that time revolutionizing Judaism along similar innovatory lines.
Philo interiorized Mosaic law by presenting it as the allegorical outer

expression of what should be freely chosen inner moral action. In the same manner, Jesus discounts the purity laws so central to Judaean society, and at times even sets them at nought. According to the Gospel of Thomas, when the disciples asked him, "Is circumcision beneficial or not?"

> He said to them, "If it were beneficial, their father would beget them already circumcised from their mother. Rather, the true circumcision in spirit has become completely profitable." (Thomas 53)

For observant Jews it was encumbent too for fasting to take place after a death; but when the Baptist's disciples demurred at the unconventional behavior of Jesus' disciples on such an occasion, Jesus asked, using the ritual language of a baptismal Mystery:

> How can the sons of the Marriage Chamber mourn while the Bridegroom *(nymphios)* is with them? The time will come when the *nymphios* will be taken from them; then they will fast.[21]

And in similar vein, when the disciples suggested, "Let us fast and pray," as was required of the strictly observing Jew,

> Jesus said: "What is the sin that I have committed, or wherein have I been defeated? But when the bridegroom leaves the bridal chamber then let them fast and pray." (Thomas 104)

And again, concerning the dietary laws he said:

> If you fast, you will give rise to sins for yourselves; and if you pray, you will be condemned; and if you give alms, you will do harm to your spirits. When you go into any land and walk about in the districts, if they receive you, *eat what they will set before you,* and heal the sick among them. For what goes into your mouth will not defile you, but that which issues from your mouth—it is that which will defile you. (Thomas 14) (author's italics)

If Thomas's reportage is to be believed, Jesus was on a direct collision course with the temple establishment in Jerusalem and with its strict ritual requirements. His negligence toward the purity laws, his manifest air of spiritual authority, his heterodox views and exceptional occult powers by which even the strongest spirits were controlled must surely have polarized and excited the pious folk of Palestine to an extent considered highly dangerous by the authorities. But even more importantly, Jesus was condemned for his betrayal of temple secrets to which only the highest initiates were permitted access. Although his authorization to teach had come from the highest source, from the Holy Spirit itself, the sect of the Mandaean/Nazareans leveled similar accusations against him in their scriptures: "Jesus," they said, "was a rebel, a heretic who led men astray, [and] betrayed secret doctrines . . ."[22] So it would appear that Jesus drew to himself a great deal of anger and calumny because of his opening up of the merkavah science and its secret Gnosis of the heart, disclosing it to large numbers of followers unqualified in the eyes of the Elect. For that reason alone, once Jesus entered on his radical teaching mission, his death was probably a foregone conclusion.

THE HEART AND ITS TRANSCENDENT FUNCTION

The heart is the key to the entire Christian message. Neurocardiologists are only now beginning to explore the mystery of the heart and to recognize its true function as a higher guiding center of the body/mind complex. Through their work we can approach the Christian mystery with a new understanding. Scientific research has found that the heart carries on an intricate dialogue with the brain, the body, and the world at large, playing a role whose holistic, synthesizing function has not been understood by scientists until the last few decades. Surprisingly, its traditional role as a pump for the circulation of blood is true only to a very limited extent. Neurophysicists have been astonished to discover that the heart is primarily an organ of intelligence like the brain, more than half of it being composed of neurons of the same nature as those that make up the cerebral system. In *The Biology of Transcendence,* Joseph Chilton Pearce, author of several books on the developmental needs of children and human society in general, comments on the extraordinary nature of the heart as now being discovered by science. He calls it "the major biological apparatus within us and the seat of our greatest intelligence."[23]

> Some reports claim 60 to 65 per cent of heart cells are neurons, all of which cluster in ganglia, small neural groupings connected through the same type of axon-dendrites forming the neural fields of our brain . . . An ongoing dialogue takes place between the heart and the brain through these direct neural connections.[24]

But the heart is not only the center of a form of intelligence hitherto unacknowledged by science, and which we are beginning to know as *emotional intelligence;* it is also the source of the body's strongest electromagnetic field. Each heart cell is unique in that it not only pulsates in synchrony with all the other heart cells, but also produces an electromagnetic signal that radiates out beyond the cell. Indeed, an EEG that measures brain waves shows that the electromagnetic signals from the heart are so much stronger than brain waves that a reading of the heart's frequency spectrum can be taken from three feet away from the body, without placing electrodes on it. The heart as a whole is found to emit electromagnetic energy that arcs out from and back to the heart in the form of a torus or field that extends as far as twelve to fifteen feet from the body, a far greater area than that of the cerebral field. The axis of this heart torus extends through the length of the body, from the pelvic floor to the top of the skull, and the whole field is holographic, meaning that information about it can be read from each and every point in the torus.

The three brain centers in the head, a cerebral complex that can operate independently of the heart's intelligence, have been studied for much longer. The neuroscientist Paul MacLean, head of the Department of Brain Evolution and Behavior at the U.S. National Institutes of Health, has found a striking similarity between the three neural

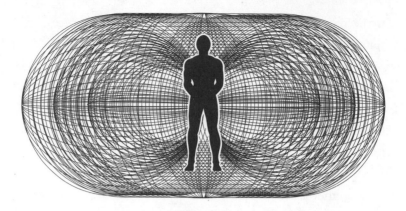

Fig. 3. The heart torus

head centers and those of the three major animal groups of evolution: reptilian, old mammalian, and new mammalian. "For more than half a century," says Joseph Pearce, "he [MacLean] and his staff traced these parallels and showed how each of our neural systems carries within it the blueprint of potential intelligences, abilities, and capacities developed during each of these evolutionary epochs."[25]

Our hindbrain, the ancient reptilian brain at the base of the skull, consists of the sensory-motor system, the instinctual center that directs the basically brutal fight-or-flight survival skills perfected by our ancestors. The old mammalian or emotional-cognitive brain is far more complex, adding to the reptilian senses those of smell and hearing, the herd instinct, a nurturing instinct for our young, and all forms of relationship skills, and resides chiefly in the thalamus or midbrain. Last, there is the neocortex or new mammalian brain, the verbal-intellectual center that introduces language and thinking into the system as well as the ability to observe these activities objectively. This high brain "occupies five times more skull space than the reptilian brain and the old mammalian brain combined and consists of some hundred million neurons."[26] Pearce points out that the abilities of the cortical brain are limitless; it can translate input from the world out there to imaginative thinking within, and is a center of intellectual creativity and novelty, analysis, and interpretation.

Furthermore, MacLean has furnished recent evidence for a further spurt of neocortical growth in the prefrontal lobes behind the brow, producing what seems to be the beginning of a mysterious fourth modality in brain development. This secondary aspect of the neocortex is still little explored and is not acknowledged in all academic circles, but the general consensus is that the prefrontal lobes constitute the supreme evolutionary cerebral center, the regulator and monitor for all the brain's other neural structures. Some attribute to the prefrontal cortex the higher human virtues of love and compassion as well as the most advanced intellectual abilities. Pearce believes this still-evolving cognitive center is of a highly intuitional nature, introducing a moral dimension into human development, in that, as he says, it is "related to the two roads we humans can take—both the path of violence and the path of transcendence . . ."[27] It relates to the spiritual "third eye" and completes a complex cerebral system that can actually operate autonomously without any connection to the heart.

To this accumulating knowledge about the highly specialized brain structure, Paul MacLean brings his findings of the entirely different kind of intelligence seated in the heart—a universal intelligence quite different from the cerebral intellect—and one that science has previously known nothing of and whose distinctively holistic and intuitive qualities it has vigorously disputed. Over many years of research, the neurological connections between the brain and the heart, and their ongoing dialogue, were studied under grants from the National Institutes of Health, in the United States, and are now being validated by the new field of neurocardiology. MacLean has gained general scientific support for his view that the heart constitutes a fifth center of intelligence that is neurally interactive with the brain center as a whole, and especially with the prefrontal lobes. Says Pearce:

> The prefrontals are nature's latest neural creation, and this orbito-frontal connection is the fourth brain's link with the ancient emotional-cognitive brain and, through it, with our heart.[28]

But as opposed to the specialized cerebral activity of the brain, the wisdom of the heart is nonverbal, prelogical, and neither linear nor digital; it is essentially holistic. Its neural ganglia are as connected to the myriad ganglia of the body as they are to those of the brain; and thus the intelligence of the heart may be thought of as a mind–body bridge that unifies the entire individual system by both neurological and hormonal means. The magnetic character of this wonderful center means that, interactive between body and mind, the heart mediates the frequency of love, for in the heart, love and wisdom are one.

"The heart," says Pearce, "is the primary mode of being and all else in our life springs from it."[29] It precedes the brain's formation, and therefore precedes the formation of the sensory-perceptual apparatus for experiencing the spacetime world at large, for in human embryonic and fetal development a rudimentary heart is the first organ to evolve, after which the brain develops and finally the body. "We do well to remember that in utero the heart, as vehicle for the frequencies of our potential world experience, forms first."[30]

The heart, therefore, furnishes the electromagnetic field that surrounds the embryo from the very beginning, while that field is itself stabilized by being surrounded by the mother's more powerful heart field. These tori are nested in a hierarchy of tori that range from the microscopic to the macroscopic. The information garnered from these nested tori, so it is thought, somehow provides the material after birth for the brain's perceptual patterning of the world in space and time. Furthermore, the activity of the heart is teleological in that it precedes the organization of the sensory organs that perceive things "out there," and can therefore foresee what is needed in the building of the body for its safety, well-being, and harmonious functioning, and relay that information to the brain. For the heart, there is no such thing as chance. The heart knows only the law of providence in creation, a foresightful guidance in relation to the All.

To understand the purposeful or teleological nature of heart intelligence and why it has a cosmic dimension—why indeed Pearce calls it an *organ of transcendence*—we need to explore further the holographic nature of its torus or electromagnetic field. Every atom has such a torus. The earth is also the center of a torus, so is the solar system, so also the galaxy, and all are holographic. Some scientists conjecture,

> [A]ll energy systems from the atomic to the universal level are toroid in form. This leads to the possibility that there is only one universal torus encompassing an infinite number of interacting, holographic tori within its spectrum . . . Because electromagnetic torus fields are holographic, it is probable that the sum total of our universe might be present within the frequency spectrum of a single torus.[31]

This means that each of us is in touch with the All. Each of us, as an organism centered in the heart torus, is nested in a hierarchy of holographic tori and thus is the center of the universe, with access to all the information it can provide at any given moment. Such cosmic information from the nurturing systems of earth, from suns, planets, and comets, and from the very life-giving galactic center itself, relayed to brain and body, ensures our harmonious compatibility with the deeds and intentions of the universe and therefore a continuing access to health, growth, and cosmic congruence. As already said, this brings a teleological factor into the development of organisms that seriously challenges the Darwinian theory of the survival of the fittest.

And there is a further dimension to this cooperative fusion of heart and brain activity, this creative blending of the particular and the universal. At its optimal, the heart's interaction with the intuitional prefrontal lobes, through the cognitive-emotional center in the cortex, creates a new and even more powerful dynamic—a single unified field, a spiritual overview of such potency that it offers the full development of our human and transcendental potential.

However, as has been remarked, there is always the possibility of a failure of the system, in that it can fall into disunity. The cerebral system can disconnect from the heart and is prone to do so under pathological conditions. "Intellect . . . can function independently from the heart," notes Pearce, "—that is, without intelligence—and can take over the circuitry and block our heart's more subtle signals."[32] The ideal cultural process can fail. Scientists can display brilliant intellects but no intelligence in inventing atomic bombs in defiance of human welfare; without intelligence, politicians can devise clever economic strategies that throw millions into penury and starvation. Civilizations can self-destruct. A society, no matter how gifted, that has no recourse to the intelligence of the heart in its policies or values is likely to wither on the vine within a short time, dying in every case by its own hand. Thus the pagan society into which Jesus was born can justifiably be defined as one that had come to function only in body and mind, without a mediating flow of love and wisdom—a condition that can be thought of as a sterile and often brutal materialism. It would seem that the Gnosis of the heart given out in the Jesus movement might have been aimed at this very problem.

"The world we see and hear in a state of fear, rage, dire emergency, or struggle," notes Pearce, "is quite different from that which we experience in a state of harmony and love."[33] According to research carried out among hundreds of workers, this latter state has been found to be achievable when the three-way connection among body, heart, and mind is coherent and unified. By learning a method called Heartmath, the establishment of emotional stability can be had, leading to happiness, transcendence, and a successful life in the midst of its manifold stresses and perils, so in time transforming the society around us.

Mae Wan Ho, Ph.D., a reader in biology at the Open University in England, studies the coherence in living organisms. Based on laboratory research, she has found that all living organisms are liquid crystalline:

> The organism is coherent beyond our wildest dreams. Every part is in communication with every other part through a dynamic, tuneable, responsive liquid crystalline medium that pervades the whole body, from organs and tissues to the interior of every cell. Liquid crystallinity gives organism their characteristic flexibility . . . optimising the rapid intercommunication that enables [them] to function as a coherent whole.[34]

As Pearce points out, when the whole being is coherent, it can transform its lower negative states into positive ones. It can then express the full potential of a human being, its positive capacity for wisdom, dominion over the world, and unconditional love and creativity, as did the Gnostic Christians. True, the latter arrived at their sanctified state by a route very different from the analytical and empirical methods, primarily cerebral, of our scientists and psychologists; but on the other hand, their heart-centered spirituality, which demanded a high order of faith rather than intellect, achieved prodigies of healing and other miracle-working effects to which Heartmath doesn't aspire and cannot. The coherence of the whole achieved in the bridechamber sacrament evidently took the initiate farther along the road of sanctifying transcendence than anything we could dream of reaching, and by a mysterious additional factor that will be explored in later chapters.

This brief summary of one of today's most important scientific discoveries offers convincing testimony that Jesus was already teaching it two thousand years ago. The Gnosis of the heart was ancient then. In the postglacial period, shaman masters were already employing it in their genetic science. We have only to study the dynamics of the Chinese civilization, which is more than three thousand years old and still virile, as well as that of the ancient Egyptians, a peaceful, humane, and brilliantly creative society lasting nearly three thousand years, to realize that *heart knowledge* in conjunction with head knowledge was understood from the beginning of history to be essential for the enlightened government of human societies. Jesus was but seeking to seed a more universal understanding of something that had been known to the few, the privileged illuminati, since Paleolithic times.

This is a realization that only deepens the mystery of Jesus' identity. As the Son of God, what relationship did he have to those primeval Sons of God of Lebanon who were pursuing a similar practice in their forest sanctuaries, creating genetic modifications to the human race that would make us what we are today, for good or ill? What linked Jesus to this immeasurably old tradition?

WHO WAS JESUS?

It has long been a matter of puzzlement to scholars that, unlike John the Baptist, Jesus seems to have been quite unknown to his pagan contemporaries. He appears in no known pagan account as the founder of the Christian movement, no Roman historian of the time mentions him (with perhaps the exception of Tacitus, who would later name "Chrestus" as the instigator of Christian riots in Rome), nor does the literature of any of the contemporary Jewish sects such as the Essenes refer to him. Who, then, was this man who was able to say with such prophetic percipience: "I have cast fire upon the world, and see, I am guarding it until it blazes" (Thomas 10)? And why has it proved so difficult to place him in any known spiritual tradition?

Since the early Christian centuries, Jesus' persona has undergone many dramatic changes, and never more so than in recent years. Today an astoundingly wide range of definitions and spiritual roles are being applied to one of the most commanding religious figures in history. He has been seen as a Cynic philosopher, a Zealot freedom fighter, a sorcerer, a shaman, and a rabbi, a Buddhist, an Essene, a proto Pharisee, a Freemason. In the latest contribution to the list, it has even been proposed that he was not a follower of Judaism at all but a pagan priest of Isis.[35] Yet although the founder of Christianity fits certain aspects of all these categories, it is a matter of frequent puzzlement, and indeed in the view of one writer "something of a scholarly bad joke"[36] that he cannot be satisfactorily identified with any one of them.

Almost the only thing we do know about Jesus that has never been concealed or disputed is that he was a Nazarean (Matthew 2:23), and that his early followers were also called Nazareans (in Hebrew Notzrim) as in the *Clementine Recognitions,* or alternatively Nazoreans or again Nazarenes. In Acts 24:5, Paul, arraigned by temple officials before the Roman governor Felix, is called "a ringleader of the sect of the Nazarenes." For centuries, variations of this name persisted in the Middle East as descriptive of Jesus in particular and of Christians in general, but the term is actually an ancient sectarian one and confirms Jesus as having belonged to a religious brotherhood closely linked to the Essenes. The brotherhood was also connected to the sects of the Ebionites and the Mandaeans, both of which in the first century called themselves Nazareans. Thus Kurt Rudolph, today's premier authority on the Mandaeans, writes:

> The earliest self-designation to be found in Mandaean literature are "elect of righteousness" *(bhiri zidqa)* and "Nasoreans" *(nasuraiyi)*, i.e., "guardians" or "possessors" of secret rites and knowledge. "Mandaeans" *(mandayi)* is of more recent date but refers back to the ancient Mandaean word for "perception, knowledge, Gnosis" *(manda);* it therefore means "the knowing ones, the gnostics."[37]

Jesus, then, belonged to this ancient Nazarean community of "knowing ones" or Gnostics, those who possessed the Gnosis. The standard belief that he was a native of Nazareth, at that time a hamlet in the south of the Galilean province, arose, it would seem, purely because the Gospel of Matthew claimed that the term Nazarean derived from the name of that site, but it is now widely recognized that this is not so. Some biblical scholars, it is true, still persist in the outdated view put forward by Matthew, ignoring the fact that his interpretation has been discredited. In Matthew 2:23, Jesus is specified as *nazoraye* (Syriac translation *nasraya*), but, says Geo Widengren, "*nasarayos* is not the natural adjectival form of Nazareth, and the assertion has lost as yet none of its validity."[38] Leading authorities agree with him.

Indeed until 1956 it was doubted that Nazareth, described in the Christian scriptures as a city with a synagogue, existed at all in the first century, some archaeologists referring to it as nothing more than a collection of ancient cave dwellings. Josephus, who commanded the Israelite army for a time in the northern provinces and therefore should know, never mentions it. But in 1956, further excavations were undertaken under the present prosperous city of Nazareth, exposing the first-century remains of a hamlet of a few poor hovels built on a site previously used by cave dwellers. Some of the most rudimentary tools for peasant life were uncovered, but nothing that associated the place with Jesus' family. Only at a later level was archaeological evidence found of Christian Nazareans and their worship of the holy family, evidently after the spread of the Christian message had popularized the place.[39]

In his monumental work *Against Heresies,* St. Epiphanius of Salamis in Cyprus (ca. 315–403) writes that the cradle of the Nazarean sect was a town called Cochaba in the Galilean-Damascene region—that is, in the Transjordan, east of the Sea of Galilee. Cochaba, the bishop tells us, was the place from which "the roots of the Ebionites and the Nazareans sprang."[40] On occasion he goes even further, equating two groups, the Essenes and the Nazareans, with each other and calling both Jessaeans; and no doubt the Ebionites could be included in this larger grouping. The term Nazarean gives us the most crucial information we possess concerning Jesus' identity as an initiate, "a true heir of an age-old religious line,"[41] as Geza Vermes says, and signals his place in the underground Mysteries of the day.

The word can be traced to the ancient Babylonian language and may have entered the Hebrew tongue at the time of the Babylonian Exile. The Assyriologist Heinrich Zimmern has shown that Nazarean is related to the term *nasaru* (or *nasiru*), which in ancient Babylonian meant "Keepers or Preservers of divine secrets,"[42] and says that it was associated in the Near and Middle East with esoteric fraternities dedicated to guarding sacred knowledge. Like the Nazareans, these fraternities were believed to be descended from the discredited prophetic orders, once so influential in the region.

Jesus the Nazarean was widely recognized as heir to the prophetic tradition. The early Christians identified him with the prophet Enoch, and the Ebionites also regarded Jesus as a prophet. According to the testimony of Clement, the Ebionites taught that Jesus was a human being like any other, but one on whom the Christ Spirit, an archangelic being of the highest hierarchy of angels, descended at the time of Jesus' baptism. The Ebionites believed in reincarnation and revered Jesus as the

True Prophet, an incarnation of the ancient Iranian prophet Zarathustra. It was only in Zarathustra's final embodiment as Jesus the Hebrew, so these sectaries believed, that the great seer received the full revelation of the Divine:

> Since the creation of the world, the True Prophet hastens through the centuries, changing his name and form of appearance. He incarnates himself again and again . . . Jesus is the true incarnation of this Prophet.[43]

The Mandaeans, a separate branch of the Semitic stock who survive to this day as the last gnostic sect in existence, likewise portray Jesus as a prophet. These sectaries declare that John the Baptist was their preeminent spiritual teacher and prophet, and that Jesus too, as one of John's initiates, was originally of their number. Their recently translated texts further assert that Jesus broke away from John's school to form his own, taking with him some of his master's followers and causing much resentment by openly teaching many of the secret Mandaean doctrines. The relevant point is that the Mandaeans are a strictly organized sect that comprises a hierarchy of three initiatory grades: the laity (mandayi), the middle rank of cult priests (tarmidi), and the highest rank of initiates, prophets, or magi (nasoraiyi), whose duty it is to preserve the Gnosis. John was a Nasurai—that is, a Nazarean prophet, say the Mandaeans—and so was Jesus.[44] Both belonged to the sacerdotal class qualified to officiate at the Mandaeans' holiest and most secret rite, that of the bridal chamber. In the baptism of the bridechamber, say the Mandaeans, every Nasurai received his prophetic office—as did Jesus.

But if Jesus was so commonly designated a prophet, why do the gospels not accord him the dignity of his rank? Indeed, we might ask further why Hebrew prophecy itself suddenly vanished from the annals of religious history, seemingly ceasing to exist long before Jesus was born. At this point the suspicion arises that both the Hebrew scriptures and the Christian scriptures may be very political documents. The checkered course of the Hebrew prophetic vocation from the post-Exilic centuries onward is a direct reflection of the massive power struggle waged between the Persian and the Greco-Egyptian Empires in the same period. Even in our present secular world, the great political power blocs tend to play out their wars in terms of religion, as we see the United States and the Middle East doing today, and the same pattern existed in antiquity. It reinforces the notion that, despite our current secular worldview, religion is still an important driving force of civilization.

The Zoroastrian, patriarchal worldview of the Persians that had been imposed on ancient Israel was in direct opposition to the Isis-and-Osiris religious tradition of Egypt, which even in Jesus' day reflected the predominantly matriarchal Goddess-centered worldview of the Bronze Age. Even the essentially monotheistic Solar cult of Re-harakhty in Heliopolis, Egypt, retained its reverence for the Divine Couple. Consequently, the political tension between these two great empires was played out between the new "Persian" Judaism and the old "Egyptian" Judaism—that is to say, between Zoroastrian Reformed Judaism and the Old Religion of the Hebrews under the pharaohs. In that struggle, it would appear that the prophets lost out.

In Palestine the prophets had long guided the people as wise elders from their communities outside the towns, maintaining such hallowed sanctuaries as Jericho, Bethel, Sinai-Kadesh in the south, and Mount Carmel in the north as repositories of the sacred wisdom of their race. In conformity with the Egyptian sacerdotal tradition, the high priest in the Jerusalem temple was traditionally a prophet, a Zadokite, one whose office had been passed down for hundreds of years in the House of Zadok and given royal status by King Solomon himself. But by the fourth century BCE, the Persians had conquered Palestine and redirected its religious outlook toward Zoroastrian ideals. Thereafter, the traditional accord among the three initiatory ranks—that of monarch, prophet, and priest—began to crumble in Judaea. By the third century BCE, kingship had lapsed and the Zadokites of the Old Religion were fatally at odds with the rising Levitical cult priests of the Reformed temple.

According to Gaalyah Cornfeld, the Levitical priesthood misled many of the religious with assurances of salvation through the mere slavish performance of the purity rituals and the practice of tithing, caring little for the erudite and contemplative practices of the prophets. Moreover, prophecy was a vocation traditionally exercised by closed orders or brotherhoods that extended without ethnic boundaries into every nation, and this global reach was seriously at odds with Israel's growing nationalism. For both reasons, the prophets had become politically marginalized.

Alarmed at the turn of events, the prophetic orders in Judaea called for a radical return to the earlier, esoteric traditions of Israel, but in this they were defeated, forbidden to exercise their vocation under pain of death and forced into exile in the Syro-Palestinian wilderness. Laws were passed: any man who assumed the role of prophet later than Ezra—by writing scripture, for example, or instructing the people—was, according to Zechariah 13:3, "to be thrust through by his own mother and father."[45] Hence a plethora of anonymously written pseudepigraphical scriptures falsely attributed to ancient prophets—ones living before Ezra—began to appear from the fourth century BCE onward, since this was the only way the prophetic voice could be heard. It would thus appear, says Cornfeld,

> that the prophets were bitterly and increasingly at odds with the Levitical priesthood of the Temple, and that the eclipse of the prophetic tradition and the rise to power of the Levites in the period of the second Temple must be regarded as the sign of some kind of Levitical power seizure.[46]

Josephus records that at the time of writing, the tradition of true prophetic succession had indeed lapsed in Judaea. Many charismatic self-styled prophets—fortune-tellers, scribes, and such—remained attached to the temple, but without being able to claim an accredited line of transmission.[47] It was therefore a dangerous exercise for any Hebrew prophet from the north to come openly preaching and healing in lands under Levitical jurisdiction, but much more so for Jesus, who was believed to have risen in rank *beyond the grade of prophet*.

In the Egyptian Solar temples, the still unbroken prophetic lineage led back to the Horus kings, to their ancestors the Shemsu-Hor, the initiate Companions of Horus, further back again to the legendary Watchers, the great priest-kings of the Neolithic age who were also called Divine Souls, and thus to the headwaters of the lineage, the Sons of God.[48] It was therefore still possible in principle for a prophet of this illustrious and timeless lineage to rise through the various grades to the supreme status of a Son of God. This was what traditionalists like the Ebionites believed. They taught that although Jesus was a human being like any other, he was chosen

> and thus called by election Son of God, Christ having come upon him from on high in the form of a dove. They say that he was not begotten by God the Father, but that he was created, like the archangels, but greater than they.[49]

Over a hundred years ago, Édouard Schuré first voiced the notion, shocking at the time, that Jesus was a high-ranking Essene initiate whose status as a Son of God had been misunderstood. In his work *The Great Initiates,* this radical French author and esotericist said, "I have tried to illumine with its own light that part of Jesus' life which the gospels have left in obscurity or hidden beneath the veil of legend."[50] The book was published in 1889 and was greeted by the press and Church authorities with what Schuré called "an icy silence." In 1909, in his introduction to one of the numerous new editions of the book, the Austrian mystic and clairvoyant Rudolf Steiner said:

> [This book] speaks about the "Great Illuminated," the Great Initiates, who have looked deeply into the background of things, and from this background have given great impulses for the spiritual development of mankind. It offers historic proof that the essence of religion is not to be separated from the concept of "initiation" or "illumination."[51]

The concept of initiation, Schuré believed, should be a guiding principle in any in-depth consideration of Jesus' life history. The proclamation that he was a Son of God actually revealed the Savior's supreme initiatory status. The official doctrine of Jesus' Divine Sonship rests on the Gospel accounts concerning the descent of the Holy Spirit at his baptism by John. "Thou art my beloved Son," the gospels say, "in thee I am well pleased" (Matthew 3:16–17; Mark 1:10–11). But the alternative reading in the Gospel of the Ebionites, cited in Luke 3:22, states, "Thou art my Son; *today* I have begotten thee," and is probably the truer one, being a direct quotation from Psalm 2:7, where it applies to King David. According to Schuré, the latter reading was an initiatory formula employed in the ancient Mediterranean Mystery temples that gave any initiate, if accounted worthy, entrance to the highest spiritual grade. This system of Mystery grades was uniform throughout the Near East:

> In the language of the temples, the term "son of woman" designated the lower stage of initiation, woman meaning here, nature. Above these were "sons of men" or initiates of Spirit and Soul, the "sons of the gods" or initiates of cosmogonic science, and "Sons of God" or initiates of the supreme science.[52]

The four initiatory grades of the Mystery temples appear to have been the equivalent of the four sacerdotal grades that once governed Hebrew society: that of priest, prophet, king, and messiah or avatar. Hence the prophet Enoch was called a Son of Man until raised to the eminence of royalty, whereupon he achieved the angelic Son of God status. And Jesus too, having risen from the prophetic rank, was an initiate of "the supreme science" and therefore could bear the title of priest-king and Son of God like others of the same grade.

There is support for Schuré's contention in the literature of antiquity. For example, an Essenic fragment of text designated 4Q246 that was found in 1958 in Cave 4 at the Qumran site suggests that the Aegian Mystery grades had their parallels in the Hebraic Mystery tradition.

Translated from the Aramaic, the fragment tells us that the Essenes' Teacher of Righteousness of the Last Days "will be called Son of God, and they will call him Son of the Most High . . . His kingdom will be an eternal kingdom."[53] Since the words call into question the Christian claim that Jesus' Divine Sonship was unique, this Dead Sea text was suppressed by the Vatican authorities for more than thirty years, and is therefore still little known. It would appear that Jesus might have been not only a Son of Man, of the grade of "Spirit and Soul," as frequently declared in the gospels, but also one of a number of advanced Hebrew initiates then living called Sons of God or "initiates of the supreme science." He seems, however, to have preferred to retain the lower title of Son of Man in his public office.

This term as an initiatory title was apparently unknown in the first-century world of Judaism, and according to Geza Vermes was not used except in the grammatical sense of self-reference, meaning "I" or "I myself."[54] If it was dangerous to be openly known as a prophet, it was far more so to be known as a Son of God, and so we find Jesus employing the safer title of Son of Man, knowing that the esoteric meaning of the term will be understood only by the very few. In other words, he is using it as a disguise. The veil of anonymity that has shrouded Jesus for so long may have been spun deliberately by Jesus himself.

Yet, one wonders why it is still so difficult to place Jesus in any known spiritual tradition. Strangely enough, the very fact that this difficulty persists proves to be one of the most valuable clues about him, for it points us toward a fact well known to Sufis. The one kind of person who defies classification, who crosses all boundaries and belongs to no particular religio-social category yet is at home in all, as is Jesus, is the highest rank of initiate trained in an esoteric order. Such a spiritual adept is proverbially classless, chameleon-like, and multifaceted. Open to scrutiny, his very training, by a paradoxical logic, hides him from view.

The modern esotericist Julius Evola says in *The Mystery of the Grail* that sacred kingship is a defining characteristic of the primordial Gnosis. The ruler's role, when validated by heaven, is essentially a unifying

one that correlates all the different belief systems and faiths existent in
the world under one primordial spiritual tradition.[55]

> Within the dimension of the Primordial Tradition, the king dem-
> onstrates his ability to rule with power and wisdom when he attains
> high degrees of initiation into universal gnosis.[56]

Shimon Halevi concurs with this ancient view of the sacred ruler's task
as being essentially a unifying one, whether he is Jewish, Christian, or
Sufi, and indeed whether or not he can claim a royal bloodline. To the
end of harmonizing the many different spiritual viewpoints that exist
in the world, the highest grade of initiate is expected to undertake the
study of other spiritual traditions and to be perfected in many different directions. This is the true criterion of kingship and is possible
because the higher the initiate goes, the less important are the outer
forms. Mystics, says this Muslim writer, "meet in a spiritual world that
is above form."[57]

That is precisely why it is so difficult to classify such a person. It is
the privilege of the supreme initiate to be proficient in many different
areas, to comprehend and to a certain degree embody every level and
degree of spiritual and worldly activity. This necessitates the breaking
of caste and religious taboos, and is what we find most clearly exemplified in Jesus. Only the setting aside of the Mosaic purity laws that
covered taboos regarding caste, women, diet, and certain kinds of occupation could have drawn so many different types of people to his side,
from merchants to freedom fighters, temple priests to prostitutes, Sanhedrin officials to despised tax collectors, lepers to Pharisees.

René Guénon calls such an initiate Universal Man or Transcendental Man, the Adam Qadmon of the Hebrew Qabalah, the King (Wang)
of the Far Eastern tradition. Universal Man, Guénon says, is the final
goal of the Mediterranean Greater Mysteries and the highest grade in
the Taoist and Hindu hierarchies. "He is that being who, in full and
conscious possession of his celestial identity, appears in this world as
the *Avatar*."[58] And the Judaic *messiah* has the same meaning, as Gué-

non points out. From the Hebrew *mashiah,* "anointed one," the term has in the Hebrew Bible the meaning of a priest-king or savior prince (Hebrew = *nasi*) whose function is universal, embodying a spiritual prowess so comprehensive that it includes within itself all the secular as well as the spiritual categories. The Gnostic Gospel of Philip stresses this state of universality in the Anointed One:

> He who is anointed possesses the all. He possesses the resurrection, the light, the cross, the Holy Spirit. As the Father gave him this in the bridechamber, such a one received it. (Philip 83:18–22)

Whether Jesus' family genealogy was such that he could claim dynastic descent from the ancient kings of Israel is unknown, although certainly that is what Bishop Eusebius of Caesarea asserts in his fifth-century *Ecclesiastical History* (*Ecc. Hist.* 1, vii). But that Jesus accepted his royal designation as a Christ or Anointed One, a title given to high priests of Zadokite lineage as well as Israelite kings, seems to be confirmed in the gospel account of a coronation ritual in which he participated. The account is in Mark 14:3, in which Jesus is anointed with an expensive unguent of spikenard by a woman most believe to have been Mary of Bethany, also known as Mary Magdalene. It is undoubtedly one of the most significant passages in the Christian scriptures.

> And while he was at Bethany in the house of Simon the leper, as he sat at table, a woman came with an alabaster flask of ointment of pure nard, very costly, and she broke the flask and poured it over his head. But there were some who said to themselves indignantly, "Why was the ointment thus wasted? For this ointment might have been sold for more than three hundred denarii [about 10,000 dollars by today's standards], and given to the poor . . ." But Jesus said, ". . . You always have the poor with you . . . but you will not always have me. She has done what she could; she has *anointed my body beforehand for burying.*" Then Judas Iscariot, who was one of the twelve, went to the chief priests in order to betray him to them. (Mark 14:3–11) (author's italics)

The entire drama of the immolated god-king of the Mysteries, his coronation by anointing with oil and his ritual death, lies hidden deep within this passage and its symbolism cannot be ignored. In what is clearly an integral part of the tapestry of events, Judas Iscariot then reports to the authorities the seditious coronation ceremony he has just witnessed.

But was he betraying Jesus or simply obeying the orders of his Master? This is now a hotly contested point. In view of the account given in the Coptic Gospel of Judas, an archaeological discovery of the last century, which was recently unveiled by the National Geographic Society, we can probably conclude that Judas did so collaborate with his Lord. Written in the second century as part of a larger Gnostic document, this apocryphal gospel has caused a sensation in the theological community by claiming that Judas was Jesus' favorite disciple and simply did Jesus' bidding in handing him over to the Romans for crucifixion. Has history done Judas a terrible injustice?

The testimony from the authenticated two-thousand-year-old Gnostic document tends to confirm the thesis of this book. From the beginning to the end of the tragic drama, Jesus in effect deliberately enacted the role of a sacrificial god-king and ordered his own execution—as indeed the voluntary victims of ritual regicide did in antiquity. Why the church fathers chose to overlook the wealth of gospel pointers to the truth is not altogether clear, but is no doubt related to their aversion for all things Gnostic. At the same time, it is possible that a grain of truth resides in the hitherto mainstream interpretation of Judas's actions as a heinous betrayer of the Messiah.

In fact, this interpretation has long been questioned in some quarters. In the Last Supper scene in John's Gospel (13:21–30), Jesus claims one of his disciples will betray him and then says to Judas: "Go! What you are going to do, do quickly!" From this alternative account of Judas's role has arisen the idea that he was perhaps not a betrayer but a secret collaborator with his Master, deliberately helping to set the stage for his arrest and execution at Jesus' own behest. In *The Meaning of the Dead Sea Scrolls,* Dr. Powell Davies suggests, as did Professor S. G. F. Brandon before him, that Judas was a Zealot. In some old Latin manuscripts he is actually called Judas Zelotes—that is, Judas the Zealot;[59] and the Zealots were a revival of the rigorously fundamentalist and nationalist Maccabean movement.[60] Judas would therefore have been in all likelihood as narrow and exoteric in his religious views as were the Maccabees and as fervent as they in hoping for the overthrow of Roman domination.

In the coronation ceremony, not only was Mary filling the forbidden role of a high priestess—she who was accustomed in bygone days to crown and administer the last rites to the dying god-king—but the ceremony's overall potential for state treason of the most dangerous kind could well have shocked Judas. He would not be the first man to misinterpret his leader's agenda and be disturbed on realizing his mistake. His deep conflict of loyalties may well have been obvious to his Master, who could read the most secret thoughts of his flock, and therefore have made Judas psychologically the obvious choice for carrying out Jesus' secret plans. In that sense, Judas would have been at least potentially the classic betrayer of Christ that mainstream history has always declared.

Following the Bethany ceremony, Jesus once again identified himself with the god-kings of antiquity by making a triumphal entrance into Jerusalem on an ass. In the same manner, King David once rode into the city on an ass as a ruler and peacemaker, accompanied by the fervent palm-waving acclaim of the people. And he too ascended the throne through spiritual merit rather than blood inheritance. Accordingly, the prophet Zechariah declaims in the book of Zechariah (9:9–11):

> *Rejoice, rejoice, daughter of Zion,*
> *shout aloud, daughter of Jerusalem;*
> *for see, your king is coming to you,*
> *his cause won, his victory gained,*
> *humble and mounted on an ass, on a foal,*
> *the young of a she-ass.*
> *He shall banish chariots from Ephraim*

and war horses from Jerusalem;
He shall speak peaceably to every nation,
and his rule shall extend from sea to sea,
from the River to the ends of the Earth.

As we have seen, in the Book of Enoch initiates were known as kings as well as angels and true human beings, and it may have been in this symbolic rather than literal sense that Jesus presented himself to the people as a monarch. In any case, we know he declared himself the heir of a great Davidic royal line renowned for its spiritual puissance as well as its mundane knowledge, political competence, and ability to protect the nation militarily. As Universal Man, Jesus presented himself as a spiritual teacher and social reformer as well as a monarch, a type of adept that has no modern equivalent but can be traced back thousands of years to the Neolithic Sons of God, who founded the ancient East's dynastic lines of kings. Jesus can also be likened to the Buddha, who by the universality of his nature was able to found both a religion and the material civilization that expressed its central principles.[61] Jesus' curiously ambiguous, many-faceted ability to be all things to all men suggests that he was of a similar universality. His actions and personality bear all the hallmarks of a spiritual master who has moved extensively in a diversified milieu such as Alexandria, among many different schools and philosophies. In this way he has acquired and distilled the wisdom of each one, so achieving an extraordinarily wide spiritual competence.

THE SOLITARY ONES

With our new familiarity with Eastern religions, we in the West are now recognizing that the transmission of *higher psychospiritual energies* rather than purity laws or blind dogma is the foremost business of religion, and in that light Jesus' hierophantic role was, as already said, like that of the Buddha: he was a spiritual Awakener. His mission was to awaken new spiritual energies and initiatives as widely as possible among the people, to plant a seed of higher knowledge among them that would germinate and spread of its own accord to cover and transform the whole of Israel. For as he said,

> the Kingdom of the Father will not come by waiting for it. It will not be a matter of saying Here it is or There it is. Rather, the Kingdom of the Father is spread out [already] upon the earth, and men do not see it. (Thomas 113)

Jesus freed the cult from its local context and from the dead hand of the ritualists. He abrogated Jewish collective law in innumerable ways, giving emphasis not to the intercessory rites of the temple but to the freedom of the individual to approach God directly and without priestly mediation. Again and again the sayings of "the living Jesus," recorded under the name of the apostle Thomas, emphasize the efficacy of the initiate as the solitary one, the individual who lays down a new Way. "Blessed are the solitary and elect, for you will find the Kingdom. For you are from it and to it you will return" (Thomas 49). And again in that most famous of Jesus' sayings:

> Men think, perhaps, that it is peace which I have come to cast upon the world. They do not know that it is dissension which I have come to cast upon the earth: fire, sword and war. For there will be five in a house; three will be against two, and two against three; the father against the son, and the son against the father. *And they will stand solitary.* (Thomas 16) (author's italics)

Yet again Jesus said: "Many are standing at the door, but it is the single ones who will enter the bridalchamber" (Thomas 75). This Saying concerns those who have become unified. In other words, through the bridechamber rite they have overcome the psychic divisions of inner/ outer, male/female, soul/spirit, and so on, and achieved wholeness or individuation. They are in touch with the All. In such Sayings we hear the voice of the true mystic, the one outside the collective who abides by his own inner law. The Gnosis of the heart cannot be found by ceremony or catechism, fasting, sacrifice, or rote learning, but only by solitary introspection illumined from within. Yet the term *solitary* as used here is possessed of an even deeper meaning than psychic integration.

The term seems to echo the teaching of King Jaibali in the earliest of the Upanishads, or "Forest Books." These were written in India around the sixth century BCE by the yogic descendants of the Indus Valley culture. The text is in the form of instruction to the Brahmin priests, who are forced to profess their ignorance of spiritual truths. The King enlightens them by likening every sleeper, however wretched, however destitute and despised, to a king in his majestic solitude. In solitude, says King Jaibali, the Self reigns supreme over every object of sense and mind—over every social distinction and the demanding ordinances of priests, over all their liturgies, laws, and sacrificial rites. In solitude the sleeper is one with the gods.[62] Similarly, Jesus says that it is the one who has established the Self as the supreme *locus of control,* the solitary one, the royal anointed, who is entitled to enter the bridechamber.

Nowhere in Jesus' teachings is there the concern for outer institutionalization that was to grip the Church after his death. He advised those seeking the Kingdom of God simply to "[a]sk and it will be given to you; seek and you will find; knock and the door will be opened for you" (Matthew 7:7). This was new. Such freedom from the mediation and supervision of a priestly hierarchy was unknown in contemporary Judaism, even among the esoteric sects; and indeed it was unknown anywhere. And related to this freedom of the individual was the importance Jesus gave to the spirit rather than the Law in the observance of the Mosaic ordinances, emphasizing the inner intention rather than the outer rite. He said, "Why do you wash the outside of the cup? Do you not realize that he who made the inside is the same one who made the outside?" (Thomas 89).

It can perhaps be said that Jesus' most precious gift to his people was this gift of inner freedom of conscience that we treasure so much today. "Whoever finds himself," he declared, "is superior to the world" (Thomas 111).

Gnostics said that certain of Jesus' sayings they heard in trance after his death, receiving them from the spirit of Christ in heaven whom Jesus had embodied on earth. Other sayings, notably those of the Gospel of Thomas, some of which were included in the canonical gospels, may well have been uttered by the earthly Jesus and recorded by the apostle himself. But whatever their source, whether pre-Crucifixion or transmitted by spiritual vision after Jesus' death, such teachings perplexed the uninitiated and were roundly condemned by those hostile to the Gnostics as a travesty of the Lord's true message. Yet it is possible for us who are entering the third millennium of Christianity, so rich in new information both esoteric and historical, to recognize that in offering the world a Mystery teaching of great antiquity, Jesus opened up a new path of initiation. He established a new Way that could be prepared for or actually entered by all men and women wishing to do so, regardless of race, gender, wealth, or social status. Nothing like it had previously been known.

So was Jesus' mission meant for Israel alone or for the Gentiles as well? Once its intrinsic universality is recognized—its implicit freedom from the cultic, socio-legal, and theological constraints that confined humanity's God to one particular race and one particular religion—Jesus' teachings were foreordained to spread beyond Israel. Although undoubtedly slanted toward his own Hebrew people, they were bound to take root in the wider world, where revolutionary currents were already stirring, bound to arouse interest not only among Jews but also among the uncircumcised God fearers. These were believing Gentiles who frequented the Jewish assemblies without becoming fully observant Jews.[63]

In the diaspora, particularly in Egypt, where the scriptures of the wealthy Jewish community had long been read only in Greek, the cosmopolitan currents of Greek, Persian, and Egyptian thought had been flowing for centuries. These currents achieved an expansion of Hebrew thought undreamed of in parochial Judaea and attracted large numbers of disaffected Gentiles. Expatriate Hebrews were among the most highly esteemed races in the Greco-Roman world, their services sought not only for their administrative and fiscal skills but also for their knowledge of the secret occult arts. They were learned in astronomy and were expert astrologers, diviners, and healers, and their prowess in all the hidden areas of Qabalistic magic was proverbial. Consequently, their synagogues customarily drew large numbers of pagans anxious to learn the secrets of Judaism without committing themselves to full membership in it. Remaining uncircumcised, they frequented the fringes and forecourts of the closed Jewish assemblies, or else flocked to the pagan Mystery schools, hoping for admittance there.

Profound spiritual unrest had been sweeping the inhabited world for several centuries, and schools of philosophy engaged in the occult sciences and revivals of ancient Mystery religions were endemic, presaging the vast changes to come. Yet all these esoteric movements were confined within the social constraints of their period. As we have seen, throughout most of the known world a rigid caste system prevailed; only the educated and affluent could enter the coteries of the Mystery schools—indeed only they could afford the extremely expensive rites of initation.[64] The peasantry and the masses of the lower classes in general were excluded by ironclad social and financial deterrents, and were therefore prevented from ever getting beyond the outer fertility cults to the citadels of sacred knowledge within. Spiritual enlightenment was for the very few—the rich and the fortunate. Enlightenment for all was an impossibility.

Moreover, by the first century the cults themselves were, as the Sorbonne Professor of Roman History Robert Turcan vividly reveals, narrow in outlook, usually lacking a coherent theology, often orgiastic in their rituals but empty of spiritual or social content, without vision.[65] This is particularly true of the Syrian Mother cults, which, with their bloody sacrifices and frenziedly dancing, castrated priests, flourished in the Near East in Jesus' time, and must have been well known to him. According to Turcan, the Isiac temples stood as oases of calm and dignity in a sea of Dionysiac emotionalism more cathartic than edifying, and offering little of the enlightenment and peace of soul that was promised, even for those who could afford initiation. A major religious reformation was long overdue.

The cultural climate was changing; skepticism was rampant. Under the impulsion of new social and psychological needs that were not being met, the collective mood everywhere in the known world was in turmoil, repudiating past traditions and stirring up sedition. Spiritual leaders like Jesus brought "not peace but a sword" to the old ways and thrust into direct conflict with the bastions of established tradition, offering a new way of salvation that was relevant to all peoples of the period.

The revolutionary nature of the new Christ Mystery has been obscured by the salvation theology centered on Jesus' death and resurrection. One example of the way the gospels have given unreliable testimony to the radical nature of that mission can be found in the editing of translations of their texts. The church father Jerome, writing in the fourth century, stated that in the library at Caesarea he had seen a Hebrew version of the Gospel of Matthew that was disquietingly, even alarmingly, esoteric in tone and quite unlike the strictly orthodox tone of Greek Matthew found today in the Christian scriptures. Jerome decided not to publish his find for fear it would do more damage than good among immature Christians.[66] Welburn comments: "The original version of Matthew contained 'esoteric' passages, relating to mysteries that were not regarded as suitable for the uninitiated. These passages had therefore been omitted from the Greek (as later from Jerome's Latin) translation."[67]

More generally known as the Gospel of the Hebrews, so Jerome claimed, Hebrew Matthew contains passages that highlight the discrepancies in our conventional view of Jesus' teachings. Because of this, modern scholars have been led to ignore Hebrew Matthew altogether, "especially since it contradicted their favorite theories about the text of the Greek Gospel."[68] It is ironic that while the Gospel of the Hebrews as the preferred text of the Ebionite sectaries is widely regarded as a heretical deviation from mainstream Christianity, the Gospel of Matthew, written by the same hand but edited by a Greek translator, is regarded as having a background of strict Judaic orthodoxy, quotations routinely being lifted from it to prove that Jesus was a pious and Law-abiding Jew. Thus Greek Matthew, writing when there was still hope that the two contending parties in the synagogues could reach an agreement, presents his leader as scrupulously observant of Mosaic law. "Do not think that I came to abolish the law and the prophets," his Jesus says; "I came not to abolish but to fulfill the law" (Matthew 5:17). Says Elaine Pagels,

> Thus Matthew defends Jesus against charges of laxity in Sabbath and kosher observance by insisting that he practices a *greater righteousness,* not a lesser one. According to Matthew 5 and 6, Jesus demands an enormous *increase in religious scrupulosity:* the traditional Torah is not half strict enough for him![69]

For example, where Moses' law prohibits murder, Jesus' "new Torah" prohibits even anger and insults; where Moses' law prohibits adultery, Jesus prohibits even lustful thoughts. Nevertheless, although some Jewish Christians did claim to reinterpret the Torah in its stricter sense, by thus internalizing it they gave individual conscience more authority than Mosaic law. By putting aside the ritual precepts that virtually defined Jewish society, they constituted a deep and thoroughly subversive threat to mainstream Judaism, whose very foundation was by then legal and ethnic. When such allegorizing was applied, for example, to the Mosaic dietary laws, it threatened the validity of all the social customs that differentiated Jews from Gentiles. It internalized the very concept of religion, bringing it under a new law of intra-racial unity.

Many biblical scholars have ignored this clear strain of non-ethnic, psychological "internalizing" of the Torah characteristic of Jesus' teachings, and have preferred to overlook its implications for a thorough-going religious revolution. This myopia is no longer excusable. For two thousand years the Christian scriptures have been almost our only source of light on Jesus' life and teachings; but now, with unprecedented possibilities for authoritative historical research opening up, it is possible for the first time to outline a much larger background picture. If we wish to learn more about this Nazarean rebel who said he was casting fire upon the world, we must turn to the company of the Hasidim, whose descendants are still active in modern Israel and throughout the West.

4

NAZAREANS
AND HASIDIM

*Kabbalism is the great poem of Judaism, a tree of symbolic
jewels showing forth the doctrine of the universe as a vesture of
Deity, of the community as the embodiment of Deity, and love
as the acting of God in man.*

KENNETH REXROTH

*A tree of life is she to those that lay hold of her, and every one
that firmly grasps her will be made happy.*

KING SOLOMON (BOOK OF PROVERBS)

The soil in which the Jesus movement was first seeded, in which it ger-
minated, grew, branched out, and finally differentiated itself defini-
tively from its sectarian parent body and from Judaism itself, was the
greater Hasidic brotherhood. This was a shadowy schismatic movement
that arose during the second century BCE and spread its revolutionary
tentacles throughout the Jewish diaspora. In the Hasidim we meet again
the psychological gulf that yawned between the theology of Orthodox
Judaism and that of its sectarian opponents—a gulf that has never been
adequately explained. Frithjof Schuon, the well-known Sufi esotericist
and author, remarked that Jesus "has the function of a regenerator; he
is the great prophet of inwardness, and in this respect he ought to have
been accepted by Israel as Isaiah was"[1]—that is, as an esoteric prophet

honored within the wider bounds of Judaism. Why did this not happen?

Raphael Patai declares that, unlike most world religions, Judaism has never known schism:

> Differences in doctrine among Christians led to schism. Among Jews, they led to heterodox groupings without secession, because there was no organized religious body from which to secede or which might have cut off the offending limb . . . However erroneous the ways of others appeared, such errors were never considered serious enough to warrant a formal break.[2]

Be that as it may, the historical evidence suggests that the Hasidic phenomenon in first-century Judaism more than amply provided the schismatic conditions necessary for the wholesale expulsion of Judaeo-Christians from the synagogues by the end of the second century CE. (Archaeology finds evidence of Judaeo-Christians and Jews living together in the same places in Palestine thereafter but separated by having their own synagogues, literature, liturgy, worship, and customs until the fourth century CE, after which the Church of the Circumcision went into decline.[3]) Given the nature of the Judaeo-Christian tenets, it could not have been otherwise; schism was inevitable. And the roots of the revolutionary religious ideas of the Judaeo-Christians can be traced directly to the Hasidim.

Jesus' mission was bound up with this rebel movement. Like the Buddha, who had belonged to a company of rebels opposed to the Brahmin priesthood, so too did Jesus the Nazarean play his fateful role in a larger Hasidic underground movement of reform that had spread throughout the Near East. The Hasidim's program and worldview were the very antithesis of those put forward in Judaea's synagogues and were replicated in the Nazarean brotherhood. Schism not only was inevitable, but also had probably been deliberately sought since the beginning of the second century BCE.

Some nineteenth-century authorities, like Édouard Schuré, have suggested that the Nazareans were of pre-Exilic antiquity and can be traced back to the prophet Samuel in the time of the Judges, in the eleventh century BCE.[4] But modern research renders it certain that, although claiming a Mystery pedigree going back to the legendary reigns of the first kings of Israel, the Nazareans actually emerged as a formal brotherhood at much the same time as the Essenes, in the second century BCE. Like the Essenes, they were an offshoot of the Hasidic movement that arose in the Land of Damascus at that time.

In the final pre-Christian centuries, a stream of Jewish pilgrims from Babylonia were accustomed to cross the desert tracts south of Damascus every year to offer sacrifices in the Jerusalem temple; but in this region popularly known as the Hauran, the Wilderness of the People, they were severely molested by brigands. And so in 23 BCE, King Herod came to an arrangement with a large contingent of armed Hauranites to protect the pilgrims in exchange for the whole region's freedom from the exaction of tribute. Thus the Hauran became known as a tax-free haven to which Jews of all persuasions flocked, settling there with the status of freemen and with immunity from the financial obligations incumbent on the populace elsewhere.[5] In a region that no high authority supervised, where dissidents, religious rebels, brigands, and secessionists could find refuge, liberty of conscience was prized above all else, as it always had been by the ancient *nabi'im,* the Hebrew men of God. It was where the democracy of the afflicted and exiled could flourish and where a diversity of religious beliefs could mix and interact in a climate of tolerance possible nowhere else in the Near East, except perhaps Alexandria. Here, then, was where the Nazareans and indeed most of the dissident Jewish sects constellated under the Hasidic umbrella.

It was in the Hauran on the banks of the river Dan, a tributary of the Jordan, that Enoch was said to have had his vision of the throne of God, and hereabouts that the first Essenes established their camps. The desert caravan routes leading to the river Euphrates and to Babylon ran eastward across a barren land, but the Dan passed through a fertile belt of the country and allowed many little villages and towns to flourish there. These were the primary centers of Hebrew sectarian life.

The whole Galilean and Transjordanian regions were of great

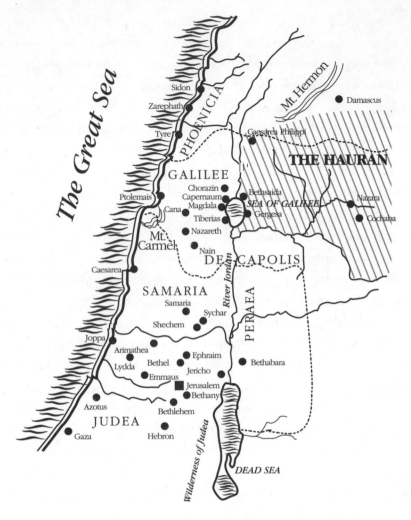

Fig. 4. Palestine in the first century CE

antiquity, with a rich spiritual history, and were an important focus both historically and geographically for the widely dispersed Hasidic movement and its messianic prophecies. Extending south to the land of Gilead, the prophet Elijah's home country, the entire region around the Sea of Galilee was, in the first century, the home of deeply held beliefs centered on the old Mystery religions. Its population had been overrun and subjugated by the Judaean army under Hasmonean command for only a little over a hundred years, and this national indignity was still resented. The people were of mixed Samaritan-Jewish stock, the psychology was independent and individualistic, and the religious and political orientation was anti-Jerusalem and anti–temple clergy. From Mount Carmel in the west to the eastern boundaries of the Upper Transjordan, the whole territory was impregnated not only with the immemorial legends and myths of this ancient land but also with the amalgam of religious doctrines and philosophies borne into it along the great trade routes from Babylonia, Persia, and India on the one hand and from the Mediterranean civilizations on the other. Various Mystery traditions were deeply entrenched and ecclesiastical visits from Jerusalem were both rare and unwelcome.

Professor Vermes has painted a vivid picture of the north–south tensions of the time: the contempt the rabbis felt for the "lawless cursed rabble" to the north, and their even greater antagonism toward the freedom-loving holy men of the region. The miraculous exploits in healing, exorcism, and rainmaking of these nabi'im were legendary, their anti-establishment influence powerfully impregnating the local messianic and insurrectionist movements. Consequently, in the eyes of the Jerusalem authorities, the Hauran was a refuge for malcontents and a veritable cesspool of apostasy, the home not only of Nazareans but also of many other equally heretical groups. It was the place where the exiled prophets and their families had long ago retreated, where sectarian communities fleeing persecution gradually constellated about the prophets, and established generations of religious opposition to the Jerusalem cult.

Rabbinic literature has depicted the lot as at best bucolic and irreligious and at worst heretical reprobates, and Josephus's history of the Jews has reinforced that impression. But these writings, for centuries our only source of information, gravely misrepresent the nature of the northern Palestinian culture and the depth of its roots in the most ancient and holy Israelite traditions. Significantly, it was also the scene of most of Jesus' missionary and healing activities.

As we have already learned, Bishop Epiphanius traced the cradle of the Nazarean sect to a town called Cochaba in the Galilean-Damascene region where Jesus grew up, describing the group as closely linked to the

Essenes.[6] He said that Nazareans were also to be found in the Decapolis, the ten Greek cities that had been built on the eastern side of the Jordan, but the region Epiphanius had mainly in mind was the Upper Transjordanian area that the Roman historian Pliny the Elder, writing in the first century (*Natural History*, v. 81), called the Nazarene Tetrarchy, adjacent to Coele-Syria.

Various groups of pre-Christian *nasaraioi* inhabited this Syro-Palestinian region, and an extremely ancient and mysterious people called the Nasairiyeh still live on the lower slopes of Mount Hermon in southern Lebanon, as did their ancestors from the earliest times.[7] All these groups, however, were probably offshoots of a single pre-Christian Nazarean fraternity centered in the Hauran. Hugh Schonfield also mentions the term *natsaraya* as the Aramaic equivalent of the word Shamerine, by which the Samaritans knew themselves, which he says has the same meaning as has Nazarean, that of Guardians or Conservers of Sacred Knowledge. This distinguished Jewish author says we now have many indications that

> the Damascus region and the Hauran were the areas where . . . in spite of many changes and vicissitudes, the Essene-Nazorean teachings and traditions were carried on from century to century.[8]

When the gospels are examined with critical modern eyes, one discovers how little of Jesus' life, family relationships, and environment is actually divulged. His provenance in northern Palestine is clearly enough indicated, but the evidence for much else that Christians have taken for granted for centuries is simply not to be found. As one commentator has remarked, it is fascinating to see "how many of the blanks in the story have been filled in, not by scripture, but by imagination."[9] Here Hugh Schonfield raises a very interesting question. He points out that all of Jesus' movements and missionary activities tend to be in the east of the Sea of Galilee rather than in the west where Nazareth lies, and he asks: Could Jesus have lived in the Hauran rather than in Nazareth of Galilee?

Dr. Schonfield, whose lifelong interest was the study of early Christian documents, believes it very possible. As we know, increasing doubt has been laid on the traditional assumption that the Christian founder came from Nazareth in the Galilean province, and the doctor makes the suggestion that Jesus' hometown may more credibly have been the Jewish town of Nazara, which was situated in the Hauran close to Cochaba and not far from Capernaum. Schonfield stresses that there is considerable warrant in the literature for such a hypothesis.

The region around Nazara was the heart of Nazarean country. In ancient times it was the land of the Aramaeans, a people whose language was said to be that of the angels. Clinging to it was a wealth of biblical mythology of messianic import, all of it reflecting in various ways the motif of the deified Redeemer. Prophecies concerning the great divinized figure of the Son of Man were preserved and circulated among the Galilean-Damascene people century after century in heavily encoded language. Thus Schonfield alludes to a prophecy in Isaiah 11:1 stating that the Messiah would come from a sprout or shoot from the stump of Jesse (the father of King David), and to another, related one from Numbers 24:17 stating that a star would come forth out of Jacob. "We find the Sprout prophecy and the Star prophecy," says Schonfield, "conjoined by the early Christians as a testimony to Jesus."[10] And Justin Martyr, a Samaritan Christian who died around 167, says, conflating his sources,

[a]nd Isaiah, another prophet, spoke thus, "A star (Heb. *cochab*) shall rise out of Jacob, and a flower (Heb. *nezer* for branch) shall spring from the root of Jesse." (Numbers 24:17)[11]

Now Epiphanius states that Cochaba had the meaning of a star, and Justin Martyr, writing around 150 CE, says that another village lay nearby to Cochaba called Nazara, meaning a sprout or branch. So these early Christian researchers, familiar with Nazarean symbology, seem to have interpreted it along the same lines as Schonfield. They located Jesus' family home in the eastern rather than the western Galilean zone, pinpointing it at Nazara, the place that had been given a messianic nomenclature that accorded with the old biblical prophecies.

In his *Letter to Aristides,* which is quoted in the fifth-century *Ecclesiastical History* of Bishop Eusebius of Caesarea, another Christian writer, Julius Africanus (160–240), deals with the genealogies of Jesus cited in Matthew and Luke. He records that Jesus' family, surviving the Roman-Jewish war of 70 CE, took pride in their Davidic descent and had composed their family tree from either memory or private records. The first-century members of the Lord's family, Julius continues, "coming from Nazara and Cochaba, Jewish villages, to the other parts of the country, explained the aforesaid genealogy as faithfully as possible from the book of Chronicles."[12]

Jesus' family had perhaps lived for generations in the Hauran in the environs of Nazara, conforming to scriptural expectations and obeying Nazarean principles and customs in the midst of a community that had a long prophetic and messianic tradition behind it.[13] Indeed, it is possible that this alternative site was known for some centuries in the underground traditions of the Apocrypha, for we note that the Gospel According to Philip declares suggestively, "Nazara means 'truth,' thus the Nazarene means 'truth'" (Philip 40:14–15). We may also add that it means "justice" or "righteousness," so perhaps linking it with Melchizedek and the Righteousness lineage.

Why, then, did the Gospel writers so sedulously hide from their readers, and from us, the very existence of a pre-Christian Nazarean brotherhood, let alone its headquarters in the land of Damascus? And why were they so eager to distance Jesus from his occult Nazarean and Hauranite roots? There may have been a complex of reasons for the omission of the brotherhood from the annals of history, including a strong desire not to identify Jesus with the heterodox Nazarean theology, so odious to orthodox Jews. But a more immediate reason may have been concern for the safety of Nazarean members. Nazareth may have replaced Nazara in the early Christian records in order to protect both the location of the brotherhood and Jesus' family from the hostile attentions of the Roman authorities, who for several generations remained highly suspicious of the family's monarchic pretensions.

We should not forget that it was in the Hauran, according to Eusebius, that the Nazarean Church set up a kind of government in exile after the war, choosing as its dynastic leader Simeon, son of Cleophas, said to be Jesus' first cousin.[14] The lost memoirs of the Christian historian Hegesippus claim that Jesus' brother James, successor to the leadership of the new movement, was murdered by Ananus, a high priest of the Jerusalem temple. James was succeeded by Jesus' brother Juda, also assassinated, and then by Simeon. Simeon was crucified by the Romans and Simeon's grandsons were interrogated under guard by the emperor Domitian Caesar in Rome. Thus the dynastic family had good cause to conceal its true whereabouts.

Another, more cogent reason may be conjectured. Only a few decades ago research uncovered the possibility that the Nazareans were merely a branch of a far greater spiritual movement that had mysteriously originated in Egypt and spread throughout the diaspora. This was the Hasidean movement, comprising a powerful coalition of Jewish dissidents that the Gospel writers, still seeking harmony within the orthodox Judaic body, might well have sought to exclude from their Judaeo-Christian records by every means possible—for, as already intimated, the Hasidim were the archenemies of the Judaic status quo.

Hasidism, Vermes avers, was a distinctive trend of apocalyptic and charismatic Judaism practiced by the holy men and miracle workers of the Hauran and the region around the Lake of Galilee. The Hasidim were mystics, prophets, healers, exorcists, and rainmakers who, like Jesus, infuriated the rabbinic herbalists to the south by working their healing miracles by no other means than the power of prayer, the laying on of hands, and the forgiveness of sins—even though, according to the rabbis, only God had the power to forgive sins. "Their supernatural powers," says Vermes, "were attributed to their immediate relation to God . . . *independent of any institutional mediation*,"[15] and were seen as of divine origin. Accordingly, they were disliked by the rabbis. In the final two centuries before Christ, the Hasidim coalesced around learned prophetic centers that were a breeding ground for the Qabalah, and laid the foundations for the heretical, or at best deviant, Judaic stream to which Jesus belonged.

"Jesus was a Galilean Hasid," Vermes asserts confidently, "a charismatic healing and exorcising Hasid from northern Palestine."[16] Today the Hasidim are one of the most ultraconservative Judaic parties in Israel, and Vermes may be under the impression that such was the case two thousand years ago; but it was not. The course of Hebraic religious history is still far from clear, but Raphael Patai's researches into the ubiquitous presence of the Goddess throughout the life of the Hebrew people is providing evidence that the Hasidim were heirs to a long indigenous tradition of prophecy that was in direct opposition to the patriarchal second-temple theology. The name given to these protesting Pious Ones—the Hasidim, or "Asidaeans," as the Book of the Maccabees transcribe the word—can be traced etymologically right back to the Essenes, who constituted another Hasidic branch, established around 159 BCE, at much the same time as the Nazarean brotherhood emerged. Stephan Hoeller explains:

> The Greek word *Essenoi* is of uncertain derivation, but it is related by scholars to the Hebrew *Asah* (he acted), *Hazah* (he saw visions), as well as to the Aramaic *Hasaya* (pious) and *Asa* (he healed). The modern Talmudic Hebrew word *Hasid* (pious) may also be reckoned among the cognate words . . . [The Essenes, especially in Egypt,] were also frequently called *Therapeutae,* meaning physicians or healers.[17]

The network of dissident Jewish sects that had spread across northern Palestine in late antiquity was long regarded by historians as an unsolved mystery. Why had it arisen? What was the relationship of the various groups to each other, to the Hasidim, to the second temple, and to Christianity? What was their core belief system? And why were they not recorded in Jewish history? In his 1983 work, Robert Eisenman was one of the first scholars to characterize all the sectarian groups—Maccabees, Zadokites, Christians, and Qumran—in first-century Palestine as branches of a single Hasidean movement of protest and reform.[18] Working with original documents, he traced the various names by which the authors of the Dead Sea Scrolls referred to themselves, and concluded that

> the Sons of Light, the Sons of Truth, the Sons of Zadok, or Zaddikim, the Men of Melchizedek (the z-d-k ending a variation of Zadok), the Ebionim (the Poor), the Hassidim (the Essenes) and the Notzrim (the Nazareans) are ultimately one and the same—not different groups, but different metaphors or appellations for essentially the same group, or the same movement. The primary objective of this movement seems to have been oriented towards the dynastic legitimacy of the high priesthood.[19]

Since the publication of Eisenman's work on the subject, the reality of a pre-Christian Hasidic umbrella movement encompassing most if not all of the disparate Judaic sects has been accepted by an increasing number of biblical commentators. The various dissident groups emerge as no more than different designations of a single great movement diffused throughout Egypt, the Holy Land, and Syria and dedicated to opposing the ruling Hasmonean party in the second temple in Jerusalem. Eisenman correctly states that Christianity arose out of this Hasidic (Zadokite) movement, but claims that the latter was of a fundamentalist, supra-orthodox nature. This is erroneous, although commonly asserted. On the contrary, Hasidism rejected the fundamentalist zealotry of the Maccabean takeover and was as secretly heterodox as the prophetic tradition to which it was a late-outlawed expression. There is reluctance in Jewish circles to admit to this fact.

The story of these ancient Hasidim is still almost unknown and many of its details are contested; indeed until the discovery of the Dead Sea Scrolls, there were as many versions as there were scholars to reconstruct it. Nor, as we have already learned, is it admitted by all scholars that any such schism in the Jewish faith ever existed. Nevertheless, there is now enough documentary evidence to show that a major politico-theological rift did occur in the fabric of Judaism, irrevocably altering its original character, and was one that subsequent rabbinic writings have sought to conceal. After the fall of Jerusalem, the Talmudic rabbis ruthlessly expunged from their records every mention of the Hasidic sects, even of their very existence, but the Dead Sea Scrolls have resurrected them, thus throwing a revealing new light on the past.

THE MACCABEES: ZADOKITE REVELATIONS

The Zadokite crisis in Judaism first became known to modern historians because of the sensational discovery in 1910, in a Cairo *genizah* (storeroom for old documents), of fragments of an ancient Jewish work that came to be known as the *Damascus Document*. It was published and presented to Cambridge University under the title "Fragments of a Zadokite Work."[20] Later, the same work was found among the Dead Sea Scrolls in Qumran and created an even greater furor than the first had done, for the sect that wrote it, believed by most scholars to be the Essenes, claimed to be of the true spiritual lineage of the high priest Zadok exiled in Egypt, while the Hasmonean dynasts ruling at that time in the second temple were illegitimate upstarts who called themselves Zadokites, but falsely so.

The Zadokite high-priestly office was regarded by Jews as sanctified to the highest degree by immemorial links with Israel's golden past. Traditionally, the high priest ruling in the Jerusalem temple was of the dynastic house of Zadok, founded in the tenth century BCE by King Solomon. Zadok had royal status bestowed on him in the high days of the Davidic court, when the first of his line had allegedly crowned its kings (1 Kings 1:39), and his pedigree was consequently the most illustrious in Israel. Indeed, his high-priestly office could be traced even further back, so legend declared, to the learned Jebusite priesthood that had officiated in Jerusalem before the Hebrews took over the town, and even further back to Abraham and the Jebusite Order of Melchizedek (see appendix 1). Throughout Jewish history, from Abraham to the present day, there have been tantalizing glimpses of a continuous theme woven around the Hebrew word *zedek* or *zadok* or *zaddik* (a Zaddik still leads today's esoteric Hasidic schools), meaning righteousness or justice, thus relating it to the Righteousness Order of El Elyon, whose high priest was Melchizedek.

But the Damascus narrative asserted that the high priests currently reigning in the Jerusalem temple, the Maccabees (or Hasmoneans, as they preferred to call themselves, after an ancestor called Hasmon), were false Zadokites who had abolished the hieratic tradition begun by Israel's kings, seizing the high-priestly office for themselves and forcing the true incumbents into exile.[21] The document claimed moreover that the Hasmonean ascension to power, culminating in the coronation of the last of the dynasty as priest-king of Israel, was linked to the sect of the Sadducees, an aristocratic group supporting the Hasmonean pretenders and also falsely claiming to be of Zadokite descent.[22] It was hinted that these Sadducees, who were amassing unrighteous wealth stolen from the needy, were claiming a legitimacy to which they had no right.

The discovery of the *Damascus Document* has been an explosive one. It queries the assumption traditionally held (and reinforced by Josephus's eulogistic history of the Maccabees) that the Hasmoneans' claim to the high-priestly throne was a legitimate one, and that their fundamentalist anti-Hellenic stance had been endorsed by all of Israel. But to the contrary, Gaalyah Cornfeld stresses that the issue had split the nation down the middle. The legitimate high priests of the house of Zadok, who were still reigning in the Jerusalem temple in the third century BCE, had been strong Hellenists in favor of bringing the Jewish culture and religious law more into line with contemporary international life, a reform introduced by Alexander the Great after conquering Palestine.[23] It was one favored by the better-educated Jews and already under way throughout the Jewish diaspora; but religious purists in Judaea, led by the violently fundamentalist priest Mattathias Maccabaeus and his five sons, had been outraged by moves toward modernization and began a holy war against all Hellenizers, including the Syrian Seleucid ruler himself.[24]

After hard-won victories that ensured Israel freedom of worship, the five valorous Maccabaeus boys cleansed the temple of its Hellenistic pollution and had then, as Joseph Campbell describes in *The Masks of God,* raged through the land with drawn swords, enforcing circumcision on countless victims and assassinating backsliders from the Judaic faith in their "zeal for the Law." They then instigated a bitter temple power struggle that allowed them to seize the sacred office of high priesthood for themselves.[25] Palestine was thus plunged by these Zealots into nearly two hundred years of internecine strife and instability.

The course of events that precipitated this dire situation is contested, but many scholars, including Gaalyah Cornfeld and Philip Davies of Sheffield University, support the thesis first put forward by Professor H. H. Rowley in 1952. It all began, Rowley suggests, in response to a politico-theological temple coup in about 196 BCE that deposed the reigning high priest, Onias IV of the house of Zadok, in favor of his brother Jason, who was of even stronger Hellenistic sympathies.[26] (We must note here that Schonfield claims it was not Onias IV but his father Onias III who was deposed, and that is probably the case.) According to the researches of the well-known author Michael Baigent in his recent book *The Jesus Papers,* Onias III was indeed a reigning high priest of the Jerusalem temple, whereas his son, Onias IV, was not a high priest but an army commander. In any case, Onias then withdrew to northern Egypt with a company of followers and under the patronage of Ptolemy I built a temple in Leontopolis (today's Tel al-Yahudiyah, the Hill of Jewry) to rival that of Jerusalem.[27]

What little we know about this Egyptian Jewish temple, which replaced an ancient temple to the god Bubastis, reveals that it was in effect a replication of the Solomonic temple on Mount Zion transported to Egypt. We know that it preserved the Hebraic Old Religion, which worshipped the Divine Couple and therefore would have retained many of the ancient Mystery rites, doctrines, and laws of pre-Exilic Judaism, and an effective order of priestesses and female prophets.[28] The town of Leontopolis lay on the Nile in the Central Delta, not very far from modern Cairo, and its Judaic temple, consecrated by the high priest Onias, survived until a year after the destruction of Jerusalem, when it was destroyed in its turn by the Romans.

In Jerusalem the unprecedented waiving of the royalist tradition, whereby Onias had been deposed and exiled, challenged for the first time the right of hereditary succession to the high priesthood, and allowed impostors like the Maccabees to take advantage of the power vacuum. Cornfeld asserts that the break in royal tradition led to the first step in the formation of a powerful Hasidic movement in support of the exiled high priest.[29] After Onias's departure to Egypt and the ascension of the Levitical priesthood to power in the Jerusalem temple, Zadok's loyal adherents left behind in Palestine were bewildered and rudderless until the Teacher of Righteousness *(Moreh-zedek)* appeared to lead them. This mysterious figure was apparently an adept of the Zadokite Righteousness lineage whom Vermes says had priestly affiliations.[30] He was later persecuted and martyred by the New Jerusalem dynasts.

Unlike the Maccabees, the Hasidim favored a degree of Hellenization and the modernization of Jewish culture as long as freedom of worship was respected—as did the landed gentry, rich merchants, and priestly aristocracy. But the Hasidim had seen the accession of Jason as an ominous drift from sacred tradition toward secularization of the state and at first sided with the Maccabees. But before long, finding the Maccabean cause uncongenial, they separated themselves from it. According to the *Damascus Document,* they were then ruthlessly persecuted by the Wicked Priest, whom Vermes identifies with Jonathan (r. 160–143 BCE), the first Maccabee to assume the high-priestly office.[31]

As a consequence, the Righteous Teacher and his followers were forced to flee into the wilderness of the land of Damascus, where they established camps and organized themselves into a spiritual community of Hasidim, owing loyalty to Leontopolis and in direct opposition to the Jerusalem party. According to the testimony of Philo, Josephus, and to a lesser extent the Roman historian Pliny the Elder, many of the Hasidim and their families also settled in increasing numbers in the cities and towns surrounding the Wilderness, both in Palestine and in Egypt. As the party grew, it split up into the Pharisees and Essenes, the latter group including the Therapeutae of Egypt. A number of other branches were spawned at the same time, such as the Nazareans, the Ophites, and the Ebionites.[32] Some Hasidim formed a community in Qumran near the Dead Sea, and Pliny reported one near Engaddi, another location not far from the Dead Sea shores.

The immediate aim of the Hasidim was to reinstate the Davidic line on the throne of Israel and the rightful Zadokite high priesthood to the Jerusalem temple, but beyond these goals they sought the return of the prophetic tradition in new Qabalistic guise. The Gnosis, the Hasidim insisted, must return to Israel; the messianic ideal must be enshrined again in the heart of Judaism and the Goddess given new meaning, dignity, and relevance as the Angel of Wisdom.

This, then, was the movement to which a number of Jewish scholars besides Vermes believe Jesus indisputably belonged. The New Covenant that the Teacher promulgated among his followers throws a great deal of light on the revolutionary social principles that later came to inform the young Christian Church. The Hasidic relaxing of the Jewish race laws meant an acceptance into their brotherhood of such "fringe observants" as the Samaritans and Nabateans, races to which many of the most notable Christian scriptures figures, such as Simon Magus and St. John the Apostle, would later belong. The Hasidim opposed the racial exclusivity that drove Orthodox Judaism, and so contributed greatly to the approaching national crisis.

All the region's sectarian groups, whatever they called themselves, shared the revolutionary social ideals of the New Covenant as well as the same gnostic, messianic, and apocalyptic ideas; all were related by bonds that went back to Israel's old Mystery tradition; all were in protest at what they saw as the debasement of their religion by the Hasmonean high priesthood; and all bitterly resisted the imposition of its narrow ideology on the rest of Palestine. And at the very heart of the dispute, the hidden engine that drove it, lay the Hasidic opposition to a patriarchal religious creed that failed to give due honor to the Mother of the World.

For Jewish sectaries, the cosmos had become pitifully shrunken. Zoroaster had demonized the intermediate divinities who throughout antiquity had peopled the spaces between God and man: the hierarchies of angels, devas, lesser nature gods and goddesses, as well as the teeming earth elementals that humans had always propitiated and revered. Zoroaster had banished all these intermediaries to outer darkness as base remnants of polytheism and the very personification of everything cruel, sense-based, and primitive. The cosmos was poorer for their going. Thenceforth the Good God ruled the universe alone—male, omnipotent, sole Creator of heaven and earth—the prototype of all the monotheistic Creator Gods to come.

But in the centuries bracketing the Common Era, the God question, fueled by messianism, had become critical among the Jewish sects, an all-consuming religious passion that joined with the nationalistic struggle against the Romans. The burning question concerning the true nature of the Divine accompanied a mounting concern about the meaning and function of evil, and whether the forces of evil could prove stronger than those of good. Both sides of the north–south ideological divide believed the ungodly were flourishing: Satan roamed the land, seducing the unwary. The battle lines were drawn; the *Damascus Document* drawn up by the Essenes informs us that the armies of the Sons of Light, composed of the sectaries themselves, were already massing in preparation for the decisive war against evil, against the Sons of Darkness. As the age of Aries ended, these preoccupations were a rehearsal, so to speak, of the new deific and moral issues that would engage the whole of the troubled Piscean age then dawning, an age that would be firmly based on principles of confrontation, conflict, and alienation.

Yet behind these moral concerns lay the more fundamental religious issue that was dividing the Jewish nation. A people's conception of God lies at the very heart of its culture; no other single factor so powerfully arbitrates its shape and direction. God is the X factor in its life, the great causal Unknown that it continually clothes in its own image. The orgiastic Mother cults of Syria would seem to us today grotesque parodies of religious worship, with their bloody castrations and ritual slaughter, but they celebrated in a degenerate and literalized form the cosmogonic truths of the old Mystery cycle that Zoroaster had replaced, and were therefore immensely popular. Mother worship fed something essential in the human spirit that could not easily be replaced.

To the Hasidic way of thinking, the impoverishment of life that had come with the Persian reforms was anathema because it was based on a false premise. The Good God *was not* at the summit of Creation, nor did he reign without the Good Goddess. Beyond and above him and her was the Absolute, the transcendent and impersonal Divine Spirit, formless and nameless, the plenum from which all Beings of form issued in their descending hierarchies. As Karl Luckert stresses, the pagan conception of deity was not polytheistic as assumed today; it posited unity as the supreme religious principle. The pantheons of gods that preoccupied folk worship were not, as the people thought, at the apex of the divine hierarchy; beyond these archetypal groupings, overarching them, lay the Supreme Self-emanating Principle, pure and transcendent Spirit, One, unknowable, formless, and eternal: the womb of all. This was the Syro-Palestinian God tradition in which Jesus was reared, trained, and initiated. It was believed among his fellow sectaries that without such a true monism society degenerated, and that nothing would change for the better until Israel's ancient prophetic religion was reinstated. The Western Qabalist Will Parfitt sums up this archaic yet new view of God:

> Although the Jewish religion (and its Christian offshoot) became patriarchal in its present form, its secret inner teachings, as expressed through the Qabalah, are equally inclusive of both male and female . . . The creation of the universe as understood Qabalistically is not about a single male God creating everything, but rather a complex unfolding of principles and energies originating from a source that includes both "male" and "female" energies.[33]

Furthermore, Parfitt reminds us, "Everything in the Qabalah is seen in terms of trinities . . . The Mother-Father Deity is simultaneously Male and Female and the creation is the Child, thus creating a threesome."[34]

According to the Apocryphal Gospels, this was the alternative cosmogonic model to which, as a Nazarean initiate and a Hasid, Jesus had subscribed. In the Apocrypha, Jesus offers his worship primarily to the divine Father, but his recognition of the divine Mother is unequivocal. In the Gospel of Thomas, Jesus says:

> Whoever does not hate his father and his mother as I do cannot become a disciple to me . . . for my [earthly] mother [gave me death] but my true mother gave me life. (Thomas 101)

In such writings the Mother is frequently characterized as the Holy Spirit (Hebrew *ruah*), known as the Shekhinah in Judaism. Thus the esoteric Gospel of Matthew, otherwise known as the Gospel of the Hebrews, has Jesus speaking of "my Mother, the Spirit." In a passage in the Greek-derived Gospel of Matthew it says that "Jesus was led by the Spirit into the wilderness," but in the Hebrew original, cited by Origen but omitted from the text with which we are familiar, Jesus said:

> Even so did my mother, the Holy Spirit, take me by one of my hairs, and carry me away to the great mountain Tabor. (Matthew 4:1, Gospel of the Hebrews)

Being caught up by the hair was known in mystical circles as an expression of inner rapture, used, for example, by Ezekiel. Again, one Gnostic group claimed to have received a secret tradition from Jesus through James and Mary Magdalene, and so prayed in the Qabalistic manner to both Father and Mother and to their Son, humanity: "From thee, Father, and through Thee, Mother, the two immortal names, Parents of the divine being, and Thou, dweller in heaven, humanity of the mighty name" (*Hippolytus, Refutation of All Heresies* 5:6).

In the Hebrew language, the term for spirit, *ruah,* is a feminine noun, and so according to the Gospel of Philip, whoever becomes a Christian has "both father and mother" (52:24) for the Spirit is "Mother of many" (59: 35–60).[35] As Elaine Pagels says,

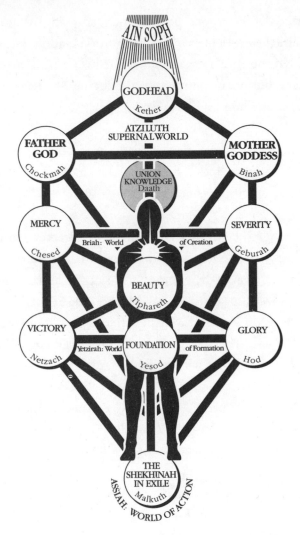

Fig. 5. The Holy Trinity: Father–Mother–Child.
*In this instance, the father is shown on the right of the son (the human figure
in the middle) and the mother on the left, a reversal of the two outside pillars
of the Tree of Life (per A. E. Waite,* The Holy Kabbalah*).*

Gnostics agreed that the divine is to be understood in terms of a harmonious, dynamic relationship of opposites—a concept that may be akin to the Eastern view of yin and yang, but remains alien to Orthodox Judaism and [Orthodox] Christianity.[36]

In Orthodox Christianity the Trinity is composed of two masculine Persons and a neutral third, the Holy Spirit (Greek: *pneuma*), so that the Son is conceived of as the offspring of a masculine and neuter coupling. But, as we have seen, the Gnostics regarded the Holy Spirit as a maternal element in the Trinity—that is, as the Spirit of Life. They therefore worshipped Christ the Son as the archetype of humanity, the offspring of the divine Father and the divine Mother, as in the Qabalah. The Apocryphon of John (literally, the Secret Book of John), which purports to reveal "the mysteries and the things hidden in silence" that Jesus taught to John (1:2–3), tells how the apostle, fleeing the horror of the Crucifixion in great fear, had a mystical vision of the Trinity within a heavenly light, and the Savior's voice said to him: "John, John, why do you doubt, and why are you afraid? . . . I am the one who [is with you] always. I [am the Father]; I am the Mother; I am the Son" (Apocryphon of John 2: 9–14).

And the same voice went on to describe the divine Mother as an emanation of the supreme Godhead: "She is . . . the image of the invisible, virginal, perfect spirit . . . She became the Mother of everything, for she existed before them all, the mother-father *(matropater)* . . ." (Apocryphon of John 4:34; 5:7).

Thus between the Jerusalem clergy and the confederation of the Hasidim there yawned an absolute and irreconcilable chasm. On one side lay a patriarchal God concept of strict monotheism and on the other an essentially matriarchal and hierarchical one, the latter expressing a limited monotheism that included both male and female principles. It was a fundamental difference of theological viewpoint, a schismatic parting of the ways that was incapable of being resolved by anything less than secession. Dr. Thompson has explored this theological gulf exhaustively in his survey of the Bible as history. He has labeled one side of the chasm *exclusive* monotheism and the other *inclusive* monotheism, the latter form including many polytheistic and matriarchal beliefs rejected by the Judaic orthodoxy. However, even this summation hardly does justice to the absolute, irreconcilable opposition inherent in the two positions.

Such fundamental issues as the reunification of Yahweh and the Goddess were of primary concern as far back as the return of the Jews from Babylon, and were those that the high priest Onias took with him to Leontopolis. The exile of a hereditary high priest to Egypt is a fact of enormous significance in Jewish history, yet in modern accounts is usually mentioned in a garbled way only briefly, as of no importance. As Baigent points out, there has undoubtedly been a rabbinic policy aimed at keeping the whole episode hidden. But Onias was the last legitimate high priest of the House of Zadok ever to reign in the Jerusalem temple, and carried in his person a divine mandate ostensibly passed down from the reign of Solomon. As the head of the temple hierarchy, Zadok was also the head of the Judaic prophetic orders, ranked above the Levitical priesthood, and served as the consecrated link between the people and God. Traditionally, moreover, he was the only priest authorized to crown a Jewish king. His defection was of grave significance for the future of the Jewish nation.

Onias's departure from Jerusalem struck at one of the most sacred elements in Jewish life, for there is a sense in which he took with him to Egypt the living heart of Judaism. Deeply unsettling to previous conceptions of Jewish history, this event, which saw the transference of much of Jerusalem's spiritual authority to the Leontopolis temple, has in general been given inaccurate, vague, and misleading treatment. For example, Baigent, Leigh, and Lincoln, who have based their version of events on Robert Eisenman's interpretation,[37] claim that in the middle of the second century BCE the fiercely nationalistic Maccabees "reinstated" the Zadokite high priesthood, which had lapsed, and became the legitimate leaders of a Hasidic movement dedicated to fighting Hellenism and preserving the exclusivist Jewish orthodoxy centered on Mosaic law.

But the legitimate Zadokite lineage had not lapsed; it had merely relocated to Leontopolis. And the Hasidim were not anti-Hellenism but anti-fundamentalism; they were not against the Law but against its tyranny. They claimed that the Maccabees had usurped the Zadokite lineage without authorization; nor were the Maccabees the leaders of the Hasidim as 1 Maccabees avers, although the latter were a part of that movement for a certain limited time. The undisputed leader of the Hasidim was the Teacher of Righteousness. And finally, at that period of history, the Hasidim were not an insular and reactionary political body as Baigent, Leigh, and Lincoln state, but one dedicated to liberalizing reforms. Most of the confusion surrounding this extraordinary religio-political upheaval in Judaism must be attributed to the apologetics of three primary sources of information, 1 and 2 Maccabees, from which Josephus drew his material, and his historical work *The Antiquities of the Jews,* which sought to glorify the Hasmonean dynasty and all its works at the expense of the older Zadokite lineage.

The true Hasidim, for whom Josephus shows little sympathy, had three goals: one was freedom of worship for observant Jews under Seleucid (Greek) rule, the second was restitution of the hereditary Zadokite high priesthood and the return of the hereditary monarchy, and the third was the reinstatement of the Judaic Mysteries. Only the first goal was of interest to the Maccabees. The Hasidim supported them until it had been achieved, but thereafter the two parties were on a collision course. The liberal Hasidim, steeped in a long tradition of prophecy, and the fanatic Maccabees, sons of a priestly father who knew little beyond the Levitical cult ordinances, precepts, and rituals, became only too soon bitter enemies, as the testimony of history makes clear.

The story goes that at a dinner given by the Hasmonean high priest John Hyrcanus I (135–104 BCE), one of the Pharisee elders, named Eleazar, spoke up, saying that "if he [John Hyrcanus] truly wished to be righteous he should lay aside the priesthood, to which his family properly had no claim."[38] From then on the Pharisees lost favor with the Hasmonean rulers. The latter—all of them of narrow bigoted outlook and outstanding venality—were, however, fully supported by the rich Sadducees with their Zadokite pretensions, and increasingly had little interest in anything but wealth and political power. Joseph Campbell recounts that what ensued was a hundred years of ceaseless Hasmonean military conquest, bigotry, xenophobia, forced conversions, social turmoil, corruption in high places, and cultural stagnation throughout

Hebraic Palestine.[39] This was undoubtedly the root cause of the hostility maintained by the rest of the country toward "the lawless Jews" so evident in the gospels. Judaeans were unpopular long before Jesus' crucifixion for their militaristic leanings, and taking into consideration Jesus' great theme of forgiveness of one's enemies, it is doubtful that the crucifixion was ever the main cause of the general ill feeling.

For almost two centuries, xenophobic policies, enforced by the Maccabees and accompanied by constant ethnic wars, were pursued by the Jerusalem hierarchy as a means of constellating Jews around a sense of exclusive ethnic and religious identity. But these policies were to bring great suffering to the little nation. Contempt for foreign authority and an unrealistic view of its own high destiny and historical importance without doubt contributed to Israel's ultimate fall. In the course of their formation, the Hebrew scriptures underwent extensive revision after 164 BCE,[40] following the Maccabean wars against Samaria, and cannot be relied on to reflect a true picture of Judaic history. Indeed, these scriptures give so little hint of the religious bigotry introduced by the Maccabees, the acrimonious ethno-religious pogroms and forced conversions they encouraged, and the resultant discord that convulsed the Hebraic-Palestinian world for several centuries, that one can only surmise deliberate censorship has been at work.

As a consequence of the Maccabean policies, the Hasidic movement grew ever more widespread, embracing in Egypt, northern Palestine, and Mesopotamia many sectarian branches dedicated to opposing the Jerusalem upstarts. As Gaalyah Cornfeld says, "The aim of the House of Zadok under the Greek Seleucids had been diametrically opposed to that of the Hasmoneans, being to bring the Jewish nation out of its exclusivist isolation into the greater commonwealth of Hellenic peoples without sacrificing its freedom or style of worship."[41] This was the ideal the Hasidim continued to favor, while at the same time working to preserve intact their ancient royalist and mystical traditions in the face of brutal persecution by the new priest-kings.

From the beginning of the second century BCE to the end of the first century CE, the spiritual heirs of the Zadokite prophets became known by their enemies as the *minim,* the rabbinic name for heretics. Related to the Righteousness lineage of Melchizedek, all these sects, including the Nazareans and later the Judaeo-Christians, were apocalyptic fraternities that lived always in a state of siege under fanatical oaths of secrecy; taught an alternative worldview deriving from the old Solomonic Mysteries; disdained the sacrificial cult of the Jerusalem temple; and preserved their own fraternal organization, ascetic practices, Solar calendrical knowledge, and merkavah Wisdom tradition. From their Wilderness camps in remote parts of Syro-Palestine or in the suburbs of Alexandria, they never ceased to look to the Day of the Lord, the day of reckoning when true kingship would return, their enemies would be routed, and there would be a restitution of the sacred earthly order ordained by heaven. At that time, the Hasidim declared, the Kingdom of God would be established in the hearts of men.

The resultant pogroms forced the Hasidim to flee Judaea, as we have seen, whereas in Egypt, among the Greek-speaking, highly educated Jewish émigrés, they were able to thrive and multiply, and to resuscitate without hindrance the traditional Solar ideology of the prophets. A permanent rupture was thus created in the Jewish religion, resulting in two diametrically opposed forms of Judaism, one Gnostic/Qabalistic and ultimately Christian, the other Mosaic and Torah centered, leading to modern Israel.

And what of the Pharisees, who get such a bad press in the Christian scriptures? In spite of their more conservative views, the Pharisees were a genuine part of the Hasidic movement. They remained, however, with the usurping regime in Jerusalem, although at times strongly opposing it and pushing through many enlightened reforms in the synagogues.[42] Strangely enough, whether by accident or design, the Hasidim appear in this way to have adopted a well-known stratagem in the international inner brotherhoods. The British esotericist J. G. Bennett describes how in the thirteenth century the Sufis of Turkestan, foreseeing the Mongol invasion, divided into three groups: one went into exile, one went underground, "preserving [its] tradition intact by disguising its outward form,"[43] and one openly joined the enemy, subverting it from within.

It is possible that the Hasidim deliberately dispersed in a similar triune way, one branch to the Therapeutae in Egypt and one in "underground" Palestinian groups, while that of the Pharisees represented the last-named type, which subverted the enemy from within its own ranks. If so, the Pharisees suffered for their sacrifice under a most cruel regime. One of the last Hasmonean priest-kings, Alexander Jannaeus (r. 103–76 BCE), enraged at an armed Pharisaic uprising against him, is said to have watched the crucifixion of eight hundred Pharisees and the strangling of their wives while drinking wine and enjoying his concubines.[44] There can be little doubt that the Sons of Darkness mentioned in the War Manual found among the Dead Sea Scrolls refer to these last dissolute scions of the Hasmonean dynasty.

But proximity to the venal influence of the Hasmoneans followed by such a punishment seems to have changed the nature of the Pharisaic sect in a fundamental way.[45] With the decline of the ruling dynasty, the Pharisees gained power, and then, as Joseph Campbell tells it, "the internecine tide only ran the other way. New purges, fratricides, betrayals, liquidations, and miracles kept the kingdom in uproar, . . ."[46] until at last, in 63 BCE, Pompey's army entered Palestine and the country passed into the sphere of Rome, after which the Hasmonean dynasty ended and the equally notorious Herodian high priesthood was installed in the temple. Thereafter, the Herodians in their turn became the target for the Hasidim's reformist agenda.

THE LIGHT OF THE BRIDECHAMBER IS EXTINGUISHED

In *The Bible in History* Dr. Thompson has candidly chronicled his difficulties in getting his research on the hidden aspects of Jewish history accepted in academia. For ten years no publishing house, either in America or Europe, would publish his work.[47] Not until Sheffield's Professor of History Philip Davies opened up a broad debate on the history of Israel and Palestine, and in general on the limited historicity of the Hebrew Bible, did the situation change. Since then Dr. Thompson's seminal work has been able to throw a revealing light on the many gaps and anomalies in Jesus' life story and the subsequent history of his movement.

By the time Epiphanius was writing his history of Christian heresies, the Nazarean Church of Jerusalem had been dispersed and great changes had overtaken the Christian religion. Its leaders no longer identified with the Nazareans and the Hasidim had apparently disappeared from public history, not to reappear until the eighteenth century to trouble Judaism anew. Many of the followers of Jesus who had been dissatisfied with the continuing observance of Mosaic law in the Jamesian church in Jerusalem had long since sought a more liberal climate in Syria and the Transjordan, among those Nazarean groups, which had managed to retain the original gnostic form of Christianity.

Indeed it is noteworthy that after his visionary conversion to Christianity on the Damascus Road, Paul immediately sought to study all he could of the new faith from this same land, Roman Arabia as it was then called. "A master of Jewish mystical teaching, instructed in the *Lore of Creation*,"[48] as Schonfield says of Paul, the apostle was already conversant with Jewish occult teachings, especially those of the Alexandrian philosopher Philo, and would have been very much at home in the rarified metaphysical climate of the Wilderness sects. As Andrew Welburn says, it is hard to see how Paul has gained his reputation for dogmatism and bigotry:

> Behind all of Paul's writings stands his strong sense of the universality of the Christian transformation, taking him out of the Jewish sphere into the wider culture of his time.[49]

Far from turning to the Jamesian church in Jerusalem, we learn it was to Nazarean and Essene country in Nabatea that Paul straightaway repaired, visiting Jerusalem only once in fourteen more years (Galatians 1:15–23). He evidently believed that the spiritual instruction and Christological initiation he received was not available in the Judaean capital, where the legalism of the synagogues had infected James's leadership of the young Church.[50] But ironically, by the fourth century these original Judaeo-Christians who had clung to the old customs and nomenclature found themselves described as heretics and ex-communicants. What could have happened to bring about such a complete volte face?

Epiphanius followed the current ruling of the Roman Church in regarding the original desert communities, which could be traced back to the most primitive stage of the Christian faith, as vile nests of heresy, and accused members of disseminating their "filthy" teachings "like poison from an asp." He mentions with modest pride that he himself, while serving in Syro-Palestine, had expelled from the local congregation one Peter the Hermit, an elderly monastic ascetic of Cochaba, for contaminating the flock with his "loathsome" gnostic doctrines.[51]

In the same historical work there is some kind of explanation for the bishop's disgust. Epiphanius describes a sectarian belief that he personally finds incomprehensible, which obliges Gnostics to collect the particles of wisdom's Light in the form of "soul" dispersed in all living things and bear it back with them in their ascension to the divine Source. Very clearly this is a reference to the classic Qabalistic doctrine that concerns the billions of sparks or holy Light monads that are emitted from the Divine Light and scattered into the cosmos, ensouling all existent things until they are gathered up by a redemptive process that reunites them in the Light that sent them forth. According to Epiphanius, the Gnostics claimed "no matter what we eat, whether meat, vegetable, bread, or anything else, we are doing a favor to created things by collecting soul from all things and transporting it with us to the above."[52]

Qabalists say that in this way humanity, by a transformative exchange of energies, can help to "redeem" Nature's lower kingdoms. Monastic Sufis teach the same doctrine, as did the ascetic Mani, and Jesus too hinted at this great redemptive secret:

Jesus said, "This heaven will pass away, and the one above it will pass away. The dead are not alive, and the living will not die. In the days when you consumed what is dead, you made it what is alive . . ." (Thomas 11)

And he said again: "Blessed is the lion which becomes man when consumed by man; and cursed is the man whom the lion consumes, and the lion becomes man." (Thomas 7)

In short, the higher can redeem the lower by ingesting it—that is, by accepting and transmuting it—but not vice versa. But Epiphanius, "whose avowed desire," according to Professor Layton, was "to discredit and destroy the sect,"[53] had little understanding of this subtle principle. He interprets in licentious terms the redemptive activity of the Nazarean-Christians, describing it as a literal gathering-up of semen eaten in sexual orgies secretly conducted during their communities' love feasts. As Layton says, Epiphanius's accusation against the Gnostics is extremely hard to justify in the light of the elevated doctrine he describes. His diatribe was probably motivated by ignorance and an overheated imagination. It was, however, an interpretation widely shared by the Orthodox Christians of the bishop's day and is often given as a major reason for the demise of Gnosticism in a cloud of salaciousness, scandal, and righteous outrage. But behind it lay the truer reason, a violent backlash against the Nazarean celebration of the mysterious bridechamber rite, whose underlying principle may well be called the metaphysics of sexuality.

Like Mandaeism, Gnostic Christianity once taught in its closed circles that the sacred wedding of the king and the high priestess in the Mysteries is a symbol for spiritual rebirth, the destiny of every soul. It showed that the way to enlightenment, to the Lightworld of the Kingdom of Heaven, is via the act of love, the ancient principle of the hieros gamos. Sexuality abides at every level of being. At every level it is necessary to marry the polarities, reconciling, wherever they occur, good and evil, reason and heart, heaven and hell, spirit and matter . . . as well as man and woman. There is no other way to God, Jesus taught, than by the way of transcendence, the way of love transmuted by the fire of mind: the way of the reconciliation of opposites. But Epiphanius's diatribes reveal all too clearly that the Christian majority found such a teaching outrageous, alarming, and even obscene. It awoke dark inner conflicts too challenging for consciousness to bear. Perhaps it had come too early. Perhaps it was only a seed that Christ sowed at the birth of Pisces, intending it to germinate in the darkness of the coming age and sprout in Aquarius. At any rate, the bridechamber teaching did not survive. Nor did Hasidism in its original form.

After the fall of Jerusalem, the world of Jewry needed above all to regroup and reunite; there was little place in it for a dissident sectarian movement like Hasidism. Consequently, the main Hasidic vehicle of expression, the Hebrew Qabalah, remained an underground spiritual current in Europe until the thirteenth century, and even after that time its study was confined to a very few aficionados. Yet after centuries of repression, charismatic Hasidism in all its original mood of ecstatic mysticism sprang to life again in the eighteenth century in Poland and the Ukraine, erupting as a popular religion that swept like wildfire throughout the Jewish world. Much to the consternation of the Orthodox majority, two different popular Qabalistic sects claimed the Zohar or the Work of the Chariot as their authority and began to proclaim once more the ancient processive creed. They were eruptions from the past, revivalist movements that give us an illuminating glimpse into the underlying principles of Hasidism in late antiquity.

One was the sect of the New Hasidim, or Pietists, followers of Israel ben Eleazar, called Baal Shem (Master of the Divine Name, 1700–1760).[54] Baal Shem is regarded by many as the greatest Jewish saint of the last few centuries. His movement spread into all the Slav countries and in the nineteenth century included nearly four million adepts,[55] all as rebellious as those of Jesus' time.

> They rejected the Talmud, together with external forms, and were
> zealous in the practice of Contemplative Prayer, as recommended by
> the Zohar to those who are in search of inward knowledge concern-
> ing Divine Mysteries . . .[56]

The second Pietist sect was also Zoharist and anti-Talmudic. It was established by one Jacob Frank and before long embraced Christianity.

Both these movements scandalized Orthodox Jewry by openly resur-recting the idea of the feminine principle as part of an androgynous Deity, and their literature makes it clear that the bridechamber rite, as they believed it to be practiced in King Solomon's temple, was cen-tral to their worship. The feminine aspect, says Patai, although always present to some extent in Judaism (particularly among Sephardic and Oriental Jews), had come to be rejected in European Jewry, more espe-cially among the Orthodox Ashkenazi Jews, because of its sexual impli-cations, its intimations of erotic ecstasy. So after the Haskala or Jewish Enlightenment spread throughout Europe in the nineteenth century, the Pietist movement was regarded as shameful and was fiercely sup-pressed. The feminine principle was more forcibly eliminated than ever from the God concept among Reform, Conservative, and non-Hasidic Orthodox Jews, "leaving it," says Patai, "centered upon a strictly spiri-tual, but nevertheless, inescapably masculine Godhead, upon 'our Father in Heaven.'"[57] Such a God was equated with moral purity, whereas an androgynous God was equated with impure contaminations.

In fact, the idea that God created man himself as an androgyne was one that had appeared centuries before in an early rabbinic midrash, being no more than a revival of the primordial Gnosis. As Patai points out, it suggests that since God created man in His own image, God Himself must be hermaphroditic in nature, although official Judaism has never pursued this line of thought to its logical conclusion. The Qabalist Moses Cordovero (1522–1570) says of the hermaphroditic nature of deity as expressed in the Qabalah: "The Crown [of the Qaba-listic Tree of Life] itself is comprised of Male and Female, for one part of it is Male, the other Female."[58]

This view of deity has been given articulate expression only in modern times, under the appellation of panentheism. Panentheism is a theological model that breaks away entirely from the classical monothe-istic conception of deity.

A new day seems to be dawning in religious thought, which for sev-eral centuries has been struggling to free itself from the intellectual chains in which Aristotelian and so-called Platonic or neo-Platonic influences have long held it confined.[59]

The philosopher Charles Hartshorne introduced the radical notion of panentheism or *processive monotheism* in a 1967 thesis as an alternative to the tradition of patriarchal or static monotheism that Christianity has inherited from Reformed Judaism. However, Raphael Patai's researches offer the possibility that this theosophical formula of Hartshorne's is actually extremely ancient and reflects the Qabalistic conception of deity that has always been held by the true Hasidim.[60] It is one in which God androgynously includes both the masculine and the feminine principles in such a manner as to transcend both. It implies moreover a motion at the core of reality, a pulse or heartbeat, such that a rhythmic oscillation occurs between unity and duality.

Thus in the second century, Clement of Alexandria, in his esoteric work the *Stromateis,* claimed that for the Gnostic initiate the Godhead was surrounded by an impenetrable cognitive darkness: the Divine Spirit could be known only by its image in manifested existence, the world of space and time.[61] And like Clement, who became the head of the Christian catechetical school in Alexandria, which followed the lines of the Greek *paideia,* the Hasidim believed that from the Godhead residing androgynously in the Unmanifest there issues eternally into the world of form two mighty deities who can be known, named, and mythopoetically given gender.

These two personifications, called Alpha and Omega by Clement, are vast centers of cosmic energy that together in union create the visible universe. One is a center of creative cosmic energy, the Father God, and the other a center of magnetic cosmic energy, the Mother Goddess. Together in creative union, as One, they engender the Creation, and separating rhythmically as Two, the Divine Couple. They govern and maintain the Creation as Images of the Godhead. This immutable cosmic process is the essence of what Hartshorne has called panentheism or processive monotheism.

The theological problem introduced by Zoroaster is absolutely central to the temple power struggle in Jerusalem and the unresolved Zadokite mutiny that followed. And it has cast a deep shadow over the whole of consequent Western religious history, because it has not been resolved in Christianity either. The Hebrew prophets rejected the absolute separation of God and His creation inherent in Zoroastrianism. The Hasidim followed the prophets. They believed that God gave humanity the power to influence his condition for good or ill, therefore *to limit* God's sovereignty and absolute power. As an androgyne, as One, He was omnipotent, but no longer omnipotent in His plural phase. This was a notion impossible in a classical monotheistic belief system in which God is separate, omnipotent, and remote from the vagaries and suffering of his creation. The Pietists rescued the notion from an underground stream that had survived since the Hasidim left Palestine.

Almost immediately after Jesus' crucifixion, a great exodus of the Hasidim began. We can assume that this was due to the fact that the secretive style on which they had depended for so long was no longer possible. Jewish persecution, which Dr. R. Macuch dates to about 37 CE,[62] drove thousands of them to flee Judaea, many northeastward toward Mesopotamia, Persia, and beyond; some to Arabia; others by boat to southern Gaul; but most to the Middle East. Schonfield says of Bishop Epiphanius's later researches into these migrations:

> The variety of Jewish and Judaeo-Christian sects flourishing in the Middle East was evidently very extensive and considerably interrelated. We meet not only with the familiar Pharisees, Sadducees, Essenes, and Nazoreans, but also with Elchesaites, Sampseans, Ebionites, Hemerobaptists, Dositheans, etc., etc.[63]

Many of these migrant Hasidic sects joined forces with the nascent Sufi stream in Arabia, but there was also a drift farther east toward India. A large community of the Nazareans settled in Afghanistan, where they are still known as the Nasara or Nusairijeh.[64] All except the Mandaeans have abandoned the heterodox beliefs of the Hasidim that made life so difficult for Judaism, Christianity, and finally militant Islam. As Thomas Thompson notes, knowledge of the exact nature and dynamics of the fracturing within the Judaic body in late antiquity that led to such massive migrations has been almost entirely lost, replaced by an uncritically accepted Jewish mythology.

For example, a recent, otherwise well-researched work on Hermetism, again by Baigent and Leigh, informs us that at the dawn of the Christian era Alexandria's Jews "looked to Jerusalem for spiritual leadership and paid their annual tax to the Temple there . . ."[65] Without qualification this is a highly misleading statement. It disregards the vast numbers of the Samaritan faithful quartered in the Delta city who were loyal to their own temple on Mount Gerizim, not to mention all the disaffected Hasidim and the Coptic contingent whose consecrated temple in Leontopolis functioned as an official center of Judaic worship in Egypt.[66] But it illustrates how thoroughly two thousand years of historical mythmaking has conditioned us to take for granted the sole legitimacy and spiritual authority of the Jerusalem temple. At that time, at the beginning of the first century CE, it was actually elsewhere, in Egypt, that Judaism's real command center lay. It was there that the critical change of direction in the Jewish religion was already taking place, which would lay the foundation for the birth of the Christ Mystery.

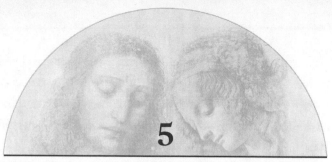

5

OUT OF THE EAST: PROPHECIES AND STAR LORE

Before Christ came there was no bread in the world. Like the Paradise, the place where Adam was, it had many trees as food for the beasts. [But] it had no wheat as food for man. Man fed like the beasts. But when Christ, the perfect man, came, he brought bread from heaven that man should feed on the food of man.

THE GOSPEL OF PHILIP

Jesus entered the stream of history on a groundswell of messianic prophecies that had been spreading westward for the past two centuries, borne thence by rumors about the strange oracles of the Zervanite magi of Persia. These astronomer-priests who comprised the esoteric arm of Zoroastrianism believed there was a High God beyond light and darkness, beyond good and evil, whom they revered under the name of Zervan, and it was their transcendent Zervanite philosophy that preoccupied the thought of the breakaway mystical circles in Egyptian Judaism in the two centuries before Christ.

Zoroastrian wisdom told of two primordial spirits of Light and Darkness, Truth and Falsehood, Good and Evil, who were fated to be antagonists to the death and to wage perpetual war on the stage of history—a dualistic doctrine that has ever since the second century CE been imputed to all Christianity's enemies, in particular to the Gnostics, despite the same dualism being inherent in Christianity itself. But because of the Oneness of the Divine, the Zervanites preached a transcendent unity, which would bring peace to the battle of good and evil here below, a surcease to strife in the sphere of Time. That victory, they proclaimed, was imminent and would soon be made possible by an incarnating Saoshyant, a great avatar or embodiment of Mithras, the Babylonian Sun god. And so there grew across the world an intense preoccupation with the idea of a coming Illuminator, a Savior prince who would once again disseminate the primordial Gnosis and end the warfare of good and evil. In ancient Persian traditions, says Andrew Welburn,

> it was said that the messianic prince would be born when a star fell to earth as a meteor or lightning flash . . . But the prophecies were connected above all with the End-time, and the saviour prince was expected to appear from the summit of a sacred mountain: the spectacular Mount Hukhairya in the Elburtz range, south of the Caspian Sea . . . Birth in a cave too corresponds to the myths of Iran about the future Saviour, who was to be born from the seed of Zarathustra.[1]

These ideas about the coming of a great Savior, the "Holy One of Truth," began to circulate in the second and first centuries BCE, and are believed to have been received and later reworked by Jewish baptizing sects, such as the Mandaean/Nazarean communities living on the borders between Persia and Mesopotamia. But the magi were also appearing in Alexandria by then, astonishing the toga-wearing inhabitants by their trousers and Phrygian caps as well as their strange oracular teachings. Their proclamation of the wondrous possibility of a coming Illuminator resulted in a mood of hope and spiritual expectation abroad, which reached fever pitch among the Hasidim.

According to the Apocalypse of Adam, which was found among the Dead Sea Scrolls and is thought to be Mandaean in origin, the Persian magi had long intimated that the series of incarnations of the great prophet Zarathustra, the founding Illuminator of their line, would culminate in his final, thirteenth rebirth as the expected Saoshyant. Thus there would be brought to earth a hypercosmic Being far greater than the Prophet himself.[2] Twelve incarnations of Zarathustra had already appeared in various races, while the thirteenth was soon to come; and, according to ancient Persian traditions collected by the baptizing sects, this climactic event was destined to take place in Palestine.[3] Later Sethian texts like the Chronicle of Zuqnin and the Sacred Book of the Invisible Great Spirit found at Nag Hammadi identified the coming Savior prince with the Hebrew Messiah.

It was this prophetic fertilization from the Persian/Babylonian sphere that contributed to the return of the Mysteries to Judaism. Numerous religious leaders arose in Palestine both before and after the ministry of Jesus claiming to be the long-awaited Holy One, the Messiah, the Savior or Anointed One predicted by the wise men from the East, and much civic excitement and unrest was provoked throughout the provinces. The Hebrew race had been chosen, had been honored, to be the cradle of a new-world revelation! Who would wear the crown? There was not only speculation but also intense argument among the various competing regions and religious parties, and a mounting disquiet in political circles in Jerusalem. It was imperative, said some, that the Messiah belong to Jerusalem, the hub of the Hebrew world. But not all agreed.

The turmoil that accompanied the separation of the Christian movement from its Judaic antecedents was only the final stage in a rupture, strand by strand, that had been going on among the conflicting elements in Judaism for more than three centuries. Indeed, some modern sources believe this spiritual fission within the Judaic body was prepared for, and even perhaps fostered over a long period, by initiates who had the new Christ Mystery in view. British editor David Ovason refers numerous times in his book *The Zelator* to the preparation for the Christ Mystery that went on in Egypt over the pre-Christian centuries.[4] Others, like Professor Thompson, see the spiritual fission in Judaism as essentially a rift between northern and southern Palestine brought on by political rivalry and ambition, but which played itself out in dramatically moral terms as an apocalyptic war between good and evil.[5] There is no doubt that the messianic prophecies about a coming savior and king who would bring back the Mysteries to Judaism played a large part in the ongoing conflict between Judaea and the northern provinces.

The two cultures had so little in common, were so fundamentally unsympathetic to each other's worldview, that they were bound to seek a divorce. The northern provinces, including Samaria, were the product of the old sophisticated Ugaritic empire and the Egyptian-imbued culture of the great port cities of Tyre and Sidon nearby—in effect, the cultural sphere of Solomon. Judaea, on the other hand, had been molded by a far more conservative Bedouin culture to the south, a culture steeped in the strict spiritual mores of the Arabian desert and with little sympathy for the intellectual currents emanating from abroad, especially from Egypt.

This may be why Jesus' association with Egypt is so played down in the gospels. The only reference in the Christian scriptures to his sojourn in that land is in Matthew 2:13, where it is said that after Jesus was born in Bethlehem, his father Joseph, in obedience to an angelic warning that King Herod would kill the child, fled with Mary and his son into Egypt, where the family stayed until the king's death. An old Coptic tradition claims additionally that the family visited Heliopolis for a time and then continued south and settled for several more years in a town called Assyut, where a church known as the Mattariya now stands on the site at which they stayed.[6] Indeed, in his researches into Christianity's origins, the British author Desmond Stewart lays little store on the reliability of the legend of Jesus' birth in Bethlehem and considers it more likely that he was born in Egypt, probably near the Mattariya (now in northern Cairo). After the birth, Stewart postulates, the holy family would have traveled down the Nile to Leontopolis, where the baby would have been presented for circumcision.[7]

According to this author, Jesus, regardless of where he was born, probably spent his youth in Egypt, possibly in Alexandria, only later returning to Palestine with his family. "Has this brief addendum to the nativity tradition of Christ Jesus," Stewart asks, "been intended to hint at the broader nativity of Christian theology in Egypt?"[8] If so, if Jesus studied in Egypt in his formative years, he would have found there an alternative Judaic tradition that had already put down deep roots in its adopted land, and he might well have been nourished by its revolutionary themes.

By at least the seventh century BCE, the Hebrew religion was well established in ancient Egypt and possibly also in Ethiopia and Arabia, and was already leaving its idiosyncratic stamp on international culture. At that time Hebrew military colonies populated by mercenaries and their families were settled at Elephantine and Hermopolis on the Nile, where temples to Yahweh and his consort, the Lady of Heaven (thought to be the "virgin goddess" Anath-Astarte), were erected. And after the destruction of the first Jerusalem temple in the following century, many thousands more Goddess-worshiping Hebrew deportees gathered in Egypt, shipped there by Babylonian and Persian conquerors.

These immigrants, as we learn in the book of Jeremiah, entered into a heated argument with that long-suffering old Yahwist prophet, who had also been deported. Jeremiah, whom the Hebrew Bible uses as a mouthpiece of Reformed Judaism, upbraided them severely, declaring they would never have suffered such a national catastrophe if they had not strayed from the path of righteousness by following foreign gods and goddesses. He therefore exhorted them to forsake idolatry and avert further national catastrophe by returning to the worship of Yahweh as the one and only true God. But the people were not impressed. They answered defiantly, believing that their abandonment of the Goddess because of the monotheistic reforms instituted in Jerusalem had brought them only disaster:

> As for the word you have spoken to us in the name of Yahweh—we shall not listen to you. But we shall without fail do everything as we said: we shall burn incense to the Queen of Heaven, and shall pour her libations as we used to do, we, our fathers, our kings and our princes, in the cities of Judah and in the streets of Jerusalem. For then we had plenty of food, and we all were well and saw no evil. But

since we ceased burning incense to the Queen of Heaven and to pour
her libations, we have wanted everything and have been consumed
by sword and famine. (Jeremiah 44:15–19)

From then on the people ignored the reforms of Jerusalem's Levitical
priesthood, continuing to worship the Divine Couple in the old manner
and to "see no evil." There is no evidence that the majority of Egyptian
Jews were ever in principle to depart from this resolve: their Judaic tradition was thereafter based on it. Around 407 BCE, a letter written in
Aramaic and sent to the governors of both Samaria and Judaea by one
Yedoniah, a Jewish priest of Elephantine, reveals that the people there
were still worshipping gods of Syrian and international origin, both
male and female, as well as Yahweh, and regarded the temples in both
Samaria and Jerusalem as equally worthy of their loyalty.[9] And in the
fourth century BCE, Hellenized Egypt, as already mentioned, was further flooded by many thousands of Samaritan deportees of heterodox
views who settled in the Delta, the traditional homeland of the Egyptian Semites, where they continued to practice the ancient polytheistic
rites of their fathers. This mixed expatriate community of Alexandrian
Jews was the largest Jewish community in the world, making up about
a third of the city's population, as well as growing to be the wealthiest,
most literate, and most influential element in its polyglot citizenry. The
Jewish contribution to the Hellenic arts, sciences, and religious philosophies that opened up in Egypt after the Greek conquest was enormous.

Arriving only a few decades after the building of Alexandria, the
advent onto the scene of the Zadokite high priest Onias III, with his
Hellenistic sympathies and his large retinue of temple officials, prophets, and other learned followers, must have given a huge further impetus
to the evolution of a distinctively intellectual Egyptian Judaism. It is
highly probable that the high priest Zadok already had close traditional
ties with the Heliopolitan priesthood and that his studies included the
Heliopolitan Solar theology. But even apart from his heterodox background, Onias's divinely mandated powers and erudition would have
been immense. Zadok represented the Judaic Mysteries. He took with

him to Egypt a vast knowledge of the arcane Chariot tradition of the Hebrews; his authority alone ratified the coronation of Jewish kings; he alone carried the bloodline of the priestly Messiah of Israel and stood therefore in close association with the royal Davidic Messiah, whose coming the people of Israel awaited. Zadok was in truth the very pulse of the spiritual life and hopes of the Jewish nation, and the magian prophecies could only have enhanced his standing among his Zadokite followers in Palestine.

Philip Davies wonders why we know so little about this Zadokite lineage. There is considerable evidence that the high priest, traditionally responsible for the entire priestly ceremonial and cult of the temple, was himself drawn from the highest and most learned of the Hebrew prophetic orders, in emulation of the Egyptian sacerdotal system. But under Persian domination and then under the even greater tyranny of the Maccabees, all mention of the prophets of the Righteousness lineage was deleted from the text of the Hebrew Bible, which was being written from circa 400 BCE. In this manner the historical role of Zadok in Israel's temple affairs was almost obliterated and the Levitical cult priests were raised to an altogether new eminence. As Dr. Davies comments:

> Zadok is a mystery, though it is widely conjectured that he belonged to the old Jebusite priestly class. It was Zadok who triumphed [over the Levitical priesthood] under Solomon, his dynasty ultimately a monopoly of the high priesthood after the exile, as the sole eligible group . . . The exclusive claims of the tribe of Levi to the priesthood are impossible to retrace with any confidence.[10]

Because the Zadokite high priest was the custodian of the most sacred knowledge of his race, it must be considered significant that the time of his arrival in Egypt and the setting up of a consecrated temple complex in Leontopolis signals the beginning of three centuries of unprecedented Hebrew intellectual and spiritual creativity centered in Alexandria. It was a cultural efflorescence that culminated in the Jewish Wisdom literature, the Qabalistic *gematria,* and the groundbreaking philosophy of

Philo Judaeus. In the latter, a radical alternative to the Jerusalem ideology was finally forged—a Universalist vision of God and the world—that only widened the gulf between Egyptian and Judaean Jewry. From this fertile soil centered in Alexandria grew the brilliant Egypto-Jewish syncretic tradition anathematized by the power circles in Jerusalem but embraced by the various sects of the Hasidim. Among these we must include the radical new Jesus movement, the last to emerge and the one that was to take the whole messianic development in a new and unforeseen direction.

But there was far more to the Mithraic prophecies than the expectation of a great religious event, as researchers are only now discovering. The predictions brought with them a further precious gift: the hidden stellar knowledge for which Babylon was famous, for the magian prophecies involved a wealth of astronomical knowledge that pinpointed the timing of the expected epiphany. A vast body of star lore began to pour into Alexandria. The tauroctony—that is, the pictorial presentation of the Mithraic bull-slaying scene found on the central altar of every ancient underground Mithraeum and surrounded by zodiacal signs, torchbearers, and other symbols—turns out to be more than a mythological record of the trials and blessings of a Mithraic initiate. It is also a map of certain constellations in the zodiac that acts as timekeeper of the cosmos.[11]

The map is in fact a kind of star clock. It encodes the relationship of the prophecies to a body of stellar calendrical knowledge that threw light on the zodiac and the precession of the equinoxes, projecting in very precise terms the end of a world age and the beginning of a new. This was the point at which the Saoshyant was expected to appear. Not until 1973, at the First International Congress on Mithraism, was it shown how "the tauroctony figures represent constellations lying between Antares and Aldebaran—the primary stars in Scorpio and Taurus,"[12] and how the coming of the Saoshyant had been regarded by the magi as intimately related to the position of these stars and constellations in the heavens. John Major Jenkins, a noted esotericist and author, cites a number of scholars who supported through the 1970s and 1980s this startling new explanation of the Mithraic tauroctonies.[13]

The Apocalypse of Adam, from the Nag Hammadi texts, reveals that in the sixth century BCE the Mithraic cult was founded by Zaratas, a Babylonian prophet and reincarnation of Zarathustra, but it was the Stoics, an intellectual community in the town of Tarsus in southeastern Turkey, who are known to have devised the Mithraic rites in the second century BCE in a form suitable for citizens of the Roman Empire. Posidonius (315–240 BCE) was the most influential of these Greek philosophers and taught astrological doctrines that involved a knowledge of the seven planets of the solar system and seven celestial spheres.

Posidonius probably had much to do with the establishment of the Mithraic rites mentioned by Plutarch in 67 BCE. These rites were apparently derived from the older Perseus cult of Tarsus, and the philosophic community there recognized, in connection with them, a Great Year of cosmic time, lasting 26,000 years, in which four world ages had their allotted periods.[14] This knowledge rested in turn on the discovery of precession by Hipparchus, a Greek astronomer who proved in 128 BCE that the vernal point shifts and that the sphere of stars, hitherto believed by the Greeks to be eternally fixed, actually slowly moves.[15] In point of fact, precession had been known by various races for thousands of years, and Hipparchus was merely rediscovering it. But the zodiacal star lore that developed from his labors was immense and played a large part in the origins of Mithraism. It is believed that a huge fleet of pirates from Tarsus, about 20,000 men strong who knew how to navigate by the stars, practiced the Mithraic ceremonies, and along with the Roman armies seeded them throughout the Mediterranean.[16] With Mithraism came the extensive body of astronomical knowledge that was to flood the Palestinian world.

A central tenet of Mithraism, described in the writings of Porphyry, was that the Mithraic cave symbolized the multileveled cosmos. Souls ascended to the transcendent realm or alternatively descended into physical manifestation on the rungs of the seven consecutive planetary circles, through one or the other of two equinoctial gateways located in the zodiac,[17] and the opening and shutting of these gateways were closely connected to the periodicity of the four great world ages. Such in brief was the astrological lore that accompanied the spread of the messianic prophecies, infusing them with deep cosmo-religious significance.

We can no longer wonder that Paul, a native of Tarsus and an intellectual thoroughly versed in the Stoic philosophy, rejected any notion that the teachings of Messiah Jesus could be constrained within the parameters of Jewish Mosaic law or made subject to the local authority of the Judaeo-Christian Church of the Circumcision in Jerusalem. For Paul the meaning of the prophecies was self-evidently multiracial; but furthermore, he understood that the Saoshyant/Messiah, the Christ, descending into manifestation through the celestial gateway of the zodiac at the end of the age of Aries, had necessarily inscribed on history a *planetary* rather than a national event. Christ had come for the salvation of not only Jews but also the nations and races of the entire planet. Paul's mission was therefore universal: Christ must be preached throughout the world to both Jew and Gentile.

It is a melancholy exercise to reflect how deeply Western civilization sank into ignorance after the ascendancy of Christianity, and how many centuries it took for the cosmological worldview of the Greco-Roman epoch to return to anything like its former level of brilliance. The indifference to high intellectual performance—as against mere scholasticism—that plunged Western culture into darkness virtually until the nineteenth century probably goes a long way to explain its strangely flat and incurious approach to Jesus' life story. Intensive research into the rich, multifaceted culture flooding Palestine in late antiquity really began only about fifty years ago. Since then many have found it increasingly difficult if not impossible, in the face of these new realities, to equate the founder of Christianity with the figure of the illiterate and untutored tradesman of Galilee so uncritically accepted by official Christian history. If we are to accept recent historical reconstructions, Jesus was at the very least a Hasid of the Nazarean persuasion, a prophet, a supporter of the Zadokite lineage, and a teacher of illumined knowledge about the cosmos intended for all peoples.

A NEW HEAVEN AND A NEW EARTH

We now know that Jesus lived and taught in a cultural climate not so very different from that of the nineteenth century in Europe and that in two thousand years we have forgotten far more than we could ever have imagined. By the first century, privileged knowledge had the very highest cachet in sectarian Palestine. Under the Hellenic aegis, esoteric/scientific information and occult learning were at a peak and had become the new means of sectarian power—not only the occult sciences pouring in from Greece and Egypt—but also the esoteric astronomy from the Persian Empire to the east. The latter bore with it the concept of a multileveled universe, a great celestial Ladder of Being whose visionary outline was being incorporated into the Qabalah. In the Nag Hammadi Library an important work is the Secret Book of John, which discloses how keenly early Christians were interested in esoteric astronomy and related subjects. Welburn describes Secret John as

> a primary Gnostic cosmological treatise giving an account of the earliest, purely spiritual phases of world evolution, followed by the origin of the material world and the molding of man's physical body. The cosmic-angelic powers, which govern his life, are described, as is the descent of the spiritual Christ to redeem him.[18]

There is also similarly apocryphal material deriving from astronomy in *The Nature of the World Rulers* (or *Archons*), and in a book called *On the Origin of the World*. In the school of Valentinus we find the Gospel of Truth, which again assumes a detailed knowledge of esoteric cosmology applied to the deeds of Christ.[19] Furthermore, the genre rejects Yahweh as the Creator God of Judaic tradition in favor of a greater hypercosmic Power, the Sun behind the sun that Philo Judaeus seems to identify with the galactic center. The distribution of this new treasure house of knowledge preoccupied all the Palestinian spiritual leaders in the centuries bracketing the Common Era, and not least Jesus, whose quarrel with the Pharisees centered on this very point. He was clearly well aware of the floodtide of new metaphysical speculation pouring into his country and believed its benefits should be shared with as great a proportion of the ordinary people as possible. For this reason he complained that

> [t]he Pharisees and the scribes have taken the keys of Knowledge and hidden them. They themselves have not entered, nor have they allowed to enter those who wish to . . . (Thomas 39)

To the Galilean populace, the Judaean ecclesiastics, the scribes, and the Pharisees were in general reactionary, insular, and self-serving, concentrating on trivia while ignoring the larger evolutionary issues. Jesus called them "a nest of vipers" and "whited sepulchres," castigating them for their nitpicking formalism and hypocrisy. He was expressing what was probably a widespread hostility among the populace to the fact that the Pharisees in particular, always intensely secretive, had become even more so by the first century, and outside their small esoteric coteries were preoccupied solely with political power and with ensuring their own survival. As we have seen, they accordingly taught little in the synagogues except the laws of ritual purification and table fellowship, thus seriously neglecting the teaching of further stages of spiritual growth through higher knowledge. Yet such teachings, Jesus frequently implied, were the right of all human beings:

> Woe to the Pharisees, for they are like a dog sleeping in the manger of oxen, for neither does he eat nor does he let the oxen eat. (Thomas 102)

History, however, has been kind to the Pharisees even if the gospels have not. Except for the Therapeutae of Egypt, they were probably the most humane and enlightened, and certainly the most learned, of all the Hasidean sects, and their secrecy was no doubt necessary in the face of their perilous relationship to the Jerusalem authorities. The gospels recount that they extended fraternal hospitality to Jesus, their fellow initiate, and appear to have held closely argued discussions with him on the merits of the Hasidean agenda for reform. But the meeting of minds foundered. Possibly the Pharisees were alarmed that their maverick brother wanted only to tear down the pillars of the House of Israel, while Jesus, quite at home in the upper reaches of Jewish society, offended his hosts by his outspokenness and his overriding concern for the spiritually poor and underprivileged masses. The idea of sharing their cosmological knowledge with the populace must have been a startling confrontation to the upper classes of those times, although it proved to be one of the most important ways by which early Christianity outshone and outclassed every other mystery cult then in existence.

These were the Last Days, a coded term for the ending of an astrological cycle: in this instance, the death of the age of Aries and the birth of Pisces—a time pregnant with apocalyptic promise. The Jesus movement promised a great awakening of heart intelligence, leading to a new and vastly expanded cosmology. This new condition of enlightenment made possible by the Gnosis of the heart was a vital aspect of the faith that may have first manifested at Pentecost in the fiery visitation of the Paraclete. It was in such a state of illumination, Jesus prophesied, that the Kingdom of Heaven would reveal itself as the divine substratum of the material world, the mighty underlying Power that projects and upholds the phenomenal cosmos. The Kingdom was the primal state underlying and energizing all things, both humans and universes. "You came forth from thence," Jesus tells his disciples, "and you shall go there once again" (Thomas 49).

Jesus himself was the supreme example of the heart intelligence that made such a revelation possible. Discussing the apocryphal Gospel of Truth, a Valentinian treatise, Stephan Hoeller speaks of "the revelation of the secret unity within the knowledge of the heart,"[20] which is indeed the key to a knowledge of the Kingdom, for although the heart's brain is prelogical, it is holistic. Some scientists conjecture that all energy systems are toroid, from the atomic to the universal, suggesting the possibility that there is only one universal torus encompassing an infinite number of interacting tori within its spectrum. Arguably, then, the heart's torus may put it in touch with the entire universe.

> An individual torus may participate holographically within a universal torus over a wide range, from the simple wave particle to the incredible complexities of our heart, brain, and body, all of which are electromagnetic by nature. One implication of this is that each of us centered within our heart torus is as much the center of the universe as any other creature or point, with equal access to all that exists.[21]

Furthermore, because of its powerful magnetic field, the heart is above all the primary organ of relationship. It is the center of love in the human economy; it synthesizes and unifies all the elements of the whole; it envisages the All and transmits its vision to the prefrontal lobes. The heart is therefore the organ of universality par excellence, leading the cerebral mind into transcendent realms. And the heart's language is the natural medium of Jesus' message to the world. Only the heart can fully respond to these words of his:

> I am the light that is above them all. I am the All, the All came forth from me, and the All became me. Cleave the wood, I am there; raise up the stone and you will find me. (Thomas 77)

The Kingdom, Jesus is saying, is the unmanifested substratum of everything that exists in the manifested universe, from the highest archangels to the humblest stone. It is the Whole, the All, a mystical concept that cannot be fitted into our three-dimensional cosmos, but exists in para–space-time. One of the most important insights the new zeitgeist brought to the West was the Qabalistic formulation of the universe as a continuum from unmanifested energy to manifested form. Like the Secret Book of John, the Qabalah described a New Genesis, an account of the Creation that could give earthbound humanity, previously knowing only the scriptures, a deeper, more numinous sense of the birth of the universe. In the Hebrew scriptures we learn that in the beginning God created the heaven and the earth—one world; but the Qabalistic glyph of the Tree of Life

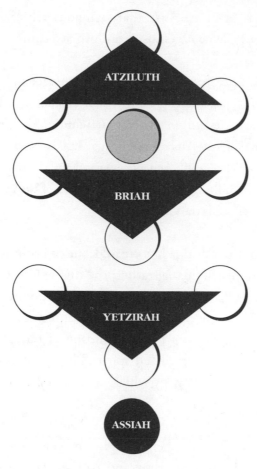

Fig. 6. The four worlds

describes a highly sophisticated process by which four worlds emanate successively from the formless abyss of Godhead. In *The Mystical Qabalah,* the Welsh Kabbalist Dion Fortune shows how a graduated concretization of Light energy descends to arrive finally at our world of physical matter.

Thus spirit itself modulates in four stages into matter, as Clement of Alexandria stressed in his Christian teachings. Creation is a cyclical process, he said, in which God and matter are one principle. "All things, all oppositions are brought together in Christ, as Alpha and Omega, the incommensurable principle in which all duality ceases to exist."[22] Andrew Itter, an Australian religious scholar who has conducted a study of Clement's Gnostic philosophy, comments:

> This *coincidentia oppositorum* assures the initiate that he/she has become Christ-like, a state of being where all contraries are resolved as complementaries within the eternal Word of God, most clearly expressed in Christ as Alpha and Omega. This is a marked feature of mystical experience, and Clement's method and doctrine are specifically designed to bring this about in the mind of the initiate, in the person Clement calls the Gnostic.[23]

In other words, the world is not created out of nothing, nor is it suddenly perfected in a Big Bang; rather, the divine Creative Power gradually externalizes space and time out of itself. It does so by progressing in four stages from the noumenal level of pure energy through three further involutionary levels to the building of our phenomenal system out of matter, or crystallized spirit. This involutionary ladder of worlds then provides a Way by which souls can return to their divine Source.

The highest of all the four cosmic realms is the archetypal world *(Atziluth)*. This supernal sphere of light and bliss is a secondary principle that gives rise to space-time and to the physical Creation itself. Below the purely immaterial world of Atziluth lies a void, an Abyss, on the farther side of which are the three descending realms of space-time that comprise the Creation proper: Briah, Yetzirah, and Malkuth, the last named being our physical world. In some alternative contexts the four worlds are given the names Saturn, Sun, Moon, and Earth, indicating the relationship of the whole to the solar system. The planets then form the rungs of a great Ladder of Being on which the soul can make its upward return journey to God.

The first cosmic level is associated with spiritual fire and with pure Will, the second with air and with Intellect, the third with water and with Emotion or Feeling, and the last with earth and with realized Action, so expressing the gradual organization of the threefold universe into a perfected expression of God in space-time. Each level, as Halevi says, "contains the qualities and activities of the one above, so that each descending level in turn is under more laws, is more complex, and is further from the source."[24] As he continues:

> It disposes of the countless arguments that have gone on over the centuries as to whether Creation was brought forth out of nothing (ex nihilo), all of which rests on an ignorance of the previous existence of the spiritual World of Divine Emanations (Atziluth).[25]

Édouard Schuré declares that this cosmology, which modulates in four steps from an inner spiritual level to an outer and purely physical one, replaces the Hebrew scriptural story of Genesis with one that had secretly been known to initiates for thousands of years. He suggests that the biblical version with which we are familiar is simply an abbreviation or summary devised by an intellectual elite for the laity. It begins at the fourth world, where the Qabalah ends. But for Qabalists themselves,

> the limitless universe was not dead matter governed by mechanical laws, but was a living whole, endowed with intelligence, soul, and will. This great divine being had innumerable organs, corresponding to its infinite faculties ... In the eyes of the ancient science *the visible order of the universe was but the reflection of an invisible order,* that is, of cosmogonic forces ... which through their perpetual involution into matter produced the evolution of life.[26]

To sum up, then: The three worlds of space-time correspond to three levels of consciousness; to three levels of involutionary descent from the spiritual to the psychic to the physical; to three states of matter; to three modalities of time; and so on. Together they form a tripartite system contained within the fourth world, the Atziluthic field, which permeates and surrounds them as a causal Whole, even as Atziluth itself is permeated and surrounded by the Ain Soph, the Godhead, itself a greater causal Whole. This basic fourfold schema provides the framework of the

Qabalah and its Ladder of Being, and pervades all the various modalities of merkavah mysticism.

In passing, the ancient prophets who propounded this system assumed that a physical science that did not incorporate the organic factors of love, intelligence, and egoic identity into the evolutionary process was inconceivable, since these were the organizing factors built into human consciousness itself. The idea of intelligent foresight built into the organism as a feature of its evolution was therefore taken for granted. As we have seen, Clement of Alexandria, who believed that philosophy was the highest path to God, taught this same Qabalistic system in carefully veiled terms. It was, he said, the philosophy of the true Christian Gnostics, "those who belonged to the golden race." Clement claimed that such Qabalistic teachings had been passed down through the apostolic tradition, and he trained a generation of Christians in the mysteries of a providential cosmic philosophy that he said had been brought into the world with the coming of Christ.[27]

Yet even the earliest of the Palestinian prophets, the wandering *ish-ha-elohim* of Israel's tribal days, must have entertained such cosmological ideas as these, for the Pentateuch's texts are full of hidden allusions to a great roadway extending between heaven and earth that initiates were able to glimpse clairvoyantly from very early times. Spiritual metaphors like Jacob's ladder, on which angels and human souls could ascend and descend, is only one of many esoteric images of the fourfold Ladder in the Hebrew Bible. Indeed, not only did such metaphors form the foundation of the Jewish Mysteries but they also were to become the fountainhead of a Qabalistic system of mysticism known to some degree, under various names, to every living metaphysician and every philosopher.

At the time of the dispersion of the Jewish people throughout the world, the secret "chain of the tradition," while still connected to the Holy Land, traveled through the Near East and down to the Yemen; it went through Egypt to North America and across most of Europe.[28]

And this is not to mention Asia Minor, Mesopotamia, Persia, and western India. Jesus therefore could hardly have failed to inherit the merkavah tradition from the still living chain of secret transmission that stretched across most of the known world. It seems impossible that, as the Messiah, he would not have sought to pass it on to his disciples, and from them to the whole world. One of the most outstanding mystics and Qabalists of modern times, Dion Fortune (1890–1946), was emphatic that the Qabalah and its cosmogony provided the original framework for Christian Gnosticism.

> This Qabalistic Cosmogony is the Christian Gnosis. Without it we have an incomplete system in our religion, and it is this incomplete system, which has been the weakness of Christianity. A very cursory acquaintance with the Qabalah serves to show that here we have the essential keys to the riddle of Scripture in general and the prophetic books in particular.[29]

Clearly Jesus believed that the role of the Messiah at the present stage of history was to extend sacred knowledge to as many races as possible. But for some in Jerusalem, the very concept of such a universal Messiah was unpalatable. He would be identical with the Sungod Mithras of Persia, creating a dangerous point of regression in monotheistic Judaism as well as favoring the beliefs of a heathen race. Constantine, for example, has frequently been accused of not being a "Christian" emperor as history claims because he venerated the Roman god Sol Invictus equally with the Jewish Christ; but for Romans familiar with the Zoroastrian prophecies, the two deities were simply synonymous. To Romans aware of the new movement, Messiah Jesus himself was a Solar being, a Sun god, a Hebrew version of Mithras.

Such Solar ideas have found an echo in the Christian scriptures. There Jesus' historical figure is given at every turn Solar associations, to the great puzzlement of scholars. "How Jesus Christ, the Logos or Word made flesh, is connected with the sun is one of the great mysteries of Christian esotericism," declares a modern commentator.[30] But it is only a puzzle if the esoteric Zoroastrian prophecies that were then flooding the world are not recognized. Adrian Gilbert quotes Philo of Alexandria as speculating that the light of the Messiah—the light that the gospels associate with Jesus, "in him was life, and the life was the light of men" (John 1:1–5)—was the spiritual Sun that shines behind the physical sun lighting our planet.

> [This Light] is the [One] star, beyond all heavens, the Source of the Stars that are visible to the senses, which it would not be beside the mark to call All-brilliancy, and from which the sun and moon and the rest of the stars, both errant and fixed, draw their light, each according to its power.[31]

This is an extraordinary statement of Philo's on two counts. It is first a revelation of the extent of astronomical knowledge circulating in privileged circles at that time, predating by twenty centuries the discovery of the center of our galaxy in 1927 by astrophysicists. There is, of course, no evidence that for Philo this Sun, this "star of stars," or master star blazing in the center of the universe, was specifically associated with our galaxy, or that he knew of such a celestial phenomenon, but his work does open up a huge train of speculation as to how much, and for how long, astronomical knowledge of an advanced kind had been available to the initiates of antiquity. John Major Jenkins believes there is clear evidence in the ancient Mithraic tauroctony of a knowledge of the Hypercosmic Sun at the center of our galaxy,[32] and it is at least certain that Philo was well aware of the ordered motion of the solar system—as Pythagoras had been five hundred years before—as traveling within a greater starry cosmos toward some unimaginably huge and incandescent center.

Second, it is even more astounding that Philo, while remaining within the mythological thought world of his time, equated the "star of stars" at the end of the world with a personified archetype that he called the Heavenly Man, the God or Primary Logos from whence came all of earth's transcendental blessings. Within this Philonic metaphysic can be found the idea entertained by all Gnostics that Yahweh was not more than a creative demiurge whose fashioning of the material world was subject to the Will of a far mightier God. To identify the Divine with a great hypercosmic center of creative energy lying behind or above the physical universe was a remarkably modern conceptualization; to apply it to the Messiah argues a metaphysical sophistication that we rarely attribute to the Hebrew thought world that Jesus inhabited.

Philo was in fact but the vanguard in the Near East of a profound intellectual awakening that covered sciences as remote from each other as astronomy and kundalini yoga, genetics and religion. But unfortunately it was a false dawn, followed in Christendom by twenty centuries of intellectual hibernation. For a time—perhaps little more than two centuries—the spiritual cosmology of the merkavah tradition, as recapitulated in the Qabalah, was kept alive in the Church by a number of brilliant Gnostic teachers from every quarter of the empire. They were soon to disappear, however, to be replaced by mediocrities.

In his analysis of pedagogic elements in the primitive Church, Morton Smith again quotes Professor Cyril Richardson. Dr. Richardson distinguishes sharply between the socially lower-class literalists and the well-to-do intellectuals with philosophic and gnostic interests who at first dominated the Christian communities.[33] By contrast with the former, these early Gnostic teachers were of the highest intellectual caliber, men and women who had apparently broken with the unspoken taboos of their class and were equipped and prepared to share their knowledge with the lower classes and to lead a new type of democratic world religion. Kurt Rudolph is another scholar who asserts that in the beginning, Gnostic Christianity was an urban religion dominated by the prosperous and well-educated intelligentsia, one that produced some of the most brilliant and original thinkers in the young Church.[34]

Marcion, Basilides, Bardesanes, and Valentinus, all prominent Christian teachers living during the second century CE, were upperclass intellectuals who created worldwide movements that survived for several centuries in the face of fierce opposition from the mainstream Church. Indeed, Rudolph has characterized Valentinus, the great gnostic poet and visionary mystic, as one of the foremost precursors of the

Persian Mani (216–276), the "Apostle of Christ" whose mystical religion of Manichaeism survived Christian and Muslim persecution for more than ten centuries.[35]

Valentinus is believed to have been born in Lower Egypt at the beginning of the second century. Renowned for his artistic genius and great eloquence, he claimed to have received a secret initiation from Theudas, a disciple of Paul. Valentinus established within the church in Rome a network of privately held, advanced metaphysical schools for qualified Christian students, which ultimately spread to every part of the Roman world and beyond. In these advanced enclaves, which were to influence the entire Gnostic genre, the initiate was given the sacrament of the bridechamber. Thereafter he was introduced to the secrets of the Christian cosmology and to appropriate psycho-spiritual meditation techniques for the furthering of his knowledge. Expelled from the orthodox Christian communities by the fourth century, these schools continued to operate as branches in an independent Valentinian Church until the eighth century.

But many of the church fathers had not been initiated into the Gnosis of the heart and were therefore unaware of its hoary age and authority, nor of the presence of its cosmological mysteries at the heart of their Lord's teachings. And so the universal truth of the Ladder of Being, which had been given the highest initiatory warrant for thousands of years, was to be ridiculed out of existence by such Church notables as Bishop Irenaeus and the Latin apologist Tertullian, who was writing his derisory polemics in the third century. As Elaine Pagel comments:

> Tertullian ridiculed the gnostics for creating elaborate cosmologies, with multi-storied heavens like apartment houses, "with room piled on room, and assigned to each god by just as many stairways as there were heresies: The universe has been turned into rooms for rent!"[36]

Such was the language of orthodoxy. Tertullian and his mainstream confreres were evidently unaware that the Gnostics were not *inventing* a multilayered cosmos but shaping their thought within the strict parameters of a cosmology that had served the Mystery religions of antiquity for thousands of years. But mainstream derision did its work; by the third century, the cosmic Ladder of Being common to all other great religious systems was already being abandoned among Christian thinkers in favor of the monoplanar flatland that the West rejoices in today.

In comparison to such distinguished mystics as Valentinus and his many eminent pupils, the heresiologists who hunted them down were in the main of much poorer quality, literalists with little interest in metaphysical thought. Clement of Alexandria and his successor Origen (ca. 185–254) were men of deep learning who stayed within the orthodox fold, but even they were denounced by their contemporaries as too radical, and were marginalized by the new breed of doctrinaire hagiographers and historians of the Church then emerging.[37] These latter arbiters of the faith founded their thought on authoritative dogma rather than the free judgment of which the pagans had been so proud, and adopted a lavish use in their literature of erudite documents, footnotes, appendices, etc., in the pagan style. They seemed to regard metaphysical ideas as deserving only of sarcasm, but were highly vocal and could use the art of ridicule to great effect. They made their literary reputation as heresiologists, vilifying as blasphemers all those more advanced Christians who disagreed with them. As the Theosophist and professor of astronomy William Kingsland says:

> The study of Christian origins is a very large and controversial question . . . but it is quite evident that the literalization of these [biblical] narratives was due to the fact that those who ultimately obtained the ascendancy of the Church Councils, and were the framers of the Creeds which have been current for so many centuries, were *not* those who were instructed in the Gnosis. They were in fact miserably ignorant, not merely of that Gnosis which . . . lies at the heart of all the allegories, myths and fables in the Christian as in other ancient and pre-Christian scriptures, but also of geographical, astronomical, and anthropological facts well known to other peoples for thousands of years.[38]

Eventually many of the so-called Fathers of the Church, those charged with the doctrinal clarification of the new religion were, as Kingsland says, the men least equipped to do so. An intellectual vacuum had been opened up in the fledgling Church, a kind of institutionalized ignorance that supported a growing preoccupation with heresy. As Joseph Pearce insists, the voice of the heart is subtle, and can be all too easily overridden by fears and anxieties triggered by something new, unknown, and possibly threatening. In such a case, there soon awakens the ancient defenses of the lower survival system in the reptilian brain at the base of the head. The higher centers are shut off and fight-or-flight mechanisms are put swiftly in place, bringing with them an entire arsenal of defensive theories and value-laden positions. In this way, reiterates Pearce,

> a sharp curtailment of connection with the higher, transcendental frequencies of heart and mind is brought about in order to shift growth toward the lower, protective survival systems.[39]

It seems incredible that such a rich treasure house of higher knowledge as Gnostic Christianity offered could have been dissipated and lost over such a short time, less than three centuries; but the power of this fear of heresy is greatly underrated. It can create myths that hold entire nations in thrall for thousands of years. Christians were struggling in an entirely new world of splintering ideologies and ambiguous moral issues. As the bridechamber sacrament was abandoned, the teaching of the metaphysics of the heart disappeared too, and the leaders of the Church found themselves wrestling with moral fragmentation and the entanglement of cerebral myths such as "original sin" and "eternal damnation"—ideas entirely without the support of heart knowledge—from which many theologians have not yet managed to extricate themselves. In fact, the cultural transition that Gnostic Christianity proposed proved far too difficult to be achieved all at once, and before long had been abandoned.

THE MESSAGE OF THE THREE MAGI

What was at issue in the new age of Pisces was the image humanity was to have of itself. The Gnostic schools believed that man existed as the image of God before the Creation: he was dual, both eternal Being and a creature bound to the wheel of Becoming. The Qabalah taught that of all beings on earth, only the human at his full potential could span the cosmic spectrum from the highest world to the lowest; he alone was the height and the depth of Creation, for he existed before it, in the Kingdom of the Father. The gnostic Apocalypse of Moses and the Nag Hammadi text the Apocalypse of Adam, both composed probably in the first pre-Christian century, present us with an image of Adam and Eve that is in harmony with the New Genesis. It is of a very different order indeed from the sinful one to which rabbinic Judaism and Judaeo-Christianity have accustomed us. Stephen Hoeller says of these Gnostic texts:

> Adam and Eve appear here as majestic, quasi-divine beings filled with glory and power, whose status is envied by the adversary angels.[40]

In the texts, Adam tells his third son, Seth, that in his and Eve's original estate they resembled the great eternal angels and were higher than the Demiurge who created them: glorious beings "created in the image of a supernal archetype [the Christ] and infused with a spirit superior to this world."[41] Far from being stained by original sin, in this initial state their bodies were no more than pure and unsullied envelopes of light only embryonically sexually differentiated, perfect images of their divine Parents. Gnostic texts present this Hermetic view of an essentially angelic humanity as being Jesus' also.

Jesus did not publicly address the issue of the hells and of the forces of evil in general, but it must certainly have been a part of his metaphysical background, in which the belief was central that all things are holy, all things are ultimately made of divine Light. But according to the Qabalah, the problem of evil is that wherever the light of the spirit shines, it casts a shadow. We call that shadow evil. Evil is a factor of life that cannot be avoided at our present stage of evolution by any means whatever, for it is a by-product of every sephirah on the Tree. Each sephirah, say Qabalists, has its unbalanced or destructive aspect, its shadow (deriving from the reptilian and old mammalian levels). If we are to pursue enlightenment, we must perforce deal with its negative, its phantom opposite, which is ignorance. It was one of the secrets of the Mystery temples that this is the inevitable concomitant of form becoming manifest to the physical senses.

> The entire theological system can be visualized as a flow of creative vitality, emanating outward from the godhead, thinning out as it flows farther from its source. Along its outer periphery this plethora of divine emanation becomes fragmented into what begins to appear as the light and shadow realm of our material world. It becomes visible.[42]

This pathology of transition, of which we are generally unconscious, applies to everything in existence and is the price of physical manifestation. Nothing can grow, change, or undergo evolution without its concomitant shadow, expressing as it does the momentary imbalance of the polarities on which all creation depends.[43] Good and evil are thus relative terms, always modulating into each other and mutually dependent—a subtle insight not lost on the early Christians, as the Gospel of Philip attests:

> Light and darkness, life and death, right and left, are siblings; it is impossible for them to separate. Accordingly, the good is not good, the bad is not bad, life is not life, death is not death. So each will be dispersed to its original source. But things that are superior to the world are indissoluble: they are eternal. (Philip 6)

Thus the Tree of the Sephiroth itself has its own infernal shadow. A phantom glyph, a reflection cast on the dark waters of chaos, this shadow Tree mirrors the sephirothic glyph above, but in all respects in reverse. Its base abutting the lowest of the sephirothic worlds, that of Malkuth, it reaches down into the abyss of *ayin* or nothingness in proportion as the Tree of the Sephiroth reaches upward. This reverse image is called the Tree of the Qliphoth, or Averse Sephiroth, whose ten malign emanations mirror precisely those of the benign sephiroth above and form in combination the foundations of the seven satanic habitations or hells. The latter, says Leo Schaya, are like "so many shadows or dark inversions of the seven earthly Paradises."[44]

The Hebrew word *qliphoth*—singular, *qliphah*—has the connotation of obscenity and refers to all those adverse and demonic forces that obstruct the work of Creation. Certain protean brute elements fundamental to the cosmos are said to have been left over from an earlier world than ours. Natural elements in process of formation, corporeal matter not yet fully crystallized, they represent a state in which the Shekinhah is not yet present. This saurian state is the foundation of Hell, and Satan, the Angel of Darkness who rules it, utilizes in his activities all its semi-formed, cruel, and unconstructive elements.[45] But Christian Gnostics believed we shall be increasingly free of their infernal influence as the frequencies of heart intelligence more strongly dominate our consciousness.

Consequently, the fundamentalist obsession with evil is mistaken; it gives evil far too much power. In the time of universal redemption, so it is said by Qabalists, God will cause the Qliphothic Tree to disappear forever like the mirage it is. The Palestinian sectaries were well aware of this truth. The biblical scholar and author Jonathan Campbell points out that according to the Dead Sea Scrolls, the sectarian Gnostic belief system, far from being dualistic, was characterized by a faith in divine unity that transcended the conflict between good and evil and found a use for both. He writes,

> Even Satan, who sometimes tricks the sectarians into sin, is mysteriously under God's control as part of the divine plan, according to the *Community Rule* 3:21–24. "The Angel of Darkness leads all the children of righteousness astray, and until his end, all their sin, iniquities,

wickedness, and all their unlawful deeds are caused by his domination *in accordance with the mysteries of God*." [46] (author's italics)

The infernal worlds are states or degrees, says Leo Schaya, citing the Zohar, that are like the links of a chain the beginning of which is joined to the end. They mirror in their circular arrangement those of the sephirothic hierarchy above, which, as we have seen, is like a serpent biting its tail. Just as Malkuth, the last sephirah, is eternally united with the first as its image, so the hells form a circle such that a soul descending through them from the upper infernal boundary will, as his cycle of purgation proceeds, eventually reascend to the point at which he began, "at the windows opening on to the Empire of holy Light." [47] He can then rejoin the main evolutionary body of his species.

Jesus understood very well this manifestation of the cyclic principle that governs all of life. When the disciples asked him, "Tell us how our end will be," he reminded them that existence is in effect a closed evolutionary circuit:

> Jesus said, "Have you discovered, then, the beginning, that you look for the end? For where the beginning is, there will the end be. Blessed is he who will take his place in the beginning; he will know the end and will not experience death." (Thomas 18)

What was of critical importance to first-century philosophers was the knowledge that an occult play of light and shadow, of good and evil, undergirds society as well as our personal lives and defines the ethical structures we have to work with. Consequently, societal evil, such as the present terrorist plague spreading across Western nations, cannot be suppressed, ignored, or extirpated by force; it can only be harmonized with its opposite principle by compensating the unbalanced force involved. In the case of terrorism, this would entail pacifying measures that address the underlying injustices or social imbalances involved, and giving full honor to the religious and societal values of others. But if these necessary adjustments are not made as the need arises—and they rarely are—a new and more dangerous situation arises. Evil becomes entrenched as a phenomenon of real power. It proliferates, condenses, and takes on the positive metaphysical aspect we associate with satanic evil, which consciously and with deliberate intent moves against the current of evolution.

> It will follow, then, that what was at first a mere overplus of force, both pure and good in its intrinsic nature, may, if not compensated, become in the course of ages a highly organized and developed center of positive and dynamic evil.[48]

Such a buildup of evil, unattended to over hundreds or perhaps even thousands of years, necessitates in the end a major social purge—such as Western civilization is now rushing toward. From all this it follows that the toxic effects on society of demonic activity are never so deadly and never so much in need of purging as in transitional periods between one form of civilization and the next, when imbalances are at their height. This happens more frequently when the world is in zodiacal transit from one age to the next, generating great social changes, as happened during the period of Jesus' ministry.

At that time, as the Arian age was passing with great turmoil into the Piscean, Satan took on a more negative and malign aspect. "No longer God's servant," says Pagels, "he begins to become what he is . . . for later Christianity, God's antagonist, his enemy, even his rival."[49] And so in first-century Israel, Satan was to become the personalized apotheosis of evil, acquiring pejorative names such as Beelzebub, Semihazah, Azazel, Belial, and Prince of Darkness, and his changed status reflected the darkening mood of the heavens.

The science of esoteric astrology was then at its height, and across the Mediterranean world astrologers were studying the stars with mounting foreboding as the age of the Ram gave way to the age of the Fish and the birth of new evolutionary energies aroused their infernal reaction. The growing spiritual turbulence created by the interference of the qliphoth was bringing great suffering to society, increasing tenfold the state of unconsciousness and ignorance among the people. Gnostic speculation was to assert that it was this blind ignorance that brought about the anguish and terror, the violence and confusion of the times, confirming the immanence of the End time. "And the anguish grew solid like a fog, so that no one was able to see," reports the apocryphal Gospel of Truth (17: 10–16). It was in such a context that Jesus grieved:

> I took my position in the midst of the cosmos and in the flesh I did appear to them. I found them all drunk; I found none of them thirsty. And my soul became afflicted for the sons of men, because they are blind in their hearts and do not perceive that empty they have come into the world and that empty they seek to exit from the world again. But for the moment they are drunk. (Thomas 28: 23–29)

In the same period, the astrological computations of Jews abroad were seeking information about the coming Initiator. Among their deliberations was a factor of a more specialist nature that added urgency to the sense of crisis, for warnings were rife not only of a period of transit between the two zodiacal ages of Aries and Pisces, bringing increased qliphothic activity, but also of the onset of an even more ominous astrological age. This was known in India as the Kali Yuga, the last of the four great world ages, or yugas, that quartered the precessional cycle or Cosmic Year of 26,000 years. Esoteric astrologers noted the Kali Yuga as a major period of transition that took place at the turning point of the Great Year, when cosmic energy was at its nadir and qliphothic mischief at its greatest.

The precessional cycle had been known and studied for many thousands of years in all the great ancient civilizations—those of the Maya, the Greeks, the Egyptian, and the Vedic peoples—in conjunction with some knowledge of the Milky Way.[50] But the heavens were not studied in the abstract fashion in which we explore them today. Integral to the stellar mythology of all these ancient cultures was the concept of two galactic gateways through which souls ascended or descended between heaven and earth, some travel stained and weary from their sojourn in purgatorial midregions, others descending bright and clean from heavenly homelands.[51] Such celestial knowledge of the soul worlds had always been held secretly within the temple orders, but was now deployed in much wider and more open circles.

The precessional cycle of 26,000 years is, as is now widely known, the period in which our planet's celestial pole traces in the heavens the great zodiacal circle.[52] The final world age of the four that make up the whole cycle, the Kali Yuga is one of abnormally unstable conditions lasting one tenth of the whole cycle and takes place when the cosmic energies are at their lowest point of entropy in the Great Year. The cycle begins with a Krita Yuga, a long golden age of high creative energies that gradually decline, followed by two more world ages of ever diminishing energies until the final yuga, the Kali or Dark age (in our Western culture called the Iron Age), brings a brief time of profoundly reduced intelligence to human society, one that is much dreaded in all civilized cultures.

Lasting about three thousand years, this age of desuetude represents a cultural midnight, a purgatorial interregnum when all deeds must receive their retribution or reward, when all debts must be paid off, when world purification is at its most intense[53] and coincides with highly catastrophic crises in world affairs and in nature. The trauma of the period concludes with an evolutionary transformation and regeneration of society, after which the cycle once again begins its ascent to the next Golden age. The Kali Yuga is therefore very much a transitional phase and the point of maximum qliphothic activity, bringing great human suffering to the earth, but at the same time providing a rare opportunity for the purification and redemption of individuals. In the first century of the Common Era, astrologers across the world were noting that such a transitional period was already upon them and would remain throughout the Piscean age.

Most of the secrets of esoteric astrology have long been lost to us, and as a consequence there are today numerous competing dates given for the beginning and end of the current Kali Yuga. The majority of astrologers believe it is either ending in our own time or has recently ended; Rudolf Steiner suggests the end of the nineteenth century, a very plausible date; Mircea Eliade, the end of the twentieth century. There are, however, those who assert that it ended nine hundred years ago, at the time of the Crusades.[54] René Guénon was noncommittal but believed it would be over in the near future. The Vedic doctrine based on astronomy underlies his acerbic belief that because of the Kali Yuga, "modern people are unconscious degenerates with little resemblance to the full human potential that our ancient ancestors manifested."[55]

John Major Jenkins, on the contrary, has adjusted the scheme proposed by Sri Yukteswar Giri, the great Indian sage of the nineteenth century, to propose that we are now only halfway through the ordeal of Kali Yuga, the end of the descending stage behind us but with another fifteen hundred years of the ascending stage still to come.[56]

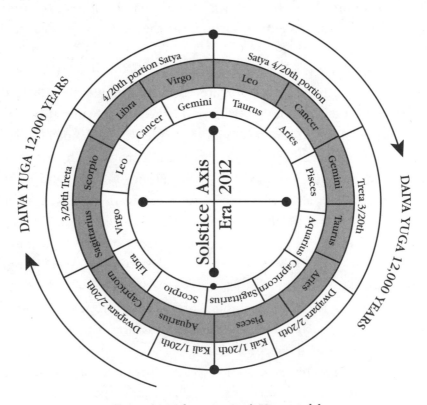

Fig. 7. Sri Yukteswar Giri's Yuga model
(adjusted to show the Kali Yuga halfway through its course)

Sri Yukteswar himself computed the end of the ascending phase to be now, at the beginning of the third millennium, and this may well be the most probable date. Whatever the truth of it, it would seem that all three religions of Semitic origin have been closely implicated in the "dark age" of Kali, goddess of death, the most evil world age in 26,000 years.[57] Therefore, for all three religions the overcoming of qliphothic evil has been their central task.

From the gospel story of the three Magi from the East who were searching for signs of the new Savior, it is clear that in the first century communications were passing among astrologers everywhere as the stars were anxiously studied. Where in Palestine would the birthplace be of the one whose divine powers would sow the seeds of the new age, its energies, its special task, its hidden destiny—the one who would successfully neutralize the qliphothic "static" already overpowering society? Like so much else in the New Testament gospels, the beautiful nativity scene in Bethlehem may well be allegorical, but there is no doubting that the three Magi arriving on their camels from Persia to greet the divine child were a coded reality, representing the gift to the new Revelator, the new Messiah, of all the wisdom and power and good wishes of antiquity.

These gifts of the Old World to the New, the Old Mysteries to the New, were talismans Jesus bore with him when he entered Jerusalem on an ass, on his way to his royal coronation with a crown of thorns. An old culture was passing away, bequeathing its many riches, its wealth of knowledge, and its spiritual powers to the new. It was a pivotal moment in history, the point at which the spiritual fission in Judaism reached completion and the new Jesus movement, propelled by its messianic destiny and bearing the solution to evil, separated out from the mother religion and took on a unique life of its own.

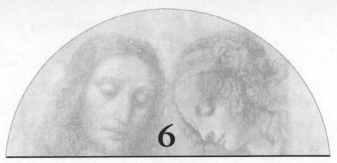

6

ENVOYS FROM THE KING OF LIGHT

*Of the universal Aeons there are two shoots . . . one is
manifested from above, which is the Great Power, the
Universal Mind ordering all things, male, and the other from
below, the Great Thought, female, producing all things. Hence
pairing with each other, they unite and manifest the Middle
Distance . . . in this is the Father . . . a male-female power . . .*

SIMON MAGUS

*The earth is like a woman and the sky like a man, for it makes
the earth fecund.*

A MANDAEAN SAYING

Except for the nativity scene in Bethlehem and the presence in it
of the three Zoroastrian astrologer-priests, there is little in the
Christian scriptures to apprise us of the great international sweep of
events that lay behind the birth of the Christian story. Were it not for
the twentieth-century discovery of the last surviving Gnostics, the baptismal Mandaean sect, and the translation of certain of their scriptures,
we would have little perspective on that critical moment in history two
thousand years ago. As descendants of the first-century Nazareans and
the only living link to Jesus' life story, the Mandaeans are therefore a
uniquely illuminating window on the past.

The parallels between Essene and Christian practices have long been noted, but those between Mandaean and early Christian practices are even more outstanding. This is especially true of their bridechamber and baptismal practices, which once included a common stress on "living" or flowing water rather than the still water of the Judaic *mikva'ot*. It is noteworthy that John the Baptist was not the only prophet to baptize in flowing water; so also did Jesus, performing his nocturnal baptisms in the stream that ran through the Garden of Gethsemene rather than in the still-water baths in Jerusalem. Kurt Rudolph gives us a vivid picture of many more of the liturgical and sacramental parallels that once existed between the Mandaean and Christian sects in the first two Christian centuries, and which are still preserved in Mandaean communities.

In 1905 and 1915, M. Lidzbarski was the first scholar to make a German translation in two volumes of the Mandaean *Book of John* or *Book of the Angels,*[1] supposedly containing John the Baptist's discourses; and in the same time frame the British scholar Lady E. S. Drower, who visited the Mandaeans in the years before the Second World War and was initiated into their mysteries, translated and studied their hitherto unknown scripture, the *Haran Gawaita,* or the *Diwan of the Great Revelation,*[2] which details their checkered history. Inevitably, it is enforcing a radical readjustment of some of our most entrenched views about Jesus and his teachings, and about his relationship to the Baptist.

Although of Judaeo-Samaritan extraction and once active in Judaea, Samaria, and Galilee, this pre-Christian sect claims that long ago its ancestors came from Egypt and that "the people of Egypt were of our religion."[3] However, J. J. Buckley, a recent American researcher, suggests it was originally a Sumerian religion carried westward to Egypt, possibly from Mesopotamia in the third century BCE,[4] which would explain its many similarities to Mithraism. We learn that because of persecution by the Jewish authorities, both the Judaeo-Christian and Mandaean sectaries fled in thousands from Judaea around 37 CE. Both parties fled to the selfsame homeland in the Hauran, but thereafter it would seem that a great ideological gulf came to divide the two sects.

Later, the Mandaeans were able to consolidate new religious bases in Parthia (now Iraq) and Upper Mesopotamia, and in the Tura d'Madai, the mountains of Media in southeastern Turkey, where they achieved their maximum prosperity and influence.[5] Coming as they did from a mixed Jewish population before gathering converts abroad, the Mandaeans included a large component of non-Jews, which has now become the dominant membership and which repudiates any Judaic associations. Yet these do exist in plenty, despite the fact that circumcision is not practiced and certain Jewish customs are unknown to the brotherhood or have been forgotten.[6] Driven by ongoing persecution at the hands of the Christians, the invading Persians, and later the Arabs, the Mandaeans were forced into continual migrations and increasing poverty. Throughout these peregrinations they took with them their precious Book of John, which they study to the present day. One of the most important sacraments of their religion remained baptism, which featured—as it still does today—a baptismal pool whose flowing water is always called Jordan. It is a testimony to the sect's ancient past in Palestine, when their members, they say, were baptized by John in the river Jordan outside Jerusalem.[7]

For hundreds of years the Mandaeans have lived in poverty and obscurity in the marshlands of southern Iraq, with somewhat more-prosperous centers in the Iraqi cities of Basra and Mosul, as well as some small communities in Iran. But over time their numbers greatly diminished; and it was feared for a while that Saddam Hussein's military assaults on the region might have decimated the sect to the point of extinction. However, J. J. Buckley reports that Mandaean communities are now living in a number of Western cities and that their number has swelled to about 100,000. A big revival is under way, in both their religious education and their cultural traditions, with an increase in initiated priests.[8] Once almost moribund, the Mandaean/Nazarean fraternity is being brought to life again, and in the process is revealing more clearly than ever its vital relationship to the great Christ-centered movement that midwifed Christianity.

Most importantly, the ethnicity so prominently displayed in the racial purity laws of orthodox second-temple Judaism is absent in the

Mandaean sect, as it is in Christianity. This striking omission has led some writers to infer that the Mandaean leadership was not Jewish at all, or at least not of the Judaic religion.[9] But this is to overlook the universal character and lack of ethnic prohibitions in the Mysteries of the early Hebrews and in esoteric Judaism generally, especially in the northern areas of Palestine where the Nazarean fraternity mainly held sway. Indeed, so alike were the two sects, the Mandaean and the Christian, that many centuries later, missionaries coming across the Mandaeans in the Middle East called them:

> "Christians of St. John," mistakenly taking them to be a strange Christian sect dedicated to St. John the Evangelist, Jesus' Beloved Disciple.[10]

The opening up of the sect's scriptures has been a great surprise to biblical scholars, who are discovering that the Mandaeans must have once commanded an influential place in the Jewish religious world. Evidently they were associated with a number of the epoch's most important spiritual movements. Mani, for example, the great Persian mystic and reformer (b. 216), who founded the Manichaean religion, drew from the Mandaean faith much of the inspiration for his new belief system. As a sage, prophet, and miracle worker in something of the mold of Jesus, Mani was a Redeemer figure proficient in all the esoteric sciences and in astrology (which in those days included astronomy), and a master of magical practices. He is reliably chronicled as having been reared until adulthood in the Mandaean/Nazarean religion followed by his princely father, and as being indebted to its cosmogonic principles as the foundation of his own messianic teachings.[11] Consequently, Manichaeism is redolent of Mandaean doctrines and terminology as well as being doctrinally close to Christianity, for Mani himself professed to be the last apostle of Jesus and a messenger of the Christ.[12]

For a time, the idea that John the Baptist and Jesus were associated with the Mandaeans was branded a blatant fabrication. It had been included in Mandaean scriptures written after the seventh century, so scholars opined, in response to Islam's conquest of the Mesopotamian region and its demand for proof that the Mandaeans were a "people of the Book."

The sect had simply purloined the figure of the Baptist from Christianity in order to give credence to a faith that had no scriptures of its own, and its suggestion that John had his own followers or church and had never belonged to the Christian tradition was therefore without the slightest foundation. However, this line of thought is strongly refuted by the Swedish scholar Geo Widengren in his history of Manichaeism,[13] in which he shows that the Mandaean scriptures were written around the second century CE and are therefore reliable indexes of the past.

And more recently, J. J. Buckley offers an even stronger refutation of the official view. She offers solid evidence that the Mandaean literature was being written down by the early part of the first century CE, contemporaneously with both John's and Jesus' missions, and may therefore be considered a reliable testimony to the events of the period.[14]

Hathem Saed, a modern, Western-educated Nasoraia or Mandaean prophet, has written comprehensively of the Mandaean belief system, which bears the imprint of considerable antiquity.[15] It seems to hark back to a time when our understanding of the laws governing the divine foundation of life and cosmos was much purer. Kurt Rudolph, in his further explorations of Mandaean knowledge, has received something of the same impression. He has said of it that it is

> a completely independant gnostic tradition . . . a revealed religion and a divinely inspired code of laws and traditions . . . [a] definitive body of knowledge and . . . theories to explain nature and the universe.[16]

The Theosophical scholar G. R. S. Mead has pointed out the striking parallels between Christian Gnostic texts and those of the Mandaeans, particularly their Book of John:[17] indeed some Gnostic sayings have actually been lifted verbatim from a Mandaean "secret scroll."[18] Andrew Welburn, who seems not to be aware that Jesus and the original Mandaeans were both Nazareans and therefore members of the same general brotherhood, nevertheless agrees with Mead. He points to the convincing evidence that Jesus

> drew on a background similar to their [Mandaeans'] Gnostic vision, as well as on Essene types of ritual practice.[19]

These findings reinforce the impression that Jesus must have been reared in a Gnostic milieu far removed from the reactionary Jerusalem school and at the very cutting edge of the new theosophies evolving in the diaspora.

As we have seen, around the turn of the Common Era a state of extreme religious anxiety gripped the nations, resulting in a marked alienation from the natural world. The theme of *salvation* or *redemption* became endemic and left an ineradicable mood of pessimism on the Mandaean worldview. Under the influence of the extreme social turbulence, the lowest in the quaternity of worlds came to be seen as hostile, as having its origin in the "chaos of the dark waters" peopled by demons and dragons of every kind and as the source of all evil and suffering.[20]

The Mandaeans said that the material world is ruled by Ptahil, the King of Darkness, a God who corresponds to the inferior God Ialdobaoth in the Christian Gnostic scheme, and who is believed to govern the entirety of this polluted physical universe. The figure of Ptahil, we may note, had been drawn from the ancient Egyptian Mystery center at Memphis, where the human-headed god Ptah, the fourth in a quaternary of deities, was the god of darkness, of shadows, the god of the dead, and also the creator of the natural world.[21]

According to the Mandaeans, this same inferior God creates the physical bodies of human beings and of all other things in the physical realm, whereas man's soul or animating substance, the "inner hidden Adam," or Light Adam, comes from and belongs to the Kingdom of Light.[22] Ptahil is therefore not represented as a Creator god, as frequently assumed, nor is Ialdobaoth in the corresponding Gnostic scheme, but in both cases Ptahil is seen as a kind of demiurge or nature deity, a creative agent of the Supreme Life.[23] He should perhaps be thought of in the Eastern sense as a great deva who assists God in the organizing and governance of his Creation. However, the Mandaeans abhor Ptahil to this day as a tyrant who forgot he was but the servant of a higher Power and became the victim of divine hubris. So too the Christian Gnostics said that

> the rulers thought it was by their own power and will that they did what they did: but the holy spirit was secretly activating the entirety through them, as it willed. (Philip 12)

The basic gnostic principle in Mandaeism is the teaching of knowledge, Manda, or Gnosis, a supernatural and direct revelation not gained through the intellect or the senses. Humanity comes from a divine Light world, a preexistent world of eternal day, before the separation of light and dark out of an original unity; and its sacred saviors, mentors, and redeemers are not historical human beings, as in other religions, but great Light-world beings in whose supernatural radiance humanity perpetually lives. It is they, not a human savior, who founded the Mandaean religion long ago and nurtures and instructs it still.

The Mandaean sect's close kinship to Mithraism and its sacraments, as well as to early Christianity, is most evident in its Solar Mystery rituals. These include baptism (masbuta) in flowing water and anointing with oil, a ritual meal, a redemptive initiation for the dying, and at its very heart the holiest and most secret rite of all, that of the bridal chamber. The spiritual marriage, culminating as it does in a profound regeneration of the whole being and an initiation into the prophetic vocation, does away with the necessity of ascetic practices (Thomas 104). Lady Drower reports that for Mandaeans this bridechamber rite is so holy that it must be performed in deepest secret so that profane eyes may not witness it, and is so potent that "the least slip, the least omission, must be expiated by baptism and may disqualify a priest for life."[24]

Evidently the ritual is powerful not only for the initiate but also for the celebrant, who must be highly qualified as a son of the bridechamber, for he too is taken up with the initiate into higher realms and imbued with the light of transformative cosmic energies. Of the similar Christian rite, the Gospel of Philip says:

> Every person who [enters] the bedroom will kindle the light . . . and it is manifest to him or her alone—hidden not in darkness and night, but hidden in a perfect day and holy light. (Philip 107)

Lady Drower's work confirms that, as Nazareans, John and Jesus must have been initiates of the bridechamber and, as such, prophets authorized to initiate others in their turn into the same high grade. It is now beyond doubt that later Gnostics were not responsible for the introduction of this potent rite into the Christian liturgy; Jesus himself must have introduced it. He himself gave his disciples the central principle whereby duality was transcended, thus laying the foundation of his new sect. Mani, too, as another Mandaean initiate, no doubt offered the same sacrament to his disciples.

The Light principle that is so dominant in Gnostic thought has a feminine connotation in Mandaeism. Symbolized by water, it relates to the creative principle of Life, which in turn is said to unite with the masculine principle of Mind to create the universe. Thus the Mandaeans speak of themselves as of "the race of Life" born of the Father-Mother. They are earthly counterparts of the archetypal Great Adam and the issue of his marriage with the Great Eve, who is described as a heavenly "Cloud of Light."

This marriage is a cosmic event as well as a human one, since all creation depends on the union of the polarities—that is, on the transcendence of all the dualities of which the material cosmos consists, whether these be the syzygies of man/woman, good/evil, dark/light, or nature/spirit.

For Mandaeans, the Supreme Being is the Great Life, and from within this primal Spirit of Life there issues a secondary creative Light principle that in turn unites with Mind to give birth to the four descending worlds of the universe and all that is in them—light and dark, good and evil, demiurgic deities both male and female, stars, demons, human beings, animals, plants, and minerals. All are contained in the limitless plenum of the Great Life.[25] The knowledge of this mystery of divine generation, which is almost a facsimile of the Qabalistic cosmological formula, the Mandaeans call the Gnosis of Life, and it is this Gnosis that saves.

Thus for the Mandaeans as for Christian Gnostics, the Great Life, the all-encompassing Godhead, is not itself the Creator; rather it is the fecund womb of those dyadic forces that, coming forth together as Cosmic Mother and Cosmic Father, create and maintain the universe. The souls of the elect therefore belong to the Kingdom of Life and Light, and Envoys, they say, are sent to earth again and again from the King of Light in order to remind souls of this redeeming knowledge and to guide them on the Path of Return back to the paradisiacal source of Life.[26]

But the Mandaean story of Creation explains much more than the birth of a religion or of personal enlightenment. It is also an attempt to describe the birth of the Cosmos outside us and its reflection within the Cosmos arrived at by introspection, both of which hold all the dualistic elements of life and death, good and evil, angels and demons, and so on. "All are connected to the essence of the Heart and Mind, and spread to the physical and spiritual actions of humans," says Hathem Saed. These Cosmoses without and within are, then, the dual source of great mysteries and powers from which, in union, springs all knowledge of Truth. However, Saed has hidden the bridechamber principle deeply under all this theology, thus succeeding in maintaining the feminine principle in her traditional state of purdah. Archetypal Eve is of the Heart, Archetypal Adam of the Mind, and Truth or Gnosis is the fruit of their marriage—but in Mandaism this mystery of the bridechamber, which is also the mystery of our human biology, is not to be spoken, not to be exposed to the light of day.

It was quite otherwise within the several movements spawned by the Mandaean/Nazareans of Jesus' day, when an unstoppable religious revolution was in the air. Their goal was to overturn the taboos of millennia and expose the truth wherever possible to the light of day.

Although everything pertaining to the religious currents in the first-century world of the Near East is shrouded today in scholarly uncertainty and controversy, it seems indisputable that John the Baptist was the first to break the seal on the secret marriage-chamber rite. Roman women were already gaining a significant place in civic affairs, but it was the Baptist and his three closest disciples who opened up to the greater *empirium* the need for the feminine principle to be liberated and brought into public view in a meaningful spiritual context. John's was probably the first major countermove in a gender war that still has no certain resolution, even in the Western world today.

THE CHURCH OF JOHN

As already noted, the Apocalypse of Adam predicted that in the End Time the Iranian Magi astrologers would see a star fall to earth, and following it would find the divine child Mithra, the Great Savior, in a cave in the Palestinian town of Bethlehem, once the site of a shrine sacred to Tammuz.[27] For the early Church this prophecy was fulfilled in Messiah Jesus. But for the Mandaeans it was fulfilled in their great mentor John the Baptist. Their teachings offer the first definitive evidence that John and Jesus must have both preached a religion of Light deriving from Zervanism, the esoteric branch of Zoroastrianism. The Fourth Gospel, redolent of Mandaean as well as Zervanite images of light and of life, conveys the truest picture of Jesus' ideological background of any of the four canonical gospels.

> And Jesus spoke to them, saying, "I am the light of the world, he who follows me will not walk in darkness, but will have the light of life." (John 8:12) . . . "While you have the light, believe in the light, that you may become sons of light." (John 12:35–36)

Taking all the parallels with the Mandaean faith into consideration, and combining them with the other factors that have come to light, it is difficult not to conclude that the organization Jesus founded simply continued Nazarean sacramental and ceremonial practices with little change, while many Nazarean doctrines that were later to become known as Mandaean were likewise carried over into Christianity.

True, dissenting voices have pointed out that there were numerous baptismal sects in the first century whose adepts went under the name of *nasaraios,* and Jesus was not necessarily associated with any of them, or with their teachings. But the baptismal ceremony of the Mandaeans is one that may be repeated numerous times in a lifetime as a greatly prized means of spiritual attainment. Thus, when we learn from the Gospel of the Hebrews as quoted by Jerome that Jesus' entire family journeyed south to the Jordan by the Dead Sea in order to be baptized by John, saying, "John the Baptist is baptizing for the remission of sins, let us go and be baptized by him,"[28] we may rest assured that it was the Baptist's Mandaean/Nazarean brotherhood and no other to which Jesus and his family had evidently belonged; and it was John's teachings and messianic aspirations they had shared, quite possibly all their lives. Hugh Schonfield too has stressed the dynastic nature of Jesus' family, suggesting its leadership of a community dedicated to John's ideal of a coming Hebrew Savior.

Could the early Church really have been ignorant of Jesus' and the Baptist's connection to the Mandaean sect? According to Lady Drower's research, that is not possible. Yet it is only now that we learn in the *Haran Gawaita* about the extraordinary importance the Mandaeans give to John as the redeeming Messiah, painting a picture of the prophet that is very different from the one detailed in the gospels. Significantly, the Mandaean portrait of John is supported by the *Clementine Recognitions,* a pseudepigraphic Christian work written in Rome in the late second century and for long dismissed by most biblical scholars as a romance of doubtful historical value.[29] However, by others, such as Hugh Schonfield, it is a reliable source that has been drawn on extensively by reputable scholars. Worthwhile bearing in mind is the fact that around 200 CE, a wealthy and well-educated class of Alexandrian Christians read as *canonical scripture* not only the Hebrew Bible and most of today's Christian scriptures but also the *Clementine Recogni-*

tions, along with other authoritative works that would before long be banned as heretical and disappear altogether.[30] In Alexandria, then, the historical veracity of the *Recognitions* must have been unquestioned, as also the "heretical" picture of John and Jesus contained in it.

The canonical gospels represent the Baptist as a hermit of the Nabataean desert. He is described as Jesus' kinsman and as a reincarnation of Elijah, and, to illustrate the point, as having come like Elijah from the wilderness dressed in rough garments of haircloth and a leather girdle (Matthew 3:4, Mark 1:6). John is depicted as a pious but uncouth "primitive" reared from birth in the desert and unacquainted with civilization, and Church tradition has upheld this depiction throughout the Christian centuries. But in startling opposition to Christian tradition, the *Recognitions* claims that John, though he may well have been reared in Nabataea and have spent some time as a hermit of the desert, was neither permanently so, nor a Christian saint. He was a man of urban erudition and international acclaim who had a number of arcane schools of his own established in Alexandria, Asia Minor, and Palestine. The headquarters of this network appears to have been based in Alexandria, with another of his schools or churches in Ephesus in Asia Minor and others along the river Jordan.[31]

John evidently grew up in the same Nazarean milieu as Jesus and was therefore of the gnostic Hasid school like Jesus. In the first century BCE, when astrological computations made it clear that the end of Aries and the beginning of the Piscean age were imminent, there emerged from northern Palestine a series of militant reformers and fiery messianists who with their followers regularly descended on Judaea to create ferment and rebellion among the people. These reformers called them to arms against the Romans or agitated against the upstart temple clergy, preaching a return to the true Way that the prophets had called for since the days of Second Isaiah. The Baptist, who had many Galilean adherents, would have been prominent among such radical figures.

In the Christian scriptures, he is said to have grown up from childhood in the wilderness, protected by the angel Uriel "until the day he appeared publicly to Israel" (Luke 1:80). From infancy to adulthood, so

Luke insists, John was miraculously sustained in the desert on his own, subsisting on locusts and wild honey. But more realistically, we may surmise he was reared by parents living in a well-populated wilderness such as the Hauran, where fertile areas, especially along the river Dan, were able to support thriving little agricultural communities. This region east of the Jordan, the heartland of the Nazarean sect, may well have been John's native habitat, as it was of the later Jewish rebel leader Bar Cosiba, for it was from here that Luke's Gospel describes John's dramatic emergence from out of the desert, a wild and commanding figure appearing in the role of the ancient prophet Elijah. Thus he takes on the semblance of a simple God-inspired hermit, but it would seem that the reality was otherwise.

The Acts of the Apostles (19:24–25) recounts that it was one of John's most learned disciples, Apollos of Alexandria, who established John's baptismal initiation and teachings in Ephesus, although later receiving the Christian baptism from Philip. If this is true, if John was indeed a spiritual leader acclaimed in Egypt and Asia Minor as well as Palestine, as the *Recognitions* also states, we can assume he was no semi-naked and wild-haired hermit but a man of intellectual and social stature whose teachings were sufficiently sophisticated to make an appeal in cities where the inhabitants were famous for being critical audiences, highly trained in pagan philosophies. Although he may have spent time "on retreat" in the desert, John, as a Nazarean initiate, a Gnostic, and an occultist schooled in the arcane tradition of the Hasidim, could not possibly have been the stern lifelong ascetic of the desert the gospels have claimed.

The *Recognitions* goes on to say that in Alexandria, John was acknowledged as a Hemerobaptist, or Day Baptist. This apocalyptic term has reference to one who proclaims the Kingdom of Light—that is, the Kingdom of Eternal Day before the great separation into the earth's polarities of light and dark. In the *Antiquities of the Jews,* Josephus speaks highly of John as a great prophet with an independent following of his own. He presents the Baptist as a revered icon surrounded by legends of divine birth and immortality, and implies that although the prophet exhorted the Jews to a life of virtue, he also taught Gentiles, as Josephus says that besides Jews, "others gathered together [around him], for they also were excited to the utmost by listening to his teachings."[32]

The Mandaeans also cherished a view of the Baptist that parted decisively from that of the Christians. In their Book of John, John the Baptist, not Jesus, was the thirteenth Illuminator, the great Savior from the King of Light.[33] It was John, not Jesus, who was conceived miraculously by his elderly and barren mother, Elizabeth; the infant John whom Herod sought to kill; John who was paid homage in Bethlehem by the three Magi. And it was John whose parents fled to Egypt to escape the murderous intentions of King Herod. For Mandaeans, John is synonymous with the Light Adam, who even now and forever, sitting at the right hand of God, shares in the government of the Creation and from time to time suffers incarnation in one race or another for the continuing welfare of the planet.[34] To this day Mandaeans believe Jerusalem was divinely punished for its persecution of this great Messenger, probably by the city's destruction in 70 CE.

Josephus says John had such a huge following in his own right[35] that his powerful influence over the masses alarmed Herod Antipas, the ruler of the Galilean and Peraean provinces, who had him beheaded "in a pre-emptive strike."[36] There is no mention in the *Recognitions* of the lurid legend put out by the Christian gospels, which tells how Herod's stepdaughter Salome demanded John's head on a platter as a reward for her seductive dancing before the king. Rather, we are presented with the Baptist as a man of eminence in the wider world: a man with friends in high places, for Josephus tells us that the Roman emperor, incensed at John's murder, thereafter banished Herod Antipas and his whole family to the Roman city of Lugdunum Convenarum in Gaul, on the outskirts of the empire.[37] This unfamiliar picture of the Baptist as a distinguished mystic and philosopher of international repute incidentally places the first-century Mandaeans in a new light, as an organization powerful enough to have been a very considerable threat to the growing young Christian movement.

Clearly a great deal of myth making went on in those early heady years of Christianity of which the figure of the Baptist has been a prime victim. Authorities have noted how the Gospel accounts marginalize him, revealing as little as possible of his life and works despite his ostensible importance to the infant Christian movement, and over-stressing his spiritual inferiority to Jesus. None of the above information as presented in the *Recognitions* has been included in Church history; none of it has been disclosed in the Baptist's spurious Christian hagiography, although it must have been familiar to the Gospel writers.

These official narrators, all writing in the late first century, must certainly have known about the greater Nazarean fraternity and of its connection to John and Jesus. We are forced to conclude that the biographical details attaching to the Baptist, a public figure of immense visibility and influence and once included in Alexandria's scriptural canon, could hardly have been simply overlooked, misconstrued, or otherwise mislaid. They could have been obliterated from Christian annals and Christian memory only by patient, thorough, and massive censorship. Not surprisingly, a large corpus of Johannine scriptures written by John's disciples once existed that might have revealed the truth, but these have disappeared entirely, as have all texts seen as inimical to Christian interests.

As has been said, conservative Church authorities have dismissed the *Recognitions* as a spurious document, probably a forgery, but there is now so much indirect evidence to support it that I believe in the matter of John the Baptist and his Egyptian school it may be taken as a true report. Not only does it give him a far more probable role as a spiritual leader and innovator, but a part career in Alexandria also places him at the hub of the Hasidean movement, where first-century Jewish Gnosticism properly belongs; and it reinforces the impression already gained of the Nazareans as an influential prophetic brotherhood of international spread. It is extremely unlikely that an unlettered hermit who had spent all his life in the Nabatean desert could have exerted as much influence over the contemporary Greco-Roman world, as we must now attribute to John. He must be credited with mystico-magical beliefs and practices entirely consonant with what we now know of the

Mandaean/Nazareans, but far removed from the naive puritan image fostered by the Christian tradition.

A number of foremost Christian scripture scholars believe that the writer of the Fourth Gospel, either John the Evangelist himself or more likely a later evangelist in his name, lifted chunks of Mandaean material, including the nativity story, from the texts concerning the Baptist and "demythologized and Christianized" it.[38] As early as 1926 the theologian H. H. Schaeder suggested that the prologue of John's Gospel was a "Mandaic hymn taken over from Baptist circles."[39] The highly esteemed German theologian Rudolf Bultmann, referring to the Fourth Gospel prologue and some of its revelation discourses, writes that these were

> believed to have been originally documents of the followers of John the Baptist who had exalted John and originally given John the role of a Redeemer sent from the world of Light. Therefore a considerable part of the Gospel of John was not originally Christian in origin but resulted from the transformation of a Baptist tradition.[40]

Andrew Welburn, on the other hand, believes the Fourth Gospel, so different from the Synoptics in its powerful mystical language and its meditative and deeply esoteric Life and Light teachings, was originally a secret oral tradition within the Nazarean brotherhood, which became accessible to both Mandaean and Christian initiates, each one applying it to his own leader. Welburn cites a number of scholars who have suggested that the Fourth Gospel was an oral tradition that was opened up and appeared among ordinary Christians as a written document only much later on in its life, at the end of the first century, and that it was accepted only with great difficulty by the mainstream Church.[41] By that time the Mandaeans had become bitter rivals of Christianity and were no doubt presenting many difficulties for the young Christian communities. The Clementine *Recognitions* records that after the deaths of their respective leaders, great ill feeling existed between Christians and Baptists, with much controversy between them over whether John or Jesus was the Messiah.[42]

In the closed world of the occult schools John was seminal, his teachings believed to have lain at the very root of the new first-century zeitgeist. It was he who at that time pioneered the rebirth of the Hebrew Mysteries and he who opened the way to a revival of the sacred merkavah sciences, which had long been forgotten. By the cognoscenti, John is seen as truly the forerunner of Jesus in that he was the one who first provided a pool of esoteric knowledge from the past from which other spiritual teachers, Jesus included, were able to draw as they would, interpreting, refining, and elaborating according to their differing briefs. If this is true, then John was the father of the powerful new movement dedicated to the rescue and elevation of the feminine principle, a movement that his foremost Jewish students initiated in various revolutionary ways.

Although all trace of the Baptist's once copious literature has been lost, and the Mandaean scriptures, immensely valuable in other ways, are too heavily adulterated by later Mesopotamian influences to be a reliable index of his teachings, we can learn something of their nature from two contemporaneous teachers, the works of whom are still extant. These teachers were the Samaritans Simon Magus and Dositheus, whom the *Recognitions* insists were John's disciples alongside Jesus.

> It was at Alexandria that Simon perfected his studies in magic, being an adherent of John, a Hemerobaptist through whom he came to deal with religious doctrines. John was a forerunner of Jesus . . . Of all John's disciples, Simon was the favorite, but on the death of his master, he was absent in Alexandria, and so Dositheus, a co-disciple, was chosen head of the school.[43]

Along with John and Jesus (and Mani), Simon and Dositheus must also have been initiates of the bridechamber, dedicated to exemplifying in their lives and teachings the unitary principle of the ancient rite. Fragments from the gnostic writings of these two spiritual leaders have been preserved by early heresiologists of the Christian Church who, eager to demonstrate the blasphemous nature of the rival literature, included tracts from it in their own works.

A PHILOSOPHY OF FIRE

Simon Magus and Dositheus were contemporaries of Jesus who were preaching in Palestine shortly after the Crucifixion. Their religious philosophy is very different from that of Jesus, yet is clearly a formative stage in the evolution of the Hebrew Old Religion into the new Christ Mystery. The modern scholar Jean Daniélou says that Dositheus (or Dosthai in the Jewish sources) came from Cochaba near Damascus, which we know was the site of Essene, Nazarean, and Ebionite communities, and that he was Simon's teacher.[44] Daniélou also suggests that the Sethians, followers of Dositheus, worshipped John the Baptist as a very great spiritual teacher and as the Righteous Teacher of the Last Days,[45] thus implying that Dositheus himself was a member of the Johannine school.

The allusion to the Righteousness lineage also points to John's Hasidean connections—even that he himself may have been in the direct dynastic line of the Zadokite high priests. However, the *Recognitions* implicitly denies that Simon, the so-called black magician who is so unjustly vilified in the Acts of the Apostles (8:9–24), was a pupil of Dositheus. Rather, it states that the two famous Samaritan adepts trained together as codisciples in John's Hemerobaptist school and succeeded him as its leaders after his death. Both were working publicly only a decade after Jesus' death, in the reign of the Roman emperor Claudius (41–54 CE).

John's Hemerobaptist teachings evidently provided a rich source of mystery material from which a number of revolutionary currents of thought were drawn, as the Hasidean movement comprised a variety of diverse schools and teachings, some more mystical than others, some hewing to an orthodox line, others more militaristic; and so the crisis of the age brought forth from the movement a cluster of Savior figures rather than one alone. Dr. Stephan Hoeller, the director of the Gnostic Society of Los Angeles and an Associate Professor of Comparative Religions at the College of Oriental Studies in that city, says of the two famous magi that after their apprenticeship to John, both Simon and Doshtai declared themselves messianic savior figures and traveled the roads of the Roman world, preaching and conferring mysteries. It is by no means unlikely that these two men, who like Jesus were initiated by John the Baptist, were infused with the power of the messianic archetype and acted as alternative savior figures side-by-side with Jesus.[46]

Simon and Dositheus became outstanding spiritual teachers in Egypt, Asia Minor, Rome, and Samaria, itinerant prophets and sages celebrated for their wisdom and magical powers and for their unprecedented support for the dignity of womanhood. Both called themselves Christs, "Anointed Ones," and preached the Gnosis revealed. The mystico-magical movements centered on them. The Sethian teachings of Dositheus found a particularly prominent place in the religious traditions of Asia Minor and Mesopotamia for about six centuries, whereas the movement founded by Simon the Magician, who was from the Samaritan village of Gitta but Greek educated in Alexandria (as well as being famous in Ephesus and Rome), was not crushed by Christianity until the fourth century. After John's death, according to the *Recognitions,* Simon took over from Dositheus the official leadership of the Johannine sect headquartered in Ephesus.

Today Simon is known mainly for being the original Faust figure, the prototype of the later heroes of Marlowe's and Goethe's plays who sell their souls to the devil in exchange for magical powers: "For devout Christians . . . the powers he [Simon] exercised were seen as emanating, by definition, from the ultimate source of iniquity, the Antichrist or the Devil."[47] Acts reports that he was baptized into the Christian faith by the apostle Philip and subsequently drew away many adherents into his own coterie; and from the beginning slander gathered about him. Thus there ensues Luke's calumny in the Acts of the Apostles, in which he has Simon attempting to buy his way into the secrets of the healing power of the Holy Spirit, so giving birth to the opprobrious term *simony.* It is a theatrical, unlikely tale and fair-minded theologians concede that Simon has probably been the victim of sectarian jealousy.

Possibly a Nazarean like John and Jesus, Simon was highly esteemed throughout the empire as a magician and philosopher of unusual spiritual power, a charismatic mystic especially famed for his magical skills. Not least among the miracle-working and magical deeds that won him such celebrity were his feats of flying, which included (according to accounts) riding in a chariot drawn by four flaming horses. In the arcane language of the time, the flying motif, like that of the chariot, was of course a metaphor for the out-of-the-body shamanic flights by which visionaries ascend to the upper worlds, even to the throne of God. The same motif found an echo in the ecstatic journeyings of the Mandaeans and many other mystics, such as the Essenes. Of the latter sectaries Josephus says that they believed that souls are immortal and incorruptible, being dragged down to the prison of the body by a kind of natural spell, but that "once released . . . as though from long servitude, they rejoice and are borne aloft." Simon's proclivity for ecstatic soul flights has been likened to that of Paul's, and some modern writers have even grouped the two mystics very closely together.[48]

But Simon was even more famous for his mythologized gnostic/ tantric teachings, and it is in these that we see how far Judaic thought, under the influence of Hellenism, had deviated by Jesus' time from the model taught in the Judaean synagogues. In *The Great Annunciation,* Simon gave voice to a metaphysical vision and a conception of God totally at odds with that of Conservative Judaism. According to this Johannine adept, the basic energy substance of the universe is Fire, which exists in two forms, one manifest and the other hidden, or occult. Six further forms of cosmic power, visible and invisible, unfold from the primal Fire, but the Seventh is as yet unknown to our race. It is associated with kundalini, which is the diminutive form of Maha Kundali, the Mother of Space and Time. Andrew Welburn tells us that

the real interest centers on the Seventh Power: for this is not yet unfolded, but lies dormant in unawakened mankind, and it subsumes into itself the working of all the other six powers. Hence the man who knows how to awaken the Seventh Power within himself, knows himself as a microcosm, a "lesser world" in which all the cosmic powers are united. In fact, the Seventh Power restores the original unity . . . of the Godhead, which is lost and divided in its cosmic manifestations, so that in reality according to Simon's system it is the Godhead, the Great Power which awakens to full self-knowledge in man.[49]

For Simon, redemption consisted in the finding and claiming of this primal Power, which he called the "supreme incomprehensible power" without name, form, or gender, the limitless and everlasting One:

> This is the meaning of the saying, "I and thou are one, thou art before me, I am after thee." This is the One Power, divided as being above and below, self-generating, self-increasing, self-seeking, self-finding, its own mother, its own father . . . unity, the root of all.[50]

And in order to vivify the unitary meaning of his ideas, Simon expounded them in a form of theater that his listeners might more readily understand. He acquired a beautiful companion and disciple consort called Helen with whom he traveled the roads of the empire, preaching his gnostic/tantric message of salvation—which was that the One is born in the human soul by transcending the universal polarities—that is, by their union.[51] According to the Christian apologist Justin Martyr (died in 167), Helen was a whore whom Simon bought from a brothel in Tyre. But Rudolph regards the accusation as probably another slanderous misrepresentation by Christians; and Picknett and Prince, who agree with him, point out that the text of the *Recognitions* suggests that Helen, far from being a harlot, seems to have been one of John's initiates before becoming Simon's devoted disciple and spiritual consort.[52]

Stephan Hoeller remarks that almost all the major features of the later Gnostic systems were present in Simon's legacy. He replaced the obsession with purity, especially sexual purity, common to the Jewish religious institutions of his day, with a libertarian philosophy based on the redemptive power of the Gnosis. The Gnosis, he said, frees the soul from the restrictive power of the material forces inherent in creation, and therefore from the law.[53] In the cosmic myth that Simon taught, he represented Helen as the embodiment of the divine feminine principle, the World Soul, even as Simon was that of the divine masculine principle, the World Mind. As the Father's First Thought, Helen longed to acquire his wisdom for herself; but for that presumption she was cast down into the "brothel of the world," where she was forced to prostitute herself, suffering in captivity until rescued by a Redeemer from on high in the form of Simon himself. In other words, for Simon the saving rebirth of the soul was due not to asceticism or to psychosomatic skills or to book learning, but to the grace of God—truly to the redeeming gift of God to all men and women who seek it.[54]

In this Gnostic myth there are many evocative echoes of the modern findings of science. The feminine heart intelligence, in the form of Helen, is placed in juxtaposition to the cerebral functions of the head, showing how the intuitive wisdom of the former can be excluded from consciousness, despised as the prompting of "a still small voice" and cast out from the machinations of the masculine intellect. In that case, as Joseph Chilton Pearce tells us, the heart's higher function is debased and it is reduced to serving the instinctual drives of the body alone, until rescued and elevated to the status of a wisdom organ by a more enlightened mind-set. Hoeller reminds us that the Gnostics were aware of this human frequency pattern two thousand years ago, and that Simon helped to proclaim it:

> The conjunction of World Soul and World Mind, of heart and head, of the relatedness of Eros with the intelligence of Logos, set the pattern that ever after was so crucial to every form of the Gnosis: the pattern of the creative conjunction of the opposites that results in freedom from limitation and the beatitude of a new and higher consciousness.[55]

But Simon has also earned a unique place in Western religious history as an outstanding innovator of his time, for it was he who first publicly elevated flesh-and-blood womanhood to the status of a divinity, to the incarnated Spirit of Wisdom. What was implicit in Jesus' teachings became openly proclaimed in Simon's, as also in the tenets of Dositheus. As we have seen, Yahweh's consort Asherah had been worshipped by the Hebrew people throughout their history, mainly in her primitive cthonic/sexual form as the great Mother, and she continued to be thus clandestinely worshipped as a fertility goddess even during the second-temple era, despite the best efforts of the Jerusalem clergy to stamp out the practice. But women in their actual flesh-and-blood reality were a different matter; they were deeply despised.

Women were regarded by mainstream Judaism as purely sexual objects and fertility vessels and as a source of defilement to men, the instruments of satanic temptation. They were a degraded element in a strongly patriarchal society. Indeed, the Dead Sea Scrolls reveal that with few rights and little dignity, Jewish women in Palestine were subjected virtually to a form of public apartheid under the puritanical regime of the second-temple priesthood. Their participation in Judaism was negligible, their position vis-à-vis that of menials and sexual servants. They were if possible not to be seen in public, nor were Jewish men permitted to speak to them in public.

Such was the transgression of human rights in first-century Judaea that women could become Judaic disciples only if their husbands or masters were rabbis willing to teach them.[56] In the synagogues women were restricted to a gallery above, unable to wear the phylactery, to carry out liturgical functions, or to be included in the priesthood (because of menstrual impurity). Indeed, one Rabbi Eliezer was quoted as saying, "Rather should the words of the Torah be burned than entrusted to a woman" (Mishnah Sotah 3, 4).[57]

But in parading a flesh-and-blood woman as divine Wisdom itself, Simon challenged this inequity. Hoeller says rightly that Simon was "the first one to devise a mythological framework for the manifestation of Wisdom [instead of Fertility] in incarnate woman-form."[58] Helen's name derives from Selene, the moon, and means a torch or light. Thus for the first time since the Bronze Age, flesh-and-blood womanhood was publicly elevated to the highest spiritual status.

Simon's tantric teachings were shared by Dositheus. The latter appears as a revelator and magician in The Three Steles of Seth in the Nag Hammadi codices.

> An angel of knowledge (gnosis) leads him into the world beyond, where various beings of light reveal to him the mysteries of gnostic or Sethian doctrine, which he is to proclaim to men.[59]

Dositheus disclosed that Seth was the third son of Adam and Eve, who, unlike his contending brothers, Cain and Abel, retained his connection with the transcendental realm of Light and its divine inhabitants. The prototype of the divine emissary, Seth was a Son of Life who fathered a mighty race of enlightened human beings. The Gospel of the Egyptians, or The Book of the Great Invisible Spirit, found among the Nag Hammadi texts, says of the wise race of Seth: "This is the vast, imperishable race that came forth from three (earlier) worlds," suggesting that many souls on earth may have come from previous cosmic systems. [60]

Thus Hoeller asserts that the Sethian race can also be understood as a fraternity of spiritual adepts who are secretly present in the world in every generation and "who possess a distinguished, luminous prehistory in their own right."[61]

Dositheus, like Simon, also had his Helen accompanying him on the roads of the empire, causing similar scandal because of his reputedly libertine practices. However, it must be borne in mind that theater, as a means of tuition of an illiterate population, was still prevalent in the first century. Just as John the Baptist probably resorted to the practice by appearing to the people in the guise of Elijah in order to emphasize that he was bearing the same message as the ancient prophet, so the two Samaritan prophets play-acted their intrinsic message with the help of their two Helens.

Their essential message was that the Hebrew scriptures' male messianic ideal was inadequate, one-sided, and false unless coupled with feminine power. Neither humanly nor spiritually speaking could woman be divorced and set aside from man: she was the man's Shakti, his creative power base. As expressed repeatedly in medieval Qabalistic theosophy, "[T]he King without the Matronit is not a king, is not great and is not praised . . ." (Zohar III, 5a, 69a). [62]

Similarly, in Hindu mythology the male god Shiva is powerful only when united with the goddess Shakti, but is unable even to stir without her. Monasticism was therefore not the highest state, according to Simon and Dositheus. Liberation of spirit and a new and higher state of consciousness were achieved rather through the redeeming power inherent in the marriage of the male and female forces. These new gnostic teachings disseminated by Simon and Dositheus profoundly modified the Samaritan religion of the time, and are still discernible in its modern form.

As savior figures twinned with their spiritual/sexual partners, the two prophets undoubtedly opened a new door on the first-century search for enlightenment. Although it is still being debated today whether their groundbreaking theosophy can be traced back to the Baptist, it certainly throws further light on Jesus' background world of ideas. Yet, that said, the differences remain profound. True, Simon and Dositheus effected an occult revolution in their transference of the crude literalism of the old fertility Mysteries onto a more inward psychological plane, thus liberating new energies into a civilization in danger of decay, but their teachings were still a reflection of the old dualistic mode of thought.

WHAT JESUS TAUGHT: "EVERY MAN AND EVERY WOMAN IS A STAR"

These words of the British Qabalist Aleister Crowley have a great deal to do with Jesus' teachings on the undivided self. In these he sounded a radically new note. His emphasis on psychic unity rendered him truly an Envoy extraordinaire from the Kingdom of Light and in many respects completely anachronistic for his generation. While the first tantric strand of the Mystery cycle is central to the teachings of Simon and Dositheus, emphasizing as it does the spiritual dialectic of the

Divine Couple, in Jesus' case it is the second messianic strand, the great hymn to death and union, that takes central place in his mission. His is the understanding of the messianic sacrifice. The joys of the senses must give way to the higher imperative of mind; the lower must be sacrificed to the higher. This was Jesus' new evolutionary message. Even so, in the ancient Egyptian funeral rites, the priests, forsaking the seat of the sexual energies that were central to the king's coronation, conducted at his death the secret ritual of "the opening of the mouth," thus activating the higher noetic energies of the Word principle.

The complex tapestry of Hemerobaptist thought as revealed in the Simonian and Dosithean doctrines, probably as taught by the Baptist himself, provided a backdrop for Jesus' teachings. Yet in all his sayings and precepts passed down to us there is a new note, an awareness of the transcendental Self, unknown as a doctrine anywhere west of the Indus Valley. Jesus stressed the autonomy of the self, from its most embryonic form in tribal group consciousness to the highly evolved super-consciousness of the sage. He saw selfhood as the central and commanding principle in the human system and as having its seat in the heart.

Thus Jesus was to give the emotional center of the heart a new and indeed supreme significance as the locus of self-awareness. In his diatribes against the learned Pharisees, he gave this governing principle a supremacy over the ordinary ratiocinating mind that was to be echoed in India in the Vedantic teachings of the sage Shankara in the tenth century C.E..

> This real self . . . is to be found in the heart of each living being, in a cavern as it were, or a space within the heart. To know it the seeker must free himself from the mind . . . he must give up willing and wishing.[63]

And long before either Jesus or Shankara were born, the Katha Upanishad had warned that

> the Self is not to be won by eloquent teaching, not by brain power, not by much learning . . . Not with the mind has man the power to

get God, nor through speech, nor by the eye . . . Nor can self-discipline reach Him, nor the most strenuous deeds.[64]

Statements about wholeness, about the state of undividedness or nonduality that transcends the opposites, run as a key refrain through Jesus' teachings and are a hallmark of the way of the awakened Spiritual Heart. "If thine eye be single," Jesus said, "thy whole body shall be full of light" (Matthew 6:22). When his disciple Salome asks him concerning himself, Jesus makes his stance clear: "I am he who exists from the Undivided. I was given some of the things of my Father." When Salome asks further concerning the condition of discipleship, Jesus does not speak of sin or virtue, but reiterates only the requirement of the disciple to be a whole and undivided person—in modern terms, a fully crystallized person.

I say that if he is [undivided] he will be filled with light, but if he is divided, he will be filled with darkness. (Thomas 61)

Joseph Chilton Pearce reminds us that we have a three-way connection among our emotional-cognitive brain, our prefrontal lobes, and our heart. In this connection, he says, lies our hope of transcendence. But the self remains weak and divided where heart intelligence is excluded from the work of the cerebral centers and relegated only to the government of the body's instinctual functions. In such a case, the lower self or ego confines its activities to the satisfaction of the instinctual self-referencing drives—the survival, sexual, and power-seeking propensities—while the higher self is unable to exercise its own proper function. Thus divided against itself, the "I" cannot govern, cannot pursue its rightful intuitional and altruistic life, cannot prevent, as it should, decay and death in the system as a whole. Consequently, we die long before we should. But most importantly, the "I" fails in its primary function as an evolutionary tool that can drive the individual toward his highest spiritual destiny.

In modern scientific terms, an individual's body, heart, and mind need to achieve synchrony in a single unified field before a truly undivided state of selfhood can be said to exist. But when it does so, unimaginable power is available. A well-known portrait of the meditating Buddha surrounded by such an introspected field and holding a vessel filled with the jewels of enlightenment seems to illustrate this point. In other words, the principle of holism—the synthesis of the outer and inner cosmos, the integration of the polarities—is absolutely essential for our evolution, for the fulfillment of our human potential.

Pearce has illustrated the principle of the threefold unified field by reference to two primitive tribes, the Senoi and the Yequana, who to the present day live in blissful social harmony far from the contaminating influence of civilization. These tribes need, he says, neither law, nor culture, nor religion.[65] The effortless goodwill of their members for each other that engenders perpetually happy children and peaceful adults is made possible by being immersed in the herd belonging of *participation mystique,* which is but another name for the heart–brain dynamic at its

Fig. 8. The threefold unified field of the meditating Buddha

most elementary. According to anthropologists, it is undeniably true that in Paleolithic times, perhaps 30,000 years ago, the whole race was involuntarily immersed in such a condition of mystical herd fellowship, and was accordingly benevolent, peace loving, and truthful—as indeed are most species of animals within their own herd.[66] Yet evolution has not been along this collective line as Pearce seems to be suggesting. Prehistorians have shown conclusively that the sorrows of earthly life really began only when selfhood began to mature. But it was not the tribal members who carried the baton of the evolution of selfhood; it was their shaman.

Thirty thousand years ago it was the shaman, the one seeking God, who began the long process of becoming an autonomous entity. It was the shaman who knew fear and pain, who knew alienation from his kind, living in isolation, often shunned by his tribe, at war with other shamans and with threatening spirits. It was the shaman who surrounded himself with objects of art, cult magic, and fetish and suffered the terrors and emotional travail that now afflict our entire race—for we are all becoming shamans.

No longer a herd animal, it was the shaman, not the ordinary tribesman, who endured the abrasive friction of differentiation that marked him off from all others as a unique and creative center of consciousness, a holon, a developing Self. The event that thus turned him into one who *stood solitary* was initiation—the awakening and fuller activation of the heart center. Thereupon the heart–mind dynamic assumed a far more advanced role; the Self grew ever stronger and more differentiated and there began the long and painful sacrificial detour that would eventually return the shaman to the undivided state in which he began.

The goal of this process of increasing self-definition takes the human condition to a state far beyond the participation mystique of the tribal personality, through pain and alienation to eventual spiritual integration on a higher level. All of Jesus' teachings were to carry this message of sacrificial service to the One. On the messianic path trodden by his disciples, the polarities were to be transcended, the mythology of the Divine Couple, however attenuated, laid to rest. There now must emerge the glorification of the One and the recognition of a new principle of synthesis arising out of the sacramental celebration of the marriage chamber. In Qabalistic terms, Jesus rose beyond the dualistic worlds in which the Divine Couple reigned and taught from the station of Da'ath, which represents spiritual Knowledge in its totality, but also union, undividedness, nonduality.[67]

From the Sephirothic Tree we gain further insights into Jesus' frequent allusions to the psychonoetic marriage that leads to integration. Although Da'ath is always placed above Tiphareth and astride the great abyss that lies between the soul world of Tiphareth and the spiritual world of Atziluth, this hidden sephirah can in practice be found anywhere on the Tree, for it represents the transcendent Whole that pervades every part. For that reason the bridechamber at Da'ath is in reality everywhere on the Tree. It is the point of union at which consciousness can register the orgasmic bliss and perfect knowledge of the Whole, the Ain Soph, the Godhead—and this bliss can in principle be experienced at any and all levels of the Tree. It can be experienced sexually, psychically, or spiritually; but the highest and most perfect expression of this rapture is spiritual, and that is why Da'ath is always placed over the abyss above Tiphareth.

Not only did Jesus transfer the old fertility dualism onto an inner psychological plane, but also, like the Hermetic philosophers, he raised it up into a numinal realm where, in the light of a higher wisdom, male and female were understood to be indivisibly one, parts of an androgynous Selfhood.

Jesus saw infants being suckled. He said to his disciples, "These infants being suckled are like those who enter the Kingdom."

They said to him, "Shall we then, as children, enter the Kingdom?"

Jesus said to them, "When you make the two one, and when you make the inside like the outside and the outside like the inside, and the above like the below, and when you make the male and the female one and the same, so that male not be male nor the female female, and when you fashion eyes in the place of an eye, and a hand in place of a hand, and a foot in place of a foot, and a likeness in place of a likeness; then you will enter [the Kingdom]." (Thomas 22)

This famous saying, the very epitome of nondualism, is Jesus' signature par excellence, which today we would think of as a networking mode of thought. Nondualism envisions a cosmic unity that transcends and includes the opposites, as in Taoism and ancient Zervanism, a unity in which the opposites are complementary rather than dichotomous elements in a mutually destructive tension. Nondualism expresses the Hermetic truth that in Reality all is interconnected; all differentiation is tending to return to the One. And because of their correspondence, the higher mirrors the lower and the lower mirrors the higher—and the inner mirrors the outer and the outer the inner "for the performing of the marvels of the One Thing," as the Emerald Tablets of Hermes Trismegistus has put it.[68] Commenting on the many such Hermetic parallels he finds in Jesus' sayings, Welburn believes "it shows that from the very beginning Mystery circles were involved in Christianity."[69]

In his nondual sayings, Jesus also made reference in a veiled way to one of the deepest secrets of the esoteric schools: the goal of union, its evolutionary purpose. The redemption sacrament, which ensured the salvation of the soul, was concerned with the creation of a bodily vehicle on the higher planes after death. Jesus gives expression to this self-same redemptive idea, that of building an inner body for the clothing of the Self, a "chariot" or vehicle of self-expression such that it will be able to sustain the high energies of the Kingdom of Light and live there in the company of the enlightened. Hence Jesus' allusion to fashioning a new spiritual light body or resurrection body, one whose organs and limbs are like those of the outer physical one in every respect but made of Light. This is the Hermetic view—"As above so below"—that developed in Egypt during the intertestamental years. It is the perspective of one who, through initiation, has attained to Da'ath on the Tree of Life and has been glorified in the bridechamber.

In a sense, the path along which Jesus was leading his disciples led ever farther from that of the Baptist. It was a way of love, of union, of individuation—not as something conveyed in a closed secret society like that of the Mithraists but as a message to be proclaimed to all men and women. Its emphasis on the loving bounty of the heart rather than prescribed ascetic practices affirmed its affinity with certain Eastern doctrines such as Hindu *bakhti* yoga, which emphasised above all the yogi's ultimate freedom from externally imposed legalistic prohibitions. And so besides Jesus' training and initiation with the Baptist, we can only suppose that in his investiture as avatar in the river Jordan he entered an altogether new sphere of influence. A divinizing mantle descended on him, clothing him in an influence mysteriously exalted, visionary, and unitive, which gave to his sayings thereafter a mystical Eastern quality unknown to Western societies at that time.

> Jesus said: "I came to make the things below like the things above, and the things outside like those inside. I came to unite them in the place." (Philip 67:30–35)[70]

There is a strangely cryptic, echoing quality to Jesus' teachings, as though they are projected over great distances toward generations yet unborn. There can be no doubt that he foresaw the great transitional crisis already speeding out of the future toward humanity, and that he seeded his message accordingly. Perhaps it is only in the third millennium, in the Aquarian age, that it will be adequately understood, for what he is signifying is not a passive condition given by nature but one that results from the long and difficult creative process of reconciling the inner polarities wherever and whenever they occur. Thus is brought about an integration of the Self under a single governing mandate. There is nothing ambiguous about this unitary work of the bridechamber; it is a work of love, the key to redemption and power.

> Jesus said, "When you make the two one, you will become Sons of Man, and when you say, 'Mountain, move away,' it will move away." (Thomas 106)

And when his disciples asked him, "When will the Kingdom come?" he offered a vision of the earth that transcended the dualities of physical place and time. Jesus taught that between heaven and hell there is nothing but a state of consciousness, an interface that can be penetrated in a nanosecond. For those who have the Gnosis, the world at this very moment is embedded, immersed, in an infinite timeless ocean of bliss, although most do not see it. For those who know themselves, who are aware of the state beyond duality, heaven and earth are luminously one, forever enfolded in love for each other. But if men and women do not know themselves, both they and the earth are heavenless; both are poverty-stricken.

> Jesus said, "If those who lead you say to you, 'See, the Kingdom is in the sky,' then the birds of the sky will precede you. If they say to you, 'It is in the sea,' then the fish will precede you.' Rather, the Kingdom is inside of you, and it is outside of you. When you come to know yourselves, then you will become known, and you will realize that it is you who are the sons of the living Father. But if you will not know yourselves, you dwell in poverty and it is you who are that poverty."
> (Thomas 3)

This vision of the primordial golden age that reigned on earth before the ethnic divisions and moral/sexual imperatives robbed man of his innocence was also reflected in the worldview of the Therapeutae and in the Qabalah, which they assiduously studied. Kieren Barry traces the development of the Qabalistic alphabetical mysticism and numerology to Alexandria during the intertestamental period, when Hebrew thought was merging with that of Greek Neoplatonism.[71] Hence in the Therapeutaean worldview we find a universe of the same harmonious order, in which "not only the angels sing: the stars, the spheres, the merkavah [Chariot-Throne] and the beasts, the trees in the Garden of Eden and their perfumes, indeed the whole universe, sings before God."[72]

In such a vision of the Kingdom of God on earth, no opprobrium attaches to the natural world. On the contrary, nature is a perfect expression of the divine. Confounding Zoroaster, the natural world is good, with no part of it evil: Malkuth the Foundation is as holy as Kether the Crown—some Qabalists say even holier—for the material universe is the ultimate receptacle and manifestation of all the divine forces and creative processes that have preceded it. Therefore, the created universe is glorified and held up as the Bride of God, for it alone represents God's most perfect unitive image.[73] This joyful worldview, so unlike the prevailing pessimism of the period, was also that of Jesus, rendering him unique among Envoys. "There are some standing here," he prophesied, "who will not taste death before they see the Kingdom of God come with power" (Mark 9:1). The earth was to be renewed, life made holy. At present, he said, there was in Jerusalem a temple full of corruption, but soon a pure temple would be established instead in each man's heart, and there the Word would reign eternally.

It is often claimed today that Jesus manifestly failed in his mission because the Kingdom of God did not materialize as promised. But the wider historical reality is that his mission was outstandingly successful. Soon after the Crucifixion, the mystical presence of the Kingdom was announced in the Pentecostal visitation of the Spirit, which descended in tongues of fire resting on the heads of thousands of assembled sectaries, transporting them in various visionary ways. Within forty years Herodian Jerusalem had been razed, the temple had been destroyed as prophesied, and its entire theocratic apparatus had been swept away forever. Judaism had been released from venal oppression, and spiritual seeds that would bear fruit over the coming age had been sown deep in the soil of historical process. A new practice, the Gnosis of the heart, had been born, and the Path of Return had been potentially opened up for every human being on earth. Jesus had promised the coming of the unitive Kingdom of Light—and in a very real sense, it had indeed come.

7

THE GOSPEL OF MARY: SACRED MARRIAGE

No one can know when [a husband] and wife have sex except those two, for marriage in this world is a mystery for those married. If defiled marriage is hidden, how much more is undefiled marriage a true mystery! It is not fleshly but pure. It belongs not to desire but to will. It belongs not to darkness or night but to the day and the light.

THE GOSPEL OF PHILIP

The mystery of the bridechamber bears the very name of a chamber of love.

STEPHAN A. HOELLER

The Coptic Gospel of Mary, found in the fifth-century papyrus codex, Papyrus Berolinensis 8502, is the only known gospel to have been written under a woman's name, that of Mary Magdalene. (An earlier Greek version once circulated, but only a few papyrus fragments of it have been found.) Mary Magdalene has always fascinated the Christian world; she holds a special place among the more exotic of the Church's hagiographic legends. As a controversial saint now emerging for the first time from the shadows of Church history, the Magdalene has become today even more important as one of Jesus' closest disciples and arguably the most magnetic and yet problematic character in the whole of the Christian story. It is becoming apparent that her importance to the development of early Christianity's mysterious bridechamber sacrament has been greatly underrated.

Mary's gospel is an exercise in first-century gender equality. Probably penned in Egypt in the late first century or early second century, it is a moving little work, tentatively self-confident, wise, and revelatory but imbued with an underlying strain of melancholy, for Mary is indubitably the epitome of the spiritual teacher who is not appreciated by her pupils. It is said in the apocryphal gospels that she knew Jesus intimately and was privy to his most secret teachings, and that it was she who comforted the Lord's discouraged and traumatized disciples after the Crucifixion. "Let us turn our hearts to him," she entreated. "Do not weep or grieve or be in doubt, for his grace will be with you all and will protect you. Rather, let us praise his greatness, for he has prepared us and made us truly human."[1]

This Enochan motif of the truly human state, as taught by Jesus also, is to reappear often in Mary's Gospel. It seems that Mary was familiar with its esoteric meaning as a purified state of consciousness beyond that of our ordinary human experience. The Hasidim, who are widely believed to have been the authors of the Book of Enoch, knew it as a state belonging to the angelic order. And along the same lines, in esoteric circles to the present day the truly human race, the race of "kings," is one believed to inhabit a fifth kingdom of Nature and the lowest or tenth in the angelic hierarchy. According to this wisdom teaching, our own fourth kingdom of Nature is a transitional one that lies between the animal kingdom (the third) and the fifth—which is why our kingdom is so subject to stress and imbalance.[2]

Clearly, Mary was a woman of wisdom possessed of many such occult secrets, and in a time of terrible crisis after the master's death she showed herself well able to lead the group. Yet as a leader, Mary is handicapped by her gender and must plead for the understanding and acceptance of her fellow male disciples. The Gospel of Mary ends on a note of uncertainty, of sadness: can she enter their charmed apostolic circle?

The document, incomplete though it is (in all, ten manuscript pages are missing), sums up the insoluble difficulty that early Christians faced in coming to terms with the union of the gender polarities that Jesus had so uncompromisingly enjoined. How could traditional Hebrew men be expected to accept the equality of women? In their ultimate inability to understand or to tolerate this strange woman disciple among them, Jesus' male disciples, led by the irascible Peter, play out the unforgiving misogyny of their era.

Despite the recent, quite dramatic feminist developments in the West, we ourselves still find it difficult to envisage what true parity of the sexes would be like, for the freedoms of Western women are still largely token freedoms. True female freedoms have as yet impregnated hardly at all the world of social archetypes, having not changed to the slightest appreciable degree the values and norms, the stable impermeable structures that continue to make up our patriarchal civilization. Yet this undeniable female imprisonment has not always existed, a fact of which spiritual leaders like Jesus, versed in the doctrines of the Old Religion, must have been well aware.

For almost four thousand years—from about 7000 BCE to 3500 BCE, in the depths of the Neolithic age—an advanced culture complex existed in which women were truly free and responsible equally with men for the building and creative organization of their society. As methods of dating become more accurate, archaeologists have found that isolated centers of Neolithic culture existed in places as far apart as eastern Europe, southern Turkey, Egypt, Palestine, Mesopotamia, and the Indus Valley, and that all shared in a single, highly developed mode of cultural expression based on equality of the sexes. The eminent researcher Marija Gimbutas has called the hub of this widespread civilization "Old Europe." Long before the heyday of the Sumerian and Egyptian civilizations, she says, Old Europe was so advanced that for a long time historians assumed that what they were unearthing were Bronze Age Greek or Roman towns.[3]

Aiding archaeological research, a wealth of beautifully executed figurines, statuary, and cult icons has been found. Spacious houses lined streets in towns of several thousand inhabitants. Agriculture and a rudimentary script existed. There were no tribal gods, only a universally worshipped Goddess. This great deity "incarnating the creative principle as Source and Giver of All" was androgynous, being depicted with a round female body and the narrow, pillarlike head of a male. Dominated by this Great Goddess, Old Europe was a matrilineal society in which descent and inheritance were through the mother. It was egalitarian, passionately artistic, and apparently entirely peace loving. No weapons have been unearthed, no defensive earthworks or hillside barricades, no evidence of an oppressive ruling hierarchy or of social conflict.

The key finding is that women participated as fully as the men in all aspects of their religious and intellectual life. With equal authority and creativity, women played essential roles in religious rituals and acted as partners in evolving the spiritual philosophy on which their civilization was built.[4] Not until the invasions of the patriarchal Kurgan peoples from the north imposed male dominance on the populace, bringing war and national power struggles to the region and competing gods to their temples, did the men and women of Old Europe demonstrate

Fig. 9. The androgynous Goddess, ca. 5000 BCE, Romania

antagonism and disunity. Until then they appear to have built the framework and evolved the structural principles of their society together, with great success, each modifying and balancing the extreme tendencies of the other.

From what we now know of the enduring legacy of the Watchers, and of Neolithic culture in general, and how their revolutionary achievements were treasured in the memory of the prophets even thousands of years later, it seems highly probable that a resuscitation of the ancient Neolithic tradition of "Old Europe" was being actively sought in first-century Hasidic circles. We can guess that Mary Magdalene's disruptive but highly creative role among Jesus' disciples was therefore not fortuitous but instead part of a deliberate policy of reform.

With the fall of Jerusalem, both the Pharisees and the Judaeo-Christians were freed from political constraints to pursue their own course, the Christians to essay for a time a radical program of gender reform, the rabbis to continue conserving the old patriarchal boundaries between men and women. At that time, Judaism was in grave peril of dying. The rabbis—the erstwhile Pharisees—were reviving their religion in a network of synagogues centered on the study of the Torah. They formed scholarly enclaves mainly in Alexandria, in old Babylon in Mesopotamia, and in Jamnia and Safed, the latter a town near Tel Aviv on the Palestinian coast; and there the Pharisees dedicated themselves to collecting and preserving the vast body of Jewish esoteric teachings, which otherwise would have been lost forever.

It is at this time that Rabbi Nehuniah, Rabbi Akiba, and other scholars of the Gnostic Emmaus School are reputed to have drawn on oral traditions to write the *Bahir,* or *Book of Illumination,* the earliest known text of the Jewish Qabalistic system, though at that time still called the Workings of the Chariot.[5] The *Bahir* contained the seed of gender equality, but this element was rejected by the Talmudic rabbis. Instead, within the first two or three centuries of the Common Era, they laid down the foundations of the conservative Judaic tradition that we know today, in which Jewish women were confirmed in their underprivileged role in relation to men.

In the same period, Christians launched into the production of both the New Testament gospels and a large corpus of Gnostic gospels, such as the Gospel of Mary, the Pistis Sophia, the Gospel of Truth, the Dialogue of the Savior, and the Gospels of Thomas, Philip, and Peter. All these apocryphal documents—and there were many others—betray Qabalistic themes centered on the rite of the sacred marriage and the new role of the feminine principle as an essential subtext in Christian discourse. The equality of the sexes is stressed, particularly in relation to the sacrament of the bridechamber, and around womanhood is drawn a numinous aura that renders the sex wholly sanctified. Yet apart from Jesus' occasional references to himself as bridegroom, the sacred marriage theme is noticeably absent from the Christian scriptures, and the disappearance of the Gnostic texts themselves for nearly two thousand years has reinforced the common assumption that Jesus' embrace of the messianic function meant that women and tantra had no place in his life, that the preeminence of one meant the demise or at least the downgrading of the other. But there is much in the rediscovered texts that contradicts this idea.

The unearthing of the Nag Hammadi treasure trove has paved the way for a new take on the long-lost feminist dimension in early Christianity. According to these apocryphal texts, Christian messianism merely overlays the tantric element in the faith, hiding without destroying it. Reality, the Gnostics suggested, always manifests in our world on two levels simultaneously; it is always a duality awaiting transcendence. Thus in their respective teachings, Simon and Dositheus emphasized by analogy the fact that the male, though dominant, is powerless without the female, degraded and recessive though she may have wrongfully become; both sexes together, united, are essential to the work of redemption.

Jesus raised the whole issue of gender equality onto a new, more wisdom-centered plane. He believed that the old fertility cults of the Goddess had had their day and made his stand clear in the Gospel parable of the cursing of the fig tree, which—as his audience would have well understood—was one of the trees sacred to the Goddess.

> On the following day, when they came from Bethany, he was hungry. And seeing in the distance a fig tree in leaf, he went to see if he could find anything on it. When he came to it, he found nothing but leaves, for *it was not the season for figs.* And he said to it, "May no one ever eat fruit from you again." And his disciples heard it. (Mark 11:12–14) (author's italics)

Thus Jesus symbolically conveyed to his followers that they were entering a new age in which much that had been sacred in the past would be so no longer. The Goddess of fertility hidden in the branches of the Tree of Life must become the androgynous Goddess. She must die and be resurrected in a new and higher form as the Goddess of Wisdom who reigns over both sexes.

Philo said that man symbolized reason and woman symbolized perception through the senses. But Jesus rejected this disparaging, judgment-laden classification. He said that, like the androgynous Goddess of old, woman must now become male as well as female, "for the sake of the Kingdom of Heaven." She must express intellectual as well as sexual creativity in order to participate fully with man in his great civilizing projects. The new woman, Jesus was saying, must not be excluded from a foundational input into her own society and culture. She must not obey laws she has never helped to frame, nor worship in temples she hasn't helped to build. Accordingly, we find that in major studies of contemporary writings on early Christianity, there are allusions to churchwomen as missionaries, prophets, martyrs, deacons, theologians, teachers, and writers. Another researcher, who has studied inscriptions and documentary papyri of the early church, notes that women acted as apostles, prophets, and teachers of theology, consecrated widows, deacons, stewards, priests, and bishops up until the tenth century.[6]

We are beginning to express similar egalitarian ideas to those of Jesus in our more scientific vernacular. In *The Heartmath Solution,* by Doc Childre and Howard Martin, the authors speak of the powerful inner teamwork evident between the brain and the heart (implicitly masculine and feminine principles within the neurocardial system), which we must now begin to honor:

> Instead of seeing the brain as the sole source of our intelligence, we begin to realize that it's a remarkable partner to our heart, not its master. When properly synchronized, it works in harmony with the heart, tuned in to "the heart's code . . ."[7]

Heartmath is a modern method for alleviating emotional stress and suffering. In its collaboration of the two intelligence systems in the human body, the brain and the heart, it shows striking parallels with the collaboration possible between the two sexes in a social context: in both cases, achieving a right relationship of equality and mutual respect can be shown to bring about an enormous increase in the harmony and well-being of the whole. Mary, then, exemplified the new woman, one who had attained to the masculine capacity for wisdom in her own holistic and intuitive style, and could therefore claim equal authority with men in affairs of state.

In first-century Hebrew society—or even in Israel today—Mary Magdalene's emancipated role is an astounding one, a declaration of a sexual revolution only now coming into prominence again in the Western world. Early Gnostic texts such as those listed above contradict the impression given in the canonical gospels that the inner circle of disciples surrounding Jesus formed an exclusive, male-only club. On the contrary, it seems that in the free Hellenic manner, both male and female disciples surrounded Jesus in his travels—the names of at least seven women disciples are mentioned—the Savior giving his attention and his affection equally to both sexes. This in itself highlights Jesus' dismissive attitude to the Levitical norms and taboos concerning the lowly place of women in Hebrew society. But even more radically, the texts are at pains to reveal that Messiah Jesus had constantly at his side a spiritual consort in the person of Mary Magdalene. Mary was not only a woman remarkably liberated for her time but she also sounded a secret tantric note as a background to the Master's dominant theme of messianic salvation.

> There were three who always walked with the Lord: Mary his
> mother, his sister, and the Magdalene, who is called his compan-
> ion. For "Mary" is the name of his sister and his mother and it is the
> name of his partner. (Philip 28)

Whereas today the word *companion* implies merely comrade and
friend in a purely platonic sense, in the original Greek it means consort
or conjugal partner in a sacred marriage that may or may not include
sexual activity. The latter is the sense in which Philip is speaking. This
is not agreeable news to many modern orthodox Christians who, interpreting Philip's message in its narrowest sexual sense, believe that as
the unique Son of God, Jesus could not, or should not, have lived as an
ordinary man of flesh and blood, subject to the same procreative laws
of the body as mere mortals.

Some researchers point out that Jesus was in fact bound to have
been married in order to conform with Judaic law, since marriage and
procreation were regarded, as they still are today, as spiritual and moral
obligations incumbent on every Jew. But this is a weak argument in
view of what we now know of sectarian celibacy and general asceticism
in Hebrew society. Celibacy *within* marriage had been a long-standing
tradition among Jews and is known to have been tacitly encouraged in
Europe in the closed Hasidic courts where the Qabalah was extensively
studied, and to which many of the later Zaddikim were drawn in the
eighteenth century. Accordingly, Jesus could still have entered a marriage and yet remained celibate. The author David Beale says that opponents of this Jewish practice of marital celibacy point to the destruction
of family life by prolonged male companionship and emotional satisfaction in the Hasidic courts. And yet, he qualifies,

> [t]he Yeshiva movement that began in Lithuania and which opposed
> Hasidism practiced exactly the same ascetic arrangement, and so did
> the *mitnagdim,* the followers of the Gaon of Vilna. These two move-
> ments studied the Torah rather than the Cabbalah, but all three
> were equally anti-marriage, anti-family; and their students, largely

celibate, could easily have seemed to an outside observer to have belonged to monastic establishments.[8]

There was also in Judaism a well-established, though informal, tradition especially relating to prophets and men of great holiness to the effect that in his later years a man should regard asceticism as spiritually obligatory and withdraw completely from cohabitation with his wife. Clearly, considerably more flexibility in the matter of celibacy existed in Jesus' day than Jewish law ostensibly allowed, particularly no doubt in Galilee and other northern provinces where the rabbinic presence was negligible and adherence to the Torah less strictly enforced.

Why, then, did Mary's presence in Jesus' life cause such scandalized turmoil and acrimony, not only among his immediate disciples but also in generations of true believers up to the present day? If Mary had been Jesus' wife and had fulfilled that role in a submissive and suitably invisible way, it would undoubtedly have been so stated in the gospels, and would probably have been understood and accepted by most readers. Many great spiritual leaders, including the Baptist, have had wives without the slightest social embarrassment, women of meekness and propriety who fade with their offspring into the domestic background with a gift for humble invisibility, leaving posterity undisturbed. But spiritual consortship is another matter altogether, a mystery, a strange kind of union unblessed by tribal law, a visible affront to full-blooded men, a possible scandal.

While marriage would not have caused anything like the incomprehension, hostility, and bewildered suspicions that we note swirled about Mary within the inner apostolic circle, her de facto relationship to Jesus did, raising many questions of impropriety. Mary offered a real challenge to male dominance. She made no pretense of fading into the background, nor was her role a lowly domestic one. The Apocrypha make it clear that she was the leader among the women disciples and at all times made her presence known, giving dissertations to the other disciples that explained the Master's teachings. But in any case, the fact was that consortship was outside the tribal pale, being always associated with the male prerogatives of initiation and sacred knowledge, as well as illicit sexual possibilities, and their association with a woman was in all senses profoundly threatening to the status quo. The fact that Jesus conferred authority and power on his consort, *on a woman,* and permitted her to transmit sacred knowledge to others, men and women alike, clearly precipitated a severe crisis among the male apostles.

The Gnostic gospels are full of their complaints. Why did the Savior love Mary more than he loved his other disciples, they asked, and why did he speak more highly of her wisdom and spiritual elevation than he did of theirs? In the Gospel of Philip the writer recounts the jealousy felt for Mary by the apostles, describing her both as Jesus' most intimate companion and a symbol of divine Wisdom:

> The companion of the [savior] is Mary Magdalene. The [savior loved] her more than all the disciples, [and he] kissed her often on her mouth [more] often than the rest of the [disciples]. They said to him, "Why do you love her more than all of us?" The savior answered and said to them, "Why do I not love you like her? If a blind person and one who can see are both in darkness they are the same. When the light comes, one who can see will see the light, and the blind person will stay in darkness." (Philip 48)

This very adroit rebuke demonstrates an attitude held by Jesus throughout all the Gnostic texts. As though deliberately fanning the flames, he invariably supports Mary against the others, elevating her to spiritual heights to which he suggests they cannot aspire. In this way he enters the gender debate, raising Mary's spiritual status as a woman to a new level undreamed of in Jewish society. By blessing Mary's innate feminine wisdom so emphatically, he is rebirthing the Goddess in all women. And so his consort remains a lonely contentious figure—a mystery woman surrounded by currents of male suspicion, argument, and discord. "How did she get to be so clever?" the apostles ask. Levi alone attempts to pour oil on troubled waters. If the Master so obviously approved of her, should not the rest of us accept the situation with good grace? he asks, as Mary, displaying considerable spiritual authority, explains to the other disciples secret visionary knowledge that the Lord Jesus has disclosed to her alone. But in the Pistis Sophia, Peter thereupon turns and complains that she talks too much. "Master," he says, "we cannot endure this woman who gets in our way and does not let any of us speak, though she talks all the time" (Pistis Sophia 36).

Elsewhere Andrew contends that her teachings are so strange they must be false: they cannot have come from the Master, who would surely not have entertained such outlandish notions (Mary 18). Nor, adds Peter, would the Savior have disclosed them to a woman without telling the rest of us. "Did he really speak with a woman in private, without our knowledge? Should we all turn and listen to her? Did he prefer her to us?" (Mary 18). Mary's response is desolate.

> My brother Peter, what do you think? Do you think I made this up
> in my heart? Do you think I am lying about the Lord?

Thus the apostles betray their overly cerebral background, their disconnection from the heart center—that subtle organ we now identify with the psyche, which has been built up over millions of years of instinctual wisdom rooted in the compassion of women rather than the logic of men. Imprisoned in their neocortical certainties, in the end the apostles go off to their various teaching and preaching missions, leaving Mary behind. The rift is apparently never healed and later church fathers reject Mary's teachings as heresy and suppress them entirely.

MARY, LIGHT-BRINGER

Who then is this light-filled woman who so unfailingly puts the cat among the pigeons—this archetype of everything in womanhood apparently most feared and rejected by Hebrew men? Even her name is something of a mystery. Her nickname, "the Magdalene" or "Mary of Magdala," has been given various meanings, the most likely being that she came from the fishing town of Magdala (Aramaic: Migdal Nunya, or "Tower of Fish") on the western shore of the Sea of Galilee, and therefore from Jesus' own region. Matthew 15:39 even makes a point of mentioning that Jesus sent away the crowds he had been addressing on the shores of the Sea of Galilee in order to visit Magdala. Another possibility is that Mary came from Magdolum in northeast Egypt; a further suggestion is that since Magdala may mean "place of the tower," or "temple tower," Mary's name could have been a title. Picknett and Prince point out that in the Hebrew scriptures in the book of Micah (4:8) there is a prophecy that declares:

> And thou, O tower of the flock [Magdal-eder], the stronghold of the daughter of Zion, unto thee shall come, even the first dominion; the kingdom shall come to the daughter of Jerusalem.

And as author Margaret Starbird notes in *The Woman with the Alabaster Jar,* a 1993 study of the Magdalene cult in southern France, "In Hebrew, the epithet *Magdals* literally means 'tower' or 'elevated, great, magnificent,'"[9] suggesting that Mary in her own lifetime may have been accorded a title of great puissance. However, the commentator Marvin Meyer, a translator and editor of the Gospels of Mary, demurs in his introduction, saying that this is a difficult interpretation and it is far more likely that Mary Magdalene is simply Mary of the city of Magdala (called Taricheae in her lifetime and renamed Magdala Nunayah after the Jewish Revolt of 70 CE) or, in her Aramaic language, Miryam of Magdala.

One of the very few things we learn about Mary from the Christian scriptures is that, according to Mark (16:9), she was one from whom Jesus had cast out seven devils. However, this doesn't tell us much, since, as we have already seen, in Mark's day all illnesses, whether physical or mental, were popularly associated with demonic forces and were commonly cured by exorcism. Mervyn Meyer simply says it "may imply that Mary faced social, mental, or spiritual issues, and that Jesus helped her address those needs."[10] But it does explain why she is so often equated with the anonymous "sinner" who, in the home of Simon the

Leper in Bethany, anointed Jesus' head and feet with a pound of costly ointment of spikenard.

On the other hand, John's Gospel (12:1–8) declares unequivocally that the anointing took place in the Bethany home of Lazarus and his sisters Mary and Martha and was conducted by Mary of Bethany. The Catholic Church identified all three women—the sinner, Mary of Bethany, and Mary Magdalene—as one until 1969, when it reversed its position,[11] perhaps wishing to distance itself from any suggestion of sinful sexual nuances in the Magdalene's relationship to Jesus. However, there are numerous indications in the gospel texts that the Church may have been right in the first place: the three women may well be one and the same.

In the Christian scriptures (Luke 8), Mary Magdalene is presented as an independent woman of means traveling along with Jesus in the company of two other women, as part of the Lord's entourage. Husbands or family members are not mentioned; the women are on their own. According to Luke, Mary and her women friends give support and assistance to the Jesus movement from their own resources. Mary therefore may well be rich and self-sufficient, perhaps a widow or divorcee living on her own—clearly a strong woman with a mind of her own. The Gospels of Mark, Matthew, Luke, John, and Peter all stress Mary's loyalty and unwavering devotion to Jesus. Mourning his death, she is the faithful witness to the Crucifixion and is acclaimed as the first person to witness the risen Christ.

The underground Christian tradition accords her a special and preeminent place in the nucleus of the new movement constellating around Jesus, and even puts her above Peter, the traditional leader of the apostles, because of her greater understanding of her master's teachings. The Dialogue of the Savior, another Nag Hammadi text, says Mary Magdalene was one of three disciples chosen to receive special teachings and was one who "spoke as a woman who knew everything,"[12] receiving from the Lord visions and insights denied even to Peter. This is entirely consonant with her consort status. Although the implications are resolutely ignored by the Church, the apocryphal texts give full support to her role as Jesus' spiritual partner. They frequently refer to Mary as Sophia, Spirit of Wisdom, and claim that Jesus gave her the title "Apostle of the Apostles," or First Apostle, and called her Mary-Lucifer, the Light-Bringer. She was to be raised above all the other apostles, men or women, and was to rule in the imminent Kingdom of Light. In the Pistis Sophia, Jesus praises her as "one whose heart is set on heaven's kingdom more than all your brothers."[13] More than one authority argues that Mary Magdalene is possibly the Beloved Disciple in the Gospel of John.

The Dutch scholar Esther A. de Boer puts forward this claim and cites a number of authors similarly convinced.[14] De Boer has particularly strong support in the detailed researches of Lynn Picknett and Clive Prince, who assert that in Leonardo da Vinci's painting of the Last Supper, the Beloved Disciple to the left of Jesus bears many undeniably feminine features and may in fact be Mary Magdalene.[15] While this suggestion can possibly be dismissed on the grounds that Leonardo also depicts the Baptist in equally feminine terms, it has served to highlight the very real possibility that the Magdalene is a candidate for the Beloved Disciple who features in the John Gospel. De Boer maintains that it is only the misogynist elements in this gospel—ones that question the authority of female discipleship—that obscure Mary's true role. Otherwise, she says,

> [Mary] would have had disciples, her testimony would have formed a community, her accounts not only of the death and resurrection of Jesus, but also of his life and teachings, would have been preserved. But not only that, her words would have been canonized and taught through the ages, and spread over the world.[16]

In the Pistis Sophia, Mary is again presented as preeminent among the disciples, giving insightful interpretations of the Master's sayings and scriptural passages and illuminating the meaning of salvation. Jesus tells Mary, "You are more blessed than all women on earth." Mary is, Jesus insists, "pure spiritual woman." And in the Manichaean *Psalms of Heracleides,* Mary is praised as one who cast the net to gather the last disciples, and she is, the poet declares, "the spirit of wisdom."[17] There is an account in the Acts of Philip concerning his spiritual sister, a woman called Mary or Mariamne who is a feminine leader in the early church, involved in healing by spiritual means as does Jesus, teaching and administering sacraments as he does, including the baptism of women. One commentator who has studied the Acts of Philip extensively is convinced this Mary/Mariamne is Mary Magdalene.[18] If so, it confirms the early Gnostic belief that Mary Magdalene took her place in the infant Christian movement as the equal, if not the superior, of all the apostles.

Mary's prestige as Light-Bringer has not only survived but also grown over the centuries and at times seems to vie with that of Jesus' mother, the Virgin Mary. Even the Church in times past has bowed (if reluctantly) to the saint's hallowed reputation, for the most famous account of the Magdalene in France is Jacobus de Voragine's *Golden Legend* (1260). De Voragine, the Dominican archbishop of Genoa, called her Illuminant and Illuminatrix, both enlightened and empowered to bestow enlightenment on others.[19]

All this emphasis on Mary's unique status in the movement points strongly to Jesus' need to draw the feminine principle into a new kind of relationship with the male, one based on parity of intelligence. Woman, Jesus is saying, is man's equal partner in the search for transcendence; and as Jesus' consort, Mary epitomizes this high destiny in her capacity for an even greater understanding of spiritual truths.

Yet the question of Mary's intimate relationship to Jesus is addressed nowhere in the canonical gospels, although this would have been of keen interest to the expatriate Jewry the gospels were mainly written for. Why the secrecy, asks our indefatigable commentator Morton Smith, if not because it belonged to arcane Mystery material? Morton Smith has put his finger on the crux of the matter. Consortship or sacred marriage in the evangelists' day was classified in the temples as one of the arcane mysteries, a part of their repository of reserved knowledge. It still is in today's underground esoteric schools, which therefore contribute by their silence to the cloud of mystery surrounding this subject.

With the recent return of the Gnosis to the public arena in the form of popular books about sacred sex, particularly in relation to the Magdalene, it would seem that the issue of her relationship to Jesus has not been resolved by the Church but merely shelved, and is now regaining its rightful prominence in best sellers like *The Da Vinci Code*. This is all the more apparent when one considers that besides the testimony of the Gnostic gospels, there is indisputable evidence of a cult of Mary Magdalene as disciple and consort of Jesus that has flourished in the Languedoc–Rousillon area in the south of France for almost as long as Christianity has existed. The beliefs of the sect of Cathars, who practiced equality of the sexes until massacred by the Church in the Albigensian Crusade of the twelfth century, certainly included the fact of such a union, though it was voiced only in the highest Cathar circles,[20] thus reinforcing the idea that it belonged to "forbidden" Mystery material. This secret belief was almost certainly shared by the Knights Templar, who are known to have had close though unpublicized links with the Cathars.[21]

Despite the Christian scriptures' deafening silence on this subject, echoes of its Mystery background cling to the gospel texts tenaciously, offering the possibility of severe offense and bewilderment to the laity. More than one biblical authority has commented on the possibility that the woman who ritually anointed Jesus' head with oil, cited in John's Gospel as Mary of Bethany and in Luke as "a woman of the city, which was a sinner," must have had the priestly authority to do so. In the Old Religion the anointing with an unguent of spikenard was an important royal sacrament, as we have seen, and could be conducted only by a priestess consecrated to the temple.[22] Consequently, in the fascinating and enigmatic legends that surround her, the Magdalene is frequently recorded as having served as a priestess in some pagan female cult, perhaps an Egyptian Isis cult, before converting to the Jesus movement, and as being already a woman of wisdom and cultic authority.[23] A more likely alternative, of course, is that she was a cult priestess in the Leontopolis temple, where the powerful female orders of the Old Religion, long suppressed in Jerusalem, seem to have been retained. Among today's orthodox congregations, such theories only heighten the impression that exotic and disreputable goddess-worshipping currents swirl around this woman whom Jesus loved.

It is more usually assumed, however, that the gospels have excised Mary Magdalene from their accounts simply because as a "sinner" she is associated with a past career of harlotry and is therefore tainted by the scandal of sexual immorality. Baring and Cashford point out that the word *harlot* was a translation of the word *quadishtu,* which in its original sense meant "sacred hierodule or priestess" rather than whore.[24] Since Jews of the second-temple era appear to have made no distinction whatsoever among whores, priestesses, and non-Jewish women generally, all being equally unclean, equally defiling to men, the sacerdotal nature of Mary's calling may well have been misconstrued. But whichever way one looks at it, the point of greatest interest in her story is undoubtedly the stubborn persistence of the legend that relates her to the pagan Mystery temples of the time and to the merkavah tradition.

THE SPIRITUAL CONSORT AND THE BRIDECHAMBER

C. G. Jung spoke of "a magic kind of love never for matrimony" and of mystic weddings that were "in reality a process of mutual individuation."[25] He was referring in effect to spiritual consortship, a love relationship that is always irregular and off the social map. Jung understood from personal experience that this unusual relationship between man and woman was essentially an inner one, the expression of a uniting of the intrapsychic polarities. Yet he saw it also at its best as archetypal, suprapersonal. The mystic character of such a union rendered it holy, and Jung deemed it one of the most beautiful of humanity's sacred mythic rites.

Late in life, Jung was granted the spiritual experience of an initiation in the bridechamber and had a vision of the hieros gamos, the marriage of Sun and Moon, of King and Queen.

Everything about me seemed enchanted . . . I myself was, so it seemed, in the . . . garden of pomegranates, and the wedding of Tifereth with

Malchuth was taking place . . . It was the mystic marriage as it appears in the Cabbalistic tradition . . . At bottom it was I myself: I was the marriage.

Gradually the garden of pomegranates faded away and changed. There followed the marriage of the Lamb, in a Jerusalem festively bedecked . . . There were ineffable states of joy. Angels were present, and light. I myself was the "Marriage of the Lamb."

That, too, vanished, and there came a new image, the last vision. I walked up a wide valley to the end . . . a classical amphitheater . . . magnificently situated in the green landscape. And there, in this theater, the hieros gamos was being celebrated. Men and women dancers came on stage, and upon a flower-decked couch All-father Zeus and Hera consummated the mystic marriage, as it is described in the *Iliad*.[26]

Thus Jung, a modern Gnostic by nature if not by profession, offers us a personal vision of the mystic sacrament, the "unsullied marriage" of the gnostics that takes place on a subtle plane known only to the Elect. We can take this numinous experience as being the foundation also of Mary's spiritual consortship, which was a part of the bridechamber tradition from the earliest times. In antiquity, especially during the Bronze Age, the god-king generally played the role of consort to the more powerful high priestess, while at other times the roles were reversed.

Although always filled with love, often of a most intense kind, the goal of the sacred marriage is not primarily procreation or emotional fulfillment but spiritual development, for which reason it may or may not encompass the first two goals, and may or may not be sexual. The hieros gamos was practiced secretly at the highest echelons of all the ancient Mystery schools and is still found today in many extant esoteric fraternities devoted to self-transformation. We find ourselves here at the threshold of a subject that will be introduced increasingly in the following chapters, the hidden yogic or shamanic dimension that underlies all religious manifestations and which played its part in the formation of the Christian religion.

The nearest we can come to an understanding of the spiritual partnership between men and women known as consortship is in Tibetan Buddhist practice. In the Red Hat tradition, based on the old pre-Buddhist Bon religion, consortship is a common spiritual discipline at a certain stage of a disciple's career, generally after a period of monasticism. It is controlled entirely by the more spiritually advanced partner, who may when the time is ripe terminate it, for it is not regarded as belonging either to the usual social canon or to the highest spiritual estate.[27] Ultimately, it must be transcended. Some Tibetan partnerships of this kind are genuine marriages producing a stable family of offspring; in many others there is transiency, with no implication of a normal worldly marriage contract or even of sexuality in its usual sense.

The dynamics of the sacred marriage have never been fully aired in the public arena even to the present day, so we are working in the dark regarding their place in the relationship of Jesus and Mary Magdalene. Picknett and Prince, who have broken intriguing new ground on this subject, making them one of the main sources for Dan Brown's *The Da Vinci Code,* make the comment that "the Gnostic gospels and other early texts have no hesitation in describing the relationship between Mary Magdalene and Jesus as being overtly sexual."[28] Strictly speaking, that opinion is not true. These gospels do indeed emphasize an intimate and loving bond between the two, but not necessarily a bond based on sexual activity. Although much has been made of the researches of Picknett and Prince into sacred eroticism in Jesus' story leading to matrimony and offspring, it must be said that fantasy and wish fulfillment frequently play a part in such speculations. In assessing them, we need to take into account the great abiding desire of most of us to draw our religious icons down to the level of ordinary humanity, to render them "one of us."

Mary points out several times to the other disciples that the Master has proclaimed "the child of humanity"—that is, the divine self-governing principle—to be the Inner Guide within each of them."[29] Although these terms will be better understood in chapter 10, when we come to consider the Gnosis of the heart, Mary is indicating that the disciples have achieved mastery of the higher cerebrospinal energy centers

critical to the birth of spiritual love. That is the criterion of a fully individuated human being—that he be one who has mastered the energic
secrets of the higher chakras—and therefore no longer needs the geni-
tal act, or even physical proximity, to establish a blissful psychospiritual
union with another human being. Such a one meets the beloved in the
bridechamber of the heart, where the true psychic marriage takes place.

The Gospel of Philip also seems to emphasize that a union may
take place on the subtle planes without ever involving the sex act or
physical contact of any kind. It is known, for example, that Francis of
Assisi had just such an inner relationship with the nun St. Clare, and it
would seem that Jesus and Mary Magdalene had likewise.

Of course endless exegetical arguments can be conducted, and are
on this very point, yet the Gnostic gospels, with their talk of images,
metaphorical garments, and symbols in general, seem to struggle continually to make their multileveled and spiritualized worldview com-
prehensible to their readers. Our flesh, says Philip, "is not true flesh but
only an image of the true" (Philip 21). He thus seems to be placing the
procreative energies on the subtle rather than the physical plane, which
he sees as only a reflection of the true shining down from above.

> Truth did not come into the world naked but in symbols and images.
> The world cannot receive truth in any other way . . . Image must arise
> through image. By means of this image, the bridal chamber and the
> image must embark upon the realm of truth, that is, embark upon
> the return. (Philip 59:9–16)

Even when Philip refers to the fact that Jesus kissed Mary often on the
mouth (if that is the correct translation), he renders it a psychospiritual
rather than a carnal expression of love. The mouth, Philip says, is the
source of the Word, and those nourished thereby are made perfect.

> The perfect conceive and give birth by a kiss. For this reason we too
> kiss one another; it is by the grace residing in one another that we
> conceive. (Philip 27:2–5)

Philip is endeavoring, rather like C. G. Jung, to bring greater definition to noetic levels of being in which physical passions have been etherealized, so to speak, into signs and symbols of the holy. Gender difference, allied as it is to the evolutionary process, is another Mystery topic that has not yet been fully opened up to public scrutiny, and so when Jesus says in the Gospel of Thomas (114) that "every female who makes herself male will enter heaven's kingdom," this is not necessarily a sexist statement. It refers rather to the need for women to develop their recessive maleness in order to bring to full maturity their own powerful female intelligence. Again, profound truths connected with the subtle realm, dealing with the specific function and gender of each chakra, are often hidden in such arcane observations. Is it coincidental that spirituality, wisdom, and intuitive creativity increase when at menopause a woman's center of gravity shifts somewhat from yin (feminine) to yang (masculine)?

As regards the sacred marriage, all emphasis on the nature of the material world as a secondary or derivative reality compared with the inner world of soul tends to bring death into the picture, and that is how the Gnostics saw it. In the bridechamber, death is annulled. The true marriage, the living marriage, they said, is not to be found in this material world where death dwells. When Eve was in Adam, according to the Gospel of Philip, there was no death. When she was separated from him (on the material plane), death came. "If she enters into him again and he embraces her" (on the inner plane of soul, in true spiritual intercourse), "death will cease to be."

In such terms do the Gnostic texts attempt to convey—not always, one must admit, with any great clarity—the interior union that is possible between compatible souls who have been adequately purified. One of the first things to strike a modern reader of ancient texts like the Gnostic gospels is the limited vocabulary and idiomatic range available to them, rendering terms like *pure* and *spiritual* misleadingly cold in tone. These terms set too great a gulf between the warm orgasmic emotions of earth and those of heaven, seeming to negate the very essence of the ecstatic harmony and "oneness" they attempt to describe. Two thousand years of increasing education and intellectual development have undoubtedly honed powers of self-expression in our Western world that were simply not available to the early Christians, particularly in the subtle psychological, yogic, and metaphysical areas of experience in which the Gnostics were especially interested.

The difficulty in articulating the subtleties of the higher dimensions of human interaction applies to all the instances in which the evangelists seek to express the nature of the bridechamber sacrament and the meaning of Jesus as Bridegroom. This is particularly so in the Gospel description of the Cana wedding (John 2:1–12). This anecdote is often cited as evidence of Jesus' marriage to Mary Magdalene, committing him to a conjugal relationship of a sexual nature, but it can equally be seen as a Midrash (a statement on two levels), as an allegory of the bridechamber sacrament.

We must remember that turning water into wine is a classical symbol of initiation, while another Cana anecdote, Jesus' dismissal of his mother—elsewhere in the gospels described as the rejection of his entire family—can also be interpreted symbolically. It is telling us that the commitment to the spiritual world demanded of an initiate is so thorough-going that henceforth his earthly relationships and tribal loyalties, once regarded as supremely binding, must now take second place.

Whatever his earlier circumstances, whether married in Cana or not, for a high adept and spiritual exemplar like Jesus, sexual polarity was one of the divisions that would have had to be transcended. In his final years on earth, Jesus would have entered into the holiest estate, that of the true avatar, the true Messiah, whose function it is to be an example of archetypal androgyny, to be fully individualized, fully autonomous, and therefore without sexual need. Unless called to have children, his completed nature would prompt him to remain "at rest"(celibate). And this in fact is the picture of the Savior that the gospels project. In them Jesus praises "those who have made themselves eunuchs for the sake of the Kingdom of Heaven" (Matthew 19:12). Says Elaine Pagels, "Luke has Jesus link marriage and death, and celibacy with eternal life."

And Jesus said to them, "The sons of this age marry and are given in marriage; but those who are accounted worthy to attain to that age and to the resurrection from the dead neither marry nor are given in marriage, for they cannot die any more, because they are equal to angels and are sons of God, being sons of the resurrection." (Luke 20:34–36)

Jesus was expressing a growing realization in radical Jewry that for "sons of the resurrection" who had achieved a certain moral strength, it was no longer necessary to be ritually segregated from the opposite sex, nor for women disciples like Mary to remain in purdah. Men and women could now afford to draw closer together without harm to themselves, a fact that was understood in Egyptian Jewry even before Jesus' lifetime. The change in the relationship of the sexes that occurred among the Therapeutae in Alexandria was an expression of the fact that a degree of individuation was already happening in Judaic spiritual circles.

THE CONSORT IN EGYPT AND GAUL

The subversive move toward gender equality so vigorously espoused by Mary Magdalene began with the Therapeutae. These Essenes had introduced their veneration of the feminine principle into Judaism nearly two hundred years before Jesus was born, instigating reforms that without any doubt prepared the way for his radical attitude toward women. Indeed, according to Hugh Schonfield, it was to these Jewish contemplatives of Egypt that the mystical secret societies of Europe could and did look back to as their true ancestral source.[30]

In their gender reforms, it is true that the Therapeutae were responsive to the Hellenic liberalism that had entered Egypt with Alexander the Great, but beyond this Greek influence there was a metaphysical imperative to mirror here below on earth the activity of the Cosmic Parents on high. William Meader, an American writer who conducts international seminars on spiritual psychology, explains the Cosmic Parents as aspects of the androgynous One Life.

From the universal perspective . . . the Father and Mother Principles represent energies that facilitate the evolution of consciousness. Yet each embodies different aspects of the One Life as that Life seeks to manifest itself as creation. Both are indispensable and equal in their support of evolution, but each plays an entirely different role in the process.[31]

Through their knowledge of the old Solomonic Religion perpetuated in the Leontopolis temple, the Therapeutae were aware of the roles played by the Divine Couple in the building of the universe. The Cosmic Father, they understood, works with energies. He is purposeful and wills the direction of evolutionary progress, thus bringing to the earth constant change and motion. The Cosmic Mother, on the other hand, is formative and works with matter in varying degrees of refinement. She brings organizational understanding to the Father's plans and materializes them in viable forms out of the substances at her disposal, thus bringing rest and stability to the earth.[32] "The Father knows what needs to be done," says Meader. "The Mother understands how to do it."[33] In this interweaving play of force and form, each Parent must yield to the other in love. The Father principle must tolerate the constant slowing down and limiting of his grand schemes, whereas the Mother principle must bear with the incessant destruction of her labors in the interests of a greater but hypothetical good.

The Therapeutae believed it was necessary to facilitate the collaboration of the divine Father and the divine Mother in their cosmic work by mirroring their interactive relationship here below. The structure of the community reflected this high commitment to gender equality. It was an outright rejection of patriarchy, and as such it gives credence to the claim that the Therapeutae were an outpost of the Leontopolis temple.

It is not known exactly when the Therapeutae established their community, but it was probably quite soon after Onias III built the Leontopolis temple. In his essay "Concerning the Contemplative Life," Philo depicts them as an informal and somewhat dilettante community of like-minded philosophers who gathered together in an affluent lakeside suburb of Alexandria to debate the metaphysical issues of the day.

They comprised people of both sexes drawn from the wealthiest and most highly educated sector of the Jewish community in Alexandria, and were renowned as students of Jewish mysticism of the more heterodox sort. Besides their tolerant outlook, they were noted for their Eastern style of mysticism, and it was this in particular that many scholars have seen reflected in Jesus' sayings.[34]

But the Therapeutae were not quite what they seemed. A closer analysis of Philo's famous essay by a Harvard research team has revealed the outlines of a quite large closed Order based on initiation and secrecy and constituted along strictly traditional lines. A small elite group of Contemplatives at the top was apparently served by a large quorum of Actives below, the latter concerned with the administration of a farming and religious community in all its many aspects.[35] As such, the dilettante character of the community disappears and in its place the dedication of a traditional Jewish Mystery school emerges. Whether it was Essene is not altogether clear. Philo does not expressly say that it was Essene, but what he does obliquely emphasize throughout his essay is that, Essene or no, these Egyptian-Jewish mystics were Hasidim dedicated to the same radical socio-religious ideals as other branches of the Hasidic movement. Behind the spare details he provides us with, one glimpses a program very similar to the Essene New Covenant, which aimed at a Judaic doctrinal and social revolution of the most far-reaching kind.

We know little more about the Therapeutae than what Philo has chosen to disclose, but there has always been informed speculation that Jesus' social agenda, his ethos, and his idiosyncratic worldview, as well as his liberal treatment of women, were influenced by the Therapeutae's ideals. The Platonic philosopher Celsus, writing in the second century, was insistent that Jesus learned from the Therapeutae, and Epiphanius likewise associated the Savior with the Lake Mareotis contemplatives (*Panarion*, xxiv). The historian and bishop of Caesarea, Eusebius (260–340), another prominent church father, believed mistakenly that the Therapeutae were a Christian sect, so alike were they to Christians in many of their ideas, customs, and precepts.

Could Mary Magdalene too have been associated with the Therapeutae? As already said, one of the Therapeutae's most revolutionary features was their acceptance of gender equality, so outlandish an idea to the Orthodox Jew that it has yet to be accepted among the Orthodox in modern Israel. The mystics of Lake Mareotis were thus the first to bring a new dignity to the feminine principle by conceiving of the numinous Sophia, the Angel of Wisdom, in the old image of Asherah, the great Hebrew Goddess of Mount Zion, and by initiating women into their Order. Philo's description of the role of women in the Lake Mareotis community and their close interaction with men on an egalitarian basis is undoubtedly unique in the history of post-Exilic Judaism until the rise of Christianity. Of the women's creative contribution to the new interpretation of their faith Philo says:

> They read the Holy Scriptures and seek wisdom from their ancestral philosophy by taking it as an allegory, since they think that the words of the literal text are symbols of something whose hidden nature is revealed by studying the underlying meaning . . . They do not confine themselves to contemplation but also compose hymns and psalms to God in all sorts of meters and melodies, which they write down with rhythms necessarily made more solemn.[36]

Such an intellectual participation in religious matters by Jewish women was revolutionary indeed, and may have been confined to Egypt, since both Josephus and Pliny the Elder claimed that the Essenes in Palestine required their members to be male, Jewish, and free-born (although this claim has recently been contested).[37] In Palestinian Judaism the antagonism to the female intellect was acute, but in the Therapeutaean community women initiates were welcomed on an equal footing with men. Equally learned and articulate, the women lived on their own in small separate houses and studied, discoursed, and composed hymns even as the men did, regularly taking part in spiritual seminars "with the same ardor and the same sense of their calling."

Philo makes clear that the women equally with the men valued free-

dom of conscience and repudiated the literal and narrowly exoteric meaning of Jewish Law in relation to the sexes. In this way they were freed
from the ancient tribal proscription that enforced subjugation of the
woman to male rule, and were able to conduct their common worship
along new lines of equality and interaction. Ritualized contact between
the sexes in sacred dance and song was encouraged on festive occasions.

> They sing hymns to God composed of many measures and set to many
> melodies, sometimes chanting together, sometimes taking up the har-
> mony antiphonally, hands and feet keeping time in accompaniment,
> and rapt with enthusiasm reproduce sometimes the lyrics of the
> procession, sometimes of the halt and of the wheeling and counter-
> wheeling of the choric dance.[38]

And finally the two groups mix and join in a single choir, "note in
response to note and voice to voice, the treble of the women blending
with the bass of the men," still presumably dancing the wheeling and
counter-wheeling of the choric dance. "Thus," says Philo, "they continue
until dawn."[39] Although nowhere stated, it is very possible that programs
of this nature in which the sexes were able to ritually mix provided a context in which the tradition of spiritual consortship was able to prosper.

The Therapeutae provided the beginning of a much wider Egypto-
Judaic reformation based on memories of the hieros gamos and the
great Goddess who reigned in Solomon's temple. It would be adopted
by all the Hasidic branches except that of the Pharisees, who chose to
remain loyal to the patriarchal Jerusalem creed. But for the rest, the
New Covenant was the seed of a new evolutionary direction. For Gnostics it led inevitably to John the Baptist's Hemerobaptist school and its
"heretical" initiates Simon, Dositheus, and Jesus; to the bridechamber
sacrament; to the cult of Mary Magdalene and the egalitarian worldview
of Qabalah—and evidently to the revival of the timeless and mysterious
tradition of spiritual consortship, of which Jesus and the Magdalene are
a classic example.

Such spiritualized relationships are still known. An initiatory union was enjoyed by Sri Aurobindo Ghose, the eminent Hindu sage and esotericist of modern fame, with his French partner Sweet Mother. The Western adept Pythagoras in the fifth century BCE married his disciple Theano, forty years his junior, on the basis of the same kind of ardent psychospiritual love, which as a matter of choice may or may not have been carnally expressed in order to find fulfillment. In both cases, the disciple, radically transformed by the experience, adopted the mantle of her Master at his death and carried on his teaching work, thus becoming a fully authorized spiritual leader in her own right.

Thus it is worth noting that there is a well-known tradition to the effect that after the Lord's death Mary Magdalene fled Palestine and, migrating to southern Gaul, became a preacher much beloved of the populace, so fulfilling the classic role of the spiritual consort.[40] In *The Holy Blood and the Holy Grail,* by Baigent, Leigh, and Lincoln, it is suggested that Jesus survived crucifixion and had a child by Mary Magdalene. The holy family then fled to southern Gaul, where it seeded a French royal dynasty.[41]

But there is no evidence that Mary ever bore a child. The many statues in southern France that depict her with a child on her lap are depicting "the child of humanity" that Mary so often extolled in her gospel. The "child of humanity" is the divine child Emmanuel, God With Us (Isaiah 7:14), the spirit of wisdom born in the human heart— but who sometimes refers to the Christ himself. Mary is revered in the lore of southern France as a hermit, a lone childless figure who became a great Teacher in the region, the inspiration for an entire medieval Gnostic culture.

According to Provençal legend, soon after the Crucifixion a shipload of fugitive relatives of both Jesus and the Baptist landed near a place in the Camargue, now a small seaside town called Les-Saintes-Maries-de-la-Mer. Among the ship's company were three Marys: Mary Jacobi and Mary Salome (supposedly Jesus' aunts) and Mary Magdalene, as well as their servant, Sarah the Egyptian, to whom the Gypsies of southern France pay deep homage even today. It's believed that two of the Marys and Sarah lived out the rest of their lives in this village and were buried in about 50 CE near a small Christian chapel they had built in the center of the village. Over the centuries the town has become an important destination of pilgrimage, noted for the antiquity of its goddess worship.

> The crypt envelops the visitor with an atmosphere of dark and earthy mystery. If this is Christianity, it's far different from its more orthodox varieties. Here, the feminine is not excluded; it is worshipped in a manner that is far more primitive than early Christianity itself.[42]

Mary Magdalene herself, so the legend goes, journeyed first to Arles, a center of Isis worship, or perhaps to Marseilles, and from there became an itinerant preacher of the Good News of the Risen Christ throughout the region, bringing Christianity to Gaul by the middle of the first century, even before Paul's early proselytizing career got under way. The prolific evidences of the Magdalenian cult are everywhere. At her death she was widely mourned by the populace, given the last rites by the then first bishop of Provence and buried in St. Maximin, the town named after him.[43]

This is by no means an improbable legend. Celtic Gaul in the first century was no barbarous place of exile but rather a civilized and populous land readily accessible by ship and graced by many Greco-Roman cities and the estates of noble families from various parts of the Roman Empire. A large Jewish colony existed in the south in what is now known as Provence and the Languedoc, and probably included many Egyptian Essenes who brought their Therapeutaean ideals to the new land. Southern Gaul would thus have been a most welcoming region for refugees from troubled Palestine. For several centuries, Jews and Christians in this part of the world and across the Pyrenees lived side by side in amity; and here shrines, chapels, and churches dedicated to the beloved Magdalene abound. The sheer number of places of worship associated with this saint, the many towns and natural features, such as miraculous springs and wells named after her, not only in the southern provinces but also throughout the rest of France and the Pyrenees, attest to her veneration. The depth of devotion she inspires and the continuing power of her charismatic image in Provençal culture makes it very evident that there are solid grounds for accepting the legends as based on fact.

Several curious associations cluster around the Magdalene cult. One is the prevalence of statues of Black Virgins and Black Madonnas found in places once devoted to pagan worship and believed by many scholars to be representations of the goddess Isis. "Time and again," comment Picknett and Prince, "these enigmatic statues and their age-old cults seem to flourish alongside that of Mary Magdalene."[44] The British psychologist and author Ean Begg has studied this phenomenon closely and notes that no fewer than fifty Magdalenian centers in the south of France also contain shrines to the Black Virgin and are sites of pagan worship.[45] He writes that the greatest concentration of Black Madonna sites in France is centered on a range of hills dedicated to the Magdalene, and that similar sites in Provence and the eastern Pyrenees are also those most intimately connected to the Magdalene legend, seeming to hark back to the far older goddess traditions of Egypt and the pagan East.

It would appear that, unlike the pure Virgin Mary, the mother of Jesus, Mary Magdalene offered the intimate and understanding solace of fertility goddesses of old like Diana and Cybele, who were also some-times portrayed as black and who had experienced the natural pas-sions of all women. In the Magdalene could be found the compassion and healing balm of the great Isis, she who as wife, lover, mother, and widow had lived to the fullness of all the joys and sorrows of earth and who, again, was sometimes depicted as black.

Unofficially involved with the Cathars, the Grail romances, and the black Madonnas were the Knights Templar, a large part of whose holdings were in Provence and the Languedoc–Roussellon area. Many Cathars were enrolled in the Templar Order, and some of these were women.[46] Clandestinely dedicated to research into esoteric and meta-physical matters, the Templars are regarded by many historians as also deeply committed to the Magdalenian cult. Bernard of Clairvaux, the chief founder of the Order, was a lifelong devotee of the Black Virgin.

He wrote numerous fervent sermons on the Song of Songs in which he identified the Bride with Mary of Bethany, thought at that time to be one and the same as Mary Magdalene. The Templars, who secretly constituted a religious initiatory Order, were known to possess and to revere a severed head called Baphomet—a name that Hugh Schonfield has decoded as Sophia—in accordance with an ancient cypher called the Atbash Cypher.[47] This head, believed to be that of John the Baptist, connects the Templars to the Grail romances in which a severed head carried on a platter, or Graal, figures prominently.

But interestingly, the Knights also owned a beautiful silver reliquary in the form of a female skull, about which Schonfield writes:

> There would seem to be little doubt that the beautiful woman's head of the Templars represented Sophia in her female and Isis aspect, and she was linked with Mary Magdalene in the Christian interpretation.[48]

We can understand the complementary relationship the Templars assigned to the two skulls only when we learn that a well-known strand of Eastern mysticism, the Tantric/Buddhist practice of the Severed Head, involves *the inner balancing of the masculine and feminine energies* of the practitioner.[49] The Templars would have become well aware of this practice and its esoteric meaning during their crusades in the Middle East.

And yet another association with the Magdalene cult was the Celtic/Arthurian tales of high chivalric devotion that had originated in Britain and taken hold across medieval Europe, giving rise to the mystical Grail legends. Again it would appear that Mary Magdalene, apostle of Christ, had the power to evoke in the medieval heart and imagination the ideal of courtly love, love etherealized to its pure essence, of which the troubadours of Provence sang in the noble courts of the late twelfth century. By the fourteenth century the Magdalene's influence had spread as far as Strasbourg in Germany, where Picknett and Prince report that a tract called *Schwester Katrei* (Sister Catherine) was published in 1330. It revealed a strong Cathar influence and was supposedly written by the German mystic Meister Eckhart, but more probably by one of his women followers. The tract links Mary Magdalene with Minne, the iconic ladylove of the troubadours or minnesingers of the region.[50]

This link is highly significant, for the troubadours of medieval Europe, as is now well known, were initiates whose line appears to have preserved against great odds the contents of the Gnostic gospels and secretly transmitted them up to the seventeenth century.[51] The only conclusion that can be drawn from such a remarkable feat (since the Gnostic gospels were irretrievably "lost" until 1946) is that the troubadours must have belonged to a continuous line of spiritual transmission dating back to the time before the gospels were outlawed in the fourth century. King René d'Anjou, count of Provence, an ardent fifteenth-century searcher for the Holy Grail, called this hidden esoteric current running through the centuries "the underground stream of lost Arcadia"—the lost Eden of Gnostic Christianity.[52] In Mary Magdalene we have a very important link in the chain of the primordial Gnosis.

Mary's gospel also sheds a great deal of light on the reason why every region that adopted the cult of Mary Magdalene, particularly southern France and the Germanic states, suffered the full brunt of the papal wrath in religious wars that left those lands devastated for centuries, and why Eden was thus lost to the Western world. Whoever wrote the Gospel of Mary did so in the language of the heart, that of the Cosmic Mother, so offering deep offense to the patriarchal Roman church. Mary is introspective, liberal in outlook, and indifferent to external authority. She rejects religious law, seems to have little use for ceremony and hierarchy, and spurns the stellar powers revered by pagans as having been set at nought with the coming of Christ.

Mary constantly reminds her listeners of the futility of crusades, for the enemy is not outside them but within. The adversaries of the saving truth are really to be found in the listeners themselves, in their passions of fear, ignorance, and anger. She is not interested in the ambitious worldly imperatives of the masculine principle at work in society, with social progress or power structures or religious hegemonies. She is interested in divine rest and bliss for the soul and peaceful cooperation for the social body. These goals, she says, can be realized by identifying the false reasoning of the rulers and understanding that the soul has been freed from its bondage by the gnosis of Messiah Jesus. Mary advises constantly against focusing on the Lord's sufferings on the cross, but instead to emphasize his greatness and his power to bring rest for the soul and peace to the nations. And indeed, it is well known that until the Church's crusades against the "heretic" Cathars, southern France was the home of Jews, Christians, and Sufis living together in harmony.

The benign simplicity of Mary's teachings is the simplicity of those of her Master as well. We learn from her gospel that after his crucifixion and resurrection, Jesus greeted the disciples and said to them:

> "Peace be with you. Receive my peace. Be careful that no one leads you astray by saying, 'Look here' or 'Look there.' The child of humanity is within you. Follow that. Those who seek it will find it . . . Do not lay down any rules other than what I have given you and do not establish law, as the lawgiver did, or you will be bound by it." When he said this he left them.[53]

The child of humanity is the Inner Guide, the intuitional faculty that catches the divine Word descending from a higher level and interprets it to the mind, which transmits it to consciousness. Thus to listen to the child of humanity is to render superfluous the dogmas and rules of an authoritarian priesthood. This passage in the Gospel of Mary constitutes the recessive matriarchal aspect of the Christian religion— yet does it not seem to presage the spiritual mood of our own times? Does it not reflect the impatience of many Western people today with protocol, dogma, and arbitrary religious rules, and highlight their belief in the absolute sovereignty of the spiritual Self?

All the "heretical" motifs contained in the Gospel of Mary are concerned with one thing—the struggle to preserve the feminine principle in an age dominated in the West by a patriarchal ideology seeking to crush it. Picknett and Prince have even postulated that the Templar Order, whose origins in the eleventh century are steeped in mystery, was created as a front for the machinations of a far older subversive organization secretly dedicated to one goal—the preservation of the feminine principle in Christianity.

In fact, the overwhelming evidence uncovered by recent research is that all thought of independent activity on the part of the troubadours, King René, the Templars, and all the other medieval esotericists and their cults should be abandoned. The heretical movements that sprang up all over Europe, uniting the alchemists of Spain, the Cathars of southern France, the Bogamils of Hungary, and the Grail mystics of Germany, had a common basis in a stream that can be traced back to the Gnostics. We are not dealing here with random cultural phenomena but with interwoven facets of one major undertaking designed to further the evolutionary plan for the new age of Pisces. A grand design—one could call it a conspiracy—engineered from above certainly seems to have been involved and to have incorporated the special teaching skills of that charismatic woman Mary Magdalene. Set in train by the Therapeutae at the very beginning of the Hellenic age in Egypt, deliberately it would seem and with a single goal in mind, and carried forward by the Magdalene cult, it was a plan that sought to preserve at all costs the essence of feminine spirituality throughout its coming period of eclipse.

8

TEMPLE CONSPIRACIES AND SECRETS

These things receive into your souls, ye mystae, ye whose ears
are purified, as truly sacred mysteries, and see that ye speak
not of them to any who may be without initiation, but storing
them away in your hearts, guard well your treasure house;
not as a treasury in which gold and silver are laid up, things
that do perish, but as the pick and prize of possessions—the
knowledge of the Cause [of all] and Virtue, and of the third,
the child of both.

PHILO JUDAEUS

Judaism was [Christianity's] father; Egypt was its mother;
Mesopotamia stood as godparent; Hellenism served as midwife.

KARL LUCKERT

I nevitably the question arises: Did the Leontopolis temple play a part in Jesus' story? There is no hard evidence of such a thing, yet there is much indirect support for it. As a Nazarean initiate, Jesus was involved in the broad esoteric movement of reform that covered the whole of the Near East and which arguably had its headquarters in Leontopolis under Zadokite direction. So how could the temple *not* have played its part in the evolution of the Christian Mystery? Far too infrequently Christians have asked themselves: If a king or a Messiah is to ascend his throne, does he not, above all, require the mandate of a legally endorsed organization prepared to validate his claims and to ritually crown him in the presence of its members? How else can royal or messianic aspirations have the slightest authority?

While the Leontopolis priesthood may well have chosen to remain a hidden influence behind events, it cannot possibly have been as uninvolved in Jesus' career as official Christian history has maintained. The Christian scriptures' Letter to the Hebrews, written in Egypt, is saturated with allusions to Jesus' close relationship to the Zadokite priesthood in which he is addressed, like King David before him, as a "high priest forever after the order of Melchizedek" (Hebrews 7:17); and even in the official gospels of the Christian scriptures there is a hint of half-seen activity behind the scenes, of a mysterious presence in high places—perhaps initiates from the Leontopolis temple—that seems to further the development of Jesus' mission.

Throughout the gospels, a shadowy company of rich and influential people seems to move unaccountably on the fringes of the narrative, coming forward briefly, enigmatically, to perform some task of which Jesus' disciples know nothing and vanishing again: the wealthy merchant and Sanhedrin official Joseph of Arimathea, Nicodemus the member of the governing council, the rich Pharisee with whom Jesus dined, the mysterious young man in white who appeared in oracular fashion at Jesus' tomb, and the wealthy group in Bethany who seem to have materially supported him, to name but a few. Taken together, they convey a curiously secretive, even conspiratorial impression and, more, a note of command, of knowledge, that is lacking in the disciples surrounding Jesus. Indeed, one gains the impression from the gospel accounts that most of his followers, with the exception of Mary Magdalene, constitute merely the foot soldiers rather than the high command of a crusade whose spiritual agenda and driving philosophy are hidden from view.

Numerous commentators have noted this phenomenon. In *The Passover Plot,* Hugh Schonfield expresses his view that the Bethany family—Lazarus and his two sisters, Mary and Martha—play a central role in some kind of clandestine group at work behind Jesus and his known followers, constituting his "base of operations."[1] According to Schonfield, the plotters' aim was to ensure that Jesus fulfilled the role of the coming royal Messiah in his public appearances, such as his entry into Jerusalem.

> The ass on which he sat, thus fulfilling the prophecy of Zechariah (John 9:9), had clearly been prearranged, complete with a password in order for it to be handed over—although Jesus' disciples knew nothing about it. (Mark 11:2–7) Then the room for the Last Supper is ready and waiting, although it is the busiest time of the year and Jerusalem is packed to overflowing. Jesus tells his disciples to go into the city and look for a *man* carrying a pitcher of water (who would have stood out like a sore thumb because only women did such menial tasks); again, passwords were to be exchanged, and he would then take them to the upper room.[2]

Such instances of clandestine activity Schonfield and others merely trace back somewhat lamely to the enigmatic "Bethany group," and take the matter no further. Yet in the light of what we now know, a more powerful and authoritative source than anything that appears in the script seems likely. Was there an organized underground in Judaea still loyal to the Leontopolis high priest? Did the Leontopolis temple support John's and Jesus' missions financially? Was the Bethany family originally from Egypt and sent to Palestine to give aid and encouragement to the two prophets—and perhaps to other rebels as well? How many of the upper class in Judaea were secretly in touch with Leontopolis and supporting Jesus? We know from Gaalyah Cornfeld's researches that many of the rich merchants and the aristocratic class, as well as some of the Pharisees, were against the Maccabean takeover from the beginning and would no doubt have been in sympathy with Jesus' aims.

Let us take but one example of this strong possibility: Of the two disciples to whom the risen Christ appeared on the road to Emmaus, one was Cleophas, who lived in that town and was a member of the governing council as well as a relative of Jesus. The two disciples were on their way to the site of the earliest-known literary rebellion against Orthodox Judaism, for it was in Emmaus that a secret Qabalistic school existed and that Rabbi Nahunia wrote his *Book of Illuminations*. In Emmaus the risen Christ ate with his disciples to prove to them his materiality (Luke 24:13). Were the disciples thus directly connected to the new Qabalistic school? The coincidences are surely significant—and may have been included in the gospel for that very reason.

If a covert power struggle were indeed raging in the Jewish world aimed at reinstating the Solomonic Mysteries to the heart of Judaism and the legitimate Davidic king and Zadokite high priest to the Jerusalem temple—then not only must Jesus' role in it be imputed but also the probability of the more distant but powerful influence of the Leontopolis hierarchy. Once again Egypt's hidden role in Jesus' life story forces its way into the foreground, a catalyst for many of the events that prepared the way for Christianity.

Yet, as already said, almost nothing is known about the Leontopolis temple. Its bare mention by Philip Davies in an article entitled "Jerusalem" and included in a 1989 journal brings a shock of surprise. In the article Davies lets drop the information that the temple was built by a high priest Onias and taught Mystery doctrines involving the Divine Couple, so giving us data available hardly anywhere else and confirming other snippets of lamentably scarce information.[3] Clearly, at Leontopolis the Old Religion still reigned. There, Jewish philosophers like Philo would be able to access ancient Hebrew texts and practice sciences of the mind unknown or forgotten in Jerusalem. The prophetic vocation and the spirituality of women would still be equally honored there and the secret wisdom of the Old Religion would still be available to the initiated.

Yet the rabbinic records of the period reveal nothing of this important piece of history, nor of other such momentous data. The spread throughout the Mediterranean world of the Gnostic movement in the wake of Alexander's conquests, and the spiritual awakening it precipitated in Judaism as elsewhere, has been dropped from Jewish history. An impenetrable blanket of censorship has fallen upon the Gnostic crisis in Jerusalem in the final pre-Christian centuries, and the entire Hasidic episode that brought it to a head has been consigned to oblivion.

Furthermore, in the first seven centuries of the Christian Era, a series of pogroms by Romans, Christians, and Muslims were to decimate and eventually burn to the ground the great Alexandrian library whose works might have revealed so much to us. Talmudic scholars, working mainly in Babylon and Syria, were unwilling or unable to repair the historical breach. They are silent on the flight of Onias to Egypt and on the birth of the Hasidim; they have no word to say on the Therapeutae, on Egyptian Judaism, on the Qumran archives by the Dead Sea, or on the Palestinian Essenes and Nazareans—even that they existed—nor do they mention the growing threat of a Hellenic-inspired Judaic revolution that had stemmed from Egypt.

As a consequence, only very recently have scholars awakened to the possibly crucial role the wisdom of Egypt and Egyptian Judaism played in the birth of Christianity. In the twentieth century, a surprisingly large number of writers have broken the silence enshrouding this subject, insisting that in many respects primitive Christianity displayed more affinity with the Mystery religions of Egypt than with the rabbinic Judaism of Jerusalem—the latter based as it was on Persian/Zoroastrian patriarchal principles—but this fact has as yet made little popular impact. The whole topic of intertestamental Egypt is like a riverbed that has been choked with silt for so long that few now remember it was once a cataract of life-giving water. Karl Luckert, who has made a major study of the influence the Egyptian religion has had on later cultures, says:

> Our old Egyptian mother died in the centuries during which her vigorous offspring emerged and began prospering in the Mediterranean world . . . Throughout her life of almost two millennia, this Christian daughter born of Mother Egypt has remained relatively well informed about her ancient Hebrew paternal tradition . . . [but] to this day has not been told about the identity of her deceased mother religion.[4]

The author draws many telling parallels between Egyptian soteri-
ology and the gospels' doctrine of salvation, particularly that of John's
Gospel. Luckert suggests that an intimate knowledge of the mysteries of death and resurrection, associated specifically with the Osiran
rather than the Greek temples, was what aided the success of the
Christian story in the Hellenic world. But other historians have gone
further. The Oxford scholar Desmond Stewart points to the closeness
of the Leontopolis temple to Heliopolis, and remarks that this circumstance would have given the young Jesus, his outlook already molded
by the Zadokite Mysteries in Leontopolis, ready access to the Solar
wisdom of the Heliopolitan priesthood, its doctrines deeply influenc-
ing his own.[5] J. M. Robertson also emphasizes the debt Christianity
owes to paganism:

> Like Christ and like Adonis and Attis, Osiris and Dionysus also
> suffer and rise again. To become one with them is the mystical pas-
> sion of their worshippers. They are alike in that their mysteries give
> immortality. From Mithraism Christ took the symbolic keys of
> heaven and assumes the function of the virgin-born Saoshyant, the
> destroyer of the Evil One . . . In fundamentals, therefore, Christian-
> ity is but paganism reshaped.[6]

We have no reason to suppose that after their altercation with Jeremiah, the expatriate Hebrews of Egypt did not continue to preserve
and honor the very similar Mystery traditions of ancient Israel as they
remembered them. Would they not have commemorated the time
when women's prophetic orders in the old country were as powerful
as Egypt's female Isiac priesthood? And would they not have proudly
declared that legendary Hebrew leaders of valor like Miriam and Deborah, and seers like Huldah the prophetess—all servants of the Great
Goddess, all officiants in the ancient royal courts of Schechem and
Jerusalem—were just as dedicated to the secret rites of the bridechamber and the worship of the Divine Couple as the priestesses and proph-
etesses of Isis?

We know that some of these Hebrew colonists migrated south to Ethiopia, where they established the old Goddess-worshipping Judaic faith in their new homeland, and that many others intermarried with native Egyptians and colonizing Greeks, so further enriching the original Hebrew Mystery strain.[7] New waves of immigrants into the land of the Ptolemies, new ideas, and new religious innovations, especially after the Greek conquest and the arrival of the high priest Zadok from Jerusalem, must have additionally transformed the original Hebrew religion from the simple fertility cult of pastoralists into an Egypto-Judaic world religion of impressive metaphysical and spiritual depth—one that was to grow more virile for its constant fertilization by new influences. Joscelyn Godwin comments that in Alexandria "some Jewish philosophers sought to reconcile their ancestral faith with the wisdom of other peoples,"[8] and refers to the reformed Judaism of Egypt during the Leontopolis years as producing the wonderful Wisdom literature of the late centuries BCE, in which

> the Jewish perspective extends over the whole of humanity, dividing mankind not into Jews and Gentiles but rather into the Wise and the Foolish. The piety of the heart is stressed more than obedience to the Mosaic law, and Jehovah is seen as the Lord over the whole earth who has created and ordered all things visible and invisible.[9]

In similar vein, Valentinus, who was born in Lower Egypt and educated in Alexandria, advised his community that, as the Church of Christ, it shared its wisdom with a universal inner tradition belonging to all mankind and accessible to all Gnostics. In a homily "On Friends," he said:

> Much that is written in the generally available books is found written also in the church of God. That which is common is this: the words which come from the heart, the law which is written in the heart. This is the people of the Beloved, who are loved by him and who love him.[10]

So it would seem that Christianity's Egyptian school led by luminaries like Valentinus followed a type of universal Gnosis taught only in the Judaism of Leontopolis. It has been remarked before in this book that the three-century reign of the Zadokite priesthood in Egypt and the syncretic flowering of Hebraic philosophy and religion in precisely the same locale and time frame cannot be attributed to coincidence. Zadokite influence had become immense. It must be seen as active behind the scenes in the known collaboration of Greek, Egyptian, and Hebraic scholars in the compilation of the Hermetic Mysteries in Alexandria. These Mysteries were an updating of the philosophy implicit in the Bronze Age semi-matriarchal religions, in which the goddess Isis in Egypt and the goddess of the double ax in Crete and Mycenae were the dominant influences on their society (see appendix 2).

It is significant that only the Leontopolis priesthood would have been ready or qualified to participate in such a collaboration across religious boundaries; and equally we must postulate the presence of the Leontopolis priesthood behind the massive work being done in Alexandria by Jewish luminaries like Philo Judaeus in reinstating the Mysteries to the heart of Judaism. Consequently, the hypothesis of a Leontopolis priesthood powerful enough to set in motion a long-standing conspiracy aimed at the birth of a new religious movement is by no means implausible.

There is more than a hint in the gospels of the Christian scriptures that the writers may have known more about the Egyptian temple background of the new faith than they were prepared to divulge. The canonical gospels, as we have seen, are peculiarly opaque and hidden documents written on two levels—that is to say, as Midrashes. The authors were evidently familiar with the symbolic language and hermeneutic techniques of the Mystery temples whereby spiritual meaning was conveyed under cover, so to speak, through concealing allegories, parables, codes, and other literary masking devices. For example, a wedding feast signified the highest initiatory grade, walking on water was the arcane expression for mastery over the emotional sphere, a meal of loaves and fishes had to do with spiritual instruction, and so on. And it is just this kind of codified doublespeak that can be sensed throughout the gospel narratives, particularly in the synoptics. It is therefore eminently possible that the evangelists' silence concerning the life details of the historical Jesus was based not on ignorance but on obedience to the traditional temple policy of strict secrecy, which in the case of Leontopolis seems to have been especially severe.

The Midrashic method of instruction by analogy was a singularly apt one for disseminating a Jewish religious revival in a covert way, for every relevant scriptural passage to which synagogue worshippers were directed reawoke memories in them of the Old Religion, illumined by its reinterpretation and refocusing on Jesus. The books of Isaiah and Zechariah especially, so rich in their evocation of the ancient world of the princes of Israel, would have spoken to the congregation with a new meaning and eloquence about the royal Suffering Servant and his messianic mission, about the Tree of Life and the mystical teachings of the vanished prophets. No better method could have been devised if Judaism's Mystery tradition was to be resurrected. It may well be argued, therefore, that behind the creation of the Gospel narratives, invisibly guiding them, a very skilled conspiratorial hand was at work in the land of Egypt.

Thoroughly Hellenized, Egyptian Judaism flourished for a time at the cutting edge of the most advanced religious, philosophic, and theurgic thought of its period, the very flower of Jewish culture. It is in the Egypto-Judaic schools such as that of the Therapeutae that we find the true cradle of the Qabalah and the creator of Sophia as the biblical Spirit of Wisdom.[11] The language and imagery of the sacred marriage with its poetic emphasis on the love between man and woman infuses the whole of Alexandrian Judaism, distinguishing it sharply from the Levitical Judaism of Jerusalem. In defiance of the latter, in Alexandria the Hebrew Goddess continued to be extolled as "more beautiful than the sun, and above all the order of stars: being compared with light, she is found before it" (Apocrypha: Wisdom 7:29). In her new noetic role, the Cosmic Mother has full authority in the universe as the executive power of the Divine, gifted with the creativity of a supreme craftswoman who gives body to life. She is both the unifying Light from

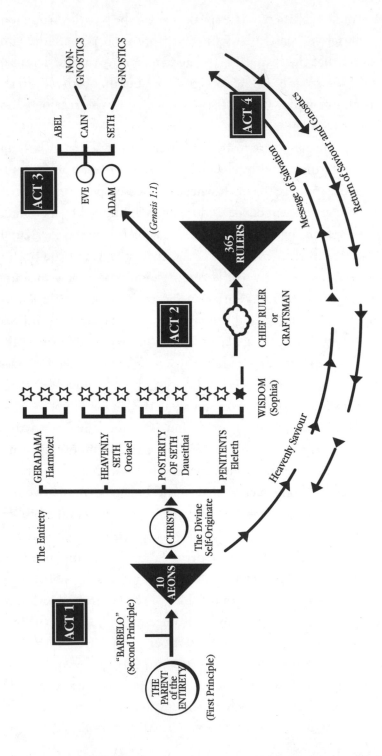

Fig. 10. Gnostic cosmology in the Secret Book According to John

which Creation emerges and the multiple forms that clothe it. And in *Ben Sirach* she sings the wonderful song that begins:

> I came out of the mouth of the Most High, and covered the earth as a cloud. I dwelt in high places, and my throne is in a cloudy pillar. I alone encompassed the circuit of heaven, and walked in the bottom of the deep. I had power over the waves of the sea, and over all the earth and over every people and nation.

Thus does the Goddess metamorphose in Egypt into the Gnostics' Angel of Knowledge. In her Mystery literature she "appears as mother and bride," say Baring and Cashford, "the consort of the father god; the image . . . of light, truth, law, insight, understanding, compassion, and justice."[12] The radical Jewish Wisdom writings,[13] based largely on the vast Wisdom literature of ancient Egypt, Phoenicia, and Mesopotamia, included *Koheleth* (Ecclesiastes), *Ben Sirach* (Ecclesiasticus), *Chokmah* (Wisdom of Solomon), Proverbs, Job, and Enoch, some of these works being compilations of much older Mystery material. And at the same time as the Qabalah was evolving, the Christian Gnostics were weaving the figure of Sophia into their own, very similar cosmology.

The brilliant Egypto-Jewish school had in fact long outshone its sister school in Jerusalem. Evolving over hundreds of years, Egyptian Judaism had acquired a conceptual power that gave it immense authority, and by the first century CE its Wisdom writings and Septuagint Bible, not to mention Qabalistic works on spiritual philosophy, astrology, magic, and proto-alchemy, had won it an international prestige equal to that of the great Greek and Persian Wisdom schools. The genre withered only after the fall of Jerusalem, when the wrath of Rome fell upon every Jewish community in the diaspora, including Alexandria. And after the Judaeo-Egyptian revolt in 117 CE, Jews, expelled in huge numbers from Egypt, became discredited and persecuted citizens of the empire and were for the most part scattered abroad, some migrating as far east as Afghanistan.[14]

"Why," asks Professor Thompson, "is so little now known about the vast yet relatively unexplored field of Egypto-Semitic mysticism, which was still flourishing when the evangelists were writing their gospels?" Today we hear only about rabbinic Judaism, as though no other form of the religion had ever existed, and yet Thompson asserts that Jerusalem's claim to exclusive cult legitimacy and orthodoxy is meaningless, having been created by rabbis only after the destruction of the temple in 70 CE "as a metaphor for a future and heavenly Jerusalem."[15] How, then, did it happen that all other forms of Judaism have been forgotten?

> Why is it that the rabbinic traditions of the Talmud—arguably reflect-ing traditions of the second to the fourth centuries CE—know so little of the immense world of the Jewish Diaspora: a Judaism that was so wholly Hellenized and Greek-speaking? And how was this interna-tional culture—so well reflected in the Septuagint and in many of the pseudepigraphic traditions—eventually lost to the Jewish world?[16]

How indeed? The answer can lie only at the door of the same pall of censorship that eventually lost the Egypto-Judaic mysteries to Christen-dom as well, obliterating all record of Egypt's primary role in the birth of the new world. From the third century on, all references to the Leon-topolis temple and its Hasidic progeny—the Essenes, the Mandaeans, the copious "John" literature, the popular books of Enoch, the Ther-apeutae, the Nazareans and all the rest—were expunged from the Christian annals and all evidence of them "lost," which is to say, prob-ably destroyed or hidden from view in secret archives. A virtual state of amnesia for the whole of the first century in the Near East, the most critical period in Western history, has been the result.

And yet if we read between the lines, there is evidence that long before Jesus' birth the Egyptian Hasidim were clandestinely aiming at the reformation of Judaism under Zadokite leadership. The *Damascus Document* clues us to this possibility. It claims that after the exile of the high priest Zadok, the Judaean sectaries supporting him were fugitive and leaderless in the Hauran for twenty years, and were then joined by the mysterious Teacher of Righteousness (Moreh-Zedek). This Righteous Teacher organized them into a brotherhood of protest called the Sons of Light, which was dedicated to vanquishing the Sons of Darkness under the banner of a New Covenant with God, and was himself martyred in the cause.

Now a study of 1 Maccabees reveals that the appearance of this Teacher of Righteousness in the land of Damascus can possibly be dated to around 175 BCE, in the Time of Wrath, when the Seleucid ruler Antiochus IV Epiphanes came to the throne[17]—in fact, exactly twenty-three years after Onias III had withdrawn to Egypt. It is tempting therefore to speculate that the exiled high priest—the last legitimate high priest of the Jerusalem temple ever to reign there—was none other than the incognito Teacher of Righteousness. This, in fact, is what Professor H. H. Rowley contended in his series of British lectures.[18]

Such a scenario is extremely persuasive. There is, however, an alternative theory, perhaps the most likely of all, provided by Josephus and espoused by Geza Vermes. The Teacher of Righteousness could have been Onias the Righteous—presumably a descendant of the Onias who fled to Egypt in 198 BCE—who, according to the Jewish historian, was stoned to death in 65 BCE, by either the Sadducees or the Pharisees.[19] (Both parties were opposed to Onias and each accused the other of the crime.) In such a case, one can speculate that Onias the Righteous returned to Palestine as the True Teacher at this much later date in order to mobilize his Essene followers, perhaps to attempt a recovery of the high priesthood in Jerusalem, and was then martyred by his enemies as the *Damascus Document* relates. Or perhaps he came as the Moreh-Zedek of the Last Days, a long prophesied office later imputed to both John the Baptist and Jesus by their respective followers.

Whatever version we favor, we are led inevitably to the conclusion that conspiratorial activity from Leontopolis, aimed at deposing Jerusalem's upstart rulers and reinstating the legitimate line, may well have been a longstanding point of conflict between Egypt and Judaea. And our search for conspirators in the birth of Christianity can be taken even further, for behind the succession of Leontopolis high priests stood the Order of Melchizedek from which they were drawn, a secretive and shadowy Righteousness brotherhood that spanned the generations and the centuries. Was this Righteousness Order the real prime mover at the heart of events, masterminding the entire affair from an impregnable position of command?

Andrew Welburn, who cites the Testament of Levi (one of the set of Testaments of the Twelve Patriarchs), speculates that the Melchizedek Order was of critical sacerdotal significance in Jerusalem, for in order to legitimize themselves as Zadokite high priests, the Maccabees would have had to invoke the hieratic figure of Melchizedek in their borrowed initiation rites. By this action they were officially confirming the existence of a secret Order to whose Solar lineage they hoped to belong. Receiving the insignia of royalty, they endowed themselves in this manner with a Zadokite legitimacy to which they had no right whatsoever.[20] So why do we know nothing about this all-important Melchizedek brotherhood, which apparently figured in Israel's pagan past long before Abraham was initiated into it? Although, as we see, on occasion the name of the priest-king Melchizedek crops up with a mysterious resonance in the Hebrew scriptures, the Righteousness fraternity that Melchizedek fronts ranks to the present day as one of the best-kept secrets in Jewish history. Why? What is being concealed?

To begin with, Z'ev ben Shimon Halevi writes in *The Kabbalah: The Tradition of Hidden Knowledge* that Melchizedek initiated Abraham into the knowledge of the esoteric tradition concerning man, the universe, and God—that is, into the esoteric principles of the Old Religion.[21] This fact on its own would have been abhorrent to the Jerusalem hierarchy.[22] But further, the Righteousness Order of Melchizedek was at odds with Jewish nationalist aspirations, for it was a foreign fraternity whose influence, associated in the book of Genesis with only biblical Canaan and the Jebusite people, actually spread far beyond Palestine and was still internationally powerful in the time of Jesus. Indeed, some of today's cognoscenti say the Order still exists.

The British author Tim Wallace-Murphy, in his official history of the Knights Templar, cites reliable esoteric sources in stating that the Order of Melchizedek was active in pre-Christian times in Asia Minor, where it fathered the Celtic fraternity known as the Kibeiri of Galatia, themselves "precursors of many esoteric groups in biblical Judaism such as the Zadokites, Essenes, and Therapeutae."[23] We might add that since the Celts were also to be found in Gaul and Britain at that time, it is probable that the Melchizedek Order was active in those lands as well, quite possibly with links to the British Druids.

All this points to an organization of great antiquity and influence in religious affairs with branches in many countries and through many epochs. Superior to any local cult or priesthood and steeped in the wisdom of the primordial Gnosis, the Melchizedek brotherhood would have been eminently capable of masterminding from behind the scenes the evolution of a new religious movement emanating from Leontopolis. Here René Guénon, a metaphysician who has been called our most accurate interpreter of esoteric doctrine, contributes a key piece to the puzzle.

In *The Lord of the World,* he asserts that Melchizedek is in effect a code name the Hebrew and Christian scriptures use throughout to designate an international brotherhood of adepts whose secret headquarters, even to the present time, lie in the mountains of central Asia.[24] This brotherhood, Guénon says, was behind the Sons of the Sun or Sons of Heaven who from the third millennium onward spread a network of Solar temples around the globe. This same mysterious hierarchy also lay behind the Solar religion of the Shang dynasty in China and the religion of the Egyptian kings who, as Sons of the Sun, were closely affiliated to the Order. Guénon furthermore states that in the Letter to the Hebrews the author, Apollos of Alexandria, was correct in claiming that the Jewish priesthood as well was associated with the Melchizedek Order.[25] Apollos argues that because perfection is not attainable under the Levitical priesthood, it has been necessary for Jesus, even though he "belonged to a tribe [of Judah] from which no one has ever served at the altar," to be given the office of a Zadokite high priest.

We have this as a sure and steadfast anchor of the soul, a hope that enters into the inner shrine behind the curtain, where Jesus has gone as a forerunner on our behalf, having become a high priest forever . . . For the Lord has sworn and will not change his mind, "Thou art a priest forever, after the order of Melchizedek." (Hebrews 6:20, 7:21)

Guénon reiterates what so many other occultists assert, that it is not only Satan who walks the earth observing all that men do; so also do the Adepti. A vast hinterland of activity lies unseen behind the world we know, a landscape as broad as the planet across which bands of initiated culture bearers have always moved freely, crossing all racial, religious, and national boundaries, observing, exchanging knowledge, seeding new religious and cultural impulses wherever they are needed. All institutional religions are in this sense heterodox, including Christianity. All have been generated and fed from within by unseen syncretic currents that flow out from the inner brotherhoods in obedience to great cosmic events. Thus the British author Trevor Ravenscroft states:

> There are in fact two separate streams of history running parallel to one another. One stream is outwardly visible; the other is hidden to all eyes but those of the initiated. Only the first stream is commonly known as "history," but hidden behind it at all times is the other stream, which continually guides it and shapes it further.[26]

There are good grounds for speculating that for perhaps a hundred years or more the Leontopolis temple, under directions from above, maintained an organized opposition to the ruling clique in Jerusalem. In such a scenario the preparations for a new Christ Mystery, a new messianic initiative for the Piscean age, may have figured centrally, possibly maturing over a number of generations. In that ultimately successful work, Jesus' mission would play a key role.

EGYPTIAN JUDAISM AND THE HERMETICA

The Zadokite hierarchy, then, may have been preparing the ground for a great religious revival almost since its arrival in Egypt. Philo's mystical writings, which were already exploring the new psychonoetic *Word* principle, bring us only subterranean echoes of the tumult of independent creativity that must have been going on in the Alexandrian synagogues and Jewish philosophical schools for the two hundred or so years prior to the Christian Era, rendering the avant-garde Egypto-Jewish culture and dynamic religious outlook in some respects almost diametrically opposed to that of the Jerusalem cult.

> With the Greek language and customs came, of course, Greek thought. Some of the [Jewish] communities tolerated mixed marriages; some of their members, joining gymnasiums, exercised naked, like Greeks . . . Some even neglected circumcision . . . There were even Jews who participated in Hellenistic cults . . . Yahweh himself had received a Greek name, *Theos Hypsistos,* God the Highest—a name later used even by Philo.[27]

Magical seals of the period show, moreover, that some Jews identified Yahweh with the Anguipede, or Snake-footed God, or with the Greek god Helios or the old Egyptian god Anubis; others with the god Harpocrates, a late Egyptian form of the child Horus.[28] At the same time, a strong Hindu-Buddhist influence entered the Hellenic-Levantine world with the Buddhist missions sent to Egypt, Syria, Cyrene, and Macedonia by King Ashoka of India (r. 268–232 BCE). Simultaneously throughout the region the Hellenistic concept of humanity as an abstract totality, an entity that transcended all racial, sectarian, and national forms, came to full flower. As a consequence, Alexandria became a melting pot of cults, the site of a massive cross-fertilization of religions that were able to flourish in a climate of unparalleled creativity and transcultural commerce.

The city of Alexandria was built on the Nile Delta in 323 BCE by Alexander the Great, the Macedonian king who had been tutored by Aristotle and had acquired from that philosopher privileged access to a great deal of the secret knowledge of the Greek Mystery temples.[29] From the beginning, Alexandria reflected the spiritual aspirations and unusually deep learning of its founder and was to achieve a singular destiny. The Templars' dream of a universal religion led by Jewish Qabalists, Christian mystics, and Muslim Sufis first came into germinal existence in Alexander's great Delta port. Scholars of all races and ideologies were lured to the city by generous subsidies and the tax-free offer of free books, free lodgings, free food, and servants, and were in effect treated as honored guests. Soon competing schools, seminaries, ashrams, and gymnasia were established and flourished in the company of missionaries of most of the world religions.[30] All were welcomed. All were encouraged to ply their particular ideology without political interference and to gather together in a climate of friendly cooperation. It was to be a brief religious golden age.

At the heart of what soon became a thriving crucible of different cultures, the vast body of mystical, magical, and alchemical literature called the Hermetica was produced. It was a compendium of philosophical and magical treatises on occult topics of every kind. These ranged from astral magic or astrology, magical talismans, knowledge of the secret virtues of stones and plants to learned expositions on the meaning of the world and humanity.[31] Written in Alexandria, the Hermetica purported to be the work of Hermes Trismegistus, a priestly Egyptian sage who had lived long ago, but was in fact a skillful syncretic construct, a monument to the universalist vision of the Old Religion of the Bronze Age.

The Hermetica was a gentle and tolerant teaching, laying little stress on sin but a great deal on the Gnosis as the means of salvation. This essentially gnosticizing trend lay at the very heart of the ancient Egyptian religion, which, polytheistic though it was, had never forgotten the Supreme One, sovereign over all the gods. Indeed Karl Luckert denies that Egyptian religion was polytheistic; he speaks of Heliopolitan process theology as basically monotheistic, and the doctrines about the premier Egyptian god, the hidden Amun, as the root of all later monotheism.[32] Tracing Amun's seminal likeness to Yahweh, Luckert quotes from the Leiden Papyrus (ca. fourteenth century BCE) from the Heliopolitan archives:

Amun is one! He who hides himself from the gods . . . whose nature is unknown. His nature is not recorded in sacred scriptures; he cannot be described and taught. He is too mysterious for his power to be laid bare; he is too great to be even asked about, too immense to be perceived . . . Not even a god can call him by his name, the vital one, because his name is secret. (p. 73)

We have here a telling evocation of the invisible, nameless, incomprehensible Power worshipped by Simon Magus and the other Qabalists and Gnostics—and by the ancient line of Zadokites stationed in Leontopolis. It was precisely this same unifying trend, expressive of the mystical totality of the universe, that distinguished the first Christian teachings. Indeed the presence of Hermetic thought in Jesus' sayings is undeniable. Welburn cites the pagan Hermetic Mysteries as having had a strong influence on the beginnings of Christianity, achieving at that time

an extensive literary expression . . . [and] moving radically away from rites and sacrifices like those of the temples. It demanded a "spiritual sacrifice" and a "baptism in mind." For the root problem of man was diagnosed in inner, psychological terms rather than by pointing to his position in the world: man was as if drunk, unaware, in a stupor as regards his higher self.[33]

So also, as we have seen, Jesus speaks of the drunken state of the world in the Gospel of Thomas and humanity as lacking thirst for higher knowledge. This gospel indicates how great the influence of Hermeticism was on early Christianity, so much so that the ancient prophet Hermes, "originally the Egyptian god of wisdom, Thoth, was later honored by some Christians as a forerunner of Christ."[34] The Hermetic stress on union of the polarities was to have a profound influence on the Mithraic teachings as well as those of Jesus, and in both cases gave to the bridechamber sacrament, the very centerpiece of the Leontopolis cult, a preeminent place in their mysteries.

To gauge the importance given to the Christian sacrament of the bridechamber and its intimate relation to spiritual rebirth, we need do no more than note that in the Gospel of Philip there are as many as thirteen sayings attributed to Jesus that refer to it. Stephan Hoeller regards the mystery of the bridechamber as "the decisive event in the reunion of the divisions of the human being," the transformation into indivisible unity being the Hermetic goal toward which the whole sacramental progression tends.[35] That unity was ruptured when the personality became partly dissociated from the higher or Angel Self in the course of its earthly evolution, but the marriage of the two in the spiritual bridechamber returns the perfected one to his or her primordial state of wholeness. This process of divorce and remarriage of the autonomous parts of the whole being is symbolized by the separation of the sexes in the story of the Garden of Eden. The Gospel of Philip tells us that

> if the female had not separated from the male, she and the male would not die. That being's separation became the source of death. The anointed Christ came to rectify the separation that had been present since the beginning and join the two components; and to give life unto those who had died by separation and join them together. Now, a woman joins with her husband in the bridal bedroom, and those who have joined in the bridal bedroom will not reseparate. Thus Eve became separate from Adam because it was not in the bridal bedroom that she joined with him. (Philip 70)

This gospel further suggests that as below, so above: the earthly bridal ceremony symbolically mirrors the heavenly nuptials.

> Is it permitted to even speak of this mystery? The parents of the entirety joined with the virgin who came down, and a fire illuminated him on that day. He revealed the great bridechamber; it was for this purpose his body came into being. On that day he came forth from the bridal bedroom as from what comes to pass between a bridegroom and a bride. (Philip 73)

Just so, the text adds, "did Jesus establish everything through these mysteries."

"The transcendental bridechamber," says Hoeller, "thus is said to have united God the Father with God the Mother (the Holy Spirit), and Jesus has replicated this divine example for the benefit of divided humanity."[36] In this and numerous other examples, we see how deeply Hermetic was Jesus' thought, both in its stress on achieving the transcendence of the opposites and in the absence of the obsession with evil (especially sexual evil) that has been so peculiarly the preoccupation of the Roman Church.

We have no hard evidence that Jesus was actually initiated into the Hermetic Mysteries or indeed any other of the Egyptian cults, or even that he visited the Leontopolis temple as an adult. The latter is certainly probable; yet even if he did not, he was a Hasid and a reflection of his era. In any meaningful study of his life, it is impossible to exclude the cultural and philosophic influences that impinged on him, the great currents of thought that shaped his society and historical period. In Jesus' lifetime the brilliant new Hermetic-Qabalistic culture wave from Alexandria was flooding Palestine and impregnating all the Hasidic groups—Essenes, Sons of Zadok, Nazareans, Ebionites—and it is only in this context that we can fully understand the esoteric thrust of Jesus' teachings.

Even some of the best-known examples of Christian iconography owe their existence to old Egypt. For example, in the sixteenth century Giordano Bruno, the former friar and itinerant missionary for Hermeticism, claimed that the Christian symbol of the cross owed its origins not to the crucifixion of Christ but to the ancient *crux ansata* or *ankh* of the Egyptians, and that the same sign adorned the breast of the Egyptian god Serapis.[37] Again, in the Seti I temple at Abydos there are carvings on the granite walls of two examples of Christianity's most primitive icons, the fish and the equal-armed cross, the cross having the splayed arms later adopted by the Knights Templar. Esoteric sources attribute both these carvings to Copt priests living hundreds of years before the birth of Christ.[38] Karl Luckert believes that the Coptic priesthood, faithful remnant of old Egypt, passed on much of its wisdom to the new Christian movement.

Was the Leontopolis temple the conduit, via the Coptic priesthood, for passing on to its Hasidic groups the vast learning of old Egypt? This question brings us once again to the Therapeutae, who were almost certainly a part of the Leontopolis sphere of influence. The wide scholarship and ardor for truth imputed to the Therapeutae and their ready approach to spiritual traditions other than the Judaic indicates that they had behind them the wisdom and expertise of the Zadokite priesthood in Leontopolis. What evidence is there for this?

In his essay on the Therapeutae, Philo comments that the Lake Mareotis contemplatives were in cultic service to "the Temple." This Temple he mentions is generally assumed to refer to the one in Jerusalem, but Philo doesn't say so. He is, as ever, close lipped on the issue, probably for political reasons. But why would a Hasidic order that teaches all the seditious socio-religious ideals and practices of the Essenes give its allegiance to a temple that persecutes it and to which it has sworn enmity? Why would its members not serve at the altar of a consecrated Jewish temple both close at hand, only a short distance down a Nile tributary, and dedicated to its own passionately held beliefs? Are we being misled by hundreds of years of brainwashing—not only by rabbis but by Christian fathers as well? Philo cannot be referring to any temple other than the one in Leontopolis.

Many of Jesus' sayings are hard to fathom without understanding their background in the esoteric wisdom of the Old Religion preserved in this Judaic-Egyptian temple on the Nile, and in this respect Philo's disclosures are thought-provoking. But it is the indisputable influence of the Therapeutae themselves on Jesus' thought that most clearly evokes the hidden presence of the Leontopolis School. Jesus' compassionate philosophy and worldview, Luckert asserts, "was to be closer to that of the Therapeutae than to any other contemporary group of whom we know,"[39] for compassion, the clemency of the open heart, was to be the leitmotif of everything the Therapeutae labored to teach and practice throughout their existence. Their new covenant with God was designed to be a social reformation founded on the uniting force of compassion in every dimension, politico-social, spiritual, and cultural. Esoteric tradition has always associated them with Jesus, who expressed a comparable ideal to the highest degree in his own person and teachings.

Josephus likened the Therapeutae, and Essenes in general, to the Pythagoreans, a semireligious Greek order of mathematicians and philosophers who were strongly influenced by the wisdom of the Egyptian temples and founded their own order in 520 BCE. The Therapeutae were noted for similar arcane practices and for their deep study of Angelology.[40] The most beautiful and mystical Wisdom literature in Jewish history, as well as Hermetic-Qabalistic doctrines and practices, secret writings on the calendar and sacred numbers, and apocalypses, are also attributed to the Lake Mareotis community.[41]

Reputed to be the spiritual power center of the Jewish world in exile, the Therapeutae's radical influence radiated out from Lake Mareotis into the most diverse religious and philosophical streams. They were famous for their love of individual freedom of conscience, repudiation of priestly authority, and toleration of diversity of thought and worship at a time when such things were almost unknown.[42] These libertarian principles were to be echoed in the Jesus movement. Thus the Therapeutaean belief in assemblies based on free association among equals formed the model for the egalitarian Christian monastic tradition that was to spring up in the Egyptian deserts in later centuries. The Therapeutae interpreted the Mosaic laws allegorically rather than literally, and worshipped a universal God of all races without ethnic distinction, as did Christianity. Joscelyn Godwin writes:

> Some [Egyptian Jews] . . . questioned the fundamentalist attitude to the Pentateuch (the first five books of the Bible) and began to interpret them allegorically . . .[43] They stressed the universal rather than the exclusive character of Jewish wisdom, claiming that it is found in every land and every people, and that its vision of a divine Unity underlying the multiplicity of phenomena was beyond race or creed.[44]

In Egypt, then, a mystical Judaism was evolving that owed much to the studies of the Therapeutae, later to be reflected in the Jesus movement and almost certainly stemming from Leontopolis.

THE THERAPEUTAE AND
THE NEW COVENANT

The number of "firsts" in the list of the Therapeutaean innovations is truly remarkable. The Therapeutae were first, as we have seen, to permit an equal participation of the sexes in sacred contexts such as communal liturgy and worship. The Nag Hammadi texts reveal that the Gnostic Christians continued this practice of gender equality in their own congregations for several centuries, women being known to lead, teach, and prophesy with as much authority as men.[45]

The Therapeutae were also the first to bring to the fore the Solar theme that runs through mystical Judaism, Christianity, and Islam. It is from the Therapeutae, so Hugh Schonfield believes, that Jesus may have acquired much of the Solar Mystery wisdom of which the high priest Zadok was traditionally the guardian, and which led through Gnostic Christianity to the secret societies of medieval Europe. According to this author, after the dispersal of the Jews from Alexandria, the Therapeutae regrouped in the Middle East, affiliating with gnostic Christian schools like the Nestorians and later with the Islamic Sufis and carrying on their esoteric work in Mosul, Basra, and Harran.

> The influence of the Essenes of Egypt, known in the first century as Therapeuts, was particularly strong. Philo of Alexandria learned much from them. The Rosicrucians could look back to an Essene impetus from Egypt relating to arcane matters associated with the Sun King and Master of Wisdom King Solomon, who had created the Temple in conjunction with the Master Asaph ben Berechiah. And these things were the foundation of Freemasonry.[46]

And further quoting a French work published in Paris in 1815, Schon-

field says in *The Essene Odyssey* that during the period of the Therapeutae in Egypt, "the Essenes and other Jews founded a School of
Solomonic Wisdom, which later reunited with Ormus."[47] (According to
certain Freemasonic sources, many of the Essenes belonged to a Judaeo-
Egyptian cult called the Brothers of Ormus, one of whom was converted to Christianity by St. Mark and founded a Rosicrucian Brothers
of the East.)[48] Later still, the society divided into a number of orders
known as the Conservers of the Hermetic Secrets, the Mosaic Secrets,
etc., destined to illuminate Hermetic and Christian Gnosticism as well
as the Islamic mysticism of Sufism in later centuries.[49] Consequently,
the Therapeutae were a strong fertilizing influence not only on expatriate Judaism generally and on the future Sufi brotherhoods, but also on
the origins of Christianity as a system with marked Solar overtones.

The Solar station on the Qabalistic Tree is Tiphareth, the sephirah of beauty known too as the Seal of Solomon, and in Christian
Qabalah, Tiphareth also represents the sacrificial Christ station. "It is
in Tiphareth," says Dion Fortune, "that we find the archetypal ideas
which form the invisible framework of the whole of manifested creation."[50] Above Tiphareth, across an abyss or void, lies the supreme
world of the Spirit, which is as yet barely accessible to us, while below
Tiphareth lie the lower worlds across a veil called *parakheth,* the ana-
logue of the abyss above. And so as Christ is esoterically equated with
the Sun, he stands at Tiphareth as the very heart and soul of the sephirothic system, the point of convergence of all its paths and the bridge
from the mundane worlds below to the divine world above. He is the
mediating intelligence: Adam Kadmon, Archetypal Man. As Dion
Fortune says:

> The Messiahs and Saviours of the world are assigned to Tiphareth
> in the symbolism of the Tree, for they were the Light-bringers to
> humanity, and as all who bring fire from heaven must do, they died
> the sacrificial death for the sake of humankind. It is here, too, that
> we die to the lower self in order that we may rise in the higher self.
> "In Jesu morimur."[51]

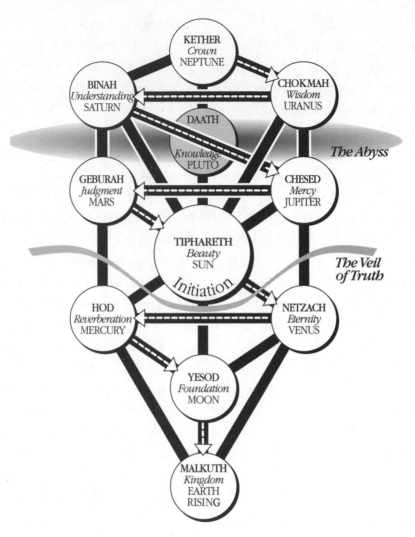

Fig. 11. The Christ station at Tiphareth

There were two areas in the Lake Mareotis philosophy that were pivotal to early Christianity as taught by Jesus, yet neither was to be retained by the church fathers. One was the Egypto-Judaic New Covenant, the engine that drove the entire Hasidic movement of social reform. Anathema to the Jerusalem cult, the New Covenant overturned, as we have seen, the Jewish caste-dominated purity laws and the inequity between classes and races. Consequently, the Therapeutae were universally admired and respected, as were the first Christians, "for the impartial passion of their love for mankind," which infused all their dealings, not only within their own brotherhood but also in their relationship with the anti-Semitic Romans. Philo says of the Therapeutae,

> They maintain a fraternal equality, believing that human brotherhood is the natural relationship of men, which has only been destroyed in society by the competition of the covetous.[52]

Both Philo and Josephus stress the fact that, although of Jewish birth and free born, these Egyptian Hasidim did not come together on a basis of race, "for one does not speak of race when it is a question of voluntary acts."[53] Rather, says Philo, they have been brought together as a brotherhood "by their zeal for virtue."[54] When we consider the kind of social ideals implicit in the New Covenant—universal brotherhood, freedom of conscience, equitable distribution of wealth, peace, and liberty for all—it is obvious that it could not have derived from the Jerusalem school, with its elitist and warlike history. The Zadokite school in Leontopolis, the very hub of the Hasidic phenomenon, is the only possible inspiration behind the Therapeutaean social reforms mirrored in those of Jesus. One wonders whether the Covenantal reforms were not the basis for Paul's mandate to preach Christ to the Gentiles of all nations in defiance of Jerusalem racism, and perhaps also for his quarrel with the rest of the apostles, more conservative than he on matters of race, for it has been largely forgotten that early Christians were also New Covenanters, the Christian New Testament being but another name for the New Covenant.

In the Gospel of Mark 14:23–24 as contained in the Revised Standard Version of the Bible, the narrative describing the Last Supper of Jesus and his disciples goes thus:

> And he [Jesus] took a cup, and when he had given thanks he gave it to them, and they all drank of it. And he said to them, "This is my blood of the Covenant, which is poured out for many."

But in the Authorized King James Version, "covenant" has been translated as "new testament." "New Covenant," says a biblical authority, "was a better word to translate the Aramaic word which Christians later translated as 'New Testament.' "[55] Thus it becomes clear that Jesus passed on to his disciples, and they to their early Christian followers, the social ethic embodied in the Therapeutae's New Covenant, an ethic that became central to all Egypto-Judaic teachings.

A new world religion invariably comes with the blueprint of a new civilization, a new social charter that will support its teachings in practice. And so it was with Christianity. The New Covenant first instigated by the Therapeutae incorporated principles of liberty, fraternity, and equality that were essentially an extension of the Hermetic ideals at its core: "as in heaven, so on earth." The essence of the program was the formulation of a new social morality central to all the Nazarean and Mandaean communities, to early Christianity, and to the Palestinian Essenes—in fact in some degree to every one of the Hasidic branches. However, soon rejected by the Christian mainstream, it achieved the fame it deserved only many centuries later, when it was adopted by the Freemasons under the banner of liberty, fraternity, and equality and became the slogan of the French Revolution. The rapid abandonment of these principles is perhaps Christianity's greatest betrayal of Jesus' teachings, leading to centuries of serfdom and oppression for the common people.

The new social principles being practiced during Jesus' lifetime and espoused by him must have been an explosive, bitterly argued political issue in Jerusalem, a challenge to the entrenched hubris of the Roman ruling machine as well as its powerful Herodian lackeys, for it was a critique of the greed of the wealthy class and a call for the rights and freedoms of an enslaved peasantry. Furthermore, at least one contemporary writer has seen in this revolutionary movement a threat to the xenophobic elements in Orthodox Judaism. Faced by such a frontal assault on the basis of their political power, it is not surprising that the Jerusalem authorities evinced fear and antagonism toward all things Egyptian, or that the subversive ideas circulating among Jesus' disciples were downplayed by the gospel writers as politically dangerous material too seditious to publish.

The libertarian thrust of the New Covenant may well have been the basis also for the tension that seems to have existed within Jesus' family—a tension hinted at in the gospels as causing a rift between Jesus and his mother and siblings that was not healed until after his death (John 2:1–4, Matthew 12:46–50).[56] It is significant that thereafter the new dynastic Church of the Circumcision in Jerusalem, headed by Jesus' family members, was largely to abandon the more radical features of the New Covenant, returning to the traditional social and cultural mores of the past. Given the subversive nature of his social agenda, it is hardly surprising that Jesus was executed so summarily as an occult teacher from Egypt, or that the Jesus movement that burgeoned after his death was seen in Judaea as creating turmoil and mayhem until ejected from the synagogues. Even the Romans sensed in Egyptian Judaism a threat to all established power structures, especially their own, and in 115–117 CE, they were quick to lay waste the Alexandrian Jewish community.

Nonetheless, in the repudiation of an old order of things, in rejecting social structures and norms central to the pagan culture of the day but now outworn or malign, the early Christian movement would find a powerful formula for world success. By moving into the current of social evolution and pressing forward to meet the more egalitarian civilizations of the future, it could not have failed to take history by storm. True, its seed idea, framed in the now famous ideals of liberty, equality, and fraternity, could not flourish for long in a violent, caste-dominated civilization so utterly hostile to it, nor hope to overcome the antipathy of a Church increasingly wedded to inordinate power and wealth. But the embryo would lie underground and survive for centuries in the hidden occult schools of Christianized Europe, germinate in the Italian Renaissance and the French Revolution, grow mightily in the struggles of the Industrial Age, and come into its own in Freemasonry and the birth of American democracy, flowering finally in a trend toward global democratization.

Whether the source of this great energizing social current set in motion by Christianity lay ultimately in the Leontopolis temple can be contested, but the same cannot be said of the spiritual science that secretly informed it. The merkavah science and the Light technology it implied—the second of Jesus' great evolutionary contributions—were rejected by the church fathers, but their transmission could have been authorized only by their official Hebrew guardians, the Zadokite high priests in Leontopolis. The part these Judaic prophets must therefore have played in the birth of the Christ Mystery has never been recognized, but in the last few decades a groundswell of religious research has begun that it is hoped will shed greater light on the issue.

Consider how the full Buddhist canon was given out to the world in three consecutive stages hundreds of years apart (in the Hinayana, Mahayana, and Vajrayana vehicles), each one of which was a flowering and deepening of the one before but at the same time a radically new revelation. The same principle of unfoldment in three revelatory stages may equally apply to Christianity. If we think of the three phases as roughly equivalent to the principles of body, soul, and spirit that animate every human being, then the first primitive stage of Christianity was an exoteric one, sacramental and cultic, while the second and more esoteric stage that emerged a thousand years later may be seen as a flowering of the mystical principle of *soul* inherent in the Grail legends, in Catharism and the Rosicrucian enlightenment of the late Renaissance. What then of the third age, the age of *spirit*?

Today, at the opening of the third millennium, some scholars are spearheading the proposition that a spiritual yoga lies at the heart of Christianity, an invisible dynamic only now emerging as the original essence of the religion.[57] The new interest in Eastern philosophies has brought us resurrected Vedantic yogas from ancient India as well as books on kundalini and the suprasensible *siddhis,* such as Gopi Krisna's groundbreaking memoirs in 1972. These acquainted us with the hitherto little-known science involving the human spinal-cerebral energy system and its chakras. And Arthur Avalon's *Serpent Power* appeared even earlier.[58] By the seventies, extensive literature on the subject was pouring into the public domain and a number of schools of Kundalini yoga, once strictly secret, had appeared. This very new and controversial insight into the occult world was made possible only in the twentieth century, when the principles of tantric yoga were opened up to the West for the first time. It is suggested here that, in a radically revised form, the merkavah science is the Gnostic seed that Jesus planted two thousand years ago and which may yet germinate as the third stage in Christianity's evolution.

If the apocryphal scriptures have anything at all to tell us, it is that in parallel with his work among the poor and disenfranchised, Jesus was disseminating doctrines of an esoteric nature to his inner circle and that these teachings were drawn from the ancient science of spiritual Power taught only in Mystery temples like the Judaic one on the Nile tributary. True, Christianity was not the only new spiritual movement demonstrating an unprecedented access to specialized yogic knowledge; so were the other Mystery cults appearing across the Mediterranean world at that time. But all these movements remained hermetically closed and backward-looking; the Christian movement was the only one that sought to overturn the embargo of millennia by opening the reserved knowledge and practices of the temples up to the common people, but by means of a reformed method appropriate to the new age. For that to happen—for the new Gnosis of the heart to be given out—the active approval and participation of the Zadokite hierarchy was essential: The Leontopolis temple *must* have been implicated.

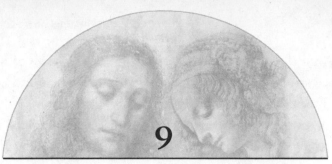

9

THE GNOSIS OF
THE HEART

*"Listen," said Krishna, "to a very great and deep secret, to the
sovereign, sublime and pure mystery. In order to reach perfection it
is necessary to acquire knowledge of oneness, which is above wisdom;
it is necessary to lift oneself to the divine Being who is above the soul
and even above intelligence. Now this divine being, this sublime
friend, is in each one of us. For God dwells within every man, but
few know how to find him. And this is the way to salvation."*

THE BHAGAVAD GITA

Jesus' mission was aimed at more than the restoration of the Judaic
Mysteries to the Jerusalem temple. The wider aim was to bring
them into the public domain, to "rend the veil" of the Holy of Holies
and to bring spiritual knowledge into the world at large, to offer a new
path of initiation that would be open to all. The key to his innovatory
teachings, their central motif and driving power, was his new Way of
the Spiritual Heart, an initiation that was to be potentially available to
every man and woman who aspired to it.

There is evidence that besides the initial baptism ceremony in
water, Jesus offered a further initiation in a secret form of fire baptism
administered to those of his followers who were ready for it.[1] Read in
this light, there is symbolic meaning in much of the gospel narratives
that otherwise remains inexplicable. The John Gospel in particular

278

with its wonderful Light terminology reveals layer upon layer of hidden meanings open to the Mystery initiate but to none other, hinting at sciences and esoteric practices that were unfamiliar to the world at large.

As already mentioned, preeminent among these advanced sciences was that of the spinal system of energies in the human body, involving various occult techniques for the holotropic transformation of consciousness. The existence in antiquity of such a science of spiritual physiology is amply confirmed by the painted temple murals in Egypt that depict the serpent power—that is, kundalini Shakti—emerging from the brows of ancient initiate kings. As well, there are scenes of enigmatic funeral ceremonies in which priests are facilitating the royal ascent to higher worlds by the application of curious implements to the king's spinal cord. Royal adepts due for death had their consciousness thereby raised to the realms of Light even while they received deep instruction

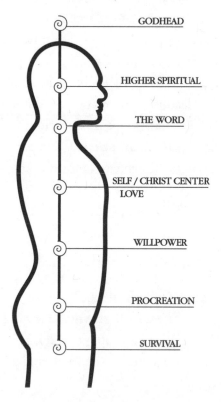

Fig. 12. The spinal energy system

in spiritual knowledge, and could then become healers, Light-bringers, and bestowers of prosperity to their people from their vantage point in the heavens.

While there is no evidence that the Levitical priesthood in Jerusalem had any real knowledge of this science, it is certain that the Leontopolis temple did. Continuing in the Hebrew Mystery tradition exported by the high priest Zadok, the temple would undoubtedly have preserved teachings in which the Zadokite Light wisdom survived in a concentrated form. Karl Luckert notes that the Light theme runs through all the Mediterranean mysteries back to the ancient Coffin texts of Egypt, and believes these highly esoteric texts "will enable us to revise our historical understanding of Hellenic philosophy, of Neoplatonism, and of the *Origins of Christendom and Gnosticism.*"[2] He bases his claim on the frank belief that "the Kingdom of Heaven movement . . . founded by John the Baptizer and Jesus of Nazareth" employed these same yogic techniques lifted from the Mystery temples and adapted them for more general use.

Morton Smith takes Luckert's proposition further. He believes the Light texts throw into relief one of the most important topics in the Christian scriptures, the source of Jesus' healing and miracle-working energy, and that they lead us to a greater understanding of the secrecy that permeates the Christian scriptures on the whole subject of spiritual physiology and its attendant science.[3] We shall see that the new mystical Way Jesus taught, which gave a unique character to Christianity, can be understood in no other way than in terms of the merkavah science taught secretly in the temples, and that it was this circumstance that was to arouse extreme antagonism in certain quarters. History has revealed again and again that when an uninformed folk culture is injected with shamanic and occult elements intrinsically foreign to it, the operation is fraught with difficulties; all too often the foreign strain is rejected, frequently with violence. So it was in Jesus' time. Two hundred years later the Persian prophet Mani, who was also to teach the new Way as "the Apostle of Christ," suffered a fate similar to that of Jesus: He was flayed alive.

Prior to the turn of the Common Era, the temples were still tiny islands of learning in a vast sea of popular ignorance illumined only by the dim verities of myth and legend. Ordinary people had no conception of the erudition that obtained in their sacred centers, nor any inkling of the powers unleashed by spiritual sciences such as that of the Chariot. Nor would their level of education have provided them with an adequate platform for understanding such things. For them the temples were indeed "mysteries" carrying the awful potency of taboo. As one commentator has observed, these citadels of supernatural power that stood like isolated lighthouses across a darkened world

> were very much aimed at the future development of mankind. Faculties such as abstract thinking were practiced there, long before they became the common property of the culture: mathematics, astronomy, and medicine were all practiced in what was for that time a future form . . . At the height of the Greek era, the mysteries were still flourishing. All the great philosophers were initiates . . . Although the content [of their thought] was kept strictly secret, the results became apparent in the culture.[4]

And therefore, however difficult, the obligation of the Mystery priesthoods at certain times in history was to siphon higher knowledge out to the people in such a way that it would be accepted and utilized in the popular culture. But rarely was this possible without a violent confrontation between resistant temple officials and those who understood that the time had come for a relaxation of the usual laws of secrecy. It was true that unless strictly monitored, extreme social and political instability was prone to follow such a venture, and it was for that reason, plus questions of personal power, that a natural caution within the temples against relaxing the laws of secrecy was liable to harden into obduracy. It is in the light of this background power struggle that went on between the Jerusalem priesthood and a series of such reforming interventions, sometimes from Egypt, sometimes from the prophet-led northern provinces, that we must understand the difficulties Jesus faced in his mission to open up a new spiritual path for the common folk.

Yet the gospels make it clear that the attempt was successful. In the lexicon of the primitive Church, a Greek word of immense potency was *exousia*. It occurs frequently in the Christian scriptures in relation to Jesus, and is translated there as "authority" or "power," as in Luke 4:36; but these translations, although nominally accurate, are misleading. They conceal the word's true meaning, that of a spiritual energy. It is really only now, when so much initiatory information is flooding into our Western culture from the East, that we can appreciate the true occult meaning of exousia as the energy or power Hindus know as kundalini Shakti—a term that is now a great deal more familiar to most Western people than its biblical equivalent. It was in this strictly esoteric and Eastern sense that Jesus succeeded in transmitting exousia first to his immediate followers and later to a rapidly widening circle of disciples committed to the new Way of the heart.

The spiritual energy of exousia derives from the merkavah science and its elucidation of the mysteries of Angelology. Since it is a concept of energy that, as the Gnostics knew, covers qualities both material and spiritual, it has no modern scientific equivalent and could not have been understood until very recently, when the West first became acquainted with the Eastern system of kundalini yoga. Exousia signifies an extraterrestrial source of energy that is crucial to the functioning of the psyche as well as of the body. In a scriptural context, it is usually translated as having something to do with rabbinic authorization, whereas its association is rather with ancient high magic, the source of the Light teachings given out in the Mystery temples under the general rubric of the Chariot tradition.

Behind the term, says Andrew Welburn, "can be discerned vastly older, Near Eastern perceptions of religious 'power,'"[5] such as that possessed by Jesus. In the primitive Church the receiving of exousia was closely related to magical power *(dynamis)* and to spiritual grace, or more specifically charisma *(charis),* which conferred the supranatural gifts of the spirit such as clairvoyance, clairaudience and prophetic, and healing powers. This supernatural Power working through Jesus was normally under his control but sometimes operated unintentionally.[6]

The "Power" is particularly effective in exorcism and is often there associated with exousia . . . The power is elsewhere described as being the "power of the Lord," the Lord here probably being God, the Highest . . . [and as] "the power from the Heights."[7]

The magician experienced exousia as a high charge of psychospiritual energy having miraculous properties that could affect matter, as has kundalini. Kundalini is the diminutive term derived from Maha Kundali, the Mother of Space and Time, and applies to the Cosmic Mother's universal presence when found in particular bodies. Thus the scholar J. M. Hull, in his monograph on the gospels and their relation to the magical healing of bodies, shows that "for Mark's readers it meant a mysterious superhuman force whereby demons were controlled and afflictions healed."[8] Exousia was, in addition, over and above the inhabiting dynamis of the magician, the divine power that was at work in the initiate kings of ancient Egypt—and therefore a secret reserved to the Mystery temples along the Nile. It is through the god whom the kings represented, Amun-Re, adored as the Hidden-and-Manifest, that we learn more about the physical attributes of exousia.

The god was conceived as a source of vital energy, filling the universe. His power floods into everything that will receive it. But in the highest degree it charges the King, who is the living portrait of the god. And by extension it flows into things connected with the King and his form, such as his garments and regalia. The source of energy in the god is infinite.[9]

Indeed, this is the essence of the secret of royal power imparted by the god Krishna in the quotation from the Bhagavad Gita that heads this chapter. The quotation is part of a dialogue being held on the summit of sacred Mount Meru between the god and Arjuna, a warrior-prince descended from the Sun kings of India. Undoubtedly Near Eastern Gnostics, too, were well aware of this same power and its supernatural manifestations, more familiarly known to Christians as the work of the

Holy Spirit. In the Gospel of Philip we learn of the relevance of exousia to the mystery of the physical body:

> The holy person is utterly holy, even including that person's body. Such a person, if picking up bread, makes it holy—likewise the cup or any of the other things, which that person picks up and sanctifies. Then how could he not consecrate the body also? (Philip 91)

Like the ancient Egyptian mystics and the yogis of Upanishadic India, the Gnostics knew that the body is one of the great secrets of the spiritualization process. Because of the interconnectedness that reigns in the universe, the supreme Life energy, when awakened by initiation, radiates outward beyond the body, so that everything a perfect master touches, his clothes, the very cup he drinks from, the chair he sits in, becomes saturated with the luminous spiritual energy emanating from his body and can be transmitted directly to others. Thus we read in the Gospel of Luke:

> As he [Jesus] went, the people pressed round him. And a woman who had had a flow of blood for twelve years and could not be healed by anyone, came up behind him, and touched the fringe of his garment; and immediately her flow of blood ceased. And Jesus said, "Who was it that touched me?" When all denied it, Peter said, "Master, the multitudes surround you and press upon you!" But Jesus said, "Some one touched me, *for I perceived that power has gone forth from me.*" And when the woman saw that she was not hidden, she came trembling, and falling down before him declared in the presence of all the people why she had touched him, and how she had been immediately healed. And he said to her, "Daughter, your faith has made you well; go in peace." (Luke 8:42–48) (author's italics)

We know from the many gospel anecdotes like the above that the secrets of the human body were well understood by Jesus. It is a subject that has long engaged the minds of Eastern thinkers. We learn from Sir John Woodroffe, a British official working in India in the early years of the twentieth century, that for Indian philosophers the body has always been a holy temple filled with deities and their servants, the angels and elementals. "Whatever of Mind or Matter exists in the universe," says Woodroffe, "exists in some form or manner in the human body."[10] There is nothing in the universe, he suggests, that is not in the human body; and moreover it is a spiritually potent magno-electrical system. The law of the universe is polarization into either static–dynamic or potential–kinetic aspects, and so it must also be in the body. "In the living body, therefore," says Woodroffe,

> there must be such polarization . . . It may be compared to a mag-
> net with two poles. In fact, the body is a vast magazine of Power
> (Shakti). The Tantras say that it is in the power of man to accom-
> plish all he wishes if he centers his will thereon. And this must be
> so, for man in his essence is one with the Supreme Lord (Isvara) and
> Mother (Isvari) and the more he manifests Spirit the greater is he
> endowed with its powers.[11]

Nor is this ancient body wisdom confined to the Orient. Hermetic initiates have long understood the potentially spiritual nature of the body, which, as the Austrian mystic Rudolf Steiner says, is "a copy of the Godhead and is shamefully belittled when looked upon as something inferior."[12] He reminds us that, on the contrary, the physical body is of supreme evolutionary importance. Only in the body can we gain control of all the forces of physical creation, only in the body can we pay off all our karmic debts contracted in the long saga of the soul's evolution, and only in such conditions can we enjoy a spiritualized body freed of all dark matter. "The redeemed physical—a level of glowing perfection—is evident in the Christian resurrectional traditions and images," asserts David Ovason.[13]

> To some extent, we all have the illusion that we understand what the
> physical is, even though the initiate is inclined to regard it as the great
> mystery . . . whose true Spiritual nature has scarcely been explored. . . .[14]

In the arcane tradition, it is maintained that in the distant future the physical body will be redeemed and spiritualized: this will be the "body of light rays," the augoedeian body in the hermetic terminology. This arcane concept was expressed in medieval art as an aura of radiations round the body of Christ.[15]

In Hermetic writings, the efficacy of exousia as a subtle animating force in the body is recognized. It is described in the literature as a cosmic Life energy, an everlasting and inexhaustible reservoir of vital energy whose influence flows down from the stars into the "womb" of the earthly elements.[16] As we have seen, the ancient Egyptians equated it with their god Amun, who was visible as the sun but was also the invisible power radiating out from the sun as an ethereal auric presence filling the world.

In Judaic Angelology, exousia is the creative power that emanates from a group of seven great Archangels called the Exousiai, who together, working as one, are responsible for building the visible universe. These great Beings, each one of which represents a biblical Day of Creation, can therefore be equated with the plural world-creating Elohim of Genesis, while behind this conception is the further Qabalistic idea drawn from esoteric astrology to the effect that the Exousiai are represented by the seven planets, chief of which is the Sun.

The Sun is conceived of as the key to the whole, the central source of spiritual as well as physical light that is reflected back by the planets on either side of it. As the primary Light-giver, the fiery Sun Spirit worshipped by Simon Magus as the Seventh Power is in this sense a Being greater than the Archangels; he is the spiritual totality, the group being conceived of as one great cosmic Entity of which the seven planets are but subsidiary outer aspects.[17] The creative power of this Solar entity is exousia and exousia is likewise the power that shines forth from the Heavenly Messiah who lives in the Sun.

The system was an early Qabalistic one in which divine/angelic names were assigned to the planetary spheres (the latter being *sphaira* in Greek and *sephiroth* in the Hebrew Qabalah), and was the most hidden element in the rabbinic vision of the cosmological and mystical forces underlying

Genesis. But these cosmic forces, it should be noted, lay beyond moral law, so creating the potentiality of evil as well as good. For as we have seen, the dual organizing principles in the universe both build forms and destroy them. Ruling both the creation and dissolution of things, they include the amoral powers of Lucifer under the planetary aspect of Venus, and thus in the opinion of some lend to the whole "work of creation" a morally dangerous ambiguity. Therefore in Pharisaic circles

> the Creation, along with the chariot-vision of Ezekiel, was a designated "esoteric" topic, to be discussed only among those "with knowledge." Even mentioning the angels could be dangerous.[18]

The higher Pharisaic echelons, like those of other Hasidic sects, were well versed in such mysteries and believed that humanity was the tenth and lowest order in the great angelic hierarchy. But among them and their rabbinic heirs a belief reigned that some things were too morally and psychologically dangerous to reveal to all, and consequently religion must be taught on two levels. Teachings acceptable on one level might imperil the soul on the other, and were therefore proscribed material whose illicit dissemination was traditionally punishable by death. It was a universally held law, one that the forest sages of Hindu India had always shared and had formulated long ago in the Doctrine of the Two Roads. In the Chandogya Upanishad, the king Jaibali, instructing a Brahmin in the yoga of the Self (Atman), refers to the way of fire and the way of smoke, corresponding to the sun and the moon, respectively, as representing two different and incompatible spiritual paths. And as Joseph Campbell notes,

> The doctrine that he taught is one of those most central to Oriental mythic thought. It is termed here the doctrine of flame and smoke, or the parting of the two spiritual ways: on the one hand, the road of flame, which leads to the sun and therewith the gods, there to abide; but on the other hand, the road of smoke, to the moon, the fathers and reincarnation.[19]

Up until the conquests of Alexander, this had been a universal tradition: the upper path of the Sun, the Road of Fire, must be hermetically sealed off from the lower Moon path, its existence scarcely suspected by the masses. But although it was therefore a topic normally forbidden outside the Mystery schools, by the first century the secrets of the Road of Solar Fire had been compromised forever. The Solar path, the path of initiation, became central to the unprecedented stream of esoterica being leaked into the popular domain. Celestial fire poured invisibly into every cranny of society, with the fateful consequences already discussed. In response, it was to take several centuries for the population to overcome its inertia, even sometimes its repulsion, and accommodate to some extent the energic revolution that was represented by Mystery cults like Christianity, which offered the Solar initiation to all those considered "mature" enough, regardless of their station in life.

Even today, two thousand years later, we are just beginning to come to grips with the complex subject of angels and with the merkavah science generally, especially its facilitation of the expansion of consciousness through the activity of spiritual energy in the spinal centers. It is still a science that to conservative Christian eyes has no valid relationship whatsoever to the modern canon of the scientifically and morally permissible. Only in the last few decades has this cosmic science been opened up in the West in books, workshops, specialized journals, and "new age" schools, cautiously at first, but with increasing prolixity and candor, and it has already generated a severe fundamentalist backlash, especially in America. Even for the more open-minded, the underlying concept of a universe-creating psychophysical Light energy that informs everything that exists and provides the basis of human consciousness is a peculiarly difficult one to accept, given the modern scientific orthodoxy that denies it any place in contemporary thought.

Indeed in some respects the gulf between the sacred and the profane in earlier centuries was not so great. Even as late as the sixteenth and seventeenth centuries, mystics like the Swiss physician Paracelsus (1493–1541) and Jacob Boehme (1575–1624), the visionary German shoemaker, were able to formulate Light-based metaphysical doctrines of a clarity and spiritual sophistication that would hardly be possible today. Boehme in particular, with his complex vision of a subtle energy body with its own laws and purposes lying behind the physical body as its hidden causative agent, foreshadowed far more boldly the tentative steps the present biological sciences are taking in the same direction. And in his radical theology that envisioned good and evil as having a single reconciling source in "the divine abyss," Boehme was able to promulgate a unified vision of life hardly possible today in the climate of frank dualism dominating the Church.[20]

INITIATION AND THE CHRIST FIRE

In Jacob Boehme's era it was possible to uncover the occult element at the root of Christianity without inviting more than the outrage of the religious; today science itself has joined the conservative forces. Nevertheless, science is itself maturing and will no doubt one day accept the idea that the unknown cosmic energy, call it exousia or kundalini Shakti, is the dynamic element in religion that has been disguised for thousands of years in a variety of mythological images. It is to be found hidden, for example, in the glyph of the Qabalistic Tree, whereon the three verticals depict the human spinal energy system.

Thus the Qabalistic glyph can be equated with the Chakra-Nadi yogic system familiar to Hindu-Buddhist Tantra. The middle Pillar of Equilibrium represents the *sushumna,* or central channel, within the spine and the side pillars of Severity and Mercy, respectively, represent the negative *ida* and positive *pingala* channels on either side, which unite in the central path. The spinal energy, says Dion Fortune, can be thought of as rising on the central pillar of the Tree, which is essentially the pillar of Consciousness in its purely dynamic, organizational, and creative function, while the two side pillars are the positive and negative factors of manifestation— that is to say, the factors of force and form, yang and yin.[21]

Fortune adds that on the Ladder of Initiation, symbolized by the Tree, the zigzag upward route of kundalini that takes in the side pillars is for the occultist and the sage, the direct route up the middle pillar for the mystic. The latter was the mystical Way of the Heart that Jesus taught his inner circle. The spiraling route is the way of the magical and ceremonial traditions, the way of talismanic magic, alchemy, divinatory rites, and the like, while the direct path of ascent is the way of love. The first is now relatively well known in Western educated circles, the second, the direct path, is hardly known at all.

This is the way of the mystic as distinguished from that of the occultist; it is swift and direct, and free from the danger of the temp-

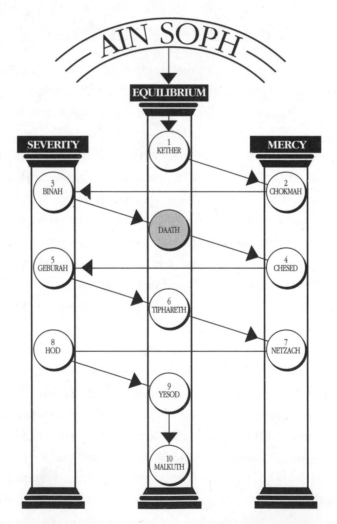

Fig. 13. The Three Pillars and the descent of the Lightning Flash of Power

tation of unbalanced force that is met with in either [side] pillar, but it confers no magical powers save those of sacrifice in Tiphareth and psychism in Yesod.[22]

Besides the Tree of Life, there are other traditional means of concealing the occult meaning of *exousia*. For example, it has been symbolized as oil in a wide array of religions. The Syriac Gnostics regarded the anointing with oil that followed water baptism as symbolizing the oil from the Tree of Life and therefore efficacious as a baptismal medium. "I have been anointed with the shining oil of the Tree of Life," runs a baptismal formula preserved in Origen (Contra Celsum VI, 27) imagery, which had profound Qabalistic significance in medieval Jewry, as oil there was symbolic of male procreative energy, as it also is in Sufism.

In his standard work, the Ilha, the famous Sufi Ghazali wrote that the four stages in dervish spiritual attainment may be likened to a walnut: There is the hard shell, the inside skin, a kernel, and oil. One by one the shell, the inner skin, and the kernel—the three bodies of the dervish—are thrown away in order to extract the oil. That is the precious thing. Says the modern Sufi Idries Shah: "The kernel is the object if one is attempting to extract oil, yet even this inner meat contains matter which is rejected in the pressing of the oil."[23]

Another common symbol for exousia has been the serpent, a deity that was revered in the Levant, as in India, for many thousands of years as the bestower of wisdom and healing. The serpent Ningizzida, supreme "Lord of the Tree of Truth" and the consort of the Sumerian Goddess, is depicted on a steatite vase from Lagash dated to ca. 2025 BCE.[24] We also know of the serpent of wisdom (see fig. 14) that winds its way up the body of the Mithraic god Zervan Akarana, "Boundless Time," the image of which was found in the Mithraic mystery temple of the Roman port of Ostia dated to 190 CE.[25]

Joseph Campbell reminds us that Yahweh too was an aspect of the serpent power and gave his servant Moses a magical serpent rod whose coiling image healed disease and divined water in the desert.[26] According to 2 Kings in the Hebrew scriptures, this bronze serpent of Moses' called Nehushtan was worshipped in the Jerusalem temple, where the people burned incense to it until the time of the reforming king Hezekiah (719–691 BCE). By then, so ambivalent had the prevailing view of the snake icon become, so dreaded was it as a supernatural symbol of healing but also of destruction, that King Hezekiah, so we are told, broke Nehushtan into pieces as a heathen idol and threw the fragments into the brook Kidron (2 Kings 18:4–5).

But the image that most nearly reflects the true nature of exousia is the one that Simon Magus popularized as the seventh Power, that of Fire. The Byzantine historian and philosopher Michael Psellus, writing

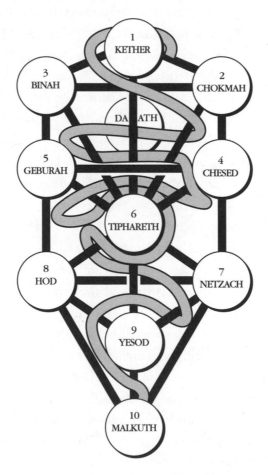

Fig. 14. The Spiral Path

in circa 1050, reconstructed a second-century Greek teaching by Julian the Theurge to the effect that Fire is the primal universe-building element in existence. At the summit of the divine hierarchy, Psellus said, is a transcendental Fire called the Father, the Hypercosmic Paternal Abyss. The Cosmic Father has "created all things in perfection, he has conceived them in the intelligible world."[27] And of course in the same vein, Acts 2:2–4, of the Christian scriptures, tells us that at the Pentecostal assembly following Jesus' death the Christ fire descended in the form of the Comforter:

> And suddenly a sound came from heaven like the rushing of a mighty wind, and it filled all the house where they were sitting. And there appeared to them tongues as of fire, distributed and resting on each one of them.

Old Jewish psalms reveal that from an early period, esoteric Judaism entertained these same ideas of supernatural power as relating to monarchy. The psalms speak of a supreme psychophysical energy that radiated from the initiate kings of Israel as a kind of inner light, a glorification.[28] After speaking with God, the skin of Moses' face likewise shone with it as he descended Mount Sinai with the tablets of the Covenant (Exodus 34:29–35). And as an initiate king representing the divine, Jesus too is a vessel of this identical cosmic power and is transformed by it in the Transfiguration scene in all three gospels (Matthew 17:2, Mark 9:2). He is one who rules by it and who casts out demons by it, "who is in touch with the creative, life-giving energy of the Father and banishes the forces of evil, death and disease."[29] The apocryphal Gospel of Peter expressly uses the term exousia to signify the presence of the divine Christ fire in the body of Jesus.[30]

"We are certainly right," says Welburn "in regarding the transference of power as one manifestation of Jesus' exousia."[31] Indeed we might call it almost the raison d'être of Jesus' mission, the key to the whole of early Christian practice. Yet despite the recent efforts of charismatic and evangelical Christians to revive the concept of exousia in its original dynamism, it is now obsolete in the mainstream Church. Indeed, to the extent that its numinous thread is no longer woven into the warp and woof of the fabric of the faith, Western religion is impotent, without credibility, for it has been robbed of its most vital component. The voices of mystics like Jacob Boehme, who intuited this power as a mighty unitive Light energy underlying all physical manifestations, have fallen silent. The Church, obsessed with tribal morals and taboos, no longer even attempts to be the organ of enlightenment it was intended to be.

Nor can science take over the Church's role. The fiery energy lying hidden at the root of all institutional religions is mightier than nuclear power, but because it reveals its full range of capabilities only to the spiritual initiate, it remains as yet unfamiliar to modern science. The initiate knows that it controls the mind, awakens all the suprasensible faculties, and governs the breath, the organs, and the connective tissues of the body. It is the basis of every human emotion and instinct and the ultimate organizer of all physical systems, underlying and comprehending all the other energies known to scientists. The one who can work with this great evolutionary power, this super force, not only has the means to heal souls and bodies and bring harmony to society but also can change the very course of history and human evolution.

And this is what Jesus, the first-century Christ-Bearer, did. The fundamental reformation Jesus brought about in religious practice was to improve the way this spiritual power was transmitted in the initiatory rite in order to open up areas of spiritual and psychological insight that were closed to the pagan world. But to understand the momentous nature of such an innovation, it is necessary to glance first at the time-honored method it was replacing, and why the change had become overwhelmingly necessary.

In her work *The Origin of Satan,* Elaine Pagels describes the Christian conversion of a thoughtful young pagan named Justin who came to Rome from Asia Minor in about 140 in order to study philosophy. Justin's philosophical reflections on the difference between paganism and the new religion of Christos tells us in traditional terms why Christianity had become necessary to the world. Pagans, said Justin, worshipped the forces of Nature as divine but were under a dangerous delusion. These mighty natural energies of mountain and sky, wind and water were represented by a pantheon of gods and goddesses whom pious human beings were taught to revere and sacrifice to from the cradle onward; but the Nature forces, or daimones, as they were called, were not divine but rather chthonic. They were related not to the upper spheres of spirit, but to the earthly and sub-earthly elements.

As Justin now saw, they were below humanity, "splendid, powerful, and dangerous realities that do not come within the sphere of morality, and are in no way concerned about the human race."[32] We moderns might call them the instinctual forces inherent in the reptilian brain, at the base of the skull. They equate with our most primitive human intelligence, which regulates the fight-or-flight responses to perceived threats from our environment—and which now generates enormous ills in society: wars, perversions, bouts of genocide, etc. However beautiful and wild these forces of Nature, Justin saw that in human beings they represented a subworld of instincts and passions that pagans, by continually worshipping, came to express more and more in their own lives, so descending ever more steeply into a darkness of the soul unlit by higher possibilities.

But Christian baptism brought illumination to mind and soul, for above Nature was a world to which humanity truly belonged, a world filled with numinous light. Here Christ reigned in the company of other divine beings of light who loved human beings and served only their greatest good. These Angelic beings raised humanity from the darkness of brute instinct into a higher and genuinely human realm of energies that conferred enlightenment, freedom from the wheel of Necessity, and a power of understanding that was beyond the comprehension of the pagan mentality. Justin realized that a true consciousness of Selfhood and its potentialities became possible only from this higher vantage point. At our birth, he said,

> [w]e were born without consciousness or choice, by our parents' intercourse. We are baptized so that we may no longer be children of necessity and ignorance, but become the children of choice and knowledge.[33]

For thousands of years the prophets had sought the rose of love in the heart of the causal Light. They knew it was to be found in the heart center, but as the Bronze Age advanced, the constricting, brutalizing effects of an agricultural way of life were felt more and more as a darkening of the soul, and the awakening of the heart center became increasingly difficult. Bearing in mind that in antiquity the temples were the sole purveyors of culture and religious consciousness in a passive, undereducated society, it is possible to appreciate how much the limitations of the pagan psyche directly mirrored the limitations of the temples. Initiates too were shackled by Nature's grip in the same way as the ordinary citizen. The only method available to initiates of antiquity was to work with the chthonic earth energies active in the three lower centers of the spinal system: those of survival, procreation, and personal power (see fig. 12, page 279). But these were the centers ruled by Nature, and few initiates indeed could rise above them to the fourth, the heart chakra.

By concentrating on the root chakras, which fueled and regulated the body and its survival and procreative powers, pre-Christian initiates sought in vain to break the ceiling above the third center and so raise exousia into the higher centers. For long sexual intercourse and willpower were the only methods known among adepts aspiring to enlightenment and are best exemplified by the Hindu tantric system handed down by the ancient Indus Valley initiate kings whom we first met in the prologue.

But this somatic yoga was a difficult and dangerous system in its ancient form, combining intensive meditation on the root chakras with breathing exercises, fasting, mudras or physical postures, sexual intercourse, or alternatively the exercise of willpower, and other specifically physiological methods, such as the use of narcotic drugs. Because of its dangers, the yoga was perforce restricted to relatively few practitioners and required secrecy, solitary conditions, arduous ascetic disciplines, and enormous dedication. Furthermore, as a matter of survival, it demanded a cult of absolute unquestioning obedience to a guru, and even then the goal of breaking through the ceiling to the fourth chakra of the heart, the *anahata* chakra, was rarely achieved.

In his classic study of the serpent power, Woodroffe unveils the

Hindu teachings concerning the primal creative energy of exousia, which is stored in the root chakra, and describes the endeavors of yogis to awaken and harness it by purely somatic means. "It is said of those who attempt it," Woodroffe reported, "that one out of a thousand may have success."[34] By the time he began to unearth its secrets, the method had outlived its evolutionary usefulness and had become virtually obsolete in India. Except for the few Hindu master yogis who had retreated into the fastnesses of the Himalayas, adepts lower down the initiatory ladder had long abandoned somatic yoga for safer paths, such as they would find, for example, in the emotional raptures of Krishna worship.

In the first century, degenerated forms of somatic yoga still dominated the religious cults in the ancient East, releasing the kind of low chthonic forces that flourished in the Dionysian orgies in Rome, in which bands of ecstatic women acolytes hunted down and tore wild animals to pieces with their teeth. The difficulty was that the physical forces, especially the sexual drive, were highly seductive and prone to corrupt, releasing animal forces that were impossible to control.[35] As Robert Turcan has shown, as a result many dangerous malpractices had entered the ancient science: Aberrant "left-path" sexual practices, sorcery, superstition and cruelty, spirit worship, black magic, necromancy, and sex magic by now infested the Near Eastern cults like so many crocodiles prowling around the would-be initiate at every turn, while even the most advanced of the Mystery schools were limited by this outworn methodology and were in decline all over the world.

Over the ages, necessary reforms have occurred within the tradition of the Gnosis, and it seems to be the task of great spiritual leaders of history like Jesus, Krishna, the Buddha, Mani, Muhammad, and others to be the vehicles of these forces of evolutionary change. But according to esoteric tradition, in order to effect such reforms the descent of divine power to earth must await the cooperation of an incarnate human vehicle. In other words, the Power can be "earthed" only by a human being already on earth prepared and able to act as a transmitting station and capable of stepping down the energy in his or her own body to a voltage safe for ordinary physical conditions. In the first century in the Near

East, precisely as the Magi had prophesied, that prerequisite was established: the new messianic impulse that would supersede the old system was able to be grounded by several great spiritual leaders, auxiliary Christs—and preeminently Jesus himself.

Jesus delivered the coup de grâce to the old form of physiological yoga, which had reigned unchallenged for thousands of years, and replaced it with a method of far greater safety, speed, and utility. This was the Way that directly opened the fourth chakra, the Spiritual Heart, without recourse to the lower centers. The descent of the Christ Spirit into incarnation had brought with it the solution to what had become an almost insoluble dilemma: how to release the primal creative energy imprisoned in the body without succumbing to the perilous seductions of animality—how to become fully human. Although ultimately in pursuit of the same goal as the old Oriental method, Jesus' new Way bypassed the lower energy centers and directly awakened exousia in the Christ center within the region of the heart, leaving to its royal discretion all further stages in the initiatory process. Thus the Sufi adept memorialized in Irina Tweedie's *The Chasm of Fire,* a diary that records her discipleship under him in India, states:

> By our system it [exousia] is awakened gently . . . we awaken the "King," the heart chakra, and leave it to the "King" to awaken all the other chakras.[36]

Initiates describe this "royal" center, which reigns supreme over the three lower chakras of Nature, as sunlike, radiating luminous multicolored rays of love and wisdom, the primary attributes of the spiritual Self. As the seat of Self-awareness and of the Inner Teacher, its awakening is the beginning of true self-government.

The new method of initiation was therefore genuinely revolutionary. It was psyche oriented rather than body oriented and was geared to self-development and individuation rather than merely to the acquisition of enhanced personal power. It fostered the wisdom of the heart, sensitivity to the emotional life, and the possibility of altruistic love, as well as a sense of personal independence, of autonomy. It was for "those who stand solitary," a term for which Jesus used the word *monachoi,* which also means "those who have become unified."[37] The new initiation required neither the use of willpower, physical proximity, extreme asceticism, or sexual congress, and was able to awaken the suprasensible functions gradually, gently, and safely, even from a great distance. It did not need solitude or arduous disciplines, was suitable for a far larger proportion of the race, and could be applied in the midst of society under ordinary, everyday conditions.

Most importantly, the new Way was proof against moral corruption. Its basis was ethical, being founded on consciousness of the initiate's selfhood with its innate faculty of conscience. His unique self-identity was thus called into action rather than his physiology, with its three instinctual drives. The new Way therefore operated above and beyond the purely egoistic goals of the past. Furthermore, it sought guidance from within, from the wisdom of the heart radiated by the Inner Teacher rather than from any external, corruptible authority. The new Way was thus a great evolutionary advance. It spelled an unprecedented expansion of consciousness as well as freedom, simplicity, and safety in spiritual practice, not merely for the privileged few but for all.

The cognitive consciousness of human beings is the very crux, the sine qua non of the evolutionary process: consciousness is really the only factor that determines progress. And there a profound change undoubtedly seems to have occurred during the Piscean age. It is easy to overlook the great gulf that separates our cognitive mind-set from that of the man of pre-Christian antiquity, yet reflection will quickly show that it does indeed exist. Modern man is more aware than was his pagan predecessor of the life of the heart, of the emotional nature, the psychic drives and instincts, and of his responsibility for them. Today he is far more firmly anchored in selfhood and historical process. The pagan individual on the other hand seemed not yet fully individualized. He was less aware of—and therefore less morally encumbered by—the iron laws of history and physical causality, and his heart center, his capacity for empathy with the pains of others, we would regard as relatively undeveloped.

In no other way can one explain the enjoyment the majority of Roman citizens experienced in watching criminals and gladiators—bought purely for their entertainment, as many as three hundred in a day—being agonizingly killed in combat or helplessly torn apart by wild beasts in the circuses held throughout the empire. Attending festive gatherings similar to our soccer matches for no other purpose than to watch the death agonies of other human beings while enjoying a lunch snack is a form of entertainment impossible to find anywhere in the world today.

The abnormal insensitivity to the pain of others that one finds widespread in antiquity seems to have been related to the fact that the dramas of the pagan's soul life, of his emotional and spiritual nature, his psyche, were not fully articulated in consciousness, but were displaced onto the doings of deified mythic figures external to himself and only vaguely related to what we would regard as the personal demands of reality. His heroes and gods cushioned the brutal impact of life on earth; they were free-floating psychic projections, naive and ahistorical, with whom the pagan could identify from a safe psychological distance, so to speak, in moral innocence.

That innocence is hardly possible today. The messianic age that dawned in the first century has everywhere brought to an end the pantheons of Nature deities, or at least diminished their enthrallment, imposing on the race instead the solitude and the burden of historical consciousness and the sorrows and conflicts of self-responsibility that pagan humanity had been spared. Today we are more empathetic toward others; we identify with them more, and to that extent are more capable of disinterested love for our fellow beings. Generalization though this may be, there are few races on the earth today whose cognitive consciousness has not been thus changed, at least to some degree, by the enormous change in the cultural climate that occurred after the birth of Christianity.

THE PHILOSOPHY OF THE SELF

In 1996, when Daniel Goleman, after exhaustive research, wrote his groundbreaking book *Emotional Intelligence,* there came the first dawning of public awareness that success in life may be based more on the ability to manage one's emotions than on intellectual capabilities—and that good emotional management may be learned. The ABC's of emotional intelligence, says Goleman,

> include self-awareness, seeing the links between thoughts, feelings, and reactions, knowing if thoughts or feelings are ruling a decision, seeing the consequences of alternative choices, and applying these insights to choices.[38]

Goleman and many other researchers after him believe that intelligence and intuition are heightened when we listen more deeply to our own heart, our emotions then becoming more educated, balanced, and coherent. Research shows that negative emotions such as anger, fear, and blame throw the nervous system out of cardiovascular balance, creating heart rhythms that appear jagged and disordered, while positive emotions such as love and gratitude increase order and balance in the nervous system and create harmonious and coherent heart rhythms.[39] Furthermore, techniques can be taught that enable a state of inner harmony and balance to be achieved at will. The results of such a program of reeducation among hundreds of workplace participants have been dramatic. They show that by cultivating care and compassion, a greater capacity to "sustain a positive perspective, balance their emotions and access an intuitive flow day to day, even in the midst of challenges," has been possible.[40] The participants have been able to retrain their systems so as to operate in greater harmony—physically, mentally, and emotionally.

Does it not appear, then, that the Christ Impulse is returning, bringing our Western culture the Gnosis of the heart once again, and the possibility of continuing the interrupted evolutionary shift begun by Jesus?

In the light of the recent scientific discoveries about the importance of listening to our heart intelligence, thus reducing stress levels and increasing our emotional performance, we can now surely begin to understand the heroic, almost miraculous sanctity of the thousands of early Christians who prayed, suffered, and died in the Roman arenas and the Egyptian and Cappadocian deserts two thousand years ago. If today the congruence of the heart–brain complex can be dramatically increased by a simple retraining method, how much more so could it have been increased by the Gnosis of the heart bathing the heart–brain complex in the transcendent energies of the bridechamber? That was undoubtedly the reason why tens of thousands of Christians flocked to the deserts in the first few centuries of the Christian Era, hoping to find the freedom there to worship far from the doctrinal tyranny of their bishops. The Vitae Patrum, a massive seventeenth-century folio recording the lives and sayings of the desert fathers, tells us as much. In the fiery horror of the deserts, infested as they were with wild beasts, the servants of Christ discovered their full spiritual potential:

> There is another place in the inner desert . . . called Cellia. To this
> spot those who have had their first initiation and who desire to live
> a remoter life, stripped of all its trappings, withdraw themselves: for
> the desert is vast . . .[41]

In *The Desert Fathers,* Helen Waddell's masterly translation from the Latin illuminates the spiritual achievements of these wonderful sons and daughters of the bridechamber:

> Of the depth of their spiritual experience they had little to say: but
> their every action showed a standard of values that turns the world
> upside down. It was their humility, their gentleness, their heart-
> breaking courtesy that was the seal of their sanctity to their contem-
> poraries, far beyond abstinence or miracle or sign.[42]

Yet miracles and signs were not absent. The abbot Agathonicus visited Poeman the solitary and asked him how he had endured sleeping the previous night in an icy cave without coverings. "How didst thou not feel so fierce a frost?" And Poeman replied: "There came a lion, and went to sleep beside me, and he kept me warm."[43] And then there is the famous account of Perpetua, a patrician girl still breastfeeding her baby, and how in the circus arena the aghast young soldier detailed to kill her could not bring himself to the deed, and how she helped him by calmly guiding his sword to her own throat. The multitude of such deeds of unearthly sanctity and moral heroism is testimony enough to the power of the bridechamber and its many Gnostic gifts.

It is quite possible that Alexander the Great and his generals had learned of the deeper potential of the tradition from the forest sages of India, who showed a great deal of benevolent interest in the visitors from the West and taught them as much of their yogic wisdom as possible. In the Old Religion worldwide it was once the kings rather than the temple priests who guarded the treasures of the bridechamber, as the earliest of the Upanishads, the Brhadaranyaka, discloses. There it is recounted that King Ajakashatru of Benares revealed to the Brahmin priests for the first time the yogic doctrine that the heart is the seat of the *atman,* the spiritual Self, and the source of dream, dreamless sleep, and the trance of mystics. From the space within the heart, said the king, 72,000 veins or nerves branch out to every part of the body, and when an individual falls asleep (or is entranced in initiation), the senses creep out through all these veins and are at rest throughout his body. He is then as great as a maharajah, as a god.

> For as a spider comes out along its thread or as sparks pour from a fire, even so, from this Self (atman) come forth all the senses, the worlds, the gods, and all being.[44]

Even as our scientists are now beginning to describe the universal knowingness of the heart nested in its hierarchy of tori and connected to the body by thousands of nerves, so the forest sages of India nearly three thousand years ago similarly described it as the center of a universal web of knowingness, and as the seat of the Self. The Greeks may have carried this Hindu philosophy of the Self westward via Ghandara, the Greek state established by Alexander in western India; and in Alexandria the method may have begun its gradual refinement among the Greek, Egyptian, and Hebrew illuminati of that city over the next two centuries, reaching its definitive flowering in the new freedoms of Christianity.

There is undoubtedly a marked similarity between Jesus' thought and the Upanishadic and Buddhist teachings on the spiritual Self that matured in India five hundred years before his birth. In the Bhagavad Gita, written about 400 BCE, only a few decades before Alexander and his army entered India, there is something of the same freedom from the social and cultural constraints imposed by the Brahmin caste to be found in Krishna's yogic rites of liberation. When Krishna says, "This deathless Yoga, this deep union, I taught Vivaswata, the Lord of Light," he is referring to the Yoga of the Self secretly taught by Jesus also. Indeed, the Anglo-Indian translator and poet Sir Edwin Arnold has said that so close is the analogy, sometimes literal, between the Christian scriptures and the teachings of the Vedantic sage Shankara, based on the Bhagavad Gita, that "a controversy has arisen between Pandits and Missionaries on the point, whether the author borrowed from Christian sources, or the Evangelists and Apostles from him."[45]

The social rigidity associated with a particularly old and venerated caste system probably accounts for the fact that in the Orient psychic consciousness remained largely centered in the collectivity and preserved the absolute authority of guru figures, as it does to the present day, whereas under the aegis of Christianity the West was to take a new evolutionary direction. Not even the ancient Greek culture, with its love of personal freedom and democratic values (which were not, however, extended to slaves, nor did they save Socrates), was to equal the spirit of moral autonomy and fierce freedom of conscience that informed the new Christian cult and which was so soon to flow into the whole of the western hemisphere.

By awakening the Anahata chakra in his nightlong secret baptism, Jesus put the one baptized into direct contact with the exalted Christ Spirit he himself embodied and who thereafter took his seat of government in the disciple's soul. Circulating through the heart organ rather than the lower centers, exousia worked in the bloodstream to purify the hereditary stains and weaknesses built up genetically in the course of generations, and drew off the poisons that had accumulated in the disciple through ignorance and wrong living over many lifetimes, replacing them with a radical new power of compassion.

The issue of spiritual power or exousia—as a high-level energy presently unknown to scientists but now accessible, in principle, to all human beings—has been consistently sidestepped by the Church, and never more so than in its teachings on love. On the path on which Jesus led his closest disciples, the sacraments were but the prelude and preparation for the reception of this exalted energy in the bridal chamber of the heart. Many passages of the recently discovered apocryphal gospels throw into new relief the depth of hidden meaning in Jesus' sermons on love, which have been frequently reduced to mere sentimentality. But they are not to be so taken: they pertain to secret knowledge; they encode the very essence of the new initiatory Christ mystery.

"All attempts to explain Christian love," says Welburn, "by deriving it from earlier forms have failed to account for its intrinsic features and new role."[46] Christian love was essentially a new moral force that began to flow with the awakening of exousia in the Anahata chakra. This great bonding power awakened by spiritual practice was, and still is, capable of surviving, neutralizing, and transforming human nature's most flawed and unregenerate aspects, working in the emotional nature a new, difficult wisdom. Jesus was undoubtedly the vessel of such a power and it formed the basis of his healing and teaching ministry. Moving beyond the conventional categories of good and evil, he said:

> You have heard that it was said, "You shall love your neighbor and hate your enemy." But I say to you, Love your enemies and pray for those who persecute you, so that you may be sons of your Father who is in heaven; for he makes his sun rise on the evil and on the good, and sends rain on the just and on the unjust. For if you love those who love you, what reward have you? Do not even the tax collectors do the same? And if you salute only your brethren, what more are you doing than others? . . . You therefore must be perfect, as your heavenly Father is perfect. (Matthew 5:43–48)

The transcending of the tribal moral code implied here does not belong to the customary order of things; it surpasses the normal possibilities of human nature. Unconditional love is simply not feasible without the entrance of a new potency in the human condition. And nor is the possession of clairvoyance and other suprasensible gifts, such as the ascension to higher planes of consciousness that Paul hints at in 1 Corinthians. Morton Smith quotes three passages in the Christian scriptures (Philippians 2:5–11, John 3:13, 1 Timothy 3:16) that suggest Jesus' close connection to Enoch and therefore to the astral journeying of the shaman, which depends entirely on empowerment by exousia. In the Dead Sea Scrolls and other scriptures of the ancient world, the perfected human being is one who, through the yoga of Light—for which we may read exousia—is so filled with unconditional love for his fellow men that he is "taken up to the heavens, transformed into a supernatural being and sent back to earth for the salvation of men."[47]

So, like Enoch, Jesus too ascends the heavenly planes, goes beyond the astral realms of the angels to the Kingdom of the All-Father, and through a trained and illumined consciousness attains his apotheosis as a fully spiritualized being, a Messiah whose love can redeem others. The gates of light are opened for him to receive what in Justin's words were "this washing we call illumination, because those who learn these things become illuminated in their understanding."[48] Although Jesus taught his ordinary followers by scripture, parable, myth, and precept, Luke's Gospel tells us that to his inner circle of disciples he transmitted spiritual power directly, passing on its secrets so that they could carry on his work.

> And he called the twelve together and gave them *power and authority* [*exousia*] over all demons and to cure diseases, and he sent them out to preach the kingdom of God and to heal. (Luke 9:1–6) (author's italics)

How, then, did Jesus effect such a transmission? Almost certainly it was by means of his secret baptismal practice, of which the scriptures tell us nothing. In the gospels there is a strange reticence surrounding this practice, which some scholars believe was related to his Kingdom of Heaven teachings. It was probably a necessary secrecy in view of the heavy death penalty exacted for any initiate disclosing such forbidden temple rites and doctrines as these. Although none of the synoptic gospels admits to Jesus baptizing anyone, the John Gospel does so in 3:26 and cites reports of his baptizing in 4:1, but in 4:2 says that Jesus himself did not baptize, but his disciples did. Why the equivocation if not a protection against the charge of breaking temple law? That this was a very serious offense is disclosed by Schonfield, who reports that in the period under discussion, any priest found serving at the altar while in a state of impurity was taken outside by young Zealot priests and clubbed to death.[49]

Morton Smith draws attention to the key to the baptism mystery, which lies in Mark's recently discovered Secret Gospel. There we find the explanatory material that throws light on the Gethsemane scene toward the end of Jesus' life, when the soldiers arrest him in the garden: "and with him there was a young man wearing a linen cloth over [his] naked [body], and they grabbed him, but he left the cloth and got away naked" (Mark 14:51f). What was he doing there?

> Through seventeen hundred years of New Testament scholarship, nobody has ever been able to explain what that young man was doing alone with Jesus in such a place, at such a time, and in such a costume.[50]

Smith believes a similar incident in the Secret Gospel gives the clue: the young man was being baptized by Jesus in the stream that ran through the Gethsemane garden. The main passage that Mark had extirpated from the canonical version of his gospel concerned the miraculous resurrection of Lazarus, who in the Secret Gospel is known only as "a youth of Bethany." In the canonical version Lazarus, as all Christians know, had lain in the family tomb for four days before Jesus came to Bethany and raised him miraculously from the dead, but in the secret version this miracle is to be taken symbolically. In a passage that appears nowhere in the canon, Lazarus comes to Jesus six days later and remains with him all night, clad only in a linen cloth, "in order to be taught the mystery of the Kingdom of God."[51] Here, as Morton Smith points out, we have the supporting evidence that the Gethsemane garden was the scene of nocturnal baptismal ceremonies conducted by Jesus. Baptism was the mystery of the Kingdom, the mystery rite by which the Kingdom was entered. But there is more.

Smith intimates that the secret Mark is divulging in Clement's letter to Theodore is that Lazarus's death was not a literal demise and resurrection but rather a mystical rite of passage, a symbolic drama of death and rebirth culminating in initiation after a six-day preparation. The relevant passages were therefore not included in Mark's canonical version, which was for general readership. "Not all true things are to be said to all men," Clement reminds his respondent.[52] He alludes to an all-night baptism by Jesus (perhaps attended by a select group of his closest disciples) as an initiation involving an ascent of consciousness to a higher world, to the Kingdom of Light—an ascent in which Jesus was able to take the neophyte with him and that conferred suprasensible knowledge of the mysteries of the Kingdom.[53] Indeed, knowledge of this spiritual realm beyond the world of Nature seems to have been the goal of the entire baptismal ceremony and to have been an intimate part of the new Way Jesus was promulgating.

One of the most curious conundrums in the gospels is why the apostles are presented as such ignorant men, even though they were participating in a time of great mental ferment and expansion of knowledge among initiates. Why, for example, is their mental baggage presented as so light that even the simple knowledge of Greek, the lingua franca of the day, was denied them until recently? We know that at least some of them had been disciples of John the Baptist and must therefore have had the wisdom background of initiates, yet little of this occult knowledge emerges in the gospel stories. Their portrayal as confused and somewhat ignorant men who milled around their Master asking foolish or irrelevant questions may not point to lack of learning, as is usually assumed, but rather suggests they were treading a different spiritual path from the majority of their fellow sectaries. Thus in the Gospel of Thomas we learn that the disciples questioned him [Jesus] and said to him, "Do you want us to fast? How shall we pray? Shall we give alms? What diet shall we observe?" Jesus said, "Do not tell lies, and do not do what you hate . . ." (Thomas 33:14–19)

In other words, the usual disciplines were to be discarded that distinguished the religious life of other Hebrews. Rules and regulations concerning kosher diet, ritual bathing, Torah study, fasting, and all the other prerequisites for the committed Jewish observant were not laid down. On an occasion when the Baptist's disciples were puzzled at the unconventional behavior of Jesus' disciples, the Master responded:

How can the sons of the Marriage Chamber mourn while the Bridegroom is with them? The time will come when the Bridegroom will be taken from them; then they will fast. (Matthew 9:15)

All that was really necessary was for the disciples to freely follow their own star in all things, untrammeled by the many strictures and cosmotheological constructions that normally accompany initiatory work on any one of the traditional paths. Freedom from the straitjacket of outer rules and proscriptions was therefore an essential ingredient of the new spiritual path. The first Christians formed small informal house churches, preserving the utmost simplicity in their liturgical and sacramental observances, and all took turns without favor in leading the congregation. But if there was a certain freedom from traditional Jewish law, it was only in order to give even more-stringent attention to inner guidance and to the creative demands of spiritual work in the world.

Consequently, unlike most learned Jewish sectaries of the first century, Jesus' disciples became not sages but practical men and women following a new dedicated way of life. The Christian scriptures present them as artists of the active life: healers, missionaries, exorcists, orators, miracle workers, dealers in ecstasy and martyrdom, but not necessarily men and women of great spiritual erudition. Even though a flood of esoterica was being released at the time, and the teachings of great masters like Appollonius of Tyana were heavily weighted with such occult sciences as thaumaturgy, talismanic magic, and astrology, this was not primarily the mystical way of the first followers of Christ. Even the considerably more sophisticated apocryphal documents of the Nag Hammadi corpus fail to remove their image as men and women of extreme intellectual simplicity.

Jesus' early emissaries embodied, among other things, a new way of heart thinking that gave wings to logic and rendered truth in images that were able to speak directly to the listener's soul. It was a mode of thought more intuitive, more imaginative and inwardly illuminated than anything the pagan world was accustomed to and enthralled audiences by its simple power to lift their insights to new heights. Indeed, this kind of reasoning imbued with heart intelligence has not been altogether lost; it survives to the present day in the best of Western esoteric thought and is burgeoning again in the new millennial climate of intellectual freedom.

The disciples were therefore blazing a new spiritual path in their very mode of thought as well as in deeds of healing. As for the Master, his was a work of pure love. By transmitting the evolutionary Life power of exousia, he could heal the bodies as well as the souls of others because his own body had already been transformed by it, the very cells and fluids charged with the fire and luminosity of one of the highest energies accessible to human beings. In Luke's case of the woman with a hemorrhage, the transmission of power from Jesus' body was for a simple healing purpose; but in the deeper initiatory process, the goal was nothing less than the inner union of master and disciple, so that all that belonged to the master belonged also to the disciple. The knowledge and power of consciousness in the one became the knowledge and power of consciousness in the other. And so when Thomas called him master, Jesus said:

> I am not your master. Because you have drunk, you have become intoxicated from the bubbling spring, which I have measured out. He who will drink from my mouth will become like me. I myself shall become he, and the things that are hidden will be revealed to him. (Thomas 13:108)

And the Gospel of Philip, in confirming the rapid transformative flow of power inherent in this method, enunciates the same truth in its broadest and most cosmic context:

> If you have seen the spirit, you have become the spirit; if you have seen the anointed (Christ), you have become the anointed (Christ); if you have seen the father, you will become the Father. Thus [here] you see everything and do not see your own self. Be there, you see yourself and what you see you shall become. (Philip 38:29–35)

In the end, the master ceased to be a master and the disciple a disciple: ideally, both came to worship God directly, without mediation, living as equals in the pure light of divinity. The disciple came to be "a disciple of his [own] mind" (Testimony of Truth 44:2). He discovered that his own mind, "the father of truth," must be his guiding principle, while accepting Jesus his master as the supreme human exemplar. Under such circumstances it was possible for the Gnostic teacher Silvanus to advise his followers:

> Have a great number of friends, but not counsellors . . . But if you do acquire [a friend], do not entrust yourself to him. Entrust yourself to God alone as father and as friend. (Teachings of Silvanus 97:18–98)

Like the sages of Hindu India, those in the Jesus movement believed that the supernatural gifts of the spirit could be acquired not by even the most arduous of mental disciplines, but only by initiation into a mystical commerce with the living Lord, one that would end in union with him. This was the non-rational, magical, visionary factor that overlaid the infant Christian religion and made it so difficult for pagans to understand or to appreciate. The movement was despised for its lack of the usual philosophical content; contempt was unfairly poured on it as a cult for slaves and uneducated artisans, and when it ultimately became the state religion under Constantine, it was widely blamed by the pagan intelligentsia for the crumbling of the empire.[54] For Gnostic Christians, on the other hand, the new current flowing through the empire carried unseen a potential of unimaginable power that they believed would reveal itself fully only in the days to come.

Although opposition abounded, by the middle of the first century in Alexandria and other great cities like Rome, Edessa, Antioch, and Ephesus, there were born the seeds of the tradition of interior exploration, self-knowledge, and internalizing of moral authority that was so singularly to distinguish the Christian movement thereafter. For the first time, Gnostics declared, an initiation existed that was independent of any outer authority, enabling a direct personal connection to be made with the higher dimensions, one that was energetically potent enough to tap the psychospiritual resources of love and wisdom that poured forth from the Christ Spirit through Jesus.

As Elaine Pagels says, the need for external guidance should be only a provisional measure: "the purpose of accepting authority is to learn to outgrow it."[55] Thus in the Valentinian Gospel of Truth, the Gnostic teacher advises those whom he addresses as "sons of interior knowledge": "Be concerned with yourselves; do not be concerned with other things which you have rejected from yourselves" (Gospel of Truth 32:31–33). And as Silvanus robustly advises,

> Knock on yourself as upon a door and walk upon yourself as on a straight road. For if you walk on the road, it is impossible for you to go astray . . . Open the door for yourself that you may know what is . . . Whatever you will open for yourself, you will open. (Teachings of Silvanus 106:30–117)

Thus the soul was freed in full consciousness from the strictures of its old separatist life by Jesus' secret nocturnal baptism. Through the mystery of the Kingdom, the initiate received the inestimable boon of a true inner freedom; the higher worlds were opened up; death held no more terrors, the Law no more tyranny.

But these benefits and insights were to find little accommodation in the developing Church. Inadequately informed about the creative force that drove their religion, many of the church fathers judged the meaning of *exousia* as it occurred in the Gnostic teachings to be a dangerous foreign heresy and a political stumbling block, seriously jeopardizing the authority of the bishops and the whole ecclesiastical structure. Consequently, they actively suppressed the concept as evil, despite the protestations of those who believed that they were thus emasculating the entire thrust of the Lord's teachings.

Jesus had resuscitated an ancient threefold Gnosis that lived on from age to age, housed always in forms appropriate to the times. The path he opened up incorporated three things: first, an *inner yoga;* second, its facilitating rites or *housing;* and third, its *right timing* according to the cosmic clock of the heavens. All too soon Sophia, the spirit of Gnosis, was banished and the threefold occult foundations on which Christianity had been built were lost to view. They were not to surface again until the twelfth century, when Bernard of Clairvaux, foremost among the medieval Christian mystics concerned with the revitalization of the Church, began the task of building a network of great Gothic cathedrals throughout Europe. The temples of the ancient world, centers of living power like Leontopolis and Heliopolis, had long been destroyed and forgotten in the tumult of the new Piscean age. The cathedrals of Europe were to be enduring new temples for the housing of Sophia and a commemoration of the lost Gnosis. But that was in the future.

Jesus' task in the first century was not finished with the laying down of the new Heavenly Temple in the hearts of coming generations. He had yet to cement it with the messianic signature, that of death and rebirth—a signature that would outlive every effacing gesture of time.

10

DEATH AND
RESURRECTION

No man leaves this world without seeing the Shekinah at the last
moment of life. The soul prostrates itself before her and praises God.
It seems then to enter a cavern wherein is a door leading to the
Earthly Paradise; there it encounters Adam, the patriarchs and all
the just, who rejoice with her and she is admitted within the Garden.
Either then or previously, she has been furnished with an envelope
other than the fleshly body but still having the form thereof.

A. E. WAITE

The Gnosis of the heart was probably transmitted formally to the world at large at the Essenes' Pentecostal festival in Jerusalem, when the Solar forces of the Christ Spirit were first unleashed like tongues of flame over the heads of the assembled sectaries. From that occasion onward, the new Way spread like wildfire in a manner unaccountable to those outside its action. Visions, healings, clairvoyance, and prophecy followed. Even as Jesus had received his power or "grace" from the Exousiai, the Angelic Authorities called "the Spirits of Creation," so now the heart center of each sectary was similarly flooded with spiritual power through the grace of the Master. Once opened to the action of the Christ Spirit, the heart center became the mediating intelligence between the procreative earth centers in the lower torso and the intellectual heaven centers in the head. Once the connection was made, once that inexhaustible reservoir of cosmic energy, of exousia, had been tapped, the disciple could then initiate others into communion with the Christ Spirit by the same method. And by the laws of sympathetic resonance, they in their turn could initiate others throughout the world.

The aim of the initiation was a very real intermingling of essences, in a sense a merging of identities. Thus Paul was able to say: "I am crucified with Christ: nevertheless, I live; yet not I, but Christ lives in me" (Galatians 2:20). And in 1 Corinthians he declares, "He who is united to the Lord becomes one spirit with him" (1 Corinthians 2:3–4).

Love was the essence of the new Way. It entailed a rite unknown to official Judaism, one that aimed at existential union with the Master, a "dying" with him and a "resurrection" with him into an altogether new level of consciousness, an elevation above and beyond the normal Nature-bound human condition. Today we might call it a transpersonal level of consciousness, its goal being identical with that of the traditional Mystery schools. In these, according to the Roman historian Plutarch, death and initiation closely corresponded.

> The primary object of these [Lesser Mystery] initiations was to take the candidate through the gates of death. The hierophant told Apuleius before his initiation that it was like a voluntary death followed by a slow recovery. As in shamanic, Masonic, and other later initiations, the candidate was placed in a trance, his consciousness taken out of his body, and in this state he experienced higher states of being and met some of the denizens of the invisible worlds. Then he would return to earth fully convinced of his immortality and prepared to meet death fearlessly, knowing it as the gate to freedom and his soul's true home.[1]

So also the soul was freed, though in full consciousness, from the strictures of its old separatist life by Jesus' secret all-night baptism. Through "the mystery of the Kingdom," the initiate received the inestimable experience of inner freedom; the higher worlds emerged; "death held no more terrors, the Law no more tyranny."

But such independence and dignity of spirit was not to last for long. Soon Jesus was turned into a heavenly Judge of sexual morals and Mary Magdalene, the Light-Bringer of the apocryphal texts, was rejected as a woman of wisdom and turned into a repentant whore. Morton Smith observes that, even by the second century, Paul's theory of charismatic baptism or *pneumatic* baptism inherited from the Master himself had become morally "dangerous" and had almost disappeared from contemporary writings. Instead, conservative Christian writers of the time represented the supernatural gifts of the spirit that accrued from the Pauline baptism as a promise for the future dependant on good behavior rather than an immediate consequence of the new yogic initiation. The extrasensory functions attendant on it were seen as

> not a present spiritual power and source of moral behavior, but a vague deposit to be protected by moral behavior. Notions of new birth, illumination, and exorcism occur, but are comparatively unimportant. The essential Pauline theme of death and resurrection with Christ is totally absent . . . The socially and morally conservative found it unsafe.[2]

Thus the existence of a mighty psychospiritual energy of Light moving in human life, expanding and illuminating its potential for evolutionary growth, remained in general unknown to all but the Mystery schools, and soon these too were to be disowned. Yet even when it was rejected by the orthodoxy that so soon replaced the primitive Christian faith, the new initiation went underground. It flourished in Gnostic and Manichaean enclaves and spread into Arabia, where seminal Sufi forces were preparing the ground for Islam. The Way of the Spiritual Heart would take over the esoteric scene in Mosul and Basra, the chief centers of Sufi mysticism; nourish Judaic Qabalah; inspire Russian Orthodox mysticism; and spread with Islam into India. And in Central Asia, heretical Nestorian Christianity would exert a deep influence on Buddhism. From the fifteenth century onward, the heart initiation was central to all the hidden esoteric traditions that illuminated Europe, despite the repressive activities of the Inquisition. Ever living, growing, and renewing itself, it was the same Way Jesus had initiated centuries before among his Palestinian disciples, as the apocryphal Dialogue of the Savior records.

> As Jesus talks with his three chosen disciples, Matthew asks him to show him the "place of life" which is, he says, the "pure light." Jesus answers, "Everyone of you who has known himself has seen it . . . " (Dialogue of the Savior 132:15–16)

When the disciples, expecting him to reveal secrets to them, ask Jesus, "Who is the one who seeks, and who is the one who reveals?" he answers that the one who seeks the truth—the disciple—is also the one who reveals it.[3]

Such sayings tell us better than any other that Jesus was directing his disciples to an altogether new and expanded sense of selfhood—almost, one might say, to a modern Jungian perspective on the self involving a process of psychological integration. This original seeding has grown over subsequent centuries into the peculiarly modern phenomenon of the Western world: the culture of the individual, psychologically aware, self-determining, morally self-responsible, and a passionate defender of human rights and freedoms, even to excess. Let us make no mistake: despite the Church's failure of nerve, despite all the obstacles, Jesus' Way of the Spiritual Heart, combining with the social charter of the New Covenant, was to work like a yeast in the collective psyche, ultimately to change the face of Western culture and at last that of much of the world.

However, although Krishna worship brought the same method to India, Hinduism elected to retain the ancient caste system and so the new Gnosis had less of a reforming impact on the Indian culture. As it turned out, the West also spurned the social implications of the New Covenant, but its caste system had always been less rigid than that of India and so has gradually given way to the Christian democratic spirit.

As we ponder Jesus' archetypal story, it becomes evident that this marvelous vehicle, the sensory body, is a two-edged boon—for the master as for the disciple. On the one hand it gives life, but on the other death. Not only has it the power to radiate the master's high spiritual energies to those in need of them, but it must also in exchange perforce receive and neutralize the lower energies it replaces—the hatred and lusts, the chattering arguments, the dead weight of inertia; these effluvia from the disciple must all be dissolved and washed away in the laboratory of the master's body. This heavy task performed by all genuine hierophants who are not merely self-appointed pedagogues leads all too often to illness or its karmic equivalent: inexplicable accidents, destructive assaults by enemies, martyrdom, or other calamitous events, as the lives of great masters have frequently testified. The Tibetan master Sogyal Rinpoche explains:

> Sometimes great masters who teach a lot, so it is said, do not live very long; it is almost as if they attract toward them any obstacles there are to the spiritual teachings. There were prophecies that if my master had put aside teaching . . . he would have lived for many more years . . . But once they found out who he was, people everywhere requested him to give teachings and initiations. So vast was his compassion that, knowing what he was risking, he sacrificed his own life to keep on teaching.[4]

Such sacrificial work almost inevitably leads the master deathward. "Surely he has borne our griefs and carried our sorrows," laments Isaiah, "yet we esteemed him stricken, smitten by God, and afflicted" (Isaiah 53:4). We can well envision that the magnitude of the task was so great, Jesus' path so exacting, that in all likelihood if he had not been crucified, he would have met death in some other way. In this sense he was indeed, as Isaiah says of the Suffering Servant, "wounded for our transgressions, he was bruised for our iniquities; upon him was the chastisement that made us whole, and with his stripes we are healed" (Isaiah 53:5).

THE CRUCIFIXION

Human sacrifice was the pivotal event in the old Mystery religions, their ritual culmination. Even when animals were substituted for humans, the event symbolized the voluntary death of the initiate king and his rebirth in a radiant Light body among the stars, from whence he would exercise his new magisterial powers for those on earth. The new Christ Mystery was to reiterate the same theme of death and ascension, but with a profoundly new meaning, for it was intended to show the way heavenward, not for the few but for every human being. The Passion of the Messiah was the Passion of humanity itself.

The gospels suggest that, no less than the taurobolium rite of the Mithraists, Jesus' death was in effect set up as a Passion play for the tuition of the people. The Apocryphon of John, or the Secret Book of John, a document believed to have been written by an unknown author early in the second century, accorded with the Gnostic tradition in depicting the Savior as a shamanistic, shape-changing adept of great magical powers who knew the secrets of the afterlife, a spiritual conjuror in league with angels. The Johannine text therefore posed for readers the burning question: Could a master gifted by such exceptional powers be crucified except by his own will? Did his very death not prove his Messiahship?

And in fact nothing we have learned since the Apocryphon was written suggests that Jesus could have been caught by inadvertence in Jerusalem's crude political toils. His death could only have been voluntary, like that of the god-kings of old; it could have come about only by intention and design as the key event in a new Mystery drama. At the very least, Jesus could have avoided drawing such provocative attention to himself as he did, or even entering Judaea at all. He could have done his work in the northern provinces, where opportunities of escape from his enemies were much greater, where, despite the example of the Baptist's fate, there were tracts of the Hauran to which judicial law rarely penetrated. Instead, we are forced by the events of history to surmise that Jerusalem and the Golgotha cross were Jesus' ineluctable, self-chosen destiny and had been embraced for the highest spiritual purpose. Early Christians were in no doubt that that high purpose was connected not so much with the redemption of sin as with Jesus' transmission of the new power of love to the world, a messianic act, which they celebrated each week in the agape, or Love Feast.

Qabalists know that to embody a principle in matter, to give it concrete material expression, is to potentiate it to an enormous degree.[5] It is the secret of all sacramental and ceremonial magic. "It should be recognized," says Dion Fortune, "that no [magical] operation is completed until the process has been expressed in terms of Malkuth, or, in other words, has issued forth in action on the physical plane."[6] The powerful effect of such magical "earthing" applies equally to religious operations, as can clearly be seen in the rich panoply of consecrated objects in the Roman and Orthodox Churches' liturgical ceremonies. Thus the drawing down of the mythic sacrifice onto the historical and physical plane of Malkuth, and showing it forth in the crucified flesh of the Redeemer, was to give a huge impetus to the new creed and guarantee its success over all the metaphors of the old Mystery religions.

Crucifixion is said to be the most painful of all deaths and in first-century Judaea the most demeaning. What kind of man, then, for whatever high purpose, submits himself voluntarily to such an agonizing fate? What extraordinary self-discipline produces the necessary purity of will and nerve, the strength of soul, to meet it? And how did an initiate of Jesus' advanced rank and powers bring himself to be executed as the lowest of criminals? Stringent prophetic training would certainly have played its part, enabling him to fulfill the teaching role for which he had been long prepared. (Instruction by analogy was, as we have already seen, a traditional method used among illiterate peoples by the prophets. The long-suffering Hosea is a prime example: Yahweh instructed him to marry a harlot in order to bring home to Israel its whoring after heathen gods.)

But the overwhelming factor in Jesus' strength of will in martyrdom was undoubtedly ideological; it was the drive to bring home to a foundering people the meaning of the Gnosis as the royal way of service and self-sacrifice. For this purpose the gospels tell us that Jesus took on the sacrificial role of the savior king "in order to fulfill the prophecies," which were predictive tracts in the scriptures long familiar to the Jews. And so Jesus allowed himself to be implicitly enveloped in the mantle of the Suffering Servant, to hang on the cross as the victim who appears in the book of Isaiah "a man of sorrows and acquainted with grief" (Isaiah 53:3).

Heir to the prophetic lineage of Isaiah and the kings of the Tophet, Jesus would have been no stranger to the sacrificial mythology of the Mysteries, in which the highest is brought willingly to the lowest and he who need not suffer does so willingly for others. It is purely in the light of the sublime philosophy underlying the custom of human sacrifice that we are enabled to see how Jesus, however terrible the cost, could have and must have willingly taken on the role of Messiah, colluding to relive on the plane of history the mythic drama of the ancient initiate kings.

Something of that surrender to the law of self-sacrifice is conveyed in another Gnostic document, the Acts of John, a Coptic translation from a Greek original also written by an unknown hand early in the second century in Upper Egypt. Formally anathematized at the Council of Nicaea, it is one of the few gnostic texts to have been known prior to the Nag Hammadi discovery. In the Acts of John, Jesus danced the ritual initiatory round dance in the upper room before his crucifixion and sang the antiphonal hymns with his disciples, as had been done in the Hebrew Mystery tradition from the earliest times. Whether the dance is to be taken literally or as an initiatory metaphor we do not know, but the whole passage, of which the following is a fragment, faithfully conveys the ecstasy and holy passion of the Suffering Servant.

> Now before he was taken by the lawless Jews . . . he gathered all of us together and said: "Before I give myself up to them, let us praise the Father in a hymn of praise, and so go forth to meet what is to come." Then he bade us make a circle, holding each other's hands, and he was in the middle. And he said: "Answer me with Amen." After which he began to sing a hymn of praise:

"Glory be to thee, Father!"

And we all, going around in a ring, answered, "Amen . . ."

"To each and all it is given to share in the dance!"

"Amen."

"A mansion I have not, and mansions I have."

"Amen."

"A torch am I to you who perceive me."

"Amen."

"A mirror am I to you who discern me."

"Amen."

"A door am I to you who knock on me."

"Amen."

"A way am I to you who pass."

"Amen."

"Glory be to thee, Father!"

"Amen."

"So as you respond to my dancing, behold yourself in me, the speaker. And when you see what I do, keep silent concerning my mysteries. You that dance, ponder what I do, for yours is this passion of humanity that I am about to suffer. For you could not at all have understood your suffering, had I not been sent to you as the Word of the Father . . . In your drive toward wisdom you have me for a bed: rest upon me . . . Had you known how to suffer, you would have been able not to suffer. See through suffering, and you will have non-suffering. What you know not, I myself will teach you . . . In me know the Word of Wisdom—say with me again:"

"Glory be to thee, Father!"

"Amen."

"Dance the round, all!"

"Amen."

And thus, my beloved, having danced with us, the Lord went forth. And like men gone astray or dazed with sleep, we fled this way and that . . .[7]

All Christendom knows the story of Jesus' subsequent death, the general outline of which is the same in all four gospels. Although we have no direct eyewitness account and no certainty that the crucifixion really took place in the way the Christian scriptures record, the gospel writers present it as a faithful Mystery reenactment. Harking back to the old Hebrew Mysteries, they recount that the crucifixion took place on the eve of the great Passover festival in Jerusalem, and that Jesus, wearing the thorny crown of immolation and carrying a reed scepter, was given the purple robe of royalty to wear and was mocked and humiliated before he died—as were the messianic kings of antiquity ritually struck, stripped of their garments, and humiliated.[8] Psalm 22 of David, which liturgically voices the ordeals of initiation, develops this same theme of the Suffering Servant:

> My God, my God, why hast thou forsaken me? Why art thou so far from helping me, from the words of my groaning? But I am a worm, and no man; scorned by men, and despised by the people. All who see mock at me, they make mouths at me, they wag their heads: He committed his cause to the Lord; let him deliver him, Let him rescue him, for he delights in him!
>
> Thou dost lay me in the dust of death. Yea, dogs are round about me; a company of evildoers encircle me; they have pierced my hands and my feet—I can count all my bones—they stare and gloat over me; they divide my garments among them and for my raiment they cast lots.

Precisely choreographed in all its minutest details, the gospels recount Jesus' ordeal on the cross—thus decisively refuting the modern charge that Paul alone, in defiance of his Master's teachings, transformed a devout Jewish cult into a pagan Mystery religion, thus becoming the first Christian. On the contrary, if we are to believe the canon, Jesus' death was a Mystery enactment from the beginning, and Jesus presented himself as a voluntary sacrificial victim. Gnostic documents present the crucifixion as primarily a reenactment of the ancient holocaust in the

Tophet. In all four gospels, Jesus, human and suffering, hung on the cross on Golgotha as an enactment of the Mystery of love, of sacrificial service.

Elsewhere deleted, in the Codex Sinaiticus Luke's Gospel records that on the Mount of Olives, while Jesus was praying before his death, "there appeared to him an angel from heaven, strengthening him. And being in agony, he prayed more earnestly; and his sweat became as it were great drops of blood falling down upon the ground."[9] The Codex Sinaiticus, discovered only in the nineteenth century, is the earliest and most reliable known rendition of the gospels, having been written in the fourth century. There is no idealized picture of Jesus as a divine being incapable of suffering or of needing the ministrations of angels, as was presented in some later, docetic literature reminiscent of Mahayana Buddhism. The docetic version is quoted below from the Apocalypse of Peter, found among the Nag Hammadi codices. Here the disciple recounts how he saw Jesus "glad and laughing" on the cross as the nails were driven into his hands and feet. The Lord explains:

> He whom you saw on the Tree, glad and laughing, this is the living Jesus. But this one into whose hands and feet they drive nails is his fleshly part, which is the substitute being put to shame, the one who came into being in his likeness.[10]

In Sinaiticus, however, Jesus is a human being in a human body facing a most dreadful death, and many of the details in this early document give the lie to the docetic interpretations of the Crucifixion that arose later.

> Now from the sixth hour there was darkness over all the land until the ninth hour. And about the ninth hour Jesus cried with a loud voice, "My God, my God, why have you forsaken me?" . . . And some of the bystanders hearing it said, "This man is calling Elijah." And one of them at once ran and took a sponge, filled it with vinegar, and put it on a reed, and gave it to him to drink. But the others said,

"Wait, let us see whether Elijah will come and save him." And Jesus cried again with a loud voice and yielded up his spirit. And behold, the curtain of the temple was torn in two, from top to bottom; and the earth shook, and the rocks were split; the tombs also were opened, and many bodies of the saints who had fallen asleep were raised . . . (Matthew 27:45–53)

There is a very real poignancy to this terrible event that cannot be romanticized in any way. And around it the gospel writers have woven the same kind of conspiratorial details noted earlier in this book. Once again, after the Crucifixion shadowy figures emerge from the background to take charge: the rich merchant Joseph of Arimathea with his new rock tomb already conveniently hewn out, the mysterious figure in white, thought to be an Essene, who guards the tomb throughout the night. All the details appear to have been thought out beforehand, even to the point of suggesting that the entombment of Jesus' body in the Gethsemane garden was intended to confirm the prophecies concerning the death of the Suffering Servant—"and they made his grave with the wicked and with a rich man in his death" (Isaiah 53:9).

The twentieth chapter of the Gospel of John is particularly redolent of such Mystery themes. There we learn that while it was still dark, Mary Magdalene was the first to come to the tomb. She saw the stone rolled away and ran to tell the other disciples that the body was gone, mourning as once the women had mourned for the death of their young god-king Tammuz. "Him of the plains why have they slain?" wept the goddess Ishtar, searching in vain for her beloved Tammuz: "The shepherd, the wise one, the man of sorrows, why have they slain?"[11] And even as the goddess Inanna once mourned for Dumuzi, and Isis for Osiris, and Aphrodite for Adonis, so Mary wept that they had taken her Lord out of the tomb, "and I know not where they have laid him."

And when she had thus said, she turned herself back, and saw Jesus standing, and knew not that it was Jesus. Jesus said unto her, "Woman, why do you weep? Whom do you seek?" She, supposing him to be the gardener, said unto him, "Sir, if thou have borne him hence, tell me where thou hast laid him, and I will take him away." Jesus said unto her, "Mary." She turned herself, and said unto him, "Rabboni;" which is to say, Master. Jesus said unto her, "Touch me not; for I am not yet ascended to my Father." (John 20:13–17)

As Baring and Cashford point out, the significance of Mary's "mistaking" of the risen Christ for the gardener "is supremely resonant, because the gardener was the name given to the son lover of the goddess in Sumer, where Inanna's tears also flowed for the loss of her Lord."[12] All these elliptical allusions in the gospels to the old Solar Mysteries and the ritual slaying and resurrection of their god-kings point unmistakably to what the evangelists saw as the symbolic nature of Jesus' death. It too, as in the pagan tradition, was intended to illustrate the supreme initiation and translation of a god-king from human to divine Solar status—but now enacted in the full glare of historical reality. And it would have been just such ritual language on the part of the gospels that alerted large numbers of Essenes and other sectaries from the various Hasidic branches to Jesus' messianic qualifications, and converted them to the new movement. For "those with ears to hear" the gospels were without doubt a clarion call to all initiates, to all those attuned to the underlying symbolism of the Mysteries.

The resurrection of Christ from the grave is Christianity's defining moment, the transcendental climax of the cycle of birth and death that epitomizes all the Mystery religions of antiquity—in them symbolically enacted, but in Christianity played out on the plane of history. In a certain sense all institutional religions are symbolic, all mythologies allegorical ways of illustrating humanity's most important evolutionary stations. The claim by his followers that after death Jesus rose to life again transformed at a stroke the significance of millennia of Mystery plays. Henceforth, men and women were exhorted to withdraw their religious energies from the larger-than-life epiphanies of myth and focus them on the adamantine reality of the human soul itself and its own potential for divinity and immortality, as Gnostics were insistent that the supreme distinction between the old Mysteries and the new Christian Mystery lay in Jesus' perfect humanity. Early Christians never thought of him as God. In the Gnostic work *The Sophia of Jesus Christ,* a papyrus codex discovered in 1896, the risen Jesus teaches his disciples concerning the mystery of the First Man:

> I desire that you understand that *First Man* is called Begetter, Mind who is complete in himself. He reflected with the great Sophia, his consort, and revealed his first-begotten, androgynous son. His male name is called "First-Begetter Son of God:" his female name is "First Begettress Sophia, Mother of the Universe." Some call her Love. Now the First-Begotten is called "Christ."[13] (author's italics)

Here we are presented with the concept of archetypal man, the perfect human being who was originally androgynous and only at a final stage of his development acquired polarity in a male or female body. Thus the idea of resurrection enshrined in the new Mysteries, connected as it was with the fate not of a god but of the perfect human being, had enormous metaphysical overtones for early Christians, with meanings no myth could fully decipher. To many of us today it is clear that death and initiation have much in common—death leads to a rebirth or resurrection into a new life on a higher plane of consciousness—in a new, more rarefied body. Consequently, it seems not improbable that this is what Christ's resurrection and ascension were meant to illustrate, that his glorification is the destiny of all of us. And yet . . . the Resurrection continues to baffle understanding, being regarded to the present day as either a New Testament hoax or its deepest mystery.

In the years after the Crucifixion, the death of the human body and indeed the body itself became the center of the most profound Gnostic enquiry, raising questions about it that had never before been posed. What was the nature of the human body? Could a dead man come back to life in his old physical flesh? Did Jesus, uniquely, really teach his apostles in the flesh after his crucifixion, walking, talking, and eating with them, or was it in some other, more subtle way?

These questions were absolutely central to the Christian faith, for the doctrine of the physical resurrection that came to be embodied in the Nicaean Creed was undoubtedly fundamental to the movement's monumental success. The proclamation that a man, "crucified, dead and buried," on the third day rose bodily from the grave was electrifying news; it was seen as a unique historical event and drew thousands of believers into the new sect. "For Jesus' followers," says Pagels "this was the turning point of history, the sign of its coming end."[14] But was it true? Or was it a simplified presentation for uneducated folk of a truth not otherwise easily assimilated?

Many theologians now openly question the bodily resurrection. As they point out, two thousand years ago people had a different mindset from our own, one more naive, less intellectually honed; facing their own death they may well have found great comfort and reassurance in the doctrine: that on the great Judgment Day at the end of time the graves would burst open and there would be a general "standing up of corpses" as promised by the Lord. But today, in a very different kind of skeptical, scientific, specializing yet well-informed culture, the literal interpretation of the resurrection story is generally regarded as absurd—and not only absurd, but also offensive and repugnant. Indeed Tertullian himself, aiming to override the shock to his readers of such a pronouncement, insisted that "it must be believed, because it is absurd!"

But Gnostics of the time were no more impressed by Tertullian's argument than the majority of men and women would be today, and controversy raged endlessly around it. Celsus, a Syrian philosopher of the second century, reported that bitter and intractable disputes regarding the resurrection were tearing apart the various Christian groups: "They slander one another with dreadful and unspeakable words of abuse, and would not make even the least concession to come to agreement; for they utterly detest one another."[15] At the beginning of the twentieth century Gilbert Murray, then Regius Professor of Greek at Oxford, summed up what he saw as the triumph of superstition such as Tertullian's over good sense:

It is a strange experience . . . to study these obscure congregations, drawn from the proletariat of the Levant, superstitious, charlatan-ridden and helplessly ignorant, who still believed in Gods begetting children of mortal mothers, who took the "Word," the "Spirit" and the "Divine Wisdom" to be persons called by these names, and turned the Immortality of the Soul into "the standing up of corpses;" and to reflect that it was these who held the main road of advance towards the greatest religion of the western world.[16]

It is now considered certain that the works called *The Letter of Barnabas* and *The Shepherd of Hermes,* once included in the canon of the Christian scriptures, were dropped from it because they opposed a bodily resurrection, a doctrine that had by then attained great popularity among the orthodox. Yet from the outset many Gnostics called it "the faith of fools," and claimed that resurrection was a purely spiritual event: Jesus, even while in his physical body, had worn the resurrected garment of Light, the shining spirit body of the higher planes that provides the model for the physical body and which outlives it, being itself immortal. Thus there is stated in the Letter to Rheginus, a treatise on the resurrection found in the Nag Hammadi corpus and believed to be from the Valentinian teachings: "We are drawn to heaven by him [Jesus] like the beams of the sun, not being restrained by anything. This is the spiritual resurrection." The letter urges Christians not to live "in conformity with this flesh . . . but to flee from the divisions and the fetters." In this way, "already you have the resurrection."[17]

The Gospel of Philip, which anthologizes many of Valentinus's sayings, insists: "While we exist in the world we must acquire resurrection" (Philip 55:15–16). Valentinus taught that physical death is irrelevant to the resurrection event. Resurrection marks a transformation in the subtle body; it occurs when exousia, coursing through the heart chakra, causes a new cognitive organ to develop like an eye opening in wonder to a world transformed. The great Gnostic teacher believed that when baptism is a truly effective initiation this wondrous perceptual awakening takes place.

> People who say they will first die and then arise are mistaken. If they do not first receive resurrection while they are alive, once they have died they will receive nothing. Just so is it said of baptism: "Great is baptism!" For if one received it, one will live. (Philip 79)

Yet three of the gospel writers—Matthew, Luke, and John—seem to reject this explanation. They insist that after his death, Jesus reappeared among his disciples in the flesh, not as a ghost, hallucination, or inner vision but as a fully physical human being who miraculously walked, ate, and talked with them in his resuscitated earthly body just as he had in life; and each of their accounts ends with much circumstantial narrative confirming the fact. Even Paul, who witnessed the living Jesus only in vision, confirms that he had it from Peter and other disciples that the Master appeared in the flesh, "first to James" and then to many of them and indeed ultimately to a crowd of five hundred people gathered together, to whom he preached (1 Corinthians 15:7).

But what of Mark, the fourth evangelist? Why is there no legitimate account of the resurrection at the end of his gospel, though some editions of the Christian scriptures have seen fit to add one? On this point, there is an item of considerable interest hidden in the academic archives that has been studied by past scholars but then buried and all but forgotten by later ones. According to the Codex Sinaiticus, Mark's gospel originally contained no reference to Jesus' appearance to his disciples after his death, but ended at chapter 16, verse 8, with the empty tomb. The last twelve verses, 9–20, although usually added on in the later received texts, are spurious. In Sinaiticus the three women disciples brought oils to the tomb of Jesus and found the stone that blocked its entrance rolled away; they were then told by a young man sitting there in a long white robe that Jesus was risen and "will go before you into Galilee and you will see him there, as he told you" (Mark 16:5–7). The women were terrified; they ran away and "said nothing to anybody." Here the scribe ends the story with a squiggle (the Greek word *gar*) and begins the Gospel of Luke.[18]

There are believed to be no authentic endings to Mark's gospel, though many have been improvised. The ending with gar is unusual and therefore many scholars believed the last sentence must continue; but examples of sentences ending in gar have now been found in Homer, Aeschylus, and Euripedes, and in the Greek version of the Hebrew scriptures. It became clear that the very earliest gospel tradition stressed only the empty tomb and ignored altogether any supposed appearances. In Sinaiticus no disciple actually sees Jesus after his death and his resurrection is of an unspecified nature. The text could have been referring to a secret burial of Jesus' body by his incognito Hasidean brothers, one of whom may well have stayed on in the tomb and spoken to Mary. The unknown young Hasid in white, who certainly seems to have known a great deal more about events than the disciples, could furthermore have been implying that Jesus will rise in the spirit rather than bodily, and in the spirit will precede his disciples on their return to Galilee, *as he had promised.* (Once again we catch that whiff of things unsaid, of prior discussions and prior arrangements by mysterious unknown agents, perhaps of many things going on in the background that the gospel narrator is not prepared to divulge.)

Matthew rather than Mark was always believed to have written the first of the synoptic gospels, so the lack of any appearance of the risen Jesus in Sinaiticus was not regarded by biblical scholars as important until the truth dawned—that Matthew and Luke had copied Mark and added their own miraculous embellishments, giving the enigmatic ending of Mark's gospel a more colorful tone, a literal interpretation, and a greater aura of piety than anything that appears in the original. Most importantly, while in Mark there is no provision for the tradition of apostolic succession, the three later gospels have very definitely created one, basing it on which disciple saw the risen Lord first—thus ensuring several centuries of bitter debate among the faithful, for as we know, although in Mark, Mary Magdalene was the first to see the empty tomb and in the other three gospels the first to see the one she took to be a gardener, she was disqualified from leading the future Church by virtue of her gender and unpopular gnostic credentials. So the disorganized and virtually leaderless Gnostics lost out to Peter in the race for apostolic primacy. Very soon, for the soundest of political reasons, it became the norm that anyone in Christendom who doubted the bodily resurrection of the Lord branded himself a heretic.

Manuscripts have been found in which the scribes themselves add a note that the last eleven verses of Mark do not appear in older copies. All the many scriptural fragments of papyruses found at Oxyrinchus in Egypt and elsewhere, and which were written before the Sinai Codex, support Mark. They too witness that originally there was no mention of a physical resurrection of Jesus or of physical appearances to his disciples after his death, or of his physical ascension to heaven. As a consequence, the British scholar C. F. Evans wrote in 1969 that "at the heart of the resurrection tradition appeared a vacuum, the nature and meaning of which scholars continue to debate."[19]

But there are more thoughtful commentators who believe Mark left out the resurrection story from his gospel because he regarded it as one of the higher mysteries.[20] Mark was the author of a secret Gnostic gospel for those "who had been initiated into the Mysteries." He knew that the literal raising of Lazarus from the dead was no more than a cypher for secret rites of initiation, and was therefore well aware that there were aspects of the Gnosis, such as resurrection, that must be revealed only to the spiritually mature. Other aspects must be either left undisclosed or camouflaged in the garment of myth for presentation to the uninitiated Christian. Morton Smith quotes Dr. Richardson, the Professor of Church History at Union Theological Seminary, in contending that Jesus' mysteries were for the true Gnostic and Mark didn't write down or divulge these.[21] Indeed, the Markan gospel explicitly states that the "secret of the Kingdom of God" is given directly to Jesus' disciples, but only via parables to "those who are outside" (Mark 4:11). Mark therefore presents a much more unorthodox point of view than many Christians realize.

We must remember that the Nag Hammadi texts were discovered only fifty years ago and made known considerably later than that. Their range and power, and the subtlety of their metaphysics, have scarcely impacted as yet on our contemporary habits of thought. But that situation will change, and is indeed already changing as Gnostic ideas regain their place in the forefront of religious philosophy. The early resurrection debate as reflected in the Apocryphon of John tells us better than perhaps any other Nag Hammadi topic how much the West would benefit from a deeper consideration of the Gnostic position.

A NEW GENESIS

From a metaphysical point of view, the most provocative of all the many layers of spiritual meaning underlying the Resurrection is to be found in the Apocryphon of John, or Secret Book of John, which deals with the spiritual genesis of the physical body. It is a strange, dense, and difficult document, one of the few instances in the history of Gnosticism that openly reveals the subtle technology underlying so-called miracles. It purports to have been written by John the Evangelist or else by John, son of Zebedee, one of Jesus' other disciples, but is now thought to have been the work of an unknown second-century Gnostic, and according to Bentley Layton was probably the basis for Valentinus's teachings.[22]

The Apocryphon implicitly supports Mark's view that the Resurrection was one of humanity's deepest evolutionary secrets preserved in the Mystery centers, and that the document written by Clement reflects a baptismal mystery beyond the competence of the average Christian to decipher. This was why it had been deleted from Mark's gospel account—not because the story was a fabrication but precisely because it was not. The British author Ian Wilson arrives at a similar conclusion.

> We seem from Clement's letter to have corroboration that there really was a "secret," "more spiritual" version of Jesus' teaching "for the use of those being perfected," just as we have suspected from Thomas.[23]

Morton Smith, who agrees, believes the more spiritual version of the Resurrection was transmitted via Jesus' secret form of baptism— the mysterious pneumatic baptism of the Gnostics tirelessly given by

Paul on his many travels. Dr. Smith's conclusion is the one contained in the Secret Book of John, which intimates that behind Jesus' tuition of those being initiated was a body of the highest teachings from the Mystery schools, and that these incorporated a secret science concerning the organization of matter and the formation and dissolution of bodies in objective space. This, says the author, is the true teaching of the Resurrection that has been transmitted to him mystically, which he has been directed to write down and keep safe for Christ's posterity.

Gnostics like John of the Apocryphon believed that after the Resurrection and before his ascension to heaven the Lord remained on earth in a spiritualized body and taught his inner circle of disciples the naked truth, unadorned by parables or metaphors. He demonstrated that the soul has a lofty destiny. After death it is not doomed to wander as a shade or ghost in the underworld paths of Sheol, as generally believed, but can rise to a high, light-filled plane of being beyond the grip of pain or sorrow. There it will be clothed in a body like the discarded earthly one, but in more ethereal or refined matter. And by a series of transmutations on even higher planes the body will eventually be glorified as a spiritual vehicle like that of the angels, sculpted out of pure crystallized Light. Thus do we recapitulate after death our original descent from spiritual to material embodiment—wherein lies the secret of resurrection.

Joseph Campbell regards the Apocryphon as having certain similarities to Mahayana Buddhism, but that in no way disqualifies it from being an authentic expression of Christ's teachings. Written perhaps only a few decades after the fourth gospel appeared, John's discourse is full of neologisms and obscure Gnostic personifications that are extremely confusing to the modern reader. But reduced to its bare essentials, it describes the four stages in the formation of the human body, from its spiritual archetype to its material manifestation, in precisely the same terms as Qabalistic Genesis describes the fourfold formation of the universe. As the greatest of the archangels, the Christ Spirit, according to John, creates his own body out of the divine Light of the Godhead. He can do this because he understands the laws of the organization of living bodies the laws of materialization, and can therefore manipulate them in the creative sculpting of Light to serve his own ends. Self-created and autonomous, his Light body is then the template for the three further stages in the manifestation of the human body in space-time: first the intellectual-spiritual body, then the emotional-astral, and last the physical-elemental, with its complex sensory system and differentiated sex.

In the case of most human souls incarnating on earth, this is a creative process they cannot as yet carry out themselves, being therefore obliged to depend on angelic agencies. John describes how in the formation of Adam's mind-body the anatomical parts are delineated in luminous soul stuff by the higher spirits of the Soul worlds and in conformity with the causal blueprint. There then follows the creation of the emotional or astral body of Light-Adam and Light-Eve, which covers the mind-body. Shining in splendor like the sun, it is again built up by angelic beings according to the template of the archetypal Light body.

Last, the material body further encases the heavenly Adam and Eve in a dark shell that covers and conceals the glory of the preceding ones. It is formed by cohorts of lower angels who model it on the archetypal body, matching it to the original organ by organ and limb by limb, but in the coarser material of the etheric and earthly elements of Nature. To the trained vision of the initiate, therefore, the death of the physical body is like a veil drawn aside to reveal the greater reality—the living glory of the Light body on which it has been modeled and which is immortal, being subject to neither spatial nor temporal limitations. The soul's awakening into perfect wholeness within that spiritual body of Light, a body not subject to death, is the true resurrection. John makes clear that in the case of the Savior, this creative process was under his own control and was instrumental in his after-death appearances to others.

It was a Gnostic belief that the avatar is one who has mastered the secret science of bodily manifestation and can fashion his own body at will, as we shall be able to do in the further course of our evolution. The outlawed Acts of John describes how, because of his conquest of the laws of matter, the Savior was capable of appearing to many people at once in an objective form, clothed not in flesh but in light. And he could appear in many and varied semblances, according to the subjective interpretation of each observer.[24]

Thus, just as Mary Magdalene mistakes her master for an unknown gardener before recognizing him as her risen Lord, so one of the disciples out fishing on the Lake of Galilee on spying Jesus on the shore sees him as a child, whereas another in the same boat sees him as a tall adult in altogether different guise. Reminiscent of the shape-changing reality shifting of the master shaman, the unearthly ability of Christ Jesus to manipulate his corporeality is noted in the canon but is nowhere explained, and is now more often than not dismissed as a mere superstitious legend. But for the unknown author of the Acts of John, it is a reality, as it is for the writer of the Apocryphon. The latter likewise says that as he was grieving after the Crucifixion, he saw a heavenly light:

> [I was afraid, and I] saw in the light [a child] . . . while I looked he became like an old man. And he [changed his] form again, becoming like a servant . . . I saw . . . an [image] with multiple forms, in the light . . . (Apocryphon of John 1:30–2:7)

And the Letter of Peter to Philip, which was discovered at Nag Hammadi, recounts that as the disciples were praying on the Mount of Olives after Jesus' death, the Lord appeared to all of them at once.

> A great light appeared, so that the mountain shone from the sight of him who had appeared. And a voice called out to them saying, "Listen . . . I am Jesus Christ, who is with you forever." (Letter of Peter to Philip 134:10–18)

Collective visions of this sort are not strange to the modern world, as the countless contemporary appearances of the Virgin Mary attest. In a similar manner, the Gospel of Philip says:

> Jesus tricked everyone; for he did not appear as he was but appeared in such a way that he could be seen. And he appeared to the great

as someone great . . . and to the small as someone small. (Philip 23:28–35)

Clearly this was a tenet firmly held by a range of Gnostic writers. Those visionaries who profess to have seen the Virgin Mary on one of her many appearances make precisely the same claim of objective reality variably interpreted by observers. *She really was there,* they insist, though in a luminous incorporeal body, a body objectively real and yet not physical, not material—a body of crystallized Light that has been self-organized on an inner plane, as John's Secret Book suggests.

Mainstream Christianity professes no knowledge of such metaphysical theories; it knows nothing of the afterlife or the laws of matter or of life prior to the birth of the earthly body. But the Gnostic conception of resurrection is supported by certain occult traditions in the East, which affirm the possibility of a conquest of the material forces as so complete that a voluntary materialization and dematerialization of the body can be achieved at will. In *The Autobiography of a Yogi,* Swami Paramahansa Yogananda (1893–1952), the Indian saint who established the Self-Realization Fellowship of America, tells of several such materializations on the part of great Hindu yogis of his own lineage. One such, he reports, appeared after death to three of his disciples in different parts of India at the same time, conversing with each in an apparently solid flesh-and-blood form.[25] Yogananda furthermore describes firsthand how his own deceased guru, Sri Yukteswar Giri, appeared to his disciples apparently in the flesh, communicating new teachings concerning the afterlife in so solid, so physical a form that they could see, touch, and even hug him. Nevertheless, this body of his, although real, solid, and objectively perceptible, was not of the same nature as theirs, but rather an apparition, a phantom body maintained for fairly short periods and which could be dematerialized at will.[26]

The Yaki Amerindian shamans, inheritors of the great Siberian shamanic tradition, are also reported to be masters of strange feats of shape changing, invisibility, and after-death visitations to the living, as the South American mystic Carlos Castaneda has testified.[27] The Yaki belief is that the shaman is one who, in order to redeem lost or afflicted souls, can cross and recross the death threshold at will through the power of his trained consciousness. For him death, or initiation, is not the end of life but instead a gateway to new life, new powers, new bodily forms (human or animal), and new and expanded experiences in other worlds. For him the life of the soul is eternal, deathless, ever verdant, springing again and again from the fiery ashes of transmutation into a new bodily abundance, in new spheres of reality that are under his control.

Tibetan Buddhism has drawn deeply from the same traditional Siberian source. The American Buddhist Tsultrim Allione, an ex-nun, describes in her book *Women of Wisdom* the incredible degree of mastery that some Tibetan adepts have demonstrated over the materialization and dematerialization of the physical body due to their shamanic training. She tells how Tibetan yogis in the Dzog Chen tradition practice a technique called Yang-Ti, which "aims at the dissolution of the physical and mental world into the body of light or the rainbow body."[28] Yang-Ti seems to have been common among Tibetan holy men and women, many reports of which occur in the recent translations of their biographies and autobiographies made in Dharamsala, India, for Western publication. This extraordinary science is especially associated with the secret wisdom of High Asia passed down from Ice Age shaman masters to the indigenous Bon religion and thence to Tibetan Buddhism.

By means of this science, yogis can dismantle their corporeal covering in such a way as to convert its elemental constituents back into the Light from which it was originally built, and to reconstitute it in a new body of Light so that nothing of the physical is left behind except the hair and fingernails. In this manner they take the rainbow body (that is, the causal or archetypal Light body) at the threshold of death, transferring their consciousness over a matter of months of intensive meditation to a higher level of being. The practice is an example par excellence of the power over matter possessed by a yoga adept's highly developed consciousness.

Once matter is understood to be energy crystallized in a pattern whose components can be broken up and reorganized by the laser beam of a highly concentrated mind, or that can be transformed to a field of finer light vibrations by the same means, the practice of Yang-Ti can be better understood.[29]

The body grows smaller and smaller until it is no bigger than a child, and finally the yogi takes on "the everlasting robe of glory" visible only to clairvoyant eyes. In the new Light form the adept can actually be seen by those disciples who are left ascending into the atmosphere and disappearing in a rainbow to join a host of other Light beings in the spiritual world. On occasion there is a return in the same way. Even as the divine Mother descends to earth for the support of her Christian children, so the departed soul of the Buddhist adept descends to earth in a cloud of sentient radiance to communicate again with the disciples remaining on earth.

> He [or she] becomes one of those beings of light of which the phi-losopher Plotinus spoke, who became visible in the Mystery initia-tions and who move invisibly in our earthly world on their errands of mercy, the Bodhisattvas of the higher regions.[30]

If the Easter climax is not merely a fictional coda to Jesus' story to add color and drama to the plain tale, could it fall into the above yogic cat-egory? Despite being foreign to the mainstream religious tradition of the West, in the case of Jesus we see from the above that there are well-attested precedents in Eastern annals for a quasi-corporeal form of resur-rection in a spiritualized body: that is to say, for a real event in objective space, but one that is not necessarily visible to everyone. There is certain evidence in the gospels, both canonical and apocryphal, that Jesus may have possessed just such a shamanistic mastery over the forces of mate-rial existence. In the Gospel of John he says:

> The good shepherd lays down his life for his sheep . . . For this rea-son the Father loves me, because I lay down my life, that I may take it [up] again. No one takes it from me, but I lay it down of my own

accord. *I have the power to lay it down and I have power to take it* [up] *again:* this charge I have received from the Father. (John 10:17–19) (author's italics)

The implication here is that after death Jesus was able to dissolve and reassemble his body at will: its life was under his command. But this supernatural ability either was not understood by his chroniclers or was suppressed as too dangerous an item of knowledge. In *Jesus the Magician,* Morton Smith ransacks the historical records to demonstrate Jesus' awesome reputation as an exorcist and magician both before and for many centuries after his death.[31] In the light of this research, it is possible that the Resurrection was another example of Jesus' shamanistic skills, exercised in order to continue on earth the dissemination among his closest disciples of higher teachings concerning corporeality.

If so, it well may be that after the Crucifixion, Christ was both buried in the flesh and arose triumphant in the spirit, appearing to his disciples from time to time over several months in the habiliments of a phantom body. Would there have been a better way to show that the shadowy underworld of Sheol was defeated? Like Christ himself, humanity had potential mastery of all the planes of being and that potentially at least, human beings were citizens of all the worlds, as was the Savior of the Apocryphon:

> *For I existed in the beginning, traveling in every*
> *   path of travel . . .*
> *Yet a third time I traveled—*
> *I who am the light that exists within the light . . .*
> *So that I might enter the midst of the darkness*
> *   and the interior of Hades:*
> *And I entered the midst of their prison,*
> *Which is the prison of the body.*
> *And I said: O listener, arise from heavy*
> *   sleep . . .*[32]

John is perhaps giving us a glimpse, a foretaste, of our own destiny. He is telling us that behind the resurrection event, there is a science of creation that all human beings on the path of perfection may acquire. They too will receive both the enlightened ethos and the evolutionary energies that were manifest in Jesus, enabling them to utilize the technology of the spirit that creates universes. The implication is that new types of civilization will arise in the future that will ensure that the mechanical technologies we know today will be used less and less, creative rapport with our own natural forces developed more and more. This will permit the control of our cellular structure, its spiritualization, in such a way that the body can live forever, manifesting or vanishing at will, and presumably able to heal itself, modify its functions, demonstrate its immunity to destruction, overcome the limitations of space and time, and in general obey the dictates of the higher human will. Achieving ever-greater autonomy, human beings may thus become increasingly self-created, self-sustaining universes capable of radiating potencies unimaginable today. As Valentinus says of humanity and its glorious future: "From the beginning you have been immortal, and you are children of eternal life . . ."

Yet the sublime vision of our potential has been lost to the Church: the notion that the Christian religion might be a storehouse of natural sciences and metaphysical knowledge has vanished as though it had never been. And similar has been the fate of the esoteric path of exousia, once a dynamic engine for self-transformation that incorporated psychosomatic techniques designed to release forces of love, creativity, and healing that would change the world. Could there not be many other such Gnostic discoveries to be made in the future?

But here we enter the zone of uncertainty that surrounds everything concerning Jesus and his true identity and role in history. It is a fact of history that the founders of great religions are strangely anonymous; they pass through our lives without leaving personal footprints, so hidden in their dealings that their life stories are rarely known. One has only to think of the Buddha, or perhaps of Zoroaster, whose very birth date falls anywhere within a thousand years' latitude. So also in the Acts of John, Jesus discloses his anonymity to his disciples even as they dance the round dance of renunciation in the upper room:

> For what you are that your see, and I have shown it to you; but what I am I alone know, and no man else. I was thought to be what I am not, not being what I was to those many others. What they will say of me is wretched and unworthy of me. Those who neither see nor name the place of stillness will much less see the Lord. First, therefore, know the Word, the inwardness, the meaning. Then secondly you will know the Lord, and thirdly, the man and what he has suffered.[33]

Thus we are invited to contemplate both the majesty and the pathos of these unknown avatars from the fifth kingdom, of which Jesus is one of the most eminent. We know he was the means of bringing greater social awareness and understanding, and a greater egalitarian freedom, into human lives, so paving the way for the liberalism of the modern Western world. We know that he imprinted onto the consciousness of an entire age the emblematic rose of Love. But who can safely categorize him? Who can say that he did not inherit many of the secrets of existence possessed by the great yogic brotherhoods such as the Sons of the Sun in Egypt, central Asia, and the Far East? Who can say that he did not have depths of knowledge we have not yet plumbed? On such issues our ignorance is profound. All that can realistically be set down in the records, and perhaps it is enough, is that Jesus, that most humble of men, fulfilled the evolutionary function of one of the greatest Lords of the Eternal ever to enter history.

THINGS TO COME

*The instrument of all human enlightenment is an educated
mind illuminated by revelation.*

JOHN MICHELL

S ince the fourth century, when Constantine turned Christianity
from a mystical Gnostic sect accused of dealings with demons into
a populist state religion, the faith has spread to every continent on earth
and numbers its membership in the millions. In that time it has hived
off into huge independent branchings and innumerable sub-branches
that have become extraordinarily powerful, politically dominant hegemonies. Yet amid the momentous social and ideological changes of the
past hundred years, Christianity seems to have stood still. For countless
people, the power of the Church's old authoritarian dogmas has waned.
In its place are dawning the psychological verities, the self-discovery,
and the self-autonomy of a new kind of processive spirituality. The
Gnosis has returned to challenge the dominance of the Aristotelian
world model on which Christian theology is still based. The revelations
now emerging of hidden sexual degeneracy among its priests reflect yet
further the impoverished intellectual core of the faith, the profound
loss of spiritual fiber and vitality.

Christianity was once aware that spiritual idealism must be yoked
to a critical intelligence, yet its present repudiation of any sound wisdom
tradition is almost as thoroughgoing as it was in 326, when Constantine outlawed the Gnostics. The tendency of all democratic rule to

descend into a tyranny of the lowest common denominator still afflicts the religion as it did in its Episcopal councils of long ago, and so too does reliance on hypnotically repeated doctrinal clichés in place of study and creative reflection. Meanwhile, Jesus himself has become a remote, stylized, mythic figure and to that extent has been diminished in the Western consciousness as a center of cosmic power; and the entire paraphernalia of saints, divinities, holy icons, and sacred festivals once intrinsic to Christendom has lost much of its magic. Despite the religion's populist spread across the world, the revelation at its heart has grown dim and for many it stands as a spent force.

David Tacey speaks for the vast majority of people in the West who have rejected formal religion when he says that the traditional Christian form of worship is primarily a group experience, communal, collective, devotional; whereas the kind of spirituality now being everywhere sought is an interior one, a cultivation of the inner life of the individual alone. "The spiritual urge seeks an inner journey and understanding," he says, "but conventional religion remains external to the self and far too historical."[1] This inner urge was precisely what drove so many Jews to embrace the Christian movement in the first place; they were "the solitary ones" who saw the Jesus revelation as the road away from communal ritual to the existential life of the self, to the personal spiritual journey.

A striking similarity confronts us when we review the spiritual climate of our Western world today and that of the Greco-Roman world of the first century. History books of the future will distinguish both as periods of major social and ideological change, transitional eras marking a struggle of epic proportions between old and new worldviews. Tacey refers to it as "a clash of paradigms." Separated by two thousand years, both eras have exhibited the evils and the advantages of what we are accustomed to call *paganism,* in which secular values and purely exoteric interests almost eclipse the soul life of a culture, yet at the same time bear witness to an intense inner urge for spiritual renewal. In short, both periods have epitomized the profound turmoil and conflict attendant on the dawning of a new zeitgeist, and in very similar ways.

The Syballine Oracle of Cumae foreshadowed the death of the pagan world with the coming of Eastern mysticism. "Now is come the Last Age of the song of Cumae, when the great lines of the centuries begin anew," sang the Sybil, prophesying that Apollo, the Sun god from the East, would now become king.[2] We too are confronting a major cultural death and rebirth. The present influx of esoteric knowledge from the East is similar to the one that flooded the Roman Empire, and it is having a very similar effect on our traditional Western culture, rapidly sweeping away the stagnant institutional piety that was standard in Christendom only a generation ago. The masking carapace of hypocrisy has been torn away as mystical new cults bring once again to the West a violent cultural turbulence, a widespread awareness of threat to the old order, of religious anxiety and breakdown—and of rebirth. As Tacey observes,

> Our age has grown weary and longs for renewal and rejuvenation. It has grown tired of the world, and seeks to return to the source of its being for life-giving water and energy. It is no longer impressed by traditional methods in health, education, religion, law, or ethics, but seeks a new answer based on direct and personal experience of the ground of our being.[3]

As early as the seventh century CE, Guru Padmasambhava predicted that the Kali yuga would end "when the iron bird flies and houses run on wheels, and the Dharma comes to the land of the Red Man [Europe]."[4] "Know then," said that great Indian sage, "that the age of darkness is ending." He foresaw that our own time, beginning in the twentieth century, would be lit by a precessional dawn, bringing with it a great tide of life renewal. Right on cue, the paradigm of the sacred that has served Christianity for so long does so no longer: today we are witnessing the birth of a new type of spirituality that seems to have little to do with institutional religion. And yet, ironically, the Gnostic model abandoned long ago by the Churches now finds its perfect fit in the new milieu. Out of the worldwide sea of secular materialism a spiritual growing tip is emerging, a small but vital minority manifesting a consciousness illumined by an altogether new and creative spiritual vision, one in which the unity underlying all the world religions is recognized. Young people are being born already possessed of transcendence, with emotional, clairvoyant, and intellectual talents already geared to a universal civilization in the making. Many are not "religious" at all in the usual sense; others profess a strong allegiance to Christ, yet reject the Christian institution. All confess to an informally lived mysticism born in the inner self.

> Within the true self God is to be discovered and engaged, and while this idea is familiar in mysticism and the mystical truths found in numerous religions and cultures, it is challenging and new to formal religion . . .[5]

For many, this modern experience of the spirit is understood to be a planetary and transreligious phenomenon that cannot be corralled within a single theological system. Where the Christian religion does come into play, rather than unreflective piety, the new paradigm demands that faith give due honor to the rigors of historical fact, that free-floating ideologies are adequately anchored in the psychological and social verities of the day, and that old doctrines, however hallowed by usage, yield if need be to new perceptions of reality and new adjustments to the march of human evolution.

But is this not the essence of Christ's original teachings—the core meaning of the Gnosis of the heart? Are we not simply rediscovering the mind-set of early Gnostic Christianity shorn of its high sacramental character?

In death, as in winter, a seed of new life is always sown. Sequestered in the darkness and secrecy of the earth, it can survive in a dormant condition indefinitely, even in the hardest and most arctic winter, to await the next season of growth. This law determining the resurrection of new life from the womb of seeming death has spiritual as well as natural force, for the ancient Greeks believed that many of their heroes were raised in similar conditions of hibernation, "to avoid the malevolent forces that sought to destroy them in their infancy."[6] In the same way, the Gnosis hidden in the underground labyrinths of the occult schools has survived the hard Byzantine winter and the premature spring of the Italian Renaissance and the Rosicrucian Awakening in Germany to preserve itself for a further five centuries, protected by invisibility from the ill will of conservative forces. In that time it has seemingly not died but grown stronger, and may yet reinvigorate the old stock. "We stand at the very beginning of Christianity," Andrew Welburn asserts, "not near its end."[7]

The first of many prophecies concerning the future course of Christianity was the book of Revelation, written after the fall of Jerusalem by John of Patmos, thought to have been an Essene priest converted to the Jerusalem Church of the Circumcision. His visionary work met with much resistance and was not included in the Christian scriptures until the fifth century. After Revelation came Celtic prophecies in the same genre. The prophetic background of the Christian legend of the Grail quest lay in ancient Celtic archetypes, its spiritual symbolism born out of Celtic history, the Celtic gift of poetry, the Celtic ideals of courage, true utterance of the word, courtesy, and honor.

After the Celtic predictions came those of Joachim of Flores, prophesying that the final third of the Piscean age would be the Age of the Holy Spirit. As a consequence, the medieval master masons of all the European cathedrals of Our Lady set about encapsulating the spirit of this predicted new age in the ornamental stonework of their structures, carving on every surface cryptic motifs from the Qabalah, the Hermetica, and alchemy, among many other forbidden arcane sources. This esoteric language in stone is believed to be the way in which the cathedral builders preserved the mysteries of the lost Celtic knowledge concerning earthly cycles governed by the stars and planets—a body of astronomical knowledge concerning the precession of the equinoxes only now being revived.[8]

The English occultist A. E. Waite was but one of many modern Western scholars who believed the secret Gnostic tradition within Christianity, lost to the West, had been preserved in the Middle East among the Mandaeans and the Sufis of Harran. The Knights Templar returning from the Crusades reintroduced the tradition into Europe. The inspiration for the wealth of arcane carvings that cover every inch of the cathedral structures is reliably attributed to these warrior monks, a message they preserved in stone for future generations. A countdown to the Aquarian age, the cathedrals were thus truly coded prophecies waiting for a time freed from religious censorship.

Following on the early Celtic and medieval prophecies, the Rosicrucians of the sixteenth and seventeenth centuries reiterated their message in more universal terms. The Rose Cross movement electrified the Western scholarly world by prophesying a day of cultural rebirth approaching that would see the renewal of the unitive hopes and values of the first Christians. The Rosicrucians cherished what they believed to be a more creative vision of the religion Jesus Christ had founded, one that conformed more truly to the holy principles he had laid down while on earth: "to gather all mankind under a universal religion of Peace."[9] It was to be a spiritual revolution in the fullest and most positive sense, an overturning of everything that had gone before—aiming, it would seem, at the uniting of the three Semitic religions under the combined leadership of Qabalists, Gnostics, and Sufis.[10]

And indeed, Baring and Cashford voice a rumor that has always had wide currency: that the esoteric schools from the three religions of Semitic origin (and probably Manichaeism also) *worked together* in Europe during the twelfth century to create the Grail legends spread by the troubadours, and to resuscitate the underlying Gnostic belief system of antiquity. So too in an even earlier age Hebrew, Egyptian, and Greek initiates are widely believed to have collaborated in Alexandria to produce the Hermetica and the Wisdom writings of the period.

The Renaissance magus Giordano Bruno had been a forerunner of the Rosicrucians, and he was rapidly followed in 1614 by their manifestos, which were

typically Hermetic, alchemical and Qabalistic, claiming to herald the advent of a new world religion, a new world order of freedom, harmony, and universal fraternity.[11]

At that future time, so it was whispered, a fraternity of initiated men and women secretly trained for the task would, like those in Wolfram von Eschenbach's Grail brotherhood, emerge under the banner of the Christ to help humanity enter a new age on a higher level of consciousness. Of that essentially Aquarian vision, Frances A. Yates writes:

> The world, nearing its end, was to receive a new illumination in which the advances in knowledge made in the preceding age of the Renaissance will be immensely expanded. New discoveries are at hand, a new age is dawning. And this illumination shines inward as well as outward; it is an inward spiritual illumination, revealing to man new possibilities in himself, teaching him to understand his own dignity and worth and the part he is called upon to play in the divine scheme.[12]

All occult traditions have contended that there is only one inner, experiential religion at the root of all the different world faiths, these being but local versions of a single esoteric tradition shared by all the initiatory hierarchies. This visionary concept runs obscurely through the entire history of esoteric Christianity from its founder onward, but at a level so deeply buried, so disguised, that its significance has scarcely surfaced to the present day. Nevertheless, the ideal of universal religious harmony under the aegis of a single, planet-wide Gnosis is arguably the implicit goal of all the Envoys sent from above. It gleams within the New Covenant; is hidden in the Hermetic teachings of Bardesanes of Edessa in the second century and those of Bishop Priscillian of Avila in the fourth—both men being early examples of "universal Renaissance Man"; flourishes for a time in the Celtic Church; struggles to reach the light of day in the twelfth-century Templar Order and in the Grail legends; and at last emerges explicitly if briefly in the late Renaissance, in the unitive ideals of some of the leading European philosophers and magi of the period.

Many of these closet esotericists, moreover, are believed to have been in touch with the Familists, a heretical and highly secret sect called "the Family of Love" founded by one Hendrick Niclaes.[13] The sixteenth-century Familists invited "all lovers of truth . . . of what nation and religion so ever they be, Christian, Jews, Mahomites or Turks, and heathen," to become part of a learned brotherhood dedicated to developing a universal theology.[14] Clearly, during the Renaissance religious universalism was very much in the air.

At that time the quest for cosmic union, for the transcendence of religious divisions, for universalist ideals, reached its zenith. The English philosopher John Dee (1527–1608), widely regarded as one of the most brilliant astrologers, Qabalists, and scientists of his time and a powerful influence in the birth of Rosicrucianism, believed the mythic symbols used in astronomy "were relics of a lost universal language that transcended national . . . and religious barriers."[15] In his Hermetic-Qabalistic book, *Monas Hieroglyphica,* Dee invented the monad, an astrological sign that he regarded as "the key to a true understanding of the unity of the cosmos"[16] and as representing the totality of wisdom, the very sign of the One. Meanwhile, his unfortunate contemporary Giordano Bruno roamed Europe, preaching "one simple divinity which is in all things . . . shines forth in diverse subjects and takes diverse names,"[17] and prophesying the advent of a new world order in which would prevail "a single true universal religion rooted in the occult tradition."[18] As we know, for his pains the renegade Benedictine monk was burned alive at the stake.

In the same period, the upsurge of Qabalism and Judaic tantra was unsettling European Jewry. There is no doubt that the Renaissance owed its universalist spirit, at least in part, to a general revival in Europe of the ideals of the Hebrew Old Religion. The Jewish Mysteries had in fact never died, nor had the ideal of one worldwide religion. The Templars merely reawakened Europe to the memories it already carried deep in its womb, for the seed of unity in humans, societies, and cosmos had been sown centuries before in the teachings of Jesus—and, behind him, in the teachings of the ancient Nazarean/prophetic tradition to which he belonged.

Today, despite the violence of the fundamentalist reaction to the new zeitgeist that is threatening to bring us to a clash of civilizations, the unitary theme running through a long line of Gnostics, Druids, Cathars, Templars, Grail bards, medieval mystics, Rosicrucians, Sufis, Buddhists, Qabalists, and others still flourishes. And in the face of the intractable religio-ethnic wars now raging across most of the planet, the longing for an end to religious divisions is likely to grow more vigorously than ever. Joscelyn Godwin speaks for countless thoughtful people today when he posits "a transcendent unity behind all religions . . . attempts, each valid for its time and place, to point the way to the true goal of human existence."[19]

In such pronouncements we can read the signs of the times. They are harbingers of a celestial renewal, the first shoots that herald the coming of the precessional springtime that Guru Padmasambhava foresaw. Approximately seventy years ago, Qabalists predicted that a worldwide cultural revolution was in the air. For the past thousand years, they said, civilization had been laboring in Malkuth, the lowest and most material sphere on the Tree of Life. But now the downward-thrusting Lightning Flash of involution ending in Malkuth is being replaced by the Serpent of Wisdom, whose coils wind upward upon the Tree, the sign of a great evolutionary reversal. The ancient image of a serpent's coils symbolizes the rising of spiritual powers in the race, an ascension of consciousness, a collective initiation. "By the path whereon the initiates have gone, ahead of their time," declares Dion Fortune, "evolution is beginning to go, taking with it the race as a whole."[20]

Can we hope that Christianity will join in the great evolutionary reversal? Will it rediscover the way of the bridechamber—and with it the lost vocation of prophecy? Although the Rosicrucian predictions of an imminent religious unity throughout the world are far too optimistic, all the world religions arguably have hidden within them a divine fiat to work for humanity's destiny in the distant future, when a unified world order will undoubtedly arise. But for Christianity, Jesus' command to work toward such a goal constituted its special God-given task. The obligation to foster a peaceful and fraternal world was explicit from its beginning, and was mandated by the Christian teachings on brotherly love. That goal has clearly not been fulfilled as yet. But we are on the threshold of great social changes that will implicate Christianity for good or ill and perhaps spur it to consider some major reforms.

Within the next fifty years the center of world civilization is going to shift to the Pacific zone, where an entirely new kind of civilization will arise, born of the interaction between the nations of East and West that ring the Pacific ocean: Indonesia, China, and Japan on one side, Canada, the Americas, New Zealand, and Australia on the other. The fluid feeling state that characterizes the Eastern psyche will have to engage with the conceptual rigidity of the West in what may well be a cataclysmic encounter; but out of it we can expect great new forces to emerge that will reshape our global society in hitherto unknown ways. Inevitably, the light of the great Euro-centered institutions, once glorious monuments to Western progress, will be eclipsed. Already a looming crisis of values worldwide, a failing of Earth's reserves and a shifting of the cultural principles and sociopolitical alignments that have underpinned our Western civilization, means that we can no longer rely on things to serve us as they have in the past. Over the next critical century, many social structures we now think of as eternal will disappear, and among them will be Christianity, unless it can institute the necessary reforms.

Among the most urgent of these reforms will be the need to return to Christianity's Gnostic roots, to resuscitate the eternal in its constitution—the ever-living sacramental and doctrinal principles laid down by its founder.

The first of such reforms must be a return to the Church's original three-tiered initiatory structure. As Tacey points out, so huge is the range of religious beliefs and attitudes in the West today that if Christian congregations are to be genuinely served, there needs to be as wide a spectrum of avenues for worship and religious study as possible. The postmodern society, he reminds us, is a fragmented plural society.

Religion in the past has been based on the idea of ministering to a gathered community. Today it has to work towards a new model,

offering guidance, support, and spiritual discernment to the scattered community.[21]

Such a model for a scattered community of pagan converts was
put in place in the Judaeo-Christian movement two thousand years
ago, when the population ranged from utterly illiterate and sometimes
enslaved to highly educated and aristocratic. Today what is needed
is a similar model of grades. There needs to be a network of populist
gatherings at one end of the spectrum similar to the great Hillsong
gatherings in America in order to satisfy the need of the majority for
emotional self-expression and feel-good aspirations; at the other end of
the spectrum there must be a network of small closed wisdom schools
for those more experienced in the spiritual quest. Priestly supervision,
whether liturgical or doctrinal, should go no farther than the second
tier, the level of ecclesiastic ceremonial such as the high mass—where
indeed its authority rightfully belongs. Beyond that level, in the informal house churches of the wisdom seekers, individual freedom of
thought and moral autonomy need to be reinstated. The dual obligation of the wisdom schools must be to encourage metaphysical studies
that will bring the Gnosis back into the modern Church and to pursue
transcendence by meditation and inner prayer.

By such a route, the revival of the bridechamber sacrament may
well become possible. It is abundantly clear that over time the marriage
chamber became in esoteric circles a metaphorical term for the heart
chakra, with its unique ability to unite body, mind, and feelings in one
spiritually transcendent field, and the task of these esoteric schools
would have to be to bring back by whatever means possible the celebration of this forgotten initiatory rite—and with it the long abandoned
grade of revelatory prophecy.

The prophetic vocation has not been known in the churches for
most of Christianity's life, but may yet return in its upper echelons,
for in fact at least one such wisdom school already exists in rural England: Anglican, accessible only by invitation and initiation, closed to
the priesthood. It suggests that already reform may be on the agenda

in certain Christian quarters, at least within the Anglican fold. Meetings are officiated by the members themselves, and several of the members in this very private enclave are healers, clairvoyants, more advanced initiates; some are looked up to as spiritual philosophers and teachers; and all play an important role in the group, virtually as prophets, in much the same sense as the prophets in Valentinian and Marcionite schools led their second-century Christian brothers and sisters. In classical times the high priest—or, as we would have it, the pope or archbishop—was selected from this higher grade, ensuring a standard of wisdom at the helm, which is not possible today.

Such closed wisdom schools are already known to exist in the Indonesian Reformed Lutheran Church as well, and are similarly clairvoyantly and prophetically active, with emphasis on healing and exorcist powers, and especially on a vital link with higher initiatory and angelic levels. Their leaders interact ecumenically with all the other Christian denominations worldwide, and moreover may also belong informally to one or other of the Sufi or Hindu-Buddhist mystical paths in the region. This strong and permitted tendency to embrace esoteric syncretism, which has been raised in the Far East to a religious principle, is one of the revolutionary contributions of the Pacific races to a newly emerging religious paradigm. Their allegiance to esoteric syncretism alone has the power to bring a brotherhood of world religions closer to realization.

There may be yet more of these prophetic third-tier schools in various parts of the Christian world, hidden behind the orthodox facade. But if so, they are at present merely exotic grace notes, in themselves of little consequence. But in days to come, when psychic abilities have become normal to a far larger percentage of the world population than at present, such schools, which open up the inner cosmos and its powers, will be essential in considerable numbers in both East and West. Already, in fact, such a development is becoming mandatory if Christianity is to maintain a relevant place and function in a society in process of deep psychic transformation. Indeed, there is a further well-known prophecy voiced by Mircea Eliade, among others, to the effect that at the end of the Kali yuga the Masters will return, the gates of initiation reopen; conditions will be favorable for a new spiritual efflorescence.[22] If that prophecy is fulfilled, might there not soon reemerge centers of Christian Mystery teachings governed, as in the days of Valentinus, by men and women initiates of a high order who will once again educate and prepare the West for the return of the sacred?

The second area of reform that will be necessary if the Church, whether Roman Catholic, Orthodox, or Protestant, is not to alienate its people beyond repair will be to transfer its obsessive control over the procreative habits and sexual mores of its flock to a consideration of the real moral issues of the day. Why have the terms of the New Covenant been so flagrantly neglected? What support, or lack of it, should the churches be giving to militarism, to global corporate ambition, and to the amassing of vast wealth and property at the expense of the third-world poor? When will the churches begin a genuinely reflective dialogue with the laity on the latter's changing worldview and rapidly dissolving religious beliefs? Why are the clergy not reevaluating their outmoded definitions of God now so perplexing to their congregations, insulting the intelligence of some and causing total rejection in the majority? Above all, in the interests of religious harmony, surely Christianity should be befriending all other world religions, including Islam, with warmth and understanding, studying their foundational principles intelligently and with the tolerance one would extend to one's own family members. Is it not time the Christian religion gave attention to the ideal of religious brotherhood, in the sense of studying and comprehending the teachings of other religions before events sweep away world peace?

Finally, the reform on which the above two crucially depend must be to reestablish the equality of the masculine and feminine principles in the very foundations of Christian life, in its values, its ideals, its basic laws and administration. There must be a true equalizing of the sexes such that women will have as much input as men into the constitutional principles and ideals of their religion, and an equal voice with men in their implementation. Women must have their own orders and mysteries and their own independent authority, as the Therapeutae once had; and women as well as men must understand their inalienable right to influence the social ethos of the day, its prevailing paradigms, its political and judicial mores. Anything less is mere window dressing.

This equality of women in the foundational principles of the Church is an issue that will soon be of far greater gravity than mere social equity, for on it will depend the kind of civilization we build for the future. The part both men and women play in any restructuring of the Christian institution will determine the kind of metaphysical and ethical pillars that support it, and these in turn will have a profound influence on the way a new civilization is constituted. The Church will need to know what will benefit the new society and what will most quickly destroy it, and thus influence those political leaders drawing up its new juridical framework.

It is a matter of historical record that patriarchal civilizations, however brilliantly they perform in the arts and sciences, are notoriously short, brutal, and self-destructive. The Assyrian and Hittite civilizations are good examples. The only long-lived and humane societies of which we have any historical record are those in which women have played as great a governing role as men. Many historians deny there has ever been a matriarchal society, and in a sense they are correct. The alternative to patriarchy is not matriarchy, but collaboration at the highest level of the two genders. Consequently, a truly matriarchal civilization is extremely rare, whereas a collaborative one was once the norm for the larger part of human history.

A patriarchal society can be defined as one lasting only a few hundred years in which the two arms of government, the secular and the religious, are both predominantly male, with a male God presiding overhead. Historically, this is a relatively late model that has engulfed all the more equitable cultures of antiquity and is now worldwide. It has spread like a disease. It accounts for much of the severe, even terminal sickness afflicting most of Earth's population and for the pathological proliferation of weaponry so destructive it is endangering the Earth itself. So persuasive is patriarchal propaganda that we take it as a normal, God-given state of affairs; yet for many thousands of years, as already said, the alternative was the norm, as expressed in such societies as the ancient Egyptian, Ural-Altaic, Chinese, and Old European.

In these societies, one arm of government, usually the religious, was female, the other male. Cooperation between the two was the norm and an androgynous Goddess or Divine Couple presided overhead. Frequently, however, there were two equally powerful religious orders, one male and the other female, as in ancient Egypt, where each authority presided over a different social function (see appendix 2). All these civilizations began in shamanism, which was once predominantly female and so powerful during the Bronze Age that the priestesses of the Mycenaean Corn Goddess Demeter and those of the Cretan Goddess of the Double Ax held absolute sway over the people, determining the life or death of rulers and able to bankrupt kingdoms[23] (see appendix 2).

The shamanic Ural-Altaic culture in northern Siberia was at its height 30,000 years ago and still active when Ivar Lissner studied the Tungus tribes in the twentieth century and marveled at their peacefulness and moral purity.[24] Old Europe, lasting peacefully for about four thousand years and dominated by female religious orders, degenerated only when overcome by the patriarchal and nomadic Kurgan peoples from the steppe lands to the east.[25] Suddenly the battle-ax and the dagger appear; warfare becomes endemic; women are frequently persecuted. Gimbutas writes:

> Millennial traditions were truncated: towns and villages disintegrated, magnificent painted pottery vanished; as did shrines, frescoes, sculptures, symbols, and script. The taste for beauty and the sophistication of style and execution withered . . .[26]

With a strongly female mythology, the Taoist and shamanic Chinese civilization began in the sixteenth century BCE in the Shang dynasty and is today mightier than ever. Although the secular arm of government has been generally masculine in China, the Taoist yin/yang (female/male) dichotomy still dominates Chinese thought. According to its most ancient scriptures, the Chinese pantheon of Immortals lies in central Asia, in the Kun Lun mountains, and is ruled by Hsi Wang Mu, the Queen Mother of the West, who is also known as Kuan Yin, the goddess of mercy.[27] Again, the ancient Egyptian civilization, rooted in the Isis religion and powerful female orders, but with the pharaonic tradition almost exclusively male, lasted over three thousand years. All these societies have been remarkably stable, healthy, and artistically brilliant cultures in their own time—and, as has been said, the Chinese culture is only now beginning its most influential phase on the world scene. None has been patriarchal in our modern meaning of the term.

Why, then, is patriarchy so inimical to the life of civilizations? Why is the equal participation of women so absolutely vital to the well-being of nations? William Meader outlines the esoteric psychology of the Father and Mother archetypes in yang/yin terms that throw a great deal of light on this thorny question.[28] The cosmic Father principle, he says, is concerned with autonomy, with the formation of selfhood and the one-pointed pursuit of evolutionary purpose. We can deduce that it is therefore self-referencing, exclusive in its interests, single-minded toward its future hypothetical progress, and instinctively inimical to anything foreign to its own nature . . . such as women. As observed in a previous chapter, the Father archetype is in fact synonymous with the cerebral system of the human brain, which can operate independently of the heart system but usually with a notable lack of that intuitive wisdom that pagan societies called *nous*—spiritual common sense. The Father calls relentlessly for the furtherance of his ideas, for greater and greater change, speed, progress, and rationality—for things ever bigger and better, faster, newer, and ever onward—and is the last to see the precipice yawning at his feet.

The cosmic Mother principle, on the other hand, is intimately connected with matter and with rest rather than motion. She is concerned not with autonomy but with relationships, with stability and quality rather than speed and novelty, and with the organization of strong viable forms. She is holistic, inclusive, hospitable to what is not herself, actively seeking union and/or cooperation between unlike natures, in the interests of which she is content to yield supremacy to her partner. The Mother principle is synonymous with the heart system, and as such a peerless organizer of groups, of societies, but prone to a deficiency in individualism. Unlike the Father, she values peace and longs for bliss. Mistress of the psyche, gateway of the soul, she is subtle and intuitive in her dealings, but also given to inertia and materialism. She is therefore at her best in tandem with the Father. If robbed of dignity, if excluded from her rightful place of authority at his side at the helm of creation, the Mother will turn to the sensory satisfactions of the physical realm and become licentious, or else hide herself in the black burka of puritanism.

As dual expressions of the creativity issuing from the Godhead, the One Primal Spirit, the masculine and feminine principles thus need each other for completion. Neither can function successfully alone. Yet our present civilization, with its economic rationalism and its all-engulfing wars, is built exclusively on the masculine principle. The foundational laws, the moral guidelines of society, and the means to their ends, both secular and religious, are worked out only by men, and the only ruling deity is male. Every vital decision concerning foreign and economic policies, every law concerning the family, criminal justice, racial attitudes, moral boundaries, and the sexual or scientific ethos is driven and controlled by men. As a result, our civilization is in the grip of a faster and faster demon of productivity, driven by a phantom called progress, overworked, out of balance, suffering vertigo and despair. The sickening of the earth, vast populations starving or perishing by genocide; crime, suicide, drug addiction, the rape of childhood, and the death of joy—all these are the inevitable consequences of rampant patriarchy and a repressed Mother archetype.

In Revelation, John of Patmos recorded his great vision of the war in heaven and on earth, and the flight of the feminine archetype into the wilderness:

> And a great portent appeared in heaven, a woman clothed in the sun, with the moon under her feet, and on her head a crown of twelve

stars; she was with child and she cried out in her pangs of birth, in anguish for delivery . . . Now war arose in heaven . . . And when the dragon saw that he had been thrown down to the earth, he pursued the woman who had borne the male child. But the woman was given the two wings of the great eagle that she might fly from the serpent into the wilderness, to the place where she was to be nourished for a time, and times, and half a time. (Revelation 12:1–15)

It is surely more than time that the Mother principle, the woman clothed in the sun, was recalled from the wilderness to give birth again and to be truly honored. She who is crowned with the twelve stars of the zodiac must be healed of her sufferings and reclaim her kingdom. But superficial medications will not do; healing can come only at the roots of this great organism we call civilization, at its very inception. There, where the bifurcation and differentiation of the polarities first occurs, is where the ancient gender conflict must be resolved. There, at the very font, the dual principles must together create the format of a future just and peaceful society; they must together frame the laws, the ethical boundaries, and the mutually acceptable priorities of the coming polity before differentiation hardens into alienation. And it is at that seminal level that Christianity can show the way forward, if it will— can point the way to the marriage chamber by dismantling much of its patriarchal superstructure in the interests of a deeper vision of truth.

Above all, the Christian religion needs to renew its ancient tryst with prophecy. But the prophetic vocation is born only in the marriage chamber, where the male and female principles must be equally honored if they are to unite. This is a fact that the history of the prophets, of whatever nation, has confirmed again and again. Where either gender is degraded, the heart of religion dies. The Gnosis withers; the evolution of the human spirit cannot go forward and the civilization dies. Yet it was for this evolution, indeed, that Christianity was brought into existence. And perhaps for this same reason it is already beginning to renew itself in the hidden mystical schools of the Far East, where the oceanic Mother principle has always held sway.

Everything is in flux today. New possibilities for the world are being born in every corner of the planet. Even in the psychological arena, the American psychotherapists Arnold and Amy Mindell are carrying out what they call Worldwork as they tour in every country, striving to bring healing and conflict resolution to every nexus of warfare, personal or corporate, regardless of race, class, political ideology, religious persuasion, or sexual preference. For expressions of their work in *The Leader as Martial Artist* they turn to Eastern paradigms, to Japanese aikido, to the flow of Ki energy.[29] It is no longer enough, the Mindells believe, to be white, middle-class, and Western: to be a true healer of the soul one must now belong to the world, one must think and act in universal terms. So also might Christianity, extended into every corner of the colonial world, approach its vocation in the third millennium. To be engaged as a leader in Worldwork is to submit to the urge to union, to become an impartial partaker of every possible viewpoint; it is for the Church to become like Christ.

Whether the traditional Christian churches will avail themselves of this radical postmodern philosophy is uncertain. Whether its lone voices and isolated reforms will be sufficient to spur to action the great Christian body as a whole remains a matter of speculation. But even if the churches are not, we can be certain that the transcendent force that brought Christianity into being, sweeping all before it, will continue its work. The waters of redemption will continue to flow, cutting new channels in the hungry land, renewing the promises of the past and bathing all things in their beneficence. We can be certain that one day, if not tomorrow as projected, the Renaissance prophecies of a coming world order based on a united brotherhood of world religions will be fulfilled. The One Primal Spirit will eventually prevail.

APPENDIX I

THE GODS OF ANCIENT ISRAEL

According to official Jewish history, Israel was divinely called to a monotheistic worship of Yahweh, the One God, from the earliest times, though often backsliding into idolatry through its commerce with the surrounding heathen nations. But Raphael Patai has presented us with an alternative and more polytheistic picture, one in which the image of Yahweh differed little in Hebrew eyes from that of other Canaanite gods. In antiquity, divinities were easily confused with each other, so that often it would have been difficult to determine whether Hebrew worship was, as Patai says, legitimately Yahwist, heretically Yahwist—or unequivocally pagan. Yahwism, moreover, was almost certainly a relatively late development, taking its place in a Hebrew society already committed to other cultic loyalties. It is to this circumstance of competing deities that we can trace the roots of the conflict in Judaism that eventually led to a terminal schism within the parent body.

In support of Patai, the British historian Robert Graves observes in *Hebrew Myths: The Book of Genesis* that although Abraham's Mount of Sacrifice, where he offered up his son Isaac as a sacrifice, is customarily identified with Mount Moriah, which in turn is identified with Mount Zion in Jerusalem, this identification is contradicted by a reliable Samaritan tradition based on Deuteronomy 11:29 ff. The scriptural passage states that Mount Moriah is Mount Gerizim in Samaria, "which overlooks the 'terebinths of Moreh,' where the patriarch Abraham had offered his sacrifice to the High Sun-God El Elyon" (Genesis 12:6).[1] It would thus appear that Mount Zion was not the locale of the original story of Abraham. Rather it was Mount Gerizim, which was in Samaria and under the rule of El rather than Yahweh. In ancient times, Graves reports, Moreh was the holiest shrine in Samaria, "visited by Abraham, blessed by Moses, and famous for Joshua's memorial stone and Joseph's grave" (Joshua 24:25ff).[2]

But after the destruction of Israel and the deportation of a large part of its population by the Assyrians, says Graves, the dominant place of worship and many early Samaritan traditions were transferred to Mount Zion in Jerusalem. The wholesale transference of old Israel's culture and very name to Judah territory and to its capital in Jerusalem included the stories of such ancient patriarchs as Adam, Abel, Noah, Enoch, and Abraham,[3] while the Goddess Asherah and her husband, El Elyon, the great Creator God of the Near East, also migrated to Jerusalem and shared their divine eminence with that of Yahweh, the desert god most popular in the southern state.

We know relatively little about this deity El Elyon, who was one of the Neolithic Old Gods at the dawn of agriculture, a vast cosmic Presence, passive but benign, who was virtually indistinguishable from the other Supreme Beings of the ancient East. (Indeed it has been argued on philological grounds that in primeval times, prior to the end of the Ice Age, only *one* divine Ruler-God presided over the whole earth.[4]) El Elyon was the God Most High whom early Hebrew pastoralists found heading the pantheon of the ruined Ugaritic Empire, that fallen bastion of High Bronze Age civilization. This High God El evolved into one of the many great Sky fathers with Solar powers and teeming progeny who could be found during the Bronze Age in Sumer, Egypt, Babylonia, Anatolia, Persia, Canaan, and Greece as well as Vedic India and the Far East. The Sky powers who created the heavens and the earth and governed their families of quarreling lesser gods and goddesses from on high were still, however, lofty, passive, and almost interchangeable deities, and were eventually replaced in their turn by even more anthropomorphized Iron Age gods who required of their devotees a much lower level of spiritual consciousness and ethic.

Yahweh seems to have been such a tribal god, although there is no complete agreement on his provenance or the meaning of his name. The historian and philologist T. J. Meek, who disputes the usual translation of Yahweh's name as I AM or I AM THAT I AM, says:

> The contention that Yahweh was of Arabian origin is clearly in accord with the Old Testament records, which connect him with the Negeb and with southern sanctuaries like Sinai-Horeb and Kadesh . . . The most probable [origin of the name] in our opinion is . . . from the Arabic root *hwy*, "to blow."[5]

A god named Jw, a son of El, has been discovered in the Canaanite Ras Shamra texts, leading Patai, like many other scholars, to believe that Yahweh was another of El's sons, a lesser bedouin god of the desert who was adopted by the Hebrews as their national deity. His image was anthropomorphic, his morality tribal and primitive, his cult animistic, and his abode a tent. His covenantal ritual consisted of desert feasts and sacrifices and burnt offerings from among the herds.[6] On the other hand, originally the Hebrews had their settlements, flocks, and farm holdings on the mountaintops overlooking the richer coastal plains of Palestine, only later moving down to win more-fertile territory for themselves: consequently, according to some authorities, Yahweh may be identified with yet another of El's sons, El Shaddai, a fierce god of mountains. Yahweh, backed by the Levitical priesthood in Jerusalem, was always to be more popular among the southern tribes of Judah that bordered the desert than among those in Samaria, where the age-old cult of El remained paramount, creating much tension between the two competing regions.[7]

In the Masoretic Text of the official Hebrew Bible, which was produced by a team of rabbis in the Palestinian town of Tiberias in the tenth century CE, a strange passage occurs in the Song of Moses in Deuteronomy 32 concerning God's actions in "the days of old." Moses recalls that in those early times, "when the Most High apportioned the nations, when he divided the sons of man, he established the borders of the peoples according to the number of the sons of Israel" (Deuteronomy 32:8). Scholars were mystified by this historical anachronism, since Moses is speaking of prehistoric times to a people still wandering in the desert and not yet formed into a nation of Israel. But when the Dead Sea Scrolls were translated, a Greek copy of the relevant Deuteronomic chapter was found that contained a significantly different wording.

The new finding was far older than the Masoretic Text. It was part of the Septuagint, translated from Hebrew and compiled in Alexandria in the second century BCE for Greek-speaking Jews, and it records that the Most High set the boundaries of the nations according to the number of the *sons of God,* not the sons of Israel. The implication of the passage is clearly polytheistic, as the American scholar Hershel Shanks points out in *The Mystery and Meaning of the Dead Sea Scrolls.*[8] It tells us that in ancient times a divine son of the Most High (El Elyon) was allotted to each of the world's peoples—Chemosh to the Moabites, Qos to the Edomites, Ba'al to the Canaanites, and so on . . . and presumably Yahweh, another son of the Most High and a kind of tribal deity, to the Israelites. Furthermore, the Temple Scroll, another sectarian Qumran discovery that had been written in the second century BCE, contains Sabbath songs to be sung in a heavenly temple mystically envisioned by the Essenes, and these songs too proclaim the existence of a pantheon of local deities, holy ones, sons of God *(elohim)* in fealty to the transcendent God Most High.

> Praise the most high God, O you high among all the gods of knowledge. Let the holy ones of the gods sanctify the King of glory, who sanctifies by his holiness all his holy ones. Princes of the praises of all the gods, praise the God of majestic praises . . . For he [is the God of gods] of all the Princes on high, and the King of king[s] of all the eternal councils.[9]

But to the Masoretic scribes, the polytheistic notion that Yahweh was not the one and only God, nor even supreme over every other god, but rather perhaps a lesser one, was evidently objectionable and had been amended in the relevant texts. Nevertheless, it was a theistic concept that had once made sense to the Hebrew people, for the Sabbath songs and the Song of Moses in the Greek/Egyptian Septuagint are unquestionably the oldest and most reliable of all the Hebrew sources now available. In further verses, the Song of Moses even seems to give additional stress to the local nature of Yahweh's sovereignty over his Chosen People, for in Moses' blessing to the children of Israel he says,

> The Lord came from Sinai, and dawned from Seir upon us; he shone forth from Mount Paran, *he came from the ten thousands of holy ones,* with flaming fire at his right hand. Yea, he loved his people; all those consecrated to him were in his hand . . . (Deuteronomy 33:1–3) (author's italics)

What is of relevance here is that the arrival of Yahweh did not preclude the continuing worship of El. They were different grades of deity, corresponding to the different ecclesiastical grades represented by prophets and lower-ranking priests. The Hebrew chieftains appear to have paid allegiance to both, and in the Jerusalem temple each deity had his own priesthood and guild of prophets, the two parties contending for dominance. Thus a religious power struggle was fought out over several centuries between the two main power centers, Samaria to the north and Judah to the south, and between their two sacerdotal factions. The battle was essentially between radically differing worldviews, social mores, and conceptions of deity. Yahweh, served by the Levitical priesthood, was an Iron Age god of conquest, a warrior deity with attractions for a people hungry for land, security, and racial identity. El, on the other hand, was a high god of prophecy from the great Ugaritic civilization that had once towered over the Near Eastern peoples. He was an archaic god of wisdom, of mystical knowledge, a god of the Solar Mysteries united to a goddess, and was served by the Canaanite Order of Melchizedek.

Other versions of this Creator God's name were El Elohim, "God of gods," and El Elohe Yisrael, "God of Israel," while Al-lah *(al-ilah)* the Compassionate One, the High God of the Quraish tribe of northern Arabia, was another.[10] It is probable that the mighty God of Job, an ancient Arabian priest-king, was not Yahweh but Allah, who, according to Philip Hitti, came to Arabia from Syria in the fifth century BCE. Allah became the Creator God and supreme provider of the northern Quraish tribe long before Muhammad reinstated him as a universal Supreme Being. Therefore, to this day Islam worships the same God the ancient Israelites worshipped as El Elohe.

By the time the Hebrew pastoralists were settling into fortified towns, El's sovereignty in the Near East was being challenged by one of his sons, the great agricultural god Ba'al (the Lord), but El was still a mighty force in the region. So it was that although for the general farming populace El lost much of his ancient mystique to Ba'al, for a small prophetic elite he remained an androgynous impersonal cosmic Power, the Mother-Father God of the whole of Creation who would one day be rediscovered by Qabalists and Christian Gnostics.

Far from being extinguished by the cult of Yahweh, the worship of El Elyon remained a very powerful influence in the princely courts of Samaria and Judah and in the legend of the United Monarchy preserved in the Hebrew scriptures (1 Samuel 2–3). In that legend, Solomon decrees that the king of Judah is to be served by a Zadokite royal priesthood that ranks above the Levitical priesthood.[11] In *The Hidden Book in the Bible,* the author Richard E. Friedman discusses at some length the royal Zadokite priesthood that dominated the Solomonic court, without, however, commenting on its Elohist background. But in fact the superior ranking of the Zadokite priesthood meant that El was to rank above all other Israelite gods, including Yahweh. Whether or not this piece of religious history (or pseudo-history) embedded in the text of the book of Samuel is true, it is of importance in throwing light on the power struggle between the Zadokites and the Levites in the Jerusalem temple in later times.

Rabbinic sources are silent concerning the powerful intrusion of

Jebusite/Canaanite/Egyptian culture into early Judaism through the prophetic lineage. It is not from the rabbis but rather from the international Elohist line of Melchizedek that we can trace the more advanced ethos and growing universalism of Judaism as taught by Hebrew prophets such as Elijah, Isaiah, Hosea, Ezekiel, Job, and others—and ultimately by Jesus and John the Baptist. After the Babylonian Exile, Yahweh gradually took over all the functions and powers of El in the new regime of Reformed Judaism, and from then on the two religious streams have merged under the sovereignty of the present Supreme God of the Jews.

APPENDIX 2

RELIGION IN THE BRONZE AGE

Egypt's Mystery cycle achieved its most spectacular flowering during the Bronze Age, when it contributed a great deal to the sudden burgeoning of high civilization that occurred over most of the planet at that time. Behind the mythologies of the walled city-states and their little hieratic courts then emerging were the great women's religious orders, monuments to institutionalized female power that rivaled and sometimes surpassed that of men.[1] Egypt strongly influenced the Mediterranean female orders such as those of the Cretan Goddess of the Double Ax and the Mycenaean Corn Goddess Demeter, both of which were influential in the development of the Greater Mysteries of Greece. The wisdom teachings of Isis that filtered through these powerful women's orders illuminated the whole of the ancient East for several millennia and inspired Hebrew religion to an extent that is only now being recognized.[2]

Under the tolerant and inclusive feminine rule during the Bronze Age, male shamans attached to the women's convents enjoyed great prestige as oracular messengers between the royal dead and the living. Nevertheless, Professor J. G. Wunderlich in *The Secret of Crete* is only one of many historians who remind us how dominant was the feminine principle in the Bronze Age, how confident and influential, both politically and ideologically, were orders like the above, which could make and break kings and bankrupt kingdoms with their claims to death dues.³ While modern research shows that it was consecrated women who dominated the religious rhythms of the Bronze Age and helped to shape the terrible yet ecstatic ideals of ritual regicide, it was the men's religious orders that flourished in the arts and sciences and built the more exoteric structures of civilization.

The level of superior scientific knowledge as well as the superb engineering skills evinced in the construction of the Giza pyramid complex (ca. 2400 BCE) has convinced a growing number of scholars that an advanced technological and scientific tradition, passed down in the Heliopolitan male priesthood, must have been responsible for shaping the Egyptian culture from a very early pre-dynastic period.⁴ Robert Bauval and Adrian Gilbert cite the Egyptologist Jane B. Sellars and the late Dr. Georgio de Santillana, historian and author of *Hamlet's Mill,* regarding the evidence these two authorities put forward for the existence of a great prehistoric civilization whose astral sciences have long been lost to us. Bauval and Gilbert suggest that the Heliopolitan priesthood was the heir to that forgotten civilization. The advanced knowledge of stellar phenomena associated with the Heliopolis temple is astonishing, and so too is its Hermetic science of correspondences known as iatromathematics, by which knowledge of the stars is intuitively correlated with the etheric chakras in the human spinal system.

In Egypt a messianic male Mystery tradition of almost unimaginable antiquity ran parallel to the female Mysteries, collaborating with them in a system whose scope and immensity of purpose are at present obscure to us. Although the male tradition was eventually to eclipse the diminishing role of the tantric female orders, there are many indications that until that time a creative accord crossing all frontiers existed between the two institutions in their great civilizing tasks. In fact, the Egyptian religion must once have been a supreme example of religio-social cooperation between the two sexes, in which every element in the community was co-opted to the great work, creating an institutional tour de force that is seemingly beyond the capabilities of modern societies. Its strength lay at least partly in the power of polarity synthesis inherent in its structure, which gave equal authority to the female and male principles, and partly in its peaceful universality. The system gave prodigally of its secrets, and so the occult sciences studied in the male orders, together with the tantric mysteries of the female orders, were made available to all the surrounding cults, including ancient Israel's.

It was this synthesizing power, now so utterly lost to our modern world, that knitted together the fabric of civilization, marrying all its modalities: the natural sciences to religion, humanity to the angelic realm, earth to the spiritual world, male spirituality to its female version, nation to nation in a web of mutuality. Backed by a sophisticated metaphysic, this emphasis on acts of love, on reconciliation and integration of the opposites, so foreign to our present ideas of religion, cemented stable social structures that were not only benign but also immensely durable, lasting for thousands of years. There can be no doubt that the cohesive force so strongly evident in the archaic civilizations rested on some kind of practical knowledge of a universal unitive energy no longer accessible to either modern science or modern religion. It is a Power that in this book has been identified with the Christian exousia or Hindu kundalini, an emanation of the divine Light.

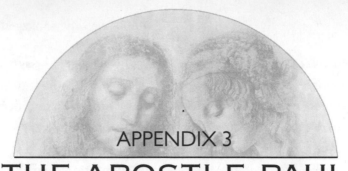

THE APOSTLE PAUL AND THE QABALAH

The gnostic teachings of the Pharisee-trained Paul have long been neglected, despite the fact that he was a Hasid through and through in his intellectual sympathies and an early Christian icon who described himself as "a steward of the mysteries of God." Of all the Pentecostal gifts of the spirit, he declares love to be the greatest, the sine qua non of the spiritual life, but also adds:

> Yet among the mature we do impart wisdom, although it is not a wisdom of this age or of the rulers of this age, who are doomed to pass away. But we impart a secret and hidden wisdom of God, which God decreed before the ages for our glorification. And we impart this in words not taught by human wisdom but taught by the Spirit, interpreting spiritual truths in spiritual language. (1 Corinthians 2:6–13)

Paul's teachings have much in common with the Qabalah, as Eisenman and Wise have noted, and echo those of the Ebionites. These Ebionites were the Hauranite Nazareans for whom Jesus Christ was the perfect human being, the vicar and guardian of Creation, but not to be equated with Almighty God. They believed Christ Jesus was

> begotten of human seed, and chosen, and thus called by election Son of God, Christ having come upon him from on high in the form of a

dove. They say that he was not begotten by God the Father, but that he was created—like one of the archangels, but greater than they. [1]

This belief about the Son of Man derives from very ancient ideas indeed.

In the *Lore of Creation (Maaseh Bereshith),* which Paul had no doubt studied, Primordial Man, Adam Kadmon, represents the visible image and firstborn of the invisible incomprehensible Godhead; he is not God but the highest expression of God in the visible universe. He is archetypal man, the Son of Man mentioned in the Mandaean *Sidra d'Yahya,* or Book of John (Section 18). There it is recounted that before John the Baptist's conception, his father Zechariah is told that the child Yohanna will be the Messiah, a God man referred to as "the youth, the Man (Son of Man) who is sent by the King." John is to be the Redeemer awaited by Israel and an incarnation of the Light-Adam who has existed in the spiritual world from before the Creation.[2] In the *Commentary on Psalm xxxvii* in the Dead Sea Scrolls, the Messiah is described as "the Man" in similar generic terms. "The steps of the Man are confirmed by the Lord and He delights in all his ways" (Verses 23–24).

The *Sepher Yetzirah* (Book of Creation) takes this idea of a human archetype or Heavenly Man further. The ten sephiroth of the Qabalistic Tree of Being trace his celestial outline. Of angelic stature, he stands astride the Tree, a vast figure spread out across the whole of the visible cosmos.

His head is a triad, Wisdom and Intelligence surmounted by the Crown representing Sovereignty. The breast which is Beauty (Tiphareth) is associated in the second triad with the right arm which is Mercy and the left arm which is Justice. In the third triad the genitalia which are Foundation govern the right leg which is Firmness and the left leg which is Splendor, which in turn make a triad with the feet which signify Kingdom.[3]

It was this Qabalistic lore concerning a heavenly Son of Man, the archetypal model for humanity, that gave Paul a more penetrating understanding of Nazarean doctrines than most of the other disciples and enabled him to express these doctrines in a Christological form intelligible to the Gentiles he was seeking to convert. It was taught in the inner brotherhoods that after death most people, still spiritually unawakened, still immersed in their narrow earthly dreams, are unable to rise beyond the astral realm of Yetzirah, remaining there in a suspended form of sleep until their next incarnation. The Elect, on the other hand, are those in process of shaking off this sleep of death; they are the resurrected ones who are following the Redeemer to the divine world through the successive Life gates of the upper planes. But the Redeemer, the Awakened One, is able to rise at once through the entire Creation to the divine world (in Qabalistic terms, the world of Atziluth) from whence he came. There he is able to participate in the government of the Creation as an agent of the Almighty—as we shall all be able to do when fully formed.

This vision of the transformation of the fully awakened and enlightened human being into archangelic form was entertained by all the Jewish sectaries and would assuredly have been passed on to Paul, for Schonfield comments insightfully that the mystery of "the Man," the one he calls Sky Man, "was one of the great secrets studied by the Essenes and other Jewish mystics."[4] But now that Western culture has disowned the multileveled cosmology of antiquity, and with it the correlated belief in a high human destiny, Paul has lost a lot of his credibility. He is even vilified for hijacking Christianity and loading it with a redemptive Christological metaphysic it was never intended to bear.

But there is no direct evidence that after his conversion on the Damascus road Paul ever departed from the mystical doctrines of Messiah Jesus, which he would have learned in the Hauran while living among those Nazarean communities most qualified to transmit them. For Paul, as for the Mandaeans, the essence of the Christian/Johannine message was a Qabalistic one: The earthly savior had to die in this our lowest world in order to assume his role in the highest as the "Son of Life," or Son of Man, whose Gnosis brings enlightenment.

NOTES

PROLOGUE. SOLOMON'S TEMPLE REVISITED

1. Hugh Schonfield, *The Pentecost Revolution* (London: Macdonald and Jane's, 1974).
2. Philostratus, *The Life of Apollonius,* trans. C. P. Jones (Harmondsworth: Penguin, 1970).
3. A. N. Wilson, *Paul: The Mind of the Apostle* (London: Sinclair-Stevenson, 1997), 44.
4. Thomas L. Thompson, *The Bible in History* (London: Jonathan Cape, 1999); also Kathleen Kenyon, *The Bible and Recent Archaeology,* revised by P. R. S. Moorey (London: British Museum Publications, 1987).
5. Ibid., *The Bible in History,* 114.
6. Ibid.
7. Raphael Patai, *The Hebrew Goddess* (New York: Avon Books, 1978), 41.
8. Ibid., 50.
9. Joseph Campbell, *The Masks of God,* vol. 1 (Harmondsworth: Penguin, 1976), 164.
10. Merlin Stone, *When God Was a Woman* (New York: Harvest/Harcourt Brace, 1976), 147; originally published as *The Paradise Paper* (New York: Virago).
11. Stone, *When God Was a Woman,* quoting Geo Widengren (New York: Harvest/Harcourt Brace, 1976).
12. Patai, *The Hebrew Goddess,* 3rd ed. (Detroit: Wayne State University Press, 1990), 128.
13. Ibid., 84.
14. Thompson, *The Bible in History,* 149.
15. Desmond Stewart, *The Foreigner* (London: Hamish Hamilton, 1981); also Karl W. Luckert, *Egyptian Light and Hebrew Fire* (New York: State University of New York Press, 1991).

16. Joseph Campbell, *The Masks of God,* vol. 2 (Harmondsworth: Penguin, 1976), 43, 69–79.

17. Ibid., 382.

18. Robert Turcan, *The Cults of the Roman Empire,* trans. A. Nevill (Oxford: Blackwell, 1992), 53.

19. Campbell, *The Masks of God,* vol. 2, 43. He is quoting Professor Henri Frankfort, *Cylinder Seals* (London: Macmillan, 1939), 75–77.

20. Anne Baring and Jules Cashford, *The Myth of the Goddess* (Harmondsworth: Penguin, 1993), 479.

21. Ibid.

22. Stone, *When God Was a Woman,* 143.

23. Cited by Cullen Murphy, *The Word According to Eve* (Harmondsworth: Penguin, 1999), 70–71.

24. Richard Elliot Friedman, *The Hidden Book in the Bible* (New York: HarperCollins, 1998), 396.

25. Martin Lings, "Old Lithuanian Songs" in *The Sword of Gnosis,* ed. Jacob Needleman (London: Routledge & Kegan Paul, 1986), 389–90.

26. Campbell, *The Masks of God*, vol. 2, 89. See also Stone, *When God Was a Woman,* 142–43.

27. Patrick Tierney, *The Highest Altar* (London: Bloomsbury, 1989), 394.

28. Ibid., 395–97.

29. René Guénon, *The Lord of the World* (Gloucestershire, U.K.: Coombe Springs Press, 1983), 33.

30. Campbell, *The Masks of God,* vol. 1, 165–66.

31. Ibid., 183.

32. Ibid., 168–69.

33. Stephen Quirke, *The Ancient Egyptian Religion* (London: British Museum Press, 1992), 159.

34. Ibid.

35. Campbell, *The Masks of God,* vol. 2, 89.

CHAPTER ONE. CHRISTIANITY:
THE GREAT DIVORCE

1. Édouard Schuré, *The Great Initiates* (New York: Harper & Row, 1961), 19.

2. William Irwin Thompson, *Passages About Earth* (London: Rider, 1975), 154.

3. John Ralston Saul, *The Unconscious Civilization* (Harmondsworth: Penguin, 1997), 3.

4. Ibid., 5.

5. David Tacey, *The Spirituality Revolution* (Sydney: HarperCollins, 2003).

6. Ian Wilson, *Are These the Words of Jesus?* (Oxford: Lennard, 1990), 166–74.

7. Morton Smith, *The Secret Gospel* (London: Victor Gollancz, 1974), 14–17.

8. Andrew Welburn, *The Beginnings of Christianity* (Edinburgh: Floris Books, 1995), 98.

9. Smith, *The Secret Gospel,* 142.

10. Ibid., 66.

11. Kurt Rudolph, trans. R. McL. Wilson, *Gnosis* (Edinburgh: T&T Clark, 1976), 32.

12. Smith, *The Secret Gospel,* 142.

13. Origen, *Contra Celsum,* 129.

14. Welburn, *The Beginnings of Christianity,* 25.

15. Ibid.

16. Bentley Layton, *The Gnostic Scriptures* (London: SCM Press, 1987), 20.

17. Smith, *The Secret Gospel.*

18. Welburn, *The Beginnings of Christianity,* 96.

19. Ibid., 141.

20. Kieren Barry, *The Greek Qabalah* (York Beach, Maine: Samuel Weiser, 1999), 105.

21. H. G. Wunderlich, *The Secret of Crete* (London: Souvenir Press, 1975).

22. Apocalypse of Peter 83:8–10, in the Nag Hammadi Library, 344.

23. Michael Baigent and Richard Leigh, *The Elixir and the Stone* (London: Penguin, 1997), 18.

24. E. R. Dodds, *Pagan and Christian in an Age of Anxiety* (Cambridge: Cambridge University Press, 1990), 106.

25. Rudolph, *Gnosis,* 245.

26. Layton, *The Gnostic Scriptures.*

27. Rudolph, *Gnosis,* 245.

28. Patai, *The Hebrew Goddess,* 76–81.

29. Ibid., 84.

30. Ibid., 93.

31. Rudolph, *Gnosis,* 245.

32. Drunvalo Melchizedek, *The Ancient Secret of the Flower of Life* (Flagstaff, Ariz.: Light Technology Publishing, 2000), 262.

33. Welburn, *The Beginnings of Christianity,* 192.

34. Ibid., 254.

35. Guénon, *The Lord of the World,* 23fn. See also Andrew Tomas, *Shambhala: Oasis of Light* (London: Sphere Books, 1976), and Victoria LePage, *Shambhala* (Wheaton, Ill.: Quest Books, 1996).

36. Lynn Picknett and Clive Prince, *The Templar Revelation* (London: Bantam, 1997), 298–300.

37. S. G. F. Brandon, "Dying God," *Man, Myth and Magic,* no. 26: 739.

38. Welburn, *The Beginnings of Christianity,* 176–77.

39. Marvin W. Meyer, ed., *The Ancient Mysteries: A Source Book* (San Francisco: Harper & Row, 1987), 8.

40. Joseph Campbell, *The Masks of God,* vol. 3 (Harmondsworth: Penguin, 1976), 262.

41. Ibid., 261.

42. Irenaeus, *Against Heresies* 4.26.3, in Elaine Pagels, *The Origin of Satan* (Harmondsworth: Penguin, 1995), 177.

43. Morton Smith, *Jesus the Magician* (London: Victor Gollancz), 1992.

44. Irenaeus of Lyons, *Libros Quinque Adversis Haereses, Praefatio,* in Pagels, *The Origin of Satan,* 17.

45. Graham Phillips, *The Virgin Mary Conspiracy* (Rochester, Vt.: Bear & Company, 2005), 147–48.

46. Ibid.

47. Rudolph, *Gnosis,* 293.

48. Ibid., 369.

49. Baigent and Leigh, *The Elixir and the Stone,* 73.

50. Cyril Mango, *Byzantium* (London: Phoenix, 1994), 49.

51. Welburn, *The Beginnings of Christianity,* 299.

52. Ibid.

53. Ibid.

54. Mango, *Byzantium,* 135–36.

55. Ibid., 67.

56. Ibid., 135.

57. Baigent and Leigh, *The Elixir and the Stone,* 103–25.

58. Frances A. Yates, *The Rosicrucian Enlightenment* (London: Routledge & Kegan Paul, 1986), 111.

59. Ibid., 28.

60. Brendan Lehane, *Early Celtic Christianity* (London: Constable, 1994), 12.

61. Ibid.

62. Baigent and Leigh, *The Elixir and the Stone,* xv.

CHAPTER TWO. FORBIDDEN PATHS

1. Percy Seymour, *The Birth of Christ* (London: Virgin Publishing, 1998), 191.

2. Adrian G. Gilbert, *Magi* (London: Bloomsbury, 1997), 61.

3. Welburn, *The Beginnings of Christianity,* 16.

4. Charles Francis Potter, *The Lost Years of Jesus Revealed* (New York: Ballentyne Books, 1962).

5. Gilbert, *Magi,* 69, 72.

6. Norman Golb, *Who Wrote the Dead Sea Scrolls?* (New York: Scribner, 1995), 380–81.

7. Margaret Barker, *The Lost Prophet: The Book of Enoch and Its Influence on Christianity* (London: SPCK, 1988).

8. Stephan A. Hoeller, *Jung and the Lost Gospels* (Wheaton, Ill.: Quest, 1989), 31.

9. Ibid.

10. Baring and Cashford, *The Myth of the Goddess,* 477.

11. Turcan, *The Cults of the Roman Empire,* 134.

12. *Cruden's Concordance* (Cambridge: Lutterworth Press, 1977), 699.

13. Barker, *The Lost Prophet,* 1.

14. Ibid., 11, from the *Book of Enoch* by R. H. Charles (Oxford: SPCK, 1912, 1917).

15. Potter, *The Lost Years of Jesus Revealed,* 94.

16. Ibid., 110.

17. Barker, *The Lost Prophet,* 18.

18. Thompson, *The Bible in History,* 256.

19. Ibid., 263.

20. Potter, *The Lost Years of Jesus Revealed,* 51.

21. Golb, *Who Wrote the Dead Sea Scrolls?,* 366.

22. Barker, *The Lost Prophet,* 109.

23. Ibid., 19.

24. Ibid., 108.

25. Ibid., 94.

26. Gaalyah Cornfeld and David Noel Freedman, *The Archaeology of the Bible: Book by Book* (New York: Harper & Row, 1976), 227.

27. Ibid., 141.

28. A. E. Wallis Budge, *The Gods of the Egyptians,* vol. 1 (London: Methuan & Co. 1904), 84, 161.

29. Raphael Patai, *The Jewish Alchemists* (Princeton, N.J.: Princeton University Press, 1994), 51–56.

30. Guénon, *The Lord of the World.*

31. Barker, *The Lost Prophet,* 27.

32. Ibid.

33. Ibid., 28.

34. Schonfield, *The Pentecost Revolution,* 59.

35. John G. Bennett, *The Dramatic Universe,* vol. IV (London: Hodder & Stoughton, 1966), 395; and *The Masters of Wisdom* (London: Turnstone Books, 1977), 37–39.

36. Jurgen Spanuth, *Atlantis of the North* (London: Sidgwick & Jackson, 1979).

37. Bennett, *The Dramatic Universe,* 250.

38. LePage, *Shambhala,* 197.

39. Barker, *The Lost Prophet,* 38.

40. Ibid.

41. Ibid., 98–99.

42. Z'ev ben Shimon Halevi, *Kabbalah: The Tradition of Hidden Knowledge* (London: Thames & Hudson, 1978).

43. David Ovason, ed., *The Zelator: The Secret Journals of Mark Hedsel* (London: Arrow Books, 1999), 554 ff.

44. Barker, *The Lost Prophet,* 50.

45. Jay Weidner and Vincent Bridges, *The Mysteries of the Great Cross of Hendaye* (Rochester, Vt.: Destiny Books, 2003), 88.

46. Ibid., 88–89.

47. Barry, *The Greek Qabalah,* xiii–xiv.

48. Ibid., 174.

49. Patai, *The Hebrew Goddess,* 299.

50. Weidner and Bridges, *The Mysteries of the Great Cross of Hendaye,* 88.

51. Barry, *The Greek Qabalah,* 176.

52. Robert Eisenman and Michael Wise, *The Dead Sea Scrolls Uncovered* (Harmondsworth: Penguin, 1993), 13.

53. Ibid., 25.

54. Ibid., 33.

55. Ovason, *The Zelator,* 446.

56. Eisenman and Wise, *The Dead Sea Scrolls Uncovered,* 213–20.

57. Hershel Shanks, *The Meaning and Mystery of the Dead Sea Scrolls* (New York: Random House, 1998), 176.

58. Ibid., 171–72.

59. Smith, *The Secret Gospel,* 82.

60. Thompson, *The Bible in History,* 296.

61. John Romer, *Testament: The Bible and History* (Melbourne: Collins Dove, 1989), 133.

62. Ibid., 83.

63. Barry, *The Greek Qabalah,* 174.

64. Eusebius, *Praeparatio evangelico,* in A. Powell Davies, *The Meaning of the Dead Sea Scrolls* (New York: Penguin, 1954), 64.

CHAPTER THREE. JESUS, UNIVERSAL MAN

1. Thompson, *The Bible in History,* 296.

2. Schonfield, *The Pentecost Revolution,* 262.

3. Smith, *Jesus the Magician,* 47–49.

4. Schonfield, *The Pentecost Revolution,* 279.

5. Cyril Mango, *Byzantium,* 43.

6. Schonfield, *The Pentecost Revolution,* 269.

7. Geza Vermes, *Jesus and the World of Judaism* (Philadelphia: Fortress Press, 1984), 6–11.

8. Baigent and Leigh, *The Elixir and the Stone,* 3.

9. Desmond Stewart, *The Foreigner,* 28.

10. A. N. Wilson, *Paul.*

11. Margaret Barker, *The Lost Prophet,* 17.

12. Carsten Peter Thiede and Matthew d'Ancona, *The Jesus Papyrus* (London: Weidenfeld & Nicholson, 1996); also Kurt Rudolph, *Gnosis,* 253–72, and John A. T. Robinson, *The Priority of John* (London: SCM Press, 1985).

13. Potter, *The Lost Years of Jesus Revealed,* 10.

14. Geo Widengren, *Mani and Manichaeism,* trans. C. Kesler (London: Weidenfeld & Nicholson, 1965).

15. Vermes, *Jesus and the World of Judaism,* chapter 5.

16. Andrew Welburn, *The Beginnings of Christianity,* 191.

17. Clement, *Protreptikos Logos,* 10m 92, in Michael Grant, *Jesus* (London: Weidenfeld & Nicholson, 1977), 39.

18. Hoeller, *Jung and the Lost Gospels,* 198.

19. Seymour, *The Birth of Christ,* 92–93.

20. Frithjof Schuon, "The Human Margin," from *The Sword of Gnosis,* ed. Jacob Needleman (London: Routledge & Kegan Paul, 1986), 440.

21. Welburn, *The Beginnings of Christianity,* 194.

22. Picknett and Prince, *The Templar Revelation,* 328.

23. Joseph Chilton Pearce, *The Biology of Transcendence* (Rochester, Vt.: Park Street Press, 2002), 54.

24. Ibid., 64.

25. Ibid., 23.

26. Ibid., 26.

27. Ibid., 42.

28. Ibid., 144.

29. Ibid., 65.

30. Ibid., 69.

31. Ibid., 59.

32. Ibid., 67.

33. Ibid., 72.

34. Ibid., 74–75.

35. Picknett and Prince, *The Templar Revelation,* chapter 16.

36. John Dominic Crossan, *The Historical Jesus: The Life of a Mediterranean Jewish Peasant* (Victoria, Australia: Collins Dove, 1993), xxvii.

37. Rudolph, *Gnosis,* 343.

38. Widengren, *Mani and Manichaeism,* 16.

39. Werner Keller, *The Bible as History,* trans. W. Neil (London: Hodder & Stoughton, 1980), 337.

40. Layton, *The Gnostic Scriptures.*

41. Geza Vermes, *Jesus the Jew* (London: Collins, 1973).

42. Elmer R. Gruber and Holger Kersten, *The Original Jesus* (Rockport, Mass.: Element Books, 1995), 204.

43. Oscar Cullman, *The Christology of the New Testament* (London: SCM, 1975), 40.

44. E. S. Drower, *The Mandaeans of Iran and Iraq* (Oxford: Clarendon Press, 1937), 100.

45. Potter, *The Lost Years of Jesus Revealed,* 27.

46. Cornfeld and Freedman, *The Archaeology of the Bible,* 141.

47. Crossan, *The Historical Jesus,* xxvii.

48. Andrew Collins, *Gods of Eden: Egypt's Lost Legacy and the Genesis of Civilization* (London: Headline Books, 1998), 126–41.

49. Epiphanius, *Panarion, XX,* 16, in Welburn, *The Beginnings of Christianity,* 87.

50. Schuré, *The Great Initiates,* 450.

51. Ibid., 25–26.

52. Ibid., 520n.

53. Eisenman and Wise, *The Dead Sea Scrolls Uncovered,* 70.

54. Vermes, *Jesus the Jew,* chapter 7.

55. John Major Jenkins, *Galactic Alignment* (Rochester, Vt.: Bear & Co., 2002), 150.

56. Ibid.

57. Halevi, *Kabbalah: Tradition of Hidden Knowledge,* 92.

58. Ibid., 97.

59. S. G. F. Brandon, *Jesus and the Zealots* (Manchester: Manchester University Press, 1967), 204, note 1.

60. A. Powell Davies, *The Meaning of the Dead Sea Scrolls,* 64.

61. David Ling, *The Buddha* (London: Temple Smith, 1985).

62. Campbell, *The Masks of God,* vol. 2, 199–200.

63. Halevi, *Kabbalah: Tradition of Hidden Knowledge,* 79.

64. Turcan, *The Cults of the Roman Empire,* 336.

65. Ibid., 334–35.

66. Welburn, *The Beginnings of Christianity,* 78–80.

67. Ibid., 79.

68. Ibid., 76.

69. Pagels, *The Origin of Satan,* 81.

CHAPTER FOUR. NAZAREANS AND HASIDIM

1. Frithjof Schuon, "The Human Margin," in *The Sword of Gnosis,* ed. Jacob Needleman, 440.

2. Patai, *The Hebrew Goddess,* 6–7.

3. Cornfeld and Freedman, *Archaeology of the Bible.*

4. Schuré, *The Great Initiates,* 425–26.

5. Schonfield, *The Pentecost Revolution,* 295.

6. Ibid., 283.

7. Ibid.

8. Hugh Schonfield, *The Essene Odyssey* (Dorset, U.K.: Element Books, 1984), 85.

9. John Shelby Spong, *Liberating the Gospels* (New York: HarperCollins, 1996), 231.

10. Schonfield, *The Pentecost Revolution*, 292.

11. Schonfield, *The Essene Odyssey*, 71.

12. Schonfield, *The Pentecost Revolution*, 292.

13. Ibid., 293.

14. Eusebius, *The History of the Church from Christ to Constantine*, trans. G. A. Williamson (Harmondsworth: Penguin, 1981), 3–19.

15. Vermes, *Jesus the Jew*, 79.

16. Ibid., 11, 27.

17. Hoeller, *Jung and the Lost Gospels*, 31–32.

18. Robert Eisenman, *Maccabees, Zadokites, Christians and Qumran* (Leiden: Brill Press, 1983), 88–92. See also A. Powell Davies, *The Meaning of the Dead Sea Scrolls*, 56.

19. Michael Baigent, Richard Leigh, and Henry Lincoln, *The Messianic Legacy* (London: Corgi Books, 1987), 88.

20. Davies, *The Meaning of the Dead Sea Scrolls*, 67.

21. Ibid., 71.

22. Ibid.

23. Campbell, *The Masks of God*, vol. 3, 273–75.

24. Ibid., 277.

25. Ibid., 277–78.

26. H. H. Rowley, *The Zadokite Fragments and the Dead Sea Scrolls* (New York: Macmillan, 1952), 62–88. Compare "The History of the Qumran Sect," *Bulletin of the John Rylands Library* 49: 63, 203–32.

27. Cornfeld and Freedman, *Archaeology of the Bible*, 241.

28. Philip Davies, "Jerusalem," in *Creating the Old Testament*, ed. Stephen Bigger (Oxford: Basil Blackwell, 1989), 180.

29. Cornfeld and Freedman, *The Archaeology of the Bible*, 241.

30. Vermes, *Jesus the Jew*, 134.

31. Ibid., 133.

32. Eisenman, *Maccabees, Zadokites, Christians and Qumran*, 19ff, 45.

33. Will Parfitt, *The Elements of the Qabalah* (Dorset, U.K.: Element Books, 1991), 44–45.

34. Ibid., 45.

35. Elaine Pagels, *The Gnostic Gospels* (London: Phoenix, 2006), 166.

36. Ibid., 74.

37. Baigent, Leigh, and Lincoln, *The Messianic Legacy*, 91.

38. Campbell, *The Masks of God,* vol. 3, 279.

39. Ibid., 278–81.

40. Thompson, *The Bible in History,* 294.

41. Cornfeld and Freedman, *The Archaeology of the Bible,* 242.

42. Baigent, Leigh, and Lincoln, *The Messianic Legacy,* 88.

43. J. G. Bennett, *Gurdjieff: Making a New World* (London: Turnstone Books, 1976), 36.

44. Campbell, *The Masks of God,* vol. 3, 280–81.

45. Margaret Barker, "Other Books," in *Creating the Old Testament,* 338.

46. Campbell, *The Masks of God,* vol. 3, 281.

47. Thompson, *The Bible in History,* xv.

48. Schonfield, *The Essene Odyssey,* 148.

49. Welburn, *The Beginnings of Christianity,* 198.

50. Spong, *Liberating the Gospels,* 231.

51. Ibid., 195, in Bentley Layton, *The Gnostic Scriptures.*

52. Ibid., 200.

53. Layton, *The Gnostic Scriptures,* 200.

54. A. E. Waite, *The Holy Kabbalah* (New York: Citadel Press, 1995), 564.

55. Leo Schaya, *The Universal Meaning of the Kabbalah* (London: George Allen and Unwin, 1971 and 1989), 63.

56. Waite, *The Holy Kabbalah,* 566.

57. Patai, *The Hebrew Goddess,* 279.

58. Moses Cordovero, Pardes Rimmonim VIII VIII 17, in "The Pomegranate Orchard," in Patai, *The Hebrew Goddess,* 125.

59. Charles Hartshorne, *A Natural Theology for Our Time* (La Salle, Ill.: Open Court, 1967), ix.

60. Patai, *The Hebrew Goddess,* 158.

61. Cited by Andrew Itter, "Esoteric Teaching in the Writings of Clement of Alexandria," in *Esotericism and the Control of Knowledge,* ed. E. F. Crangle (Sydney: Department of Studies in Religion, University of Sydney, 2004), 189.

62. Cited by Schonfield, *The Essene Odyssey,* 84.

63. Schonfield, *The Essene Odyssey,* 87.

64. Ibid., 84.

65. Baigent and Leigh, *The Elixir and the Stone,* 15.

66. Smith, *The Secret Gospel,* 82.

CHAPTER FIVE. OUT OF THE EAST: PROPHECIES AND STAR LORE

1. Welburn, *The Beginnings of Christianity,* 83.

2. Ibid., 83–84.

3. Ibid., 84–105.

4. Ovason, *The Zelator.*

5. Thompson, *The Bible in History,* 198.

6. Gilbert, *Magi,* 103.

7. Stewart, *The Foreigner,* 21–22.

8. Luckert, *Egyptian Light and Hebrew Fire,* 319.

9. Stewart, *The Foreigner,* 257–58.

10. Davies, "Jerusalem," 178.

11. Jenkins, *Galactic Alignment,* 103.

12. Ibid., 102.

13. Ibid., 103.

14. Ibid., 104.

15. Ibid., 103.

16. Ibid., 105.

17. Ibid., 106.

18. Welburn, *The Beginnings of Christianity,* 19.

19. Ibid.

20. Hoeller, *Jung and the Lost Gospels,* 224.

21. Pearce, *The Biology of Transcendence,* 59.

22. Itter, "Esoteric Teaching in the Writings of Clement of Alexandria," 205.

23. Ibid., 189–90.

24. Halevi, *Kabbalah: Tradition of Hidden Knowledge,* 37.

25. Ibid.

26. Schuré, *The Great Initiates,* 194.

27. Itter, "Esoteric Teachings in the Writings of Clement of Alexandria," 188.

28. Schaya, *The Universal Meaning of the Kabbalah,* 111.

29. Dion Fortune, *The Mystical Qabalah* (London: Aquarian Press, 1987), 27.

30. Gilbert, *Magi,* 64.

31. G. R. S. Mead, *Thrice Greatest Hermes,* vol. 1. (London: John M. Watkins, 1964), 161.

32. Jenkins, *Galactic Alignment,* 106–109.

33. Smith, *The Secret Gospel,* 66.

34. Rudolph, *Gnosis,* 293.

35. Ibid., 322.

36. Pagels, *The Gnostic Gospels,* 26, quoting Tertullian in *Adversus Valentinianos 7.*

37. Arnaldo Momigliano, ed., *The Conflict Between Paganism and Christianity in the Fourth Century* (Oxford: Clarendon Press, 1963).

38. William Kingsland, *The Gnosis in the Christian Scriptures* (London: Solo Press, 1993), 84.

39. Pearce, *The Biology of Transcendence,* 145.

40. Hoeller, *Jung and the Lost Gospels,* 140.

41. Ibid., 140–41.

42. Luckert, *Egyptian Light and Hebrew Fire,* 45.

43. Ibid., 302.

44. Leo Schaya, *The Universal Meaning of the Kabbalah,* 111.

45. Ibid., 115.

46. Jonathan Campbell, *Deciphering the Dead Sea Scrolls* (London: Fontana Press, 1996), 95.

47. Schaya, *The Universal Meaning of the Kabbalah,* 115.

48. Ibid., 303.

49. Ibid., 47.

50. Jenkins, *Galactic Alignment,* 87–92.

51. Ibid., 93.

52. Gilbert, *Magi,* 270–71.

53. Mircea Eliade, *The Myth of the Eternal Return* (New York: Princeton University Press, 1954), 113–14.

54. Melchizedek, *The Ancient Secret of the Flower of Life,* 57–58.

55. Jenkins, *Galactic Alignment,* 133.

56. Ibid., 128–32.

57. Melchizedek, *The Ancient Secret of the Flower of Life,* 124.

CHAPTER SIX. ENVOYS FROM
THE KING OF LIGHT

1. M. Lidzbarski, *Das Johnanneshuch der Mandäer,* 2 vols. (GieÞen: 1905 and 1915).

2. Drower, *The Mandaeans of Iran and Iraq,* 100.

3. Rudolph, *Gnosis,* 264.

4. J. J. Buckley, "Mandaeans in the U.S.A. Today: Tenacity of Traditions" (ARAM 7 1995), 353: also *The Mandaeans: Ancient Texts and Modern People* (Oxford: Oxford University Press, 2002), 6.

5. E. S. Drower, "Mandaean Polemic," *Bulletin of the School of Oriental and African Studies,* vol. XXV, part 3 (1964).

6. Rudolph, *Gnosis,* 363.

7. Ibid., 360.

8. Buckley, "Mandaeans in the U.S.A. Today: Tenacity of Traditions," 5.

9. Smith, *Jesus the Magician,* and Picknett and Prince, *The Templar Revelation,* 334.

10. Rudolph, *Gnosis,* 323.

11. Ibid., 25.

12. Ibid., 37.

13. Widengren, *Mani and Manichaeism,* 20.

14. Ibid., 114.

15. Hathem Saed, "*Nasiruta:* Deep Knowledge and Extraordinary Priestcraft in Mandaean Religion" in *Esotericism and the Control of Knowledge,* ed. E. F. Crangle (Sydney: Department of Studies in Religion, University of Sydney, 2004), 306.

16. Rudolph, *Gnosis,* 30.

17. G. R. S. Mead, ed., *The Gnostic John the Baptizer: Selections from the Mandaean John-Book* (London: John M. Watkins, 1924), 16.

18. Welburn, *The Beginnings of Christianity,* 175.

19. Ibid., 191.

20. Rudolph, *Gnosis,* 357.

21. Ovason, *The Zelator,* 131.

22. Rudolph, *Gnosis,* 357.

23. Ibid., 357–58.

24. Welburn, *The Beginnings of Christianity,* 175.

25. Ibid., 357.

26. Ibid., 358.

27. Ibid., 86.

28. Jerome, *Against Pelagius,* iii, 2, cited by Hugh Schonfield in *The Pentecost Revolution,* 303.

29. Layton, *The Gnostic Scriptures,* xx.

30. Ibid.

31. G. R. S. Mead, *Simon Magus: An Essay* (London, 1892; reprint, Chicago: Ares Publishing, 1979), 19.

32. Josephus, *Antiquities of the Jews*, quoted by Picknett and Prince, *The Templar Revelation*, 306.

33. Schonfield, *The Essene Odyssey*, 59.

34. Ibid., 145.

35. Ibid., 305.

36. Ibid.

37. Ibid., 86.

38. Edwin Yamauchi, *Pre-Christian Gnosticism* (London: Tyndale Press, 1973), 31.

39. Ibid., 24.

40. Ibid., 25.

41. Welburn, *The Beginnings of Christianity*, 240–42.

42. Schonfield, *The Pentecost Revolution*, 284.

43. Mead, *Simon Magus: An Essay*, 28 ff.

44. Welburn, *The Beginnings of Christianity*, 65.

45. Jean Daniélou, in S. J. Isser, *The Dositheans* (Leiden: E. J. Brill, 1976), 198.

46. Hoeller, *Jung and the Lost Gospels*, 65.

47. Baigent and Leigh, *The Elixir and the Stone*, 6–7.

48. Hoeller, *Jung and the Lost Gospels*, 72.

49. Welburn, *The Beginnings of Christianity*, 66.

50. Simon Magus, *The Great Annunciation*, in W. Foerster, *Gnosis*, vol. 1 (Oxford: Clarendon, 1972), 258.

51. Rudolph, *Gnosis*, 295, quoting Justin Martyr, Irenaeus, and Hippolytus.

52. Picknett and Prince, *The Templar Revelation*, 321.

53. Ibid.

54. Hoeller, *Jung and the Lost Gospels*, 71.

55. Ibid., 70.

56. Susan Haskins, *Mary Magdalene* (London: HarperCollins, 1994), 404–405.

57. Ibid., 12.

58. Hoeller, *Jung and the Lost Gospels*, 68.

59. Rudolph, *Gnosis*, 150.

60. Hoeller, *Jung and the Lost Gospels*, 226.

61. Ibid.

62. Raphael Patai, *The Hebrew Goddess*, third enlarged edition (Detroit: Wayne State University Press, 1990), 129.

63. Shankara, in Aubrey Menon, *The New Mystics* (London: Thames & Hudson, 1974).

64. Sisirkumar Mitra, *The Dawn Eternal* (Pondicherry, India: Sri Aurobindo Ashram, 1954).

65. Pearce, *The Biology of Transcendence,* 256–58.

66. Ivar Lissner, *Man, God and Magic* (London: Jonathan Cape, 1959).

67. Editorial note in Fortune, *The Mystical Qabalah,* 313–16.

68. Trans. Robert Powell, "Historical Note Concerning the Emerald Tablet," *The Hermetic Journal* 15 (Spring 1981), 38; also Baigent and Leigh, *The Elixir and the Stone,* 22.

69. Welburn, *The Beginnings of Christianity,* 188.

70. Wilson, *Are These the Words of Jesus?,* 106.

71. Barry, *The Greek Qabalah,* 174.

72. Aaron M. Rothmuller, *The Music of the Jews: An Historical Appreciation,* trans. H. S. Stevens (Brunswick, N.J.: Thomas Yoseloff, 1967), 175.

73. Schaya, *The Universal Meaning of the Kabbalah,* 57–59.

CHAPTER SEVEN. THE GOSPEL OF MARY: SACRED MARRIAGE

1. Marvin Meyer, *The Gospels of Mary* (New York: HarperSanFrancisco, 2004), 20.

2. William Meader, *Shine Forth: The Soul's Magical Destiny* (Mariposa, Calif.: Source Publications, 2004), 152.

3. Baring and Cashford, *The Myth of the Goddess,* 53.

4. Ibid., 56.

5. Weidner and Bridges, *The Mysteries of the Great Cross of Hendaye,* 88.

6. Meyer, *The Gospels of Mary,* 77.

7. Doc Childre and Howard Martin, *The Heartmath Solution* (New York: HarperSanFrancisco, 1999), 58.

8. David Beale, *Eros and the Jews* (New York: HarperCollins, 1992), 148.

9. Margaret Starbird, *The Woman With the Alabaster Jar* (Santa Fe: Bear & Co., 1993), 50.

10. Meyer, *The Gospels of Mary,* ix.

11. Picknett and Prince, *The Templar Revelation,* 251.

12. Meyer, *The Gospels of Mary,* xvi, *The Dialogue of the Saviour,* 139, 12–13, in the Nag Hammadi Library, 235.

13. Ibid., 66.

14. Ibid., xii.

15. Picknett and Prince, *The Templar Revelation,* 20–21.

16. Meyer, *The Gospels of Mary,* xiii.

17. Picknett and Prince, *The Templar Revelation,* 20 –21.

18. Meyer, *The Gospels of Mary,* xviii.

19. Jacobus De Voragine, *Golden Legend: Readings on the Saints,* vol. 1, trans. W. G. Ryan (Princeton, N.J.: Princeton University Press, 1993), 374 ff.

20. Picknett and Prince, *The Templar Revelation,* 93.

21. Ibid., 104.

22. Ibid., 252.

23. Ibid., 259–64.

24. Baring and Cashford, *The Myth of the Goddess,* 592.

25. Claire Dunne, *Carl Jung: Wounded Healer of the Soul* (New York: Parabola Books, 2000), 171.

26. Ibid., 129–30.

27. Tsultrim Allione, *Women of Wisdom* (London: Routledge & Kegan Paul, 1984).

28. Picknett and Prince, *The Templar Revelation,* 88.

29. Meyer, *The Gospels of Mary,* 19–20.

30. Schonfield, *The Essene Odyssey,* 166.

31. Meader, *Shine Forth: The Soul's Magical Destiny,* 22.

32. Ibid., 24–26.

33. Ibid., 26.

34. Hans Lewy, ed., *Philosophical Writings: Philo* (Oxford: Phaidon Press, 1946), 57–60.

35. Joan E. Taylor and Philip R. Davies, "The So-Called Therapeutae of *De Vita Contemplativa:* Identity and Character," in *Harvard Theological Review* 91, vol. 1, (1998), 3–15.

36. Philo, *De Vita Contemplativa,* 58.

37. Linda Bennett Elder, "The Woman Question and Female Ascetics Among Essenes," in *Biblical Archaeologist* 57 (1994), 220–28.

38. Philo, *De Vita Contemplativa,* 60.

39. Ibid.

40. De Voragine, *Golden Legend: Readings on the Saints,* 374 ff.

41. Michael Baigent, Richard Leigh, and Henry Lincoln, *The Holy Blood and the Holy Grail* (London: Corgi Books, 1983), 330–70.

42. Weidner and Bridges, *The Mysteries of the Great Cross at Hendaye,* 162.

43. Picknett and Prince, *The Templar Revelation,* 68.

44. Ibid., 78.

45. Ean Begg, *The Cult of the Black Virgin* (London: Arkana, 1985; revised edition 1996), 99.

46. Picknett and Prince, *The Templar Revelation,* 108.

47. Schonfield, *The Essene Odyssey,* 164.

48. Ibid., 165.

49. Allione, *Women of Wisdom,* 34–35.

50. Picknett and Prince, *The Templar Revelation,* 95.

51. Barbara Newman, *From Virile Woman to WomanChrist* (Philadelphia: University of Pennsylvania Press, 1995), 172–81.

52. Weidner and Bridges, *The Mysteries of the Great Cross of Hendaye,* 163.

53. Meyer, *The Gospels of Mary,* 19.

CHAPTER EIGHT. TEMPLE CONSPIRACIES AND SECRETS

1. Quoted in Picknett and Prince, *The Templar Revolution,* 240.

2. Ibid.

3. Davies, "Jerusalem," 180.

4. Luckert, *Egyptian Light and Hebrew Fire,* 29.

5. Stewart, *The Foreigner,* 21–22.

6. J. M. Robertson, *Pagan Christs,* abridged edition (New York: Barnes & Noble, 1993), 52–53.

7. Graham Hancock, *The Sign and the Seal* (London: Heinemann, 1992).

8. Joscelyn Godwin, *Mystery Religions in the Ancient World* (London: Thames & Hudson, 1981), 32.

9. Ibid., 78.

10. Rudolph, *Gnosis,* 318.

11. Godwin, *Mystery Religions in the Ancient World,* 32.

12. Baring and Cashford, *The Myth of the Goddess,* 476.

13. Godwin, *Mystery Religions in the Ancient World,* 78.

14. Schonfield, *The Essene Odyssey,* 135.

15. Thompson, *The Bible in History,* 262.

16. Ibid., 265.

17. Schonfield, *The Essene Odyssey,* 21–22.

18. Rowley, *The Zadokite Fragments and the Dead Sea Scrolls,* 62–88. Compare

Rowley, "The History of the Qumran Sect," *Bulletin of the John Rylands Library* 49, 203–32.

19. Davies, *The Meaning of the Dead Sea Scrolls,* 74.

20. Welburn, *The Beginnings of Christianity,* 41.

21. Halevi, *Kabbalah: The Tradition of Hidden Knowledge.*

22. Welburn, *The Beginnings of Christianity,* 33–34.

23. Tim Wallace-Murphy and Marilyn Hopkins, *Rosslyn* (Dorset, U.K.: Element, 1999), 44.

24. Guénon, *The Lord of the World,* 2.

25. Ibid., 33.

26. Trevor Ravenscroft and Tim Wallace-Murphy, *The Mark of the Beast* (London: Sphere Books, 1990), 75.

27. *The Masks of God,* vol. 3, 273.

28. Ibid., 277.

29. Plutarch, *Life of Alexander,* trans. I. Scott-Kilvert in the *Age of Alexander* (Harmondsworth: Penguin, 1973), 259.

30. Baigent and Leigh, *The Elixir and the Stone,* 12.

31. Frances Yates, *Giordano Bruno and the Hermetic Tradition* (London: Routledge & Kegan Paul, 1982).

32. Luckert, *Egyptian Light and Hebrew Fire,* 45.

33. Welburn, *The Beginnings of Christianity,* 187.

34. Ibid., 188.

35. Hoeller, *Jung and the Lost Gospels,* 206.

36. Ibid., 209.

37. Yates, *The Rosicrucian Enlightenment,* 63.

38. Melchizedek, *The Ancient Secret of the Flower of Life,* vol. 1, 137–38.

39. Ibid., 48.

40. Davies, *The Meaning of the Dead Sea Scrolls,* 65.

41. Godwin, *Mystery Religions in the Ancient World,* 78.

42. Ibid., 38–39.

43. Ibid., 78.

44. Ibid.

45. Meyer, *The Gospels of Mary,* 77.

46. Schonfield, *The Essene Odyssey,* 166.

47. Ibid., 167.

48. Picknett and Prince, *The Templar Revelation,* 143.

49. Schonfield, *The Essene Odyssey,* 167.

50. Fortune, *The Mystical Qabalah,* 204.

51. Ibid., 58.

52. Edmund Wilson, *The Scrolls from the Dead Sea* (London: W. H. Allen, 1955), 43.

53. Ibid.

54. Ibid., 42–43.

55. Potter, *The Lost Years of Jesus Revealed,* 13.

56. Phillips, *The Virgin Mary Conspiracy,* 103.

57. Luckert, *Egyptian Light and Hebrew Fire,* 80.

58. Gopi Krishna, *The Secret of Yoga,* also *The Biological Basis of Religion and Genius* (New York, 1972), and Arthur Avalon, *The Serpent Power* (London: Luzac & Co., 1919).

CHAPTER NINE. THE GNOSIS OF THE HEART

1. Smith, *The Secret Gospel,* 110.

2. Luckert, *Egyptian Light and Hebrew Fire,* 80.

3. Smith, *The Secret Gospel,* 108–10.

4. Bernard Lievegoed, *Phases,* trans. H. S. Lake (London: Rudolf Steiner Press, 1979), 232–33.

5. Welburn, *The Beginnings of Christianity,* 270.

6. Ibid.

7. J. M. Hull, *Hellenistic Magic and the Synoptic Tradition* (London: SCM Press, 1974), 106.

8. Ibid., 164, note 52.

9. Welburn, *The Beginnings of Christianity,* 272.

10. John Woodroffe, *The Serpent Power* (New York: Dover Publications, 1974), 50.

11. Ibid.

12. Rudolf Steiner, *Three Streams in the Evolution of Mankind,* Lecture Three (London: Rudolf Steiner Press, 1963), 58.

13. Ovason, *The Zelator,* 468, footnote.

14. Ibid., 27–30.

15. Ibid., 468, footnote.

16. Welburn, *The Beginnings of Christianity,* 272.

17. Ibid., 280.

18. Ibid., 277.

19. Campbell, *The Masks of God,* vol. 2, in the Chandogya Upanishad, 53–110 (Harmondsworth: Penguin, 1976), 201–202.

20. Jacob Boehme, *The Way to Christ,* trans. P. Erb (New York: Paulist Press, 1978), xvii.

21. Fortune, *The Mystical Qabalah,* 80.

22. Ibid., 58.

23. Idries Shah, *The Sufis* (London: Octagon Press, 1964), 307.

24. Campbell, *The Masks of God,* vol. 3, 9.

25. Ibid., 263.

26. Ibid., 30.

27. Turcan, *Cults of the Roman Empire,* 281.

28. Ibid., 270–75.

29. Ibid., 272.

30. Ibid., 275.

31. Welburn, *The Beginnings of Christianity,* 271.

32. A. H. Armstrong, "The Ancient and Continuing Pieties of the Greek World," *Classical Mediterranean Spirituality* (London: SCM Press, 1989), 66–101.

33. Pagels, *The Origin of Satan,* 116–19.

34. Woodroffe, *The Serpent Power,* 26.

35. Turcan, *Cults of the Roman Empire.*

36. Irina Tweedie, *The Chasm of Fire* (Dorset, U.K.: Element, 1983), 245.

37. Hoeller, *Jung and the Lost Gospels,* 153.

38. Daniel Goleman quoted in Childre and Martin, *The Heartmath Solution,* 12–13.

39. Ibid., 13.

40. Ibid., 14.

41. Helen Waddell, *The Desert Fathers* (London: Constable & Co., 1936), 9.

42. Ibid., 29.

43. Ibid., 257.

44. Campbell, *The Masks of God,* vol. 2, 199.

45. Edwin Arnold, preface to *The Bhagavad Gita* (London: Routledge & Kegan Paul, 1955), viii.

46. Welburn, *The Beginnings of Christianity,* 330 fn.

47. Smith, *The Secret Gospel,* 110.

48. Pagels, *The Origin of Satan,* 118.

49. Schonfield, *The Pentecost Revolution,* 263.

50. Smith, *The Secret Gospel,* 80–81.

51. Ibid., 17.

52. Ibid.

53. Ibid., 110.

54. Momigliano, *The Conflict Between Paganism and Christianity in the Fourth Century*, 92.

55. Pagels, *The Gnostic Gospels*, 138.

CHAPTER TEN. DEATH AND RESURRECTION

1. Godwin, *Mystery Religions of the Ancient World*, 34–35.

2. Smith, *The Secret Gospel*, 132.

3. Pagels, *The Gnostic Gospels*, 139.

4. Sogyal Rinpoche, *The Tibetan Book of Living and Dying* (London: Rider, 1994), 268–69.

5. Fortune, *The Mystical Qabalah*, 275.

6. Ibid., 275.

7. Acts of John 94–96, 97–102, in Campbell, *The Masks of God*, vol. 3, 371–73.

8. Leo Frobenius, in Campbell, *The Masks of God*, vol. 1, 168.

9. James Bentley, *Secrets of Mt. Sinai* (London: Orbis, 1985), 133.

10. Stuart Holroyd, *The Elements of Gnosticism* (Shaftsbury, Dorset, U.K.: Element Books, 1994), 28.

11. Stephen Langdon, "Tammuz and Ishtar," *Sumerian and Babylonian Psalms* (Librairie Paul Geuthner, 1909), 14.

12. Baring and Cashford, *The Myth of the Goddess*, 592.

13. Ibid., 629.

14. Pagels, *The Gnostic Gospels*, 35.

15. Bentley, *Secrets of Mt. Sinai*, 184.

16. Barry, *The Greek Qabalah*, 136.

17. Bentley, *Secrets of Mt. Sinai*, 185.

18. Ibid., 139.

19. Ibid., 179.

20. Wilson, *Are These the Words of Jesus?*

21. Smith, *The Secret Gospel.*

22. Layton, *The Gnostic Scriptures*, 24.

23. Wilson, *Are These the Words of Jesus?*, 87.

24. Quoted in Campbell, *The Masks of God*, vol. 3, 364.

25. Paramahansa Yogananda, *The Autobiography of a Yogi* (Los Angeles: Self-Realization Fellowship, 1981), 340.

26. Ibid., 399.

27. Carlos Castaneda, *The Active Side of Infinity* (London: Thorsons, 2000), 37.

28. Tsultrim Allione, *Women of Wisdom.*

29. LePage, *Shambhala,* 241.

30. Ibid.

31. Smith, *Jesus the Magician.*

32. Layton, *The Gnostic Scriptures,* 50.

33. Campbell, *The Masks of God,* vol. 3, 375.

EPILOGUE. THINGS TO COME

1. Tacey, *The Spirituality Revolution,* 205.

2. Schonfield, *The Essene Odyssey,* 142.

3. Tacey, *The Spirituality Revolution,* 205.

4. Weidner and Bridges, *The Mysteries of the Great Cross of Hendaye,* 415–16.

5. Tacey, *The Spirituality Revolution,* 78–82.

6. Joscelyn Godwin, *Harmonies of Heaven and Earth* (Rochester, Vt.: Inner Traditions, 1987), 2.

7. Welburn, *The Beginnings of Christianity,* 300.

8. Jenkins, *Galactic Alignment,* 71.

9. Tomas, *Shambhala: Oasis of Light,* 106.

10. Wallace-Murphy and Hopkins, *Rosslyn.*

11. Baigent and Leigh, *The Elixir and the Stone,* 134.

12. Yates, *The Rosicrucian Enlightenment,* 232.

13. Ron Heisler, "John Dee and the Secret Societies," *The Hermetic Journal* (1992), 157–60 and 187–91.

14. Hendrick Niclaes, *Evangelium Regni: A Joyfull Message of the Kingdom,* trans. C. Vitell (Amsterdam, ca. 1575).

15. Benjamin Woolley, *The Queen's Conjurer* (London: HarperCollins, 2001), 84.

16. Ibid., 55.

17. Yates, *Giordano and the Hermetic Tradition,* 197.

18. R. J. W. Evans, *Rudolph II and His World* (Oxford: Clarendon Press, 1984), 230.

19. Godwin, *Mystery Religions in the Ancient World,* 8.

20. Fortune, *The Mystical Qabalah,* 272.

21. Tacey, *The Spirituality Revolution,* 197.

22. Mircea Eliade, *The Myth of the Eternal Return* (Princeton, N.J.: Princeton University Press, 1954).

23. Wunderlich, *The Secret of Crete.*

24. Lissner, *Man, God and Magic,* 270–76.

25. Baring and Cashford, *The Myth of the Goddess,* 79.

26. Ibid., 79–80.

27. Tomas, *Shambhala: Oasis of Light,* 26.

28. Meader, *Shine Forth: The Soul's Magical Destiny,* 22.

29. Arnold Mindell, *The Leader as Martial Artist* (New York: HarperSanFrancisco, 1992).

APPENDIX ONE. THE GODS OF ANCIENT ISRAEL

1. Robert Graves, *Hebrew Myths: The Book of Genesis* (London: Cassell & Co., 1964), 178.

2. Ibid.

3. Ibid., 179.

4. Gerd Von Hassler, *Lost Survivors of the Deluge,* trans. M. Ebon (New York: Signet, New American Library, 1978), 85–88.

5. Campbell, *The Masks of God,* vol. 3, 133.

6. Philip Hitti, *The History of the Arabs* (London: Macmillan, 1970), 40.

7. Kenyon, *The Bible and Recent Archaeology,* 86.

8. Shanks, *The Mystery and Meaning of the Dead Sea Scrolls,* 151.

9. Geza Vermes, *Complete Dead Sea Scrolls in English* (New York: Allen Lane/The Penguin Press, 1997), 325.

10. Hitti, *The History of the Arabs,* 100–101.

11. Friedman, *The Hidden Book in the Bible,* 320.

APPENDIX TWO. RELIGION IN THE BRONZE AGE

1. Picknett and Prince, *The Templar Revelation,* 292.

2. Waite, *The Holy Kabbalah,* x–xi.

3. Wunderlich, *The Secret of Crete.*

4. Robert Bauval and Adrian Gilbert, *The Orion Mystery* (London: William Heinemann, 1994), 150–53.

APPENDIX THREE. THE APOSTLE PAUL
AND THE QABALAH

1. Epiphanius, *Panarion, XXV,* in Andrew Welburn, *The Beginnings of Christianity*
(Edinburgh: Floris Books, 1995), 87.

2. Schonfield, *The Essene Odyssey,* 141.

3. Ibid., 145, from C. D. Ginsberg, *The Kabbalah* (London: Routledge & Kegan
Paul, 1955).

4. Ibid., 138.

BIBLIOGRAPHY

Allione, Tsultrim. *Women of Wisdom.* London: Routledge & Kegan Paul, 1984.

Armstrong, A. H., ed. "The Ancient and Continuing Pieties of the Greek World," *Classical Mediterranean Spirituality.* London: SCM Press, 1989.

Arnold, Edwin. Preface to *The Bhagavad Gita.* London: Routledge & Kegan Paul, 1955.

Baigent, Michael, and Richard Leigh. *The Elixir and the Stone.* London: Penguin, 1997.

Baigent, Michael, Richard Leigh, and Henry Lincoln. *The Holy Blood and the Holy Grail.* London: Corgi Books, 1983.

———. *The Messianic Legacy.* London: Corgi Books, 1986.

Baring, Anne, and Jules Cashford. *The Myth of the Goddess.* Harmondsworth: Penguin, 1993.

Barker, Margaret. *The Lost Prophet: The Book of Enoch and Its Influence on Christianity.* London: SPCK, 1988.

Baron, S. W. *A Social and Religious History of the Jews,* vol. II. New York: Columbia University Press, 1952.

Barry, Kieren. *The Greek Qabalah.* York Beach, Maine: Samuel Weiser, 1999.

Bauval, Robert, and Adrian Gilbert. *The Orion Mystery.* London: William Heinemann, 1994.

Beale, David. *Eros and the Jews.* New York: HarperCollins, 1992.

Begg, Ean. *The Cult of the Black Virgin.* London: Penguin, 1985; revised edition 1996.

Bennett, John G. *The Dramatic Universe,* vol. IV. London: Hodder & Stoughton, 1966.

———. *Gurdjieff: Making a New World.* London: Turnstone Books, 1976.

———. *The Masters of Wisdom.* London: Turnstone Books, 1977.

Bentley, James. *Secrets of Mt. Sinai.* London: Orbis, 1985.

Black's Bible Dictionary. London: Adam and Charles Black, 1973.

Boehme, Jacob. *The Way to Christ.* Translated by P. Erb. New York: Paulist Press, 1978.

Brandon, S. G. F. *Jesus and the Zealots.* Manchester: Manchester University Press, 1967.

———. "Dying God," in *Man, Myth and Magic,* no. 26. New York: Doubleday, 1966.

Buckley, J. J. "Mandaeans in the U.S.A. Today: Tenacity of Traditions," ARAM No. 7 (1995).

Budge, Wallis A. E. *The Gods of the Egyptians,* vol. 1. London: Methuan & Co., 1904.

———. "Mandaean Religion," in *Encyclopedia of Religion.* Edited by M. Eliade. New York: Macmillan, 1987.

Campbell, Jonathan. *Deciphering the Dead Sea Scrolls.* London: Fontana Press, 1996.

Campbell, Joseph. *The Masks of God,* 3 vol. London: Penguin, 1976.

Castaneda, Carlos. *The Active Side of Infinity.* London: Thorsons, 2000.

Charles, H. R. *The Book of Enoch.* Oxford: SPCK, 1912, 1917.

Childre, Doc, and Howard Martin. *The Heartmath Solution.* New York: HarperSanFrancisco, 1999.

Collins, Andrew. *Gods of Eden: Egypt's Lost Legacy and the Genesis of Civilization.* London: Headline Books, 1998.

Cornfeld, Gaalyah, and David Noel Freedman. *The Archaeology of the Bible: Book by Book.* New York: Harper & Row, 1976.

Crossan, John Dominic. *The Historical Jesus: The Life of a Mediterranean Jewish Peasant.* Victoria, Australia: Collins Dove, 1993.

Cruden's Concordance. Cambridge: Lutterworth Press, 1977.

Cullman, Oscar. *The Christology of the New Testament.* London: SCM, 1975.

Davies, A. Powell. *The Meaning of the Dead Sea Scrolls.* New York: Penguin, 1956.

Davies, Philip. "Jerusalem," in *Creating the Old Testament.* Edited by Stephen Bigger. Oxford: Basil Blackwell, 1989.

De Boer, Ester. *Mary Magdalene, Beyond the Myth.* Harrisburg, Pa.: Trinity Press, 1997.

De Voragine, Jacobus. *Golden Legend,* vol. 1. *Readings on the Saints.* Translated by W. G. Ryan. Princeton, N.J.: Princeton University Press, 1993.

Dodds, E. R. *Pagan and Christian in an Age of Anxiety,* Cambridge: Cambridge University Press, 1990.

Drower, E. S. *The Mandaeans of Iran and Iraq.* Oxford: Clarendon Press, 1937.

———. "Mandacan Polemic," in *Bulletin of the School of Oriental and African Studies,* vol. XXV, part three, 1964.

Dunne, Claire. *Carl Jung: Wounded Healer of the Soul.* New York: Parabola Books, 2000.

Eisenman, Robert. *Maccabees, Zadokites, Christians and Qumran.* Leiden: Brill, 1983.

Eisenman, Robert, and Michael Wise. *The Dead Sea Scrolls Uncovered.* Harmondsworth: Penguin, 1992.

Elder, Linda Bennett. "The Woman Question and Female Ascetics Among Essenes." *Biblical Archaeologist* 57 (1994): 4.

Eliade, Mircea. *The Myth of the Eternal Return.* Princeton, N.J.: Princeton University Press, 1954.

Eusebius. *The History of the Church from Christ to Constantine.* Translated by G. A. Williamson. Harmondsworth: Penguin, 1981.

Evans, C. F. *Resurrection and the New Testament.* London: SCM Press, 1970.

Evans, R. J. W. *Rudolph II and His World.* Oxford: Clarendon Press, 1984.

Fortune, Dion. *The Mystical Qabalah.* London: Aquarian Press, 1987.

Friedman, Richard Elliot. *The Hidden Book in the Bible.* New York: HarperCollins, 1998.

Gilbert, Adrian G. *Magi.* London: Bloomsbury, 1997.

Godwin, Joscelyn. *Mystery Religions in the Ancient World.* London: Thames & Hudson, 1981.

———. *Harmonies of Heaven and Earth.* Rochester, Vt.: Inner Traditions, 1987, 1995.

Golb, Norman. *Who Wrote the Dead Sea Scrolls?* New York: Scribner, 1995.

Grant, Michael. *Jesus.* London: Weidenfeld & Nicholson, 1977.

Graves, Robert. *Hebrew Myths: The Book of Genesis.* London: Cassell & Co., 1964.

Gruber, Elmer R., and Holger Kersten. *The Original Jesus.* Rockport, Mass.: Element Books, 1995.

Guénon, René. *The Lord of the World.* Gloucestershire, U.K.: Coombe Springs Press, 1983.

Halevi, Z'ev ben Shimon. *Kabbalah: The Tradition of Hidden Knowledge.* London: Thames & Hudson, 1978.

Hancock, Graham. *The Sign and the Seal.* London: Heinemann, 1992.

Hartshorne, Charles. *A Natural Theology for Our Time.* La Salle, Ill.: Open Court, 1967.

Haskins, Susan. *Mary Magdalene.* London: HarperCollins, 1994.

Heisler, Ron. "John Dee and the Secret Societies," in *The Hermetic Journal,* 1992.

Hitti, Philip. *The History of the Arabs.* London: Macmillan, 1970.

Hoeller, Stephan A. *Jung and the Lost Gospels.* Wheaton, Ill.: Quest, 1989.

Holroyd, Stuart. *The Elements of Gnosticism.* Shaftsbury, Dorset, U.K.: Element Books, 1994.

Hull, J. M. *Hellenistic Magic and the Synoptic Tradition.* London: SCM Press, 1974.

Isser, S. J. *The Dositheans.* Leiden: Brill, 1976.

Itter, Andrew. "Esoteric Teaching in the Writings of Clement of Alexandria," in *Esotericism and the Control of Knowledge.* Edited by Edward Crangle. Sydney: Department of Studies in Religion, University of Sydney, 2004.

Jenkins, John Major. *Galactic Alignment.* Rochester, Vt.: Bear & Co., 2002.

Keller, Werner. *The Bible as History.* Translated by W. Neil. London: Hodder & Stoughton, 1980.

Kenyon, Kathleen. *The Bible and Recent Archaeology.* Revised by P. R. S. Moorey. London: British Museum Publications, 1987.

King, John. *Kingdom of the Celts.* London: Blandford, 2000.

Kingsland, William. *The Gnosis in the Christian Scriptures.* London: Solo Press, 1993.

Krishna, Gopi. *The Biological Basis of Religion and Genius.* New York: Harper & Row, 1972.

Langdon, Stephen. "Tammuz and Ishtar," in *Sumerian and Babylonian Psalms.* Librairie Paul Geuthner, 1909.

Layton, Bentley. *The Gnostic Scriptures.* London: SCM Press, 1987.

Lehane, Brendan. *Early Celtic Christianity.* London: Constable, 1994.

LePage, Victoria. *Shambhala.* Wheaton, Ill.: Quest Books, 1996.

Lewy, Hans, ed. *Philosophical Writings: Philo.* Oxford: Phaidon Press, 1946.

Lievegoed, Bernard. *Phases.* Translated by H. S. Lake. London: Rudolf Steiner Press, 1979.

Ling, David. *The Buddha.* London: Temple Smith, 1985.

Lings, Martin. "Old Lithuanian Songs," in *The Sword of Gnosis.* Edited by Jacob Needleman. London: Routledge & Kegan Paul, 1986.

Lissner, Ivar. *Man, God and Magic.* London: Jonathan Cape, 1959.

Luckert, Karl W. *Egyptian Light and Hebrew Fire.* New York: State University of New York Press, 1991.

Mango, Cyril. *Byzantium.* London: Phoenix, 1994.

Mead, G. R. S. *Thrice Greatest Hermes,* vol. 1. London: John M. Watkins, 1964.

———. ed. *The Gnostic John the Baptizer: Selections from the Mandaean John-Book.* London: John M. Watkins, 1924.

Meader, William. *Shine Forth: The Soul's Magical Destiny.* Mariposa, Calif.: Source Publications, 2004.

Melchizedek, Drunvalo. *The Ancient Secret of the Flower of Life.* Flagstaff, Ariz.: Light Technology Publishing, 2000.

Menon, Aubrey. *The New Mystics*. London: Thames & Hudson, 1974.

Meyer, Marvin W., ed. *The Ancient Mysteries: A Source Book*. San Francisco: Harper & Row, 1987.

————. *The Gospels of Mary*. New York: HarperSanFrancisco, 2004.

Michell, John. *The View over Atlantis*. London: Sphere Books, 1975.

Mindell, Arnold. *The Leader as Martial Artist*. New York: HarperSanFrancisco, 1992.

Mitra, Sisirkumar. *The Dawn Eternal*. Pondicherry, India: Sri Aurobindo Ashram, 1954.

Momigliano, Arnaldo, ed. *The Conflict Between Paganism and Christianity in the Fourth Century*. Oxford: Clarendon Press, 1963.

Murphy, Cullen. *The Word According to Eve*. Harmondsworth: Penguin, 1999.

Needleman, Jacob. *The New Religions*. New York: Doubleday, 1970.

Newman, Barbara. *From Virile Woman to WomanChrist*. Philadelphia: University of Pennsylvania Press, 1995.

Niclaes, Hendrick. *Evangelium Regni: A Joyfull Message of the Kingdom*. Translated by C. Vitell. Amsterdam: ca. 1575.

Ovason, David, ed. *The Zelator: The Secret Journals of Mark Hedsel*. London: Arrow Books, 1999.

Pagels, Elaine. *The Gnostic Gospels*. Harmondsworth: Penguin, 1982.

————. *The Origin of Satan*. Harmondsworth: Penguin, 1995.

Parfitt, Will. *The Elements of the Qabalah*. Dorset: Element Books, 1991.

Patai, Raphael. *The Hebrew Goddess*. New York: Avon Books, 1978.

————. *The Hebrew Goddess*. Third Enlarged Edition, Detroit: Wayne State University Press, 1990.

————. *The Jewish Alchemists*. Princeton, N.J.: Princeton University Press, 1994.

Pearce, Joseph Chilton. *The Biology of Transcendence*. Rochester, Vt.: Park Street Press, 2002.

Phillips, Graham. *The Virgin Mary Conspiracy*. Rochester, Vt.: Bear & Company, 2005.

Philo. *De Vita Contemplativa*.

Philostratus. *The Life of Apollonius*. Translated by C. P. Jones. Harmondsworth: Penguin, 1970.

Picknett, Lynn, and Clive Prince. *The Templar Revelation*. London: Bantam, 1997.

Plutarch. *The Life of Alexander*. Translated by I. Scott-Kilvert. *The Age of Alexander*. Harmondsworth: Penguin, 1973.

Potter, Charles Francis. *The Lost Years of Jesus Revealed*. New York: Ballentyne Books, 1962.

Quirke, Stephen. *The Ancient Egyptian Religion*. London: British Museum Press, 1992.

Ravenscroft, Trevor, and Tim Wallace-Murphy. *The Mark of the Beast*. London: Sphere Books, 1990.

Rexroth, Kenneth. Introduction to A. E. Waite, *The Holy Kabbalah*. New York: Carol Publishing Group, 1995.

Robertson, J. M. *Pagan Christs*, abridged edition. New York: Barnes & Noble, 1993.

Robinson, John A. T. *The Priority of John*. London: SCM Press, 1985.

Romer, John. *Testament: The Bible and History*. Melbourne, Australia: Collins Dove, 1989.

Rothmuller, Aaron M. *The Music of the Jews: An Historical Appreciation*. Translated by H. S. Stevens. Brunswick, N.J.: Thomas Yoseloff, 1967.

Rowley, H. H. *The Zadokite Fragments and the Dead Sea Scrolls*. New York: Macmillian Co., 1952.

Rudolph, Kurt. *Gnosis*. Edinburgh: T. & T. Clark, 1976.

Saed, Hathem. "*Nasiruta*: Deep Knowledge and Extraordinary Priestcraft in Mandaean Religion," in *Esotericism and the Control of Knowledge*. Edited by E. F. Crangle. Sydney: Department of Studies in Religion, University of Sydney, 2004.

Saul, John Ralston. *The Unconscious Civilization*. Harmondsworth: Penguin, 1997.

Schaya, Leo. *The Universal Meaning of the Kabbalah*. London: George Allen and Unwin, 1971 and 1989.

Schonfield, Hugh. *The Essene Odyssey*. Dorset, U.K.: Element Books, 1984.

———. *The Pentecost Revolution*. London: Macdonald and Jane's, 1974.

Schuon, Frithjof. "The Human Margin," in *The Sword of Gnosis*. Edited by Jacob Needleman. London: Routledge & Kegan Paul, 1986.

Schuré, Édouard. *The Great Initiates*. New York: Harper & Row, 1961.

Seymour, Percy. *The Birth of Christ*. London: Virgin Publishing, 1998.

Shah, Idries. *The Sufis*. London: Octagon Press, 1964.

Shanks, Hershel. *The Meaning and Mystery of the Dead Sea Scrolls*. New York: Random House, 1998.

Simon Magus. *The Great Annunciation*. Gnosis vol. 1. Oxford: W. Foerster, 1972.

Smith, Morton. *Jesus the Magician*. London: Victor Gollancz, 1992.

———. *The Secret Gospel*. London: Victor Gollancz, 1974.

Sogyal Rinpoche. *The Tibetan Book of Living and Dying*. London: Rider, 1994.

Spanuth, Jurgen. *Atlantis of the North*. London: Sidgwick & Jackson, 1979.

Spong, John Shelby. *Liberating the Gospels*. New York: HarperCollins, 1996.

Starbird, Margaret. *The Woman with the Alabaster Jar.* Santa Fe: Bear & Co., 1993.

Steiner, Rudolf. *Three Streams in the Evolution of Mankind,* Lecture Three. London: Rudolf Steiner Press, 1963.

Stewart, Desmond. *The Foreigner.* London: Hamish Hamilton, 1981.

Stone, Merlin. *When God Was a Woman.* New York: Harvest/Harcourt Brace, 1976.

Swidler, Leonard. *Biblical Affirmation of Women.* Philadelphia: Westminister Press, 1979.

Tacey, David. *The Spirituality Revolution.* Sydney: HarperCollins, 2003.

Taylor, Joan E., and Philip R. Davies. "The So-Called Therapeutae of *De Vita Contemplativa*: Identity and Character," in *Harvard Theological Review* 1 (1998).

Thiede, Carsten Peter, and Matthew d'Ancona. *The Jesus Papyrus.* London: Weidenfeld & Nicholson, 1996.

Thompson, Thomas L. *The Bible in History.* London: Jonathan Cape, 1999.

Thompson, William Irwin. *Passages About Earth.* London: Rider, 1975.

Tierney, Patrick. *The Highest Altar.* London: Bloomsbury, 1989.

Tomas, Andrew. *Shambhala: Oasis of Light.* London: Sphere Books, 1979.

Turcan, Robert. *The Cults of the Roman Empire.* Oxford: Blackwell Publishers, 1992.

Tweedie, Irina. *The Chasm of Fire.* Dorset, U.K.: Element, 1983.

Vermes, Geza. *Complete Dead Sea Scrolls in English.* New York: Allen Lane/The Penguin Press, 1997.

———. *Jesus and the World of Judaism.* Philadelphia: Fortress Press, 1984.

———. *Jesus the Jew.* London: Collins, 1973.

Von Hassler, Gerd. *Lost Survivors of the Deluge.* Translated by M. Ebon. New York: Signet, New American Library, 1978.

Waddell, Helen. *The Desert Fathers.* London: Constable & Co, 1936.

Waite, A. E. *The Holy Kabbalah.* New York: Citadel Press, 1995.

Wallace-Murphy, Tim, and Marilyn Hopkins. *Rosslyn.* Dorset, U.K.: Element, 1999.

Weidner, Jay, and Vincent Bridges. *The Mysteries of the Great Cross of Hendaye.* Rochester, Vt.: Destiny Books, 2003.

Welburn, Andrew. *The Beginnings of Christianity.* Edinburgh: Floris Books, 1995.

Widengren, Geo. *Mani and Manichaeism.* London: Weidenfeld & Nicolson, 1965.

Wilson, A. N. *Paul: The Mind of the Apostle.* London: Sinclair-Stevenson, 1997.

Wilson, Edmund. *The Scrolls from the Dead Sea.* London: W. H. Allen, 1955.

Wilson, Ian. *Are These the Words of Jesus?* Oxford: Lennard, 1990.

Woodroffe, John. *The Serpent Power.* New York: Dover Publications, 1974.

Woolley, Benjamin. *The Queen's Conjurer.* London: HarperCollins, 2001.

Wunderlich, H. G. *The Secret of Crete.* London: Souvenir Press, 1975.

Yamauchi, Edwin. *Pre-Christian Gnosticism.* London: Tyndale Press, 1973.

Yates, Frances. *Giordano and the Hermetic Tradition.* London: Routledge & Kegan, 1978.

———. *The Rosicrucian Enlightenment.* London: Routledge & Kegan Paul, 1982.

Yogananda, Paramahansa. *The Autobiography of a Yogi.* Los Angeles: Self-Realization Fellowship, 1981.

INDEX

BOOKS OF RELATED INTEREST

The Gospel of Mary Magdalene
by Jean-Yves Leloup
Foreword by Jacob Needleman

The Woman with the Alabaster Jar
Mary Magdalen and the Holy Grail
by Margaret Starbird

Magdalene's Lost Legacy
Symbolic Numbers and the Sacred Union in Christianity
by Margaret Starbird

Mary Magdalene, Bride in Exile
by Margaret Starbird

Gnostic Philosophy
From Ancient Persia to Modern Times
by Tobias Churton

Gnostic Secrets of the Naassenes
The Initiatory Teachings of the Last Supper
by Mark H. Gaffney

The Mystery of the Copper Scroll of Qumran
The Essene Record of the Treasure of Akhenaten
by Robert Feather

The Secret Initiation of Jesus at Qumran
The Essene Mysteries of John the Baptist
by Robert Feather

INNER TRADITIONS • BEAR & COMPANY
P.O. Box 388
Rochester, VT 05767
1-800-246-8648
www.InnerTraditions.com
Or contact your local bookseller